D1499385

Making the Majors

Making the Majors

*The Transformation of Team
Sports in America*

...

Eric M. Leifer

HARVARD UNIVERSITY PRESS
Cambridge, Massachusetts
London, England
1995

Library of Congress Cataloging-in-Publication Data

Leifer, Eric Matheson.
  Making the majors : the transformation of team sports in America /
Eric M. Leifer.
      p.   cm.
  Includes bibliographical references and index.
  ISBN 0-674-54322-X (alk. paper)
  1. Professional sports—United States—History. 2. Sports teams—
United States—History. I. Title.
GV583.L45   1995
796'.06'0973—dc20   95-13469

To my mother and my father,
an organizer and an enthusiast

Contents

Preface

Sports enthusiasts often credit their interest in major league sports to star players, winning teams, or memorable moments from games past. The Babe Ruths and Michael Jordans, the New York Yankees and Dallas Cowboys, the 1958 Colts-Giants overtime game and Celtics-Lakers showdowns loom large in the appeal of major league sports. But there is a hidden side that has never received proper credit: the quiet efforts of the major leagues to construct a framework of competition in which players and teams can be both compared and distinguished. Far from being obvious or natural, this framework has been developing since the first major league appeared in 1871.

The protagonists of this book are the organizers who transformed children's games into the stable industry of major league sports. Their organizational innovations are followed from the very beginnings of baseball in the early nineteenth century through the future prospects of the major leagues in baseball, football, basketball, and hockey. A narrower scope, focused on a single sport, would be too constraining. The organizers themselves have moved freely across sports, learning from and interlinking the development of each. Nor can teams and leagues that failed be ignored, as these have provided valuable organizational lessons for subsequent efforts. In following the path of sports organizers, as opposed to the interests of enthusiasts, I treat major league sports as an object of experimentation rather than reverence.

Instead of bringing enthusiasts closer to players they hold in awe, teams they identify with, or games they find exciting, this book examines enthusiasts' own involvement in major league sports. This involvement is, after all, what league organizers have been seeking from the very beginning. Every major extension of involvement, in the form of expanding sports publics, has been accompanied by a reorganization of competition. Today, international publics lure major league organizers.

While enthusiasts might think their current star players and champion teams are sufficient to engage the whole world, this last great expansion of the sports public will require a fundamental reorganization of competition. This book aims to prepare the enthusiast for the unsettling changes ahead.

A strange insight guides this pursuit. It is that organizational innovations in major league sports have pushed in the opposite direction from what on the surface seems to interest enthusiasts. A phenomenal regularity has been progressively achieved in major league sports. The same set of teams now play one another in the same number of games, half lost and half won, half at home and half away, season after season. Leagues have become quite sophisticated in ensuring that contending teams are balanced in their competitive abilities, each doing what the others can do. Enthusiasts, by contrast, have become increasingly intent on finding differences and mobilizing around winners. The more successful organizers have become in imposing a blanket sameness across teams and repetition across seasons, the more energy enthusiasts have come to exert in finding differences. The fewer differences there are, the more differences fans seem to find. This strange cross-pressure between organizers and enthusiasts is the foundation on which major league sports have been progressively built, and is a central theme in this book.

My own interest in major league sports extends back to my childhood days when my father, an avid enthusiast, would take me to games or call me into the television room during crucial moments in a telecast game. The players on the distant field or the images on the television, however, never seemed quite as interesting as the intense involvement of those around me at the games or the solitary fixation of my father on the screen. In my schoolbooks, sports was never treated as a serious subject. From their perspective, only politics and religion seemed to stir real passions in past and present peoples. Yet in my experience, growing up in the Midwest, nothing seemed more involving than major league sports. While religious and political arguments were rare and short-lived in my household, there were almost daily contentions over which team was better. Something was amiss between what I was learning and what I was experiencing.

My first insights for this book came while teaching at the University of North Carolina in Chapel Hill. I was struck by the intensity of support for UNC sports teams. With alumni streaming in from all over the state, attendance at weekend football games exceeded the entire population of Chapel Hill. As one of the few town residents not at the games, I sometimes faced the practical problem of estimating when the game would be over in planning to meet up with friends afterward. Not only did games vary in length, but they were often effectively over long before the official end. I quickly learned that the score was the best predictor of when people would leave the game. With more than a 20-point difference between teams—no matter which team was ahead—torrents of people would start to flood out of the stadium shortly after the fourth quarter began. The intense support that had so impressed me seemed to have vanished entirely in this mass desertion. Teams that had filled the stadium at the start of the game executed their final plays in a nearly empty stadium. How could enthusiasts so suddenly and thoroughly lose interest in something they were so passionate about?

In a close contest, the situation was much different. On average only two to three people per minute trickled out up to the last seconds of the game. From the main exit, I could hear the crowd repeatedly roar in unison. Virtually the same people who disengaged so completely when there was a 20-point difference were now unshakably involved. Any professed attachment to the UNC team had not kept them from disengaging earlier, and so could not explain their current involvement. Involvement must hinge on the menu of teams that compete with one another, which ensures close contests, and not on any particular team or set of players. This places responsibility for public involvement in the hands of the organizers who select and regulate teams engaged in sporting competition, rather than in the hands of the players and teams. There is evidently more to involvement than what enthusiasts profess.

My project gained momentum when a colleague, Peter Marsden, showed me an article on the home advantage by Barry Schwartz and S. F. Barsky (1977). The home advantage factor is compelling evidence that publics can affect outcomes, and hence publics may help induce the performance differences between teams that these researchers end up finding. Publics exert a real pressure on competition to yield winners and losers, and this pressure runs counter to that of organizers in pursuing competitive balance. To explore the effects of publics on season performance differences between teams, I carried out a computer simulation of league competition based on effects estimated from games across all four major league sports. The main finding, presented in Chapter 8, is that the entire extent of season performance inequality in the National Football League, the modern prototype for major league sports, can be accounted for by the effects of its public. (This was not the case for the other leagues, which have not fully adopted the modern prototype.) This finding for football provides support for the idea that certain types of publics can induce and sustain inequality among equals. An offshoot of the project was a scheduling program (for season schedules), which effectively convinced me of the technical difficulty facing leagues in putting and keeping teams on an equal footing (see Leifer 1990b). Leagues varied in their success here.

I began to notice important differences in the way publics and sporting competition have been organized across sports and over time. The first professional teams were independent of leagues, and they had to keep moving constantly from town to town to find audiences. Early leagues set out to cultivate local publics by attaching teams to cities. The survival of early leagues often depended on the dominance of large-city teams and on the intense loyalty of smaller-city fans who could weather long losing spells. None succeeded better than Major League Baseball. With the rise of network television, the cultivation of national publics became increasingly important to sports organizers. National publics decrease the importance of team location and make winning essential for a team to receive support. At the same time, national publics make competitive balance crucial for persuading enthusiasts of a sport to search as widely as possible for winners to support. The National Football League led the way in forging a new prototype here. Change for baseball proved difficult, a problem taken up in Chapter 7. Yet there is currently no relation between local market size and performance in any of the four major league sports, though performance inequality persists. These findings were first published in the *American Journal of Sociology* (Leifer 1990a), and appear in more detailed form in Chapters 2 through 6. They directly contradict the economic model of performance inequality, which is implicity based on an attachment of teams to cities that was achieved only by baseball, and even there only before the modern era of televised sport.

Economists, like enthusiasts, have failed to recognize the role of sports organizers in constructing the basis for public involvement in major league sports. Teams must become attached to cities before cities become potential markets. Sports organizers forged this attachment, and in the process they helped construct identities for cities. In the same way, major league sports played a pivotal role in making network television what it is today. National publics, like local publics, must be actively created. As sports organizers searched for ways to extend involvement, cities and television were targeted as convenient vehicles for creating publics. Not only does this process need to be recognized, it needs to be tapped for insights into what possibilities lie ahead. The final frontier is composed of international publics, made possible through further advances in telecommunications. Although there have been some striking successes in gathering together huge international audiences, the problem of mobilizing a stable international public has not been resolved. How will competition be organized? What new identities will emerge from the reorganization? In Chapter 9, I offer predictions grounded in lessons from the past.

A large amount of data and a variety of analyses are used. Appendix B provides an explanation of the statistics that appear in the pages ahead. For readers interested in testing their own ideas, Appendix C provides season characteristics for every league that has successfully claimed major league status (see Appendix A for a listing). Material from Chapter 7 has appeared in "Endogenizing Contents: Opportunity, Organization, and Deal Making in Major League Baseball," *Social Science Research*, 23 (1994): 263–293, and material from Chapter 8 has appeared in "Perverse Effects of Social Support: Publics and Performance in Major League Sports," *Social Forces*, 74, no. 1 (1995).

From the inception of this project, many people and institutions have provided invaluable assistance. Launching the project was a two-year National Science Foundation Grant (SES 8610363), later followed by two Columbia University Research Council awards. At the University of North Carolina, useful advice came from Peter Bearman, Peter Blau, Walter Davis, Jack Kasarda, Tim Liao, and Peter Marsden. Carol Murphree and Kent Redding gave generous assistance and comments. After I moved to Columbia University, Karen Barkey, Ronald Burt, Herb Gans, Jennifer Kiser, Loring Leifer, Marshall Meyer, Mark Mizruchi, Andrej Rus, Lisa Schwartz, Paul Temme, Dorothee von Samson, and Harrison White provided a new fount of support and advice. David Gibson and Holly Raider provided superb assistance and editorial help. Martha Collins served as a consultant on Canada in accounting for the anomalies of ice hockey. From a distance, Mark Granovetter watched and shaped the project from the very start; and at Harvard University Press, Michael Aronson and Elizabeth Gretz were invaluable in helping bring it to a finish.

My greatest debt is to the many sports historians and data compilers

I cite. The scope of this book would have been impossible without their labors. Among the historians whose work proved most helpful are George Kirsch, Lee Lowenfish, Robert Peterson, David Pietrusza, Steven Riess, William Ryczek, Harold Seymour, and David Voigt. Joseph Reichler made Chapter 7 possible with his compilation of player sales and trades in major league baseball. A book by Jerry Gorman and Kirk Calhoun came out only weeks before the completion of the manuscript for this one but was a very useful source for recent developments. Most of the materials used for this book were obtained from the research branch of the New York Public Library. I am indebted to this remarkable institution both for the materials and for providing a place of scholarly refuge in an otherwise distracting city.

New York City
March 1995

Making the Majors

$\bullet\ \bullet\ \bullet$

Introduction

Major league sports are a huge phenomenon in America, distinguished as much by their regularity as by the excitement they arouse. Four major league sports—baseball, football, basketball, and hockey—wrap around the entire year with a steady flow of over 4,200 games. In each sport, a stable set of teams compete every season, each playing the same number of games, half in the same home location. Television and radio provide thousands of hours of game coverage in slots that, like Monday Night Football, can remain the same for decades. Perhaps the greatest regularity, however, comes from the treatment of sporting outcomes as news and the regular inclusion of commentaries and feature pieces in all forms of media. Every day, at the same time and in the same places, there are words or talk about the same teams playing the same game. In between, bits and pieces of major league sports flow by in commercials, fall out of cereal boxes, or appear as logos imprinted on jackets, tee shirts, caps, and athletic footwear. Although each exposure may arouse the excitement of a one-time event, the essence of major league sports as a phenomena resides in its regularity.

Everywhere major league sports appear, there are people attending to them. Tens of thousands gather in arenas and stadiums for games, while millions can tune into sporting events on television. Countless others turn to the sports pages in the daily newspaper, listen to sports radio, watch sports news and features on television, or buy any of the thousands of products with major league logos. Along with the major league sports they follow, all of these people can be distinguished by the regularity with which they attend to sports. Rarely a day goes by without the sports enthusiast's paying some attention to major league sports, from coffee and the sports section in the morning to conversations about last night's game at work to an evening game and a wrap-up on the ten o'clock news. These large numbers of people constitute a sports public, distinguished from the crowds or gatherings of earlier times by the regularity with which they are reactivated. Underlying the regularity of major league sports is the public that follows and supports them.

There is a widely held belief among writers on sport as well as sports enthusiasts that the regular supply of major league sports follows directly from the demand for it. Because people find major league sports exciting, they wish to surround themselves with all the things that are associated with these sports. The widespread enthusiasm for a sport, as played by the very best, creates endless opportunities for others to supply enthusiasts with sporting events, sports reporting and analysis, and paraphernalia. Writers on sport cater to the appetites of enthusiasts as well by celebrating star players, victorious teams, decisive games, memorable seasons, or a sport itself.

Widely ignored, however, is the active role of major leagues themselves in shaping the nature and extent of demand for sporting competition and its by-products. In the century and a quarter since major leagues first appeared, professional versions of the sports they organized have gone from being a novelty for an idle few to being a regularity that may soon become international in scope. Not only have major leagues spread the love of professional team sports, but they have changed the way these sports are loved. In the earliest days of professional sports, independent teams could never stay anywhere for more than a few games before the interest of local "cranks" or "bugs," as early spectators were known, would disappear. By attaching teams to cities and cultivating loyal fans, major leagues made it possible for teams to settle down and play half their games in the same location, year after year. But local loyalties to city teams eventually became an obstacle as major leagues began cultivating a new attachment between network television viewers and leaguewide competition. Particularly in football, the bulk of attention gradually shifted to games between remote teams as viewers everywhere began to focus on a limited stream of nationally broadcast games. As a result of the changes brought on by major leagues, cranks who attended games became loyal fans of a team, only to change again into enthusiasts of a sport. Far from merely responding to demand, major leagues have both cultivated and transformed the publics that support their product.

The phenomenon of major league sports derives not from the intrinsic appeal of the sports themselves but from the activities of the major leagues and the publics they have cultivated. Every major extension of publics, from the crowds that gathered when a traveling independent team came to town to the local public that provided ongoing support for a home team to the national publics that now follow a limited stream of nationally broadcast games, has been associated with a reorganization of competition by major leagues. Major leagues have, in other words, extended their publics by changing their basic "product" of sporting competition. This is the main argument. It matters because major leagues are currently on the verge of cultivating international publics. If the main argument is correct, this internationalization will require more than just the current marketing efforts, however ingenious they may be. A fundamental reorganization of competition will be necessary. Instead of celebrating the past or present, the aim of this study is to use the past and present to anticipate the future.

From the start, major leagues have not limited themselves merely to supplying what publics at the time demanded. Competition has been reorganized in ways that have excluded existing publics in pursuing the opportunity to cultivate new and larger publics. Television now dictates when games start and how many times they will be stopped for commercial breaks—much to the annoyance of local fans, who would like to believe their team is playing for them. As in the past, the impending reorganization of competition will appear quite strange and unsettling to current publics. To see how major leagues can formulate and pursue plans that current sports publics neither demand nor envision, it is necessary to look at some of the distinctive problems major leagues face.

Major leagues must concern themselves with the failure of sports publics to remain involved in sporting competition. This is something enthusiasts rarely think about, because someone who loves a major league sport expects that love to endure. Yet numerous failures occur, both large and small. Cricket was eclipsed in popularity by baseball in the middle of the nineteenth century. Soccer, the world's most popular sport, did not really take hold in the United States after being launched in the 1960s. Professional football and basketball remained marginal for the first thirty years of their major league existence. Baseball was

overtaken in popularity by football in the 1960s. Of the twenty-six
leagues—in football, baseball, basketball, and hockey—that have successfully claimed major league status and provide the basis for this
study, only five survive today (see Appendix A).[1] On a small scale, involvement can cease entirely even among the most avid enthusiasts, as
it does near the end of a lopsided game or a runaway pennant race.
This shutting off of involvement may be barely noticed, or it may be
rationalized in any number of ways. Yet the very fact of the shutting
off suggests that there is something very fragile in the involvement of
fans that no profession of commitment to a sport can ever completely
remove. In beloved sports, with beloved teams, involvement can turn
off as well as on. Averting failure, in ensuring that attention returns
over and over to a sport, is a major league responsibility.

Another problem that is distinctive for major leagues derives from
all the losing that must occur among a closed circuit of teams. No team
has ever been boosted in public esteem by losing.[2] In the days of traveling independent teams, losing could quickly prove fatal. After winning
their first seventy-six games (with one tie), baseball's 1869 Cincinnati
Red Stockings folded after only four losses by the end of their second
season. Even some years after the first major leagues had formed in
each sport, losing teams continued to perish or refuse to finish their
scheduled games. As major leagues struggled to stabilize member teams
and get each to play the same number of games, they in effect generated
more losing than ever before. Unless losing teams drop out, at the end
of the season major league teams in total have lost as many games as
they have won. Somehow major leagues must accommodate this huge
number of losses. The fact that not a single major league team has
perished or failed to complete its season (aside from player strikes) in
the last forty years suggests that major leagues have been remarkably
successful.

Major leagues have managed to accommodate losing at a time when,
if anything, winning has become even more important for attracting
followers. The early loyalty of fans to local teams helped teams weather
losing spells. As television viewers became more important than stadium goers in the economics of major league sports, however, winning
became essential in attracting a viewership. Tuning out a losing team
was much easier, from many standpoints, than being disloyal to a local
team. Were major leagues merely responding to public demand, it
would be hard to account for both the increase and the accommodation

of losing at a time when winning was becoming more important to an emerging national public.

A third distinctive problem of major leagues arises from the very effectiveness with which they produce clear champions. Before major leagues appeared, numerous independent baseball teams roamed the country claiming to be world champions in order to attract a crowd. Major leagues eliminated the possibility of multiple claimants both by undermining independent teams and by providing a framework, in the pennant race, for clearly determining the champion among league teams. But this leaves major leagues with only one true winner to offer publics, and seemingly undermines the lack of resolution over who is best that draws people to sporting events.[3] With enthusiasts demanding that all the teams they support be winners, major leagues are producing more losing teams and fewer true champions than ever before. Major leagues not only must accommodate these losses but must also undermine the significance of past winning to maintain public interest in subsequent competition. The past resolutions of sporting competition must somehow not undermine the present lack of resolution that keeps publics involved.

Celebrating winners is a thrill not just for sports enthusiasts but also for victorious players, their owners, and even league commissioners, who may let slip their partiality after a championship is over. But the major leagues must soon get back to work. Here the job is to pursue a regularity in the output of their product that elicits the regularity in the publics who follow major league sports. The central challenge of the major leagues is to achieve a regularity that is not seriously disrupted by the winning and losing that sporting competition unavoidably produces. In the course of accommodating losing and undermining the significance of winning, major leagues do much more than merely supply what publics demand. They actually operate at cross-purposes with the publics they supply, imposing cross-pressures on competition to those imposed by publics. Cross-pressures are the foundation on which major league sports are built. This insight provides the basis for anticipating, or designing, a future for major league sports, one in which cross-pressures are only intensified by the international reach of major leagues and the publics they cultivate.

Cross-pressures impose on sporting competition seemingly contradictory demands. Where publics seek to find differences between teams, major leagues seek to impose a sameness across teams. Where publics seek a resolution in the struggle for supremacy among teams, major leagues seek a repetition across seasons that sustains a lack of resolution. While game and season victors are celebrated as heroes, it is up to major leagues to ensure that the victors are not really any different from the vanquished—so that when the victors and vanquished meet again, game after game, season after season, interest in the outcome will remain at least as high as when they last met. Every game looms as a potential event where something might happen, but it is up to the major leagues to ensure that nothing ever really happens. The more successful major leagues have become in their pursuit of sameness and repetition, the more energy publics have put into finding differences through events. Out of their involvement come the winners that publics celebrate, largely as a creation of the publics themselves. It is necessary to look past the pageantry surrounding winners to see the real accomplishment of major leagues, which is still very much in progress.

Pursuing Accomplishment

When people think about the accomplishments of the major leagues, two distinct types come to mind. For many the primary accomplishment is the product of the major leagues at its best, the exciting moments and participants of sporting competition. Great players and teams have emerged from this competition to take a place in the history of not only a sport but the nation as well. Books and movies are still being produced on Babe Ruth, and the 1927 New York Yankees still compete against the best baseball teams today in the imaginations of enthusiasts. Every enthusiast has particular games and seasons that are forever engraved as personal memories, and many are shared with others in speech and in writing. Most of what major leagues have produced has been long since forgotten, both in the record books and in memories, but the very best and most exciting aspects will not easily fade away.

If we judge major leagues by the best of what they produce, however, we may be in for a disappointment. Independent teams, like the 1869 Cincinnati Red Stockings in baseball or the 1925 New York Celtics in basketball, have at times been superior in ability to any the major leagues could produce. Major leagues have always been more concerned with spreading talent across teams than with concentrating it within any one team, and there are currently more major league teams than ever before to spread talent across. Only rarely, as in all-star games or basketball's "dream team" in the 1992 Olympics, will a deliberate effort to create a superteam be made, and then only on the condition that it be disbanded immediately after a single contest or tournament. Any effort to turn a major league team that is in it for the long haul into the greatest that can be assembled is as much an accomplishment of the public as it is of the major leagues.

The situation is a bit like one found in Ayn Rand's *Fountainhead.* Ellsworth (Toohey) is the public opinion shaper, and Peter (Keating) and Gus Webb are architects just like the others whose fate Toohey controls:

> "Ellsworth, why have you dropped me? Why don't you ever write anything about me any more? Why is it always . . . Gus Webb?"
>
> "But, Peter, why shouldn't it be? . . . I don't believe that any one man is any one thing which everybody else can't be. I believe we're all equal and interchangeable . . . Why do you suppose I chose you? Why did I put you where you were? To protect the field [of architecture] from men who would become irreplaceable. To leave a chance for the Gus Webbs of this world. Why do you suppose I fought against . . . Howard Roark?"

The interchangeability of the likes of Peter Keating and Gus Webb gives Toohey free rein in building and destroying "greatness" among architects. Some great independent teams of the past have stood as a threat to major leagues, much as Howard Roark is a threat to Ellsworth Toohey, and have had to be destroyed or dismantled for major leagues to ascend. While enthusiasts might imagine themselves to be looking for a Roark in following a major league sport, a Roark would only diminish their interest in the sport. Fortunately for the major leagues, interchangeability need not rest on a philosophical conviction of human equality but is something that can be actively pursued by regulating the distribution of players and revenues across teams. Teams are much more amenable to design than individuals.

Outside of looking to the major leagues for heroes, people see the large amounts of money made by players and teams as a distinctive accomplishment. Every year, when players hold out for higher salaries, television contracts are signed, or franchises are sold, it is discovered anew that major league sports is a business. The dollar values involved always seem exorbitant. Yet in purely business terms, the major leagues are not particularly large compared with the largest corporations in America. Team revenues average around $50–$70 million, and teams now sell for as much as $200 million, but even aggregated into leagues, these figures pale next to the tens of billions used to measure the largest corporate sales, assets, and acquisition prices.[4] That the finances of major league sports can upstage so many larger corporations in garnering public attention suggests that publicity may be a more important accomplishment than profits for these sports. For many owners, both corporate and individual, teams are regarded as advertising expenses rather than profit generators. Risky in profit terms, major league sports offer publicity as a sure thing.

Profits and publicity, however, derive from a larger accomplishment of major leagues, the ability to sustain the involvement of sport publics. This involvement has been extended from sporadic gatherings of rowdy young males to regular reactivations of millions of people across the entire social spectrum. Every time a person reads the sports page, tunes in to a sports broadcast, or talks about sports with friends, some credit must be given to the major leagues. Without these involvements, profits and publicity could not be had. By treating owners as "profit maximizers," economists end up seeing only the narrow issue of extraction and not how the arena for extraction is cultivated. The real genius of sports organizers does not rest on issues such as when stars are pursued in the player market or when teams are moved to the suburbs. It lies in cultivating the arena for extraction, involved publics that eagerly stand ready for regular reactivation. Although championship teams and contests attract the most attention and are the most remembered, the accomplishment (or failure) of the major leagues is most clearly evident in the daily routine of the regular season.

A look at regular season final standings for the earliest and more recent baseball and football seasons reveals a great deal about the publics major leagues have cultivated (see Table I.1). Every game that is entered in the won-lost columns is a costly production requiring some form of audience for support. The striking feature of modern standings is that not only do the same teams return each year, but each plays the same number of games every season regardless of how well or poorly it performs. This kind of regularity is missing from the early standings. In both sports, early teams doing poorly in one season tended not to survive into the next, and typically played fewer games than better-

Table I.1 Early and modern season records from major leagues in baseball and football

Early Major League Baseball					
National Association 1871			National Association 1872		
Team	Won	Lost	Team	Won	Lost
Philadelphia Athletics	22	7	Boston Red Stockings	39	8
Chicago White Stockings	20	9	Philadelphia Athletics	30	14
Boston Red Stockings	22	10	Lord Baltimores	34	19
Washington Olympics	16	15	New York Mutuals	34	20
Troy Haymakers	15	15	Troy Haymakers	15	10
New York Mutuals	17	18	Cleveland Forest Citys	6	15
Cleveland Forest Citys	10	19	Brooklyn Atlantics	8	27
Fort Wayne Kekiongas	7	21	Washington Olympics	2	7
Rockford Forest Citys	6	21	Middletown Mansfields	5	19
			Brooklyn Eckfords	3	26
			Washington Nationals	0	11
Modern Major League Baseball					
National League 1989			National League 1990		
Pittsburgh Pirates	95	67	Chicago Cubs	93	69
New York Mets	91	71	New York Mets	87	75
Montreal Expos	85	77	St. Louis Cardinals	86	76
Philadelphia Phillies	77	85	Montreal Expos	81	81
Chicago Cubs	77	85	Pittsburgh Pirates	74	88
St. Louis Cardinals	70	92	Philadelphia Phillies	67	95
Cincinnati Reds	91	71	San Francisco Giants	92	70
Los Angeles Dodgers	86	76	San Diego Padres	89	73
San Francisco Giants	85	77	Houston Astros	86	76
Houston Astros	75	87	Los Angeles Dodgers	77	83
San Diego Padres	75	87	Cincinnati Reds	75	87
Atlanta Braves	65	97	Atlanta Braves	63	97

(continued)

performing teams (either from perishing early or from simply conserving resources). It made sense that winning teams should play more games, because they drew the largest crowds, and it made sense that losing teams should perish. Only a few years earlier, independent teams had to win nearly every game to maintain a reputation that could draw out curious crowds for games against pieced-together local teams. How

Table I.1   (continued)

Early Major League Football

National Football League 1921				National Football League 1922			
Team	Won	Lost	Tie	Team	Won	Lost	Tie
Chicago Bears	10	1	1	Canton Bulldogs	10	0	2
Buffalo Bisons	9	1	2	Chicago Bears	9	3	0
Akron	7	2	1	Chicago Cardinals	8	3	0
Green Bay Packers	6	2	2	Racine	5	4	1
Canton Bulldogs	4	3	3	Toledo	5	2	2
Dayton	4	3	1	Rock Island	4	2	1
Rock Island	5	4	1	Green Bay Packers	4	3	3
Chicago Cardinals	2	3	2	Buffalo Bisons	3	4	1
Cleveland	2	6	0	Akron	3	4	2
Rochester	2	6	0	Milwaukee	2	4	3
Detroit	1	7	1	Marion	2	6	0
Columbus	0	6	0	Minneapolis	1	3	0
Cincinnati	0	8	0	Rochester	0	3	1
[plus five teams not				Hammond	0	4	1
finishing]	?	?	?	Evansville	0	2	0
				Louisville	0	3	0
				Columbus	0	7	0

Modern Major League Football

National Football Conference 1989				National Football Conference 1990			
New York Giants	12	4	0	New York Giants	13	3	0
Philadelphia Eagles	11	5	0	Philadelphia Eagles	10	6	0
Washington Redskins	10	6	0	Washington Redskins	10	6	0
Phoenix Cardinals	5	11	0	Dallas Cowboys	7	9	0
Dallas Cowboys	1	15	0	Phoenix Cardinals	5	11	0
Minnesota Vikings	10	6	0	Chicago Bears	11	5	0
Green Bay Packers	10	6	0	Tampa Bay Bucks	6	10	0
Detroit Lions	7	9	0	Detroit Lions	6	10	0
Chicago Bears	6	10	0	Green Bay Packers	6	10	0
Tampa Bay Bucks	5	11	0	Minnesota Vikings	6	10	0
San Francisco 49ers	14	2	0	San Francisco 49ers	14	2	0
Los Angeles Rams	11	5	0	New Orleans Saints	8	8	0
New Orleans Saints	9	7	0	Los Angeles Rams	5	11	0
Atlanta Falcons	3	13	0	Atlanta Falcons	5	11	0

could they even have conceived of a day when winning and losing did not affect opportunities to play or survive?

Major leagues struggled to overcome the disruptiveness of winning and losing by pushing the product of sporting competition in the direction of sameness and repetition. The first was a matter of competitive balance, or endowing teams with the same competitive ability. Competitive balance yields winners and losers in both games and seasons, but it keeps open the chance that winners will lose and losers will win in subsequent competition. This helps undermine the significance of past winning and losing by arousing public interest in upcoming competition, no matter what has happened in the past. At the same time, the major leagues pushed for repetition across time, where the same set of teams played the same number of games each year. Although new teams are sometimes added at the beginning of the season, and others move, teams no longer die. The fact that winning and losing have no consequences for the survival of teams helps provide subtle assurance to publics that they can celebrate winners without threatening the framework of teams and games from which winners emerge.

Sameness and repetition hinge on three aspects of major league organization that are closely monitored in this study. One is the structuring of leagues and pennant races, where substantial changes have occurred across time. The composition of early major leagues was shaped by complex tradeoffs between the size of population bases, travel distances, and site competition with rival leagues. The uneven size of city population bases, even among those that proved able to support franchises, became an obstacle to competitive balance because larger cities could provide more support. Only after national television publics became possible did it become less important where a team was located. Major leagues began pursuing national coverage by spreading teams throughout the country in more and, on average, substantially smaller cities. Expansion brought the restructuring of pennant races as well as the introduction of more complicated postseason playoff formats. Throughout, the challenge was to keep the largest number of people interested in the largest number of teams for as long as possible, season after season.[5]

A second important aspect of major league organization is formal authority and regulation. Once teams are selected and located, competition between them has to be carefully managed. There are ongoing struggles for authority among players, agents, unions, managers, team owners, and leagues, frequently triggering the intervention of the courts. Even authority over a seeming necessity like centralized scheduling was at one time a hard-won victory for leagues. Authority, once gained, is used to formulate and enforce regulations. Regulations like revenue sharing and the reverse order amateur draft have a direct impact on competitive balance. Other regulations, like the reserve clause in player contracts that gave teams exclusive rights to renegotiate contracts with their players, have had less clear and more controversial impacts. Changes in major league authority and the introduction of new regulations have been associated with, as both markers and causes, every major progression toward sameness and repetition.

A final crucial aspect of major leagues is their informal organization. Even when formal regulations clearly promote sameness or repetition, some owners can come to dominate within league politics and use their power to subvert formal regulations. For competitive balance to be sustained across time, the means and motivation to win have to be widely diffused throughout the league. Although formal regulations can sometimes effectively address competitive abilities, they offer no assurance regarding the motivation to win. Indeed, it is typical in any closed social group for roles to develop that make members unequal in terms of what they put into the setting and what they get out of it. It has fallen on major league commissioners to prevent such real and enduring differences from occurring, so that owners will always be poised to do what is necessary to field a winning team. In Chapter 7, player sales and trades between teams are used to explore the informal organization of owners in Major League Baseball (MLB). Unfortunately, available evidence for football, basketball, and hockey is patchy and often anecdotal.

Aspects of size and composition, formal authority and regulation, and informal organization are highly interdependent. Composition and formal regulation can determine the relative bases of power in informal organization. Owners of teams in large cities, for example, have often dominated league politics, although this has been eroded by the equal sharing of television revenues. Yet informal organization can, in turn, shape league composition and formal regulations. Revenue sharing, for example, was easy to push through in football, but effectively limited in baseball. Thus even if formal regulations like revenue sharing and the reverse draft can be related to competitive balance, we need to look at the conditions under which these regulations can be adopted. Sameness and repetition flow not from single or even multiple causes but from a coherent system.

The major leagues have varied considerably in their efforts to impose sameness and repetition on competition, and in the kinds of publics they have cultivated as a result. Only in the modern era of televised sport has full success become important, as enthusiasts must be drawn to search throughout a league for winners to support in order to focus them on a limited stream of national broadcasts. In Chapter 8, it is shown that the movement of national public attention toward winners and away from losers can actually function to stabilize winning and losing among competitive equals. In the major league most successful at cultivating these fluid national publics, the National Football League (NFL), the entire amount of actual season performance inequality can be accounted for by the effect of the public on competition. Celebrated teams that persist in winning (like the Giants and the 49ers in Table I.1) may be the accomplishment of a national public, and not the NFL. What the NFL has accomplished is a sameness across teams and a repetition across time that have kept a national public sufficiently engaged to sustain stable winners among equals.

Major leagues in the past and even in the present have thrived with a far from perfect product. One of the primary ways in practice that major leagues have overcome the disruptiveness of winning and losing has been to attach their product to an outside entity capable of arousing loyalty or commanding attention. These attachments have not only helped ensure the regularity of sports publics, but have also defined their character. The attachment of teams to cities, around which major leagues first formed, gave rise to loyal local publics willing to support their teams through long losing spells. Later, the attachment of entire leagues to network television gave rise to national publics. Although national publics have been willing to abandon a losing team, the loyalty they have had to network television has for a long time ensured large audiences for prime broadcasting slots. Currently, however, many major league cities are in decline and the networks are rapidly losing market share to cable, satellite, and pay-per-view television. In the final chapter, I propose a new major league attachment for international publics to latch on to.

Constraints on Accomplishment

Understanding the accomplishment of major leagues is a formidable task. Yet the closer we look at this accomplishment, the more we will begin to wonder why it has been so slow in coming about. From the very beginning, sports organizers have moved freely across sports. Joe Carr, a minor league baseball organizer, founded the first major leagues in both football and basketball. Maurice Podoloff, a hockey arena owner and president of the American Hockey League, founded the Basketball Association of America that later became the National Basketball Association. Cross-ownership has been around ever since there was more than one major league to buy in to. The founder of Blockbuster Entertainment, H. Wayne Huizenga, has an ownership stake in major league Florida franchises in baseball, hockey, and football. Even without the actual flow of organizers and owners between sports, organizational innovations in a setting that receives so much public attention should rapidly diffuse. But this is not the case.

Except for the first appearance of professionals, the sports that followed after baseball failed to evolve any faster in the direction of stable major leagues than those that came before them. This can be seen in the developmental time lines for the four major league sports offered in Figure I.1. Major leagues were established in baseball before the other sports had advocacies of any kind. Ice hockey originated and developed in Canada, and to this day remains dominated by Canadian players. Its slowness in penetrating major U.S. cities, a criterion for a "major" league, might be excusable. Yet football and basketball were distinctly American, and were extremely popular sports at the grassroots, school, and college levels very soon after their inceptions. But neither their widespread appeal nor the model for major league organization that baseball provided accelerated the emergence of stable major leagues in either sport. In fact, later sports were slower to develop. This peculiarity should warn us that accomplishment is more than an analytical problem, solved with a set of prescriptions for organizing. Accomplishment also entails a historical problem, as it comes about only through an uncertain struggle with and amid the by-products of past accomplishments.

Three types of constraints have been central in the evolution of major leagues. These have placed limits, at any given time, on what could be accomplished by sports organizers. First and most obvious, technolog-

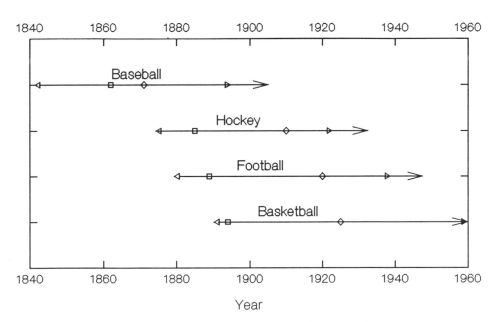

Figure I.1 Developmental time lines for the major leagues in four sports.
◁ = first appearance of adult clubs; □ = first observation of professional players;
◇ = emergence of a major league; ▷ = stabilization of league's team
composition.

ical and demographic constraints have in the past limited opportunities for mobilizing publics. To turn a sport into a viable business, the logistic problem of bringing people to games, or games to people, must be resolved. In the nineteenth century, urban growth played a crucial role in concentrating potential publics. Attaching teams to cities was a brilliant organizational innovation aimed at exploiting these new potential publics. Even within densely populated cities, however, improvements in construction, transportation, and communication increasingly helped get people, as well as teams, to ballparks that were large enough to accommodate them. With the advent of television and air travel, the emphasis shifted from bringing people to games to bringing games to people. Teams spread themselves across the entire nation, while leagues and networks steered large national audiences to single sporting events. The modern scene is distinguished by the near absence of logistic constraints on mobilizing publics. If anything, the problem current and future leagues will face is an overabundance of access to their events, something that threatens to undermine their value for television.

What is possible from a logistic standpoint seldom actually happens. Standing in the way, as a second source of constraints, is the social configuration of groups vying for control over a sport. A few decades after adult players took baseball from children, managers were to wrest the game from the players. With the formation of major leagues, struggles ensued among players, owners, commissioners, local and national politicians, courts, amateur organizations, religious and ethnic groups, and a host of others. Sunday baseball was not a logistic issue, but one involving politicians and their religious-minded constituencies. Night baseball was not introduced in the majors until the 1930s, fifty years after it was technologically possible and decades after it appeared in the minor leagues. Every innovation threatened positions defined by the status quo and hence necessitated some social struggle. What could be done was limited by how much one group could get away with vis-à-vis other groups. In this respect, the evolution of major league sports is a story of intrigue, in which various social groups vie for control over the new team sports to enhance their own standing.

Central in the historical drama is the relation between professional and amateur sport. Emerging together, each defined itself with reference to the other, and each has spawned powerful organizations to promote its own interests. The success of Major League Baseball only fueled the aspirations of amateur organizations, who, having engaged too late in the struggle over baseball, directed their newly emerging energies toward the sports that followed. Difficulties experienced by professional football and basketball leagues in emulating Major League Baseball were, in large measure, owing to the powerful amateur organizations spawned by Major League Baseball's success. It was not until the modern era of televised sports that amateur (particularly college) and professional versions became fully complementary, and hence the power of one fully reinforced the power of the other.

Current major leagues face less outside opposition and fewer obstacles to mobilizing publics than ever before. All forms of media have vested interests in the success of the major leagues. Over 25 percent of television advertising revenues are generated by sports broadcasts. State and city politicians can be made or broken by the acquisition or loss of a major league franchise to their area. Yet without the involvement of the sports publics, the dictates of which constitute the third set of constraints, the whole edifice of major league sports would crumble. And despite professions to the contrary, no sport can ensure involvement entirely through its intrinsic appeal. Despite over a hundred years of fan support, baseball owners could fear that the formation of a soccer league in 1967 or even a short player strike in 1972 might sever the sport's grip on fans. With the 1994 World Series canceled as a result of the latest baseball player strike, commentators were eerily silent on what 1995 would bring. As rock solid as major league sports seem, they are no more solid than the involvement of the publics on which they depend.

Involvement, in sports or elsewhere, is a very peculiar thing. If examined closely, it breaks down into a short-lived attention that keeps moving away from an object, only to return later. Even the most dedicated sports fan is constantly turning away from sports. At a game, attention wanders from the game to the crowd, to a neighbor, to a desire for a hot dog or beer. If the game outcome is clear, attention may cease entirely as the fan rushes to beat the crowd leaving the stadium. But attention returns with the evening news or morning paper or next game. And the same turning away and turning back occur at the level of seasons, when pennant races are effectively over and when they restart the next year. The return of attention is the crucial element of involvement, the coming back over and over from elsewhere. In the process, sports move from being an episodic novelty to a stable industry.

Most sports enthusiasts know very well what grabs their attention. They thrive on disruptions of all sorts: a big play that breaks open a game, a fight that empties the benches, an outstanding player who stands out from the rest, a crucial game that puts a team on top. But the basis for involvement is quite different from that of attention. Although attention thrives on disruptions, involvement is sustained by what endures across disruptions. Building, not disrupting, organization is where sports organizers have directed their efforts. What started as an isolated match, and then a traveling team, out to attract attention, was gradually shaped into a highly regular and ongoing series of games played out before regular publics. Close up, every game may appear unique and be billed as such. Attention may be piqued as one team stands ready to dash the hopes of another. But if we step back, the sameness and repetition are overwhelming: the same set of similarly endowed teams play the same game under similar conditions season after season. In the sameness and repetition, not the uniqueness, is the engine for producing durable involvement as opposed to short-lived attention.

The dictates of involvement have made competitive balance and scheduling regularity the central organizing principles for league sports. With the formation of major leagues, the dominance that was imperative for the survival of an independent team became disruptive. Getting attention and sustaining involvement became separate issues as regular schedules were established pairing the same teams over and over. Teams had to be good enough to draw crowds when they traveled (as had been true for the earlier independent teams), but not so good that their opponents would not be able to draw crowds when playing at home. Competitive balance was the only way to satisfy this constraint on widespread involvement.

Major leagues evolved in fits and starts. Changes were often long overdue and, once adopted, often outlived their usefulness. Over the last 125 years, only two enduring forms of organization have emerged. The first form was based on a closed circuit of professional teams attached to cities. It emerged at a time when sport revenues were derived from gate receipts and concessions, and intercity travel was by rail. Major League Baseball became the prototype in successfully attaching a set of teams to a set of cities. From 1903 to 1953, the National and American Leagues maintained the same teams and locations—across two world wars and the Great Depression. By the end of this period, however, the attachment to cities had become more of a liability than an asset. The interests that had formed around this attachment hindered Major League Baseball from exploiting new opportunities after World War II.

After 1945, the new opportunities presented by television and air travel made possible a much different form of organization. These technological changes were rapidly removing the geographical constraints on who could view or play games, thereby making truly national leagues and national publics possible. Moving from a position of marginality before World War II, the National Football League (NFL) was soon to offer a new prototype in organizing for the involvement of national publics. While President Calvin Coolidge thought the NFL's Chicago Bears were an animal act, President George Bush insisted that the NFL's Super Bowl not be interrupted by the war with Iraq. Instead of seeking only to occupy the largest cities, the NFL sought to occupy all the major television networks. In bold defiance of localism, the Super Bowl is not played in the home city of either of its contenders. Rather, it is staged almost entirely for a national television audience.

Major League Baseball and the National Football League provide the central organizational prototypes in this study, and the reversal of their fortunes after World War II provides the central event under examination. We will see that real change is possible yet extremely difficult to bring about. Moments of real change reveal the direction of major league sports. During them, a new opportunity is exploited, a new alignment in the social configuration surfaces, and the changes hold because the involvement of publics is in some way extended. Major leagues are presently entering another period of organizational transition as opportunities for creating international publics open up. None of the present major leagues has figured out how to fully exploit the new international opportunities, although there is considerable experimentation in progress. If once again past marginality provides the best springboard for change, then we must look to the National Basketball Association (NBA) or the National Hockey League (NHL) for the next momentous event in major league sports. So far, however, neither has made the necessary move beyond marketing to the reorganization of its product.

A schematic overview of the progression of major leagues can be found in Figure I.2. In the course of making the majors, both teams and publics have evolved in the way they locate each other. Traveling

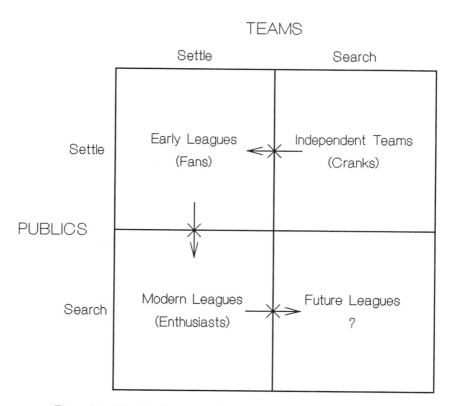

Figure I.2   The development of major leagues and their followings.

teams had to search constantly for audiences in moving from town to town. Early leagues made it possible for teams to settle in large cities and enjoy the ongoing support of local publics. With the rise of network television, however, publics could begin searching for teams to support. Modern leagues arose in an effort to focus the search on a limited stream of national broadcasts. Each transition between these search and settle possibilities marked a central event in the evolution of major leagues. The next event will carry major leagues into the future, when both teams and publics will be freed to search for each other. In the final chapter, I offer a blueprint for what lies ahead.

Challenges Ahead

In this study, many of the challenges faced by the author are analogous to those faced by a sports organizer. Both are experimenters by nature, looking for something that works. While the past provides a rich source of valuable lessons, the future is where accomplishment is sought. To bring about the future, both ideas and organizational efforts are required. Getting one step ahead of the organizer, to show the way rather than simply follow behind and interpret, is the mark of accomplishment for any science.

A major challenge lies in breaking away from past success. Major League Baseball's success in attaching teams to cities became an obstacle in adapting to the new era of televised sports. Television was seen as a threat to a way of doing things that needed to be defended and not changed. Professional football, previously a marginal sport (next to the immensely popular college version) that never really succeeded in attaching teams to cities, adapted quickly to the new media and soon surpassed baseball in popularity. Yet its success in adapting to network television now seems to be only impeding the pursuit of international publics. The National Football League's recent efforts to sponsor a "World League of American Football" seem primarily designed to avoid impinging on the sponsor's turf. Breaking away from past success is never easy. Yet every major extension of involvement has required it.

The same can be said about the study of major league sports. Economists formulated a model of league competition in the 1950s that was successful in accounting for the dominance of large-city teams in the preceding decades of Major League Baseball. In clinging to this success, researchers have since had to ignore the impact of network television and avoid empirical tests on the other major league sports (which would prove them wrong).[6] This book was initially intended to show the impact of national network television publics on league competition, with the NFL as the standard of success. At some point, however, future international opportunities began to seem enormous and current league organization, including the NFL's, began to appear inadequate. Change became more appealing than defense of the status quo. Tensions that were to be downplayed became the focus of redesign. The result is a blueprint for the future, offered in the final chapter.

Another challenge lies in dealing with the unevennesses that confront both the organizer and the author. Building any kind of organization is an immensely challenging task, fraught with obstacles. In sports, the core—the production of games—must be insulated from countless possible shocks and disruptions. Technology has been harnessed to build weatherproof stadiums, transport teams, bring more fans to games and then games to fans, reduce player injuries, and play night and indoor games. The major leagues have interfaced with colleges and minor leagues to ensure a stable flow of players and have brought in corporate backing to service growing capital needs. Sports organizers have from the beginning cultivated political connections to secure choice locations, tax concessions, city services, and favorable legislation. Over time, insulation has been achieved with ever greater effectiveness.[7]

At the time the first baseball major league emerged in 1871, games had to be finished before dark, because there were no electric lights. Cranks were crowded into wooden stadiums that were vulnerable to fire and collapse. Gamblers and ruffians had a visible presence, often trying to affect outcomes through graft, verbal taunts, bottle throwing, and once even jumping on the back of an outfielder chasing a ball. Players traveled by train and an occasional steamboat, often getting diverted in the course of their long journeys by women and liquor. Local politicians could threaten, as happened in Cincinnati, to cut a road through the ballpark. Teams came and went with such frequency that, in the 1880s, the National League stopped listing its teams on its stationery. The repetitive production of sporting events was, in short, a long way off.

Obstacles to organizing also stem from unevennesses in the actual setting. Hours of the day, days of the week, and weeks of the year differ, constraining when and where games could be played. Ballparks could not be placed just anywhere in cities, and the uneven placement of cities made an ideal league problematic. The largest cities were greatly uneven in size, and cities of the same size were uneven in the support they gave teams. Laws were uneven across states and across time. Players were uneven in ability and owners in their dispositions. Even without these obstacles, however, the very act of organizing can create unevenness. Baseball, insofar as it came first, faced a different setting than sports that came later. Professional football and basketball, besides being excluded from the summer, had to contend with the countermobilization of amateur sport triggered by the rise of Major League Baseball.

Over time, many of these obstacles have been overcome by exploiting new technologies, devising new regulations (or whole new leagues), or exerting informal social controls. The organizer specializes in overcoming obstacles and hence in effecting real change. But at any given time, far from being unimportant, the various kinds of unevenness will entirely determine the character and specifics of a major league. Every game won or lost, every team reputation, and every major league action is rooted in some unevenness. Phillip Wrigley, owner of the Chicago Cubs, refused to put lights in his stadium. Early football's Pottsville Maroons drew such large crowds from their town of 23,000 that the New York Giants chose to play them in Pottsville rather than in New York. There is no end to such examples of unevenness. Each hinges on a particular stubbornness, or location, or advantage that others lack.

For the author, there exists an avalanche of opportunities for explanation in the progression of major league sports. Many intriguing questions arise from unevennesses. Why did major league football adopt a such liberal revenue-sharing policy in the 1920s, one that helped it pass baseball in popularity forty years later? Why did amateur and professional sport merge into a single hierarchy in Canada, yet remain a dual hierarchy in the United States? Why did blacks disappear from Major League Baseball in the 1880s and professional football in the 1930s, only to reappear in 1946? Why did a national scandal break in college basketball shortly after the launching of what came to be the first successful professional basketball league? Although some answers to such questions are offered, the aim of this book goes beyond accounting for the endless specifics, or character, of leagues in terms of unevennesses of all sorts. The goal is less to explain than to explain away, in getting past the specifics to an underlying idea.

None of the central objects of this study can be seen without being pointed out. Involvement dissolves into an ever-fleeting attention when examined close up. Competitive balance, or sameness, among teams dissolves into victory or defeat in the course of any game or season. Repetition dissolves into seemingly unique events at any given moment. These objects must somehow reach across, or underlie, close-up observations to be real. In this very illusiveness lies the power of these objects. Not to be found in isolated observations, they emerge only as bridges across observations and hence promise to organize all they reach.

For the enthusiast, major league sports offer a succession of unique moments. Every game offers new thrills, every piece of sport news offers new information. Teams that win are superior to ones that lose. An industry of sportswriters and analysts, sensitive to unevennesses of all kinds, provides explanations for why some teams are doing better than others and thereby reinforces the enthusiast's perceptions. To succeed, this study must explain away these perceptions. It must show sameness where enthusiasts see winners and losers, and repetition where enthusiasts see uniqueness. In Chapter 8, it is argued that the season performance inequalities enthusiasts observe are a product of their very looking for them. To see sameness and repetition, you have to look for them as well.

Alexis de Tocqueville long ago used this same mode of explaining away in his famous book *Democracy in America*. Tocqueville, coming to America to get a glimpse of what the future might bring, sought to get one step ahead of the organizers of democracy in Europe. Tocqueville claimed to have observed equality in America, which he rather ambiguously equated with democracy, but this was easier seen back in France while writing his famous book than while trekking around America. Up close, there was only unevenness. There were slaves and women and patriarchs and nascent industrialists and men who toil, some on poor soil and some on rich soil. Even among the limited group of propertied white males eligible to vote, some were more active and persuasive in their political efforts than others. This is what Tocqueville saw, just as the modern enthusiast sees only winners and losers in major league sports. Yet through Tocqueville's brilliant explaining away we come face to face with a powerful force that, once recognized, can be seen everywhere.

Tocqueville's capacity to see what cannot be seen is hard to match. Even with his brilliant vision, current standards for science would prove much more circumscribing. Unlike in Tocqueville's time, pains must be taken to distinguish between observations and constructions. This book is based on a tremendous amount of data requiring a great deal of pointing out to help the reader see what could not otherwise be seen. Although the facts may sometimes seem to obscure the argument, the ensuing struggle will be good practice. For unlike Tocqueville's book on a distant country in a now distant century, this book is about something most people are quite familiar with. Herein lies a great challenge, to discover something in the familiar that could not otherwise be seen.

The reason for looking beyond the surface unevennesses derives from a final challenge, to generalize. In the computerized catalogue of the New York Public Library, there are 1,041 entries for baseball, 779 for football, 313 for basketball, and 188 for ice hockey.[8] Nearly all are written by fans and enthusiasts in a variety of guises, as athletes, coaches, sportswriters, and academics. Individual sports are relished, with no thought of drawing out lessons that might be applied to other sports. But sports organizers have from the very beginning moved freely across sports. What was learned in one sport could eventually be transported to others.[9] This book goes a step further in seeking principles of organizing that may be transported out of sports altogether.

In England, parliamentary government and highly regulated sport evolved together after the 1640 revolution, which had divided the upper classes. Both are viewed by Norbert Elias (1986) as part of a civilizing process, one that seeks to exclude from competition violent actions that can seriously hurt competitors. Without a strong monarchy, as in France, the upper classes were largely on their own to overcome the postrevolution heritage of hatred and fear in pursuing common interests. "Hostile factions united by a 'gentlemanly' code of sentiment and conduct learned to trust each other sufficiently for the emergence of a non-violent type of contest in Parliament" (1986, p. 31). "The 'parliamentarization' of the landed classes . . . had its counterpart in the 'sportization' of their pastimes" (p. 34). The straightforward shooting of foxes, for example, was forbidden, and elaborate rules for the fox hunt "were designed to make it less easy, to prolong the contact, to postpone the victory for a while" (p. 160). Even the fox, as a worthy opponent, was accorded some rights.

In his study of Indian cricket, Richard Cashman (1980) finds the British still acutely sensitive to the interconnectedness of the civilizing process. Accordingly, Lord Harris "believed that Indians would benefit from playing cricket partly . . . because of his political views . . . he did not look upon India as a nation . . . but rather as a loose collection of races, creeds and castes without any common bonds . . . the cricket field was a meeting point where they could engage in social intercourse while retaining their separate team and social identities . . . participation in the game would educate Indian players to a new set of colonial values which would help to create a sense of unity and purpose in a country where such ideas were weak" (1980, p. 12).

Major league sports mark a sort of culmination of the civilizing process. To see this, one needs to look beyond the verbal bloodlust and slamming bodies at sporting events to the remarkable preservation of teams in current major leagues. Victorious teams do not destroy their opposition; they come back to play them over and over in contests whose outcomes remain up for grabs. Vanquished become victors, and victors become vanquished. Behind the drama of victory and defeat, imposed by commentators and publics on the basis of differences of a few points, there is an underlying sameness and repetition. The drama of producing winners and losers is not a one-shot affair but a continuous process that strangely does not transform itself over time. Publics remain interested, leagues remain viable, owners and teams remain hopeful throughout the repetitive process of producing winners and losers. This is a remarkable achievement, one that should provide continuing inspiration for organizers of all sorts.[10]

Rather than celebrate the achievements of players and teams, this book is devoted to the major league organizers who have painstakingly built up the framework within which player and team achievements have emerged. These are the people who have given publics unremitting opportunities to make distinctions. Success, for them, lies not in the distinctions that get made but in the vigilance that goes into making them. Their peculiar genius resides in organizing for the involvement of publics. Having captured the involvement of cities, and then the nation, major league organizers now stand on the threshold of involving international publics. The challenge is to figure out how the threshold can be crossed.

1

· · ·

Laying the Groundwork

From the modern vantage point, the early days of professional sports appear ragged. The first professional teams roamed the countryside playing pieced-together local teams, billing nearly every match-up as a championship in order to attract a crowd. These independent teams were eventually displaced by early leagues, which established pennant races among closed circuits of teams. Yet for some time it was common for league teams to perish during the season, and for teams that survived to play substantially different numbers of games (see Table I.1). These early modes of organizing competition hardly seem efficient next to today's meticulously constructed pennant races. Embarrassed by the instability and irregularity of the past, most official major league sports encyclopedias suppress early league results. In terms of organizing competition, nothing makes more sense for the modern fan than the practices of today's major leagues. To look back is to wonder why the obvious was missed.

Yet if we were to go back to the ragged days when professional team sports were first emerging and look ahead, it would be modern times that appeared strange. In a business where winning was essential to attract attention, it made sense that losing teams had fewer opportunities to play and were the most likely to perish. It also made sense to play games in locations where the most fan interest could be generated. The idea of playing half one's games in the same place, regardless of local interest, and somehow never perishing would be strange indeed. To appreciate the bold innovations that made these strange practices and outcomes seem perfectly natural, we must start at the beginning of

27

professional team sports and move forward. How did something that seemed so natural at the time get displaced by something as strange as modern major league sports?

Major leagues did not appear overnight. A tremendous amount of groundwork was necessary for them to become possible. First of all, sports with widespread appeal and hence a good deal of organization had to exist. It is a curious feature of major leagues that they have never spawned new sports, and have always been dependent on outside vehicles for the early diffusion of the sports they formed around. Early associations of clubs eagerly worked to recruit new clubs in legitimating a new game. Industrialists formed teams from their workers, to raise company morale and compete among themselves. High school and college teams played a pivotal role in popularizing new sports. Traveling teams spread interest and diffused new techniques of play. Wars, as well, inadvertently served to spread team sports by intermingling unparalleled numbers of young men and affording lulls where pastimes were shared.[1] Major leagues have depended on these vehicles not only to arouse interest in a game but also to produce skilled players who could themselves attract a following.

Professionalism was another essential ingredient for major leagues. Here again the major leagues have functioned to legitimate and enhance something that developed elsewhere. Nothing has contributed more to the stature of professional athletes than major league sports, yet professionals had to establish their initial foothold without the help of leagues. It is difficult to imagine, in today's world, a time when professional athletes were regarded as unsavory mercenaries who had to be surreptitiously introduced into a sport. In an era when teams were integrally tied to preexisting groups like clubs or schools or workplaces, however, the hiring of outsiders, or "ringers," solely for the purpose of winning seemed to threaten conceptions of both the sport and the group. Professionals did not gain a foothold until teams started attaching themselves to cities, which at the time were burgeoning new entities in search of identities. Only after this foothold was established did major leagues come along and cement the bond between professional teams and cities, a subject pursued in the next chapter.

The first professionals were, of course, skilled players who enhanced the likelihood of victory. But this is not what made them essential for major leagues. By closing the circuit of competition, the major leagues had to incorporate an unprecedented amount of losing into the regimen of a set of the best teams. Enhancing victory was no longer an issue when half of all games played had to be lost. Professionals were valuable because they were free floating, moving from team to team and town to town without loyalties of any kind. This gave sports organizers remarkable latitude in the business of composing teams and regulating the movement of players between them. Clubs or schools or workplaces, in drawing from their own memberships, lacked this freedom. Unlike any other entity in the sports scene, past or present, the major leagues were amenable to design. That major leagues crystallized around professional team sports was no accident. The composition of teams provides an additional level for design, not available in individual sports, and professionals provide the ideal materials for composition. Major league sports could be boldly different by putting together what already existed in a new way.

But major leagues first had to be envisioned and organized, and to carry this out required a new type of person. In America's English past, sports were under the control of a landed elite. Sports took the form of either refined games like polo or cricket played exclusively among elites, or raucous events like cockfights or boxing matches sponsored by elites for the enjoyment of peasants, workers, and sometimes themselves as well (Gorn and Goldstein 1993). Both forms served mainly to reaffirm bonds, either among elites or between elites and the lower orders that served them. Neither carried the seeds for commercial development. It was not until an urban bourgeoisie entered the scene, in America's nineteenth century, that commerce and sports became mingled.[2]

For those rising within the new industrial order, sports were at first an object for disdain and outright opposition. The new urban bourgeoisie saw a threat in both the conspicuous consumption of leisure pursued by landed elites and the vice and disorder that spilled out among those drawn to the blood sports of commoners.[3] Aligning with Protestant evangelical movements, the bourgeoisie helped erect legal barriers to the increasingly popular pursuits of horse racing and boxing. Yet in team sports, the new orders were to find something they could rally behind. Instead of seeing in team sports an occasion for idleness or vice, they found an opportunity for skill, discipline, and order—values they prized in industry and in themselves. Thus they latched onto team sports, first as participants and later as promoters, and in the process turned the sports themselves into stable industries.

This chapter traces the origin and diffusion of four team sports to the point at which independent professional teams in each gained national attention. Hence it lays out the groundwork for the bold idea of major leagues. Baseball receives the most attention, as it came first. Professional athletes and teams were established in baseball before the other sports came on the scene. With each succeeding sport, professionals emerged more quickly than they had in baseball. Yet though the groundwork for major leagues was laid more quickly in these sports, major leagues were actually slower to develop in the sports that followed baseball. In the two chapters that follow this one, the challenges entailed in organizing a major league will be examined.

The Summer Game

Baseball evolved from the children's game of English rounders.[4] Though first mentioned as a game of "base" in the diary of a revolutionary soldier in 1778, it was not until the 1830s that references to "base ball" suggest it was widely known or played. The first open challenge documented was issued on July 12, 1825, by a group of nine men in Delaware County, New York (Rader 1992). Early enthusiasts were mostly from the urban upper middle class, including prosperous merchants, bankers, doctors, lawyers, and clerks, who played the game within athletic clubs organized along occupational lines (Adelman 1986). Intraclub matches were usually scheduled on midweek afternoons and followed by gala banquets and balls as part of social occasions rather than intense competitions. Women were eagerly invited to such occasions, and their presence became a sign that the men were not merely pursuing a boy's game (Goldstein 1989). Publicity, however, was avoided. George Kirsch (1989, p. 12) notes, "Perhaps because of their defensiveness about playing a child's game, or because they valued privacy, they did not seek publicity in the city's daily or weekly papers." Only later, in the late 1850s, was the baseball contest disentangled from a web of fraternal rituals and club activities and put forward as the focal point for players, spectators, and the press.

As the number of clubs grew in the 1840s and 1850s, numerous versions of baseball began to compete for primacy. The need to standardize rules became a major impetus for organizing the sport. Alexander Cartwright, a bank clerk and member of the New York Knickerbockers (founded in 1842), assumed a pivotal role in codifying the New York version of the game and championing it over its main rival, the Massachusetts version. Cartwright's version was safer, simpler, and easier for adults to master, substituting the tag, for example, for throwing the ball at runners to make an "out." The pace was also quickened by limiting the game to nine three-out innings (versus requiring 100 runs, or putting out an entire team), ensuring that the contests could end before evening (Kirsch 1989). The game remained much different from the modern version, however. Pitching was underhand, and batters could specify where they wanted the pitch placed and wait for the pitch they desired. Fielders wore no gloves and could let the ball bounce once before catching it. These and many other differences serve as reminders that baseball was not the immutable invention of one person, but a sport that evolved gradually through the energies of many people and groups.

Clubs fielded a number of teams of varying strengths, and early games were primarily intraclub events. The Knickerbockers' top team ventured out in 1846, but was trounced so badly that it did not play another recorded game with an external foe until 1851 (Rader 1992). By the 1850s, however, growing interclub rivalries had started attracting public attention to the teams and the sport. The first tabulated score (predecessor of the box score) appeared in the *New York Clipper* on July 16, 1853, covering a July 5 game between the Knickerbockers and the Gothams (Lieb 1951, p. 24). An informal Massachusetts championship in 1857 attracted 2,000 spectators. A growing Manhattan-Brooklyn rivalry served as a model for arousing interest. In Philadelphia, a game with the Brooklyn Excelsiors drew "a vast crowd" of 2,500 as reported in a Philadelphia newspaper. Struck by the way these spectators carried on, one reporter complained, "the crowd seemed to think that games were got up for their special entertainment and that they were conferring a favor on the players by their presence" (quoted in Seymour 1960, p. 29). The idea of baseball as a spectator sport still seemed odd to this reporter.

During these formative years, baseball was also spreading quickly among the working classes. Teams of "dudes, carpenters, and fishpeddlers" formed across the East River in Long Island, but were snubbed by the Knickerbockers as "coarse and vulgar" (Lieb 1951). Fire companies, who had for some time held competitions among themselves and had recently started recruiting boxers, enthusiastically took up baseball in the 1850s (Goldstein 1989). After considerable agitation by working-class teams for a meeting to clarify rules, in March 1858 the presidents of four of the established New York teams organized a convention. Twenty-two clubs were represented, and together they formed the National Association of Base Ball Players (NABBP). Knickerbocker members failed to get even a minor post in the new association, an exclusion that both reflected and enhanced the broadening appeal of baseball. A two-thirds vote was required for admission (by 1859, fifty clubs had been admitted). Players had to be members of a club for thirty days to play, a rule designed to prevent the borrowing, and soon the hiring, of ringers to get an edge on a rival. Because games were played on open fields and hence could be observed by anyone, no provisions were made regarding revenues.

Adults distinguished themselves from boys by refusing first entry into the NABBP, then just voting privileges, to teams of young players (Kirsch 1989). Manliness was a touchy issue, and became material for the burgeoning newspaper industry of the time. One of the first great sportswriters and champions of baseball, Henry Chadwick, took great care to portray the sport as work governed by science. Baseball was an "invigorating exercise and manly pastime" much different from the "primitive" and "simple game" of rounders, designed "only for the relaxation of school boys" (quoted in Goldstein 1989, p. 45). Chadwick's writing helped the *New York Clipper*, founded in 1853, eclipse the two-decade-old *Spirit of the Times* (circ. 100,000) as the premier sporting weekly. With the press actively involved, the issue of what was manly versus boyish came to a head over the fly rule (which required a fly ball to be caught before it hit the ground). After being defeated five times starting in the late 1850s by a coalition of "traditionalists and socially minded," the fly rule was adopted in 1865 (Goldstein 1989, p. 50).

Even Protestant clergy, previously suspicious of idle play and the gambling associated with sports, jumped on the bandwagon by developing a new gospel of "muscular Christianity" (Gutmann 1988; Kirsch 1989). With the help of press and clergy, baseball became a legitimate adult activity on a par with cricket, an undisputedly manly game that the British had brought to America. Unlike cricket, however, baseball was not controlled by exclusive clubs rooted in British sporting traditions. As the popularity of baseball grew, cricket was stymied by its exclusivity. Cricketers shunned prospective working- and middle-class players by emphasizing stately clubhouses, proper attire, correct deportment, and strict adherence to British rules (Jable 1991).

Detached from the children's game and from the control of exclusive clubs, baseball was ripe for commercial development. An all-star series was organized in the late summer of 1858 between Brooklyn and New York players, marking the first time spectators were asked to pay. The series was played at a horse-racing track where, unlike other baseball sites, spectators could be kept out. In 1860, the first great baseball tour was undertaken by Brooklyn's Excelsior Club, making good use of rapidly expanding railroads as well as the telegraph system. The Excelsiors easily beat locally prominent teams throughout their tour, which began in upstate New York and then went as far south as Washington, D.C. Jim Creighton, a pitcher for the Excelsiors, became the first player to be paid for playing, a practice that did not come out in the open until 1866 (Seymour 1960). By 1867 the press was commonly referring to "professional clubs," even though there were not supposed to be any in the NABBP (Goldstein 1989). The payment of players put pressure on teams to enclose playing fields and start charging admission.

An "enclosure movement" began in 1862, when Brooklyn's William Cammeyer converted his ice-skating pond into an enclosed baseball field as a way to generate summer revenues (Rader 1992). In deference to the Civil War then raging, he called his 1,500-seat wooden stadium "Union Grounds." The enclosure movement quickly gained momentum. By 1868, in the midst of a post–Civil War surge of baseball popularity, the eight most prominent clubs together took in as much as $100,000 in annual gate receipts from their newly built stadiums (Seymour 1960).

By the late 1860s the tremendous commercial potential of baseball had become readily apparent. Yet athletic clubs, numbering 340 at the 1868 NABBP convention, were not well suited for exploiting this potential. Large cities had numerous clubs, and there was no mechanism to limit the number of clubs in a city. Both the NABBP and the clubs were run by players, who welcomed the growth of clubs as a sign of legitimacy for the sport. While the practice of paying players began to put financial pressure on ambitious teams, the rarity of contracts extending beyond individual games limited the financial risk. Strong players who could command payment for their services "revolved" from team to team in what was often seen as a perversion of club integrity and British sporting tradition (where sportsmen were gentlemen, not working-class mercenaries). Although most clubs sought the publicity and gate receipts that came from winning, some were reluctant to abandon what, in the light of encroaching professionalism, were being articulated as amateur ideals.

The transition to professionalism within clubs was often quite subtle. Most clubs had many teams, ranging from their "top nine" to their "muffins" on the bottom. As a reward, the top nine were often exempted from club dues. This practice had the effect of making mobility between clubs easier, and fostered a businesslike relation between the exempt member-players and the club director. Warren Goldstein observes (1989, p. 99), "The vocabulary of management entered the baseball world suddenly, almost without warning in 1867." Dues-exempt members were transformed into paid employees, and club directors into managers.

Besides athletic clubs, some strong teams were attached to colleges. Intercollegiate baseball was played (coupled with a chess match) as early as 1859, at Williams and Amherst, and soon after at Harvard, Tufts, Yale, Dartmouth, and then most other major colleges. Baseball was a popular college sport, although summer vacation limited the season to less than thirty games. But sports were new to colleges, and their organization depended entirely on student initiative. Nearly all of the 180 existing colleges were church affiliated, with clergymen as presidents. Activities were strictly regulated, with compulsory chapel and study hours. In 1787 Princeton's faculty had ruled out ball playing as "low and unbecoming gentlemen" (Seymour 1990, p. 131). Only as a result of student rebellions during the 1830s were extracurricular activities such as literary societies, debating, music, and sports tolerated. With little or no financial support, faculty involvement, professional coaching (teams had player captains and a student athletic director), or convenient means of travel, there were too many obstacles to organizing intercollegiate sports on even a regional basis.[5] When the first intercollegiate sporting event was organized, a Harvard-Yale crew meet in 1852, a reporter for the *New York Tribune* commented that intercollegiate sport would "make little stir in the busy world" (Lucas and Smith 1978, p. 197).

Baseball also found its way into high schools in a similar manner. In 1859, when students in Massachusetts formed the Worcester High School Baseball Club, the first of its kind, school officials intervened to prevent students from associating the school name with a baseball club. Before long, however, the school administration came to realize the value of such sponsorship, as college administrations were also soon to do. At Princeton, the president came to see sports as "gentlemanly contests for supremacy" (Seymour 1990, p. 144). Yet as school baseball grew in popularity, both mounting abuses and growing opportunities led administrators to seek control over student-run athletic activities. Ringers had quickly appeared in both college and high school matches, raising conflicts over eligibility rules that continue to this day. Control over gate receipts and expenses was also the source of much contention.

As players and teams started to make money, corruption found its way into both club and school baseball. With virtually no regulatory systems in place, gamblers tampered with players or hired rowdies to influence game outcomes with words, bottles, or an occasional physical assault on a team member. Teams themselves engaged in "hippodroming," in which they took turns losing to each other to create the impression of being closely matched, hoping to arouse crowd interest for future contests. Players who moved from team to team would not show up for games they were paid to play, and not get paid for games they did play. Schedules were left entirely to teams, and numerous problems arose because teams sometimes failed to appear for a scheduled game, or demanded too high a money guarantee after arriving. Cooperation with the NABBP was voluntary, and there were no mechanisms to enforce rules. A student-formed American College Base Ball Association (1879) failed to work out eligibility rules, as did an agreement among college administrators four years later when students rebelled against faculty interference.

Amid the burgeoning interest in baseball, city politicians and local businessmen became interested in the sport as more than a pastime for themselves. The biographer of Al Spaulding notes, "In cities as small as Rockford and as large as Chicago, the recognition that winning baseball teams might be profitable investments while also serving as significant symbols of a city's prominence and potential propelled important changes in the game . . . clubs increasingly admitted as members anyone whose qualifications consisted of baseball talent rather than of requisite social status . . . by 1865 (when 15-year-old Spaulding joined the Rockford Club) clubs were not above charging admission, paying ballplayers, or providing them with fulltime jobs off the diamond because of their performance on it" (Levine 1985, p. 7). Spaulding took a job as clerk in a business owned by the vice president of the Rockford Club, a man "as much interested in the ball club of the town as he was in his own business" (p. 9). As early as 1866 a tournament was held for town teams in western New York with teams from Buffalo, Albany, and two from Rochester.

In some larger cities, players were placed on the city payroll in various guises. Members of the New York Mutuals, controlled by Boss William Tweed, drew a total of $30,000 annually from the street sweeping and coroner's departments (Pietrusza 1991). When, in 1868, the NABBP repealed its prohibition against teams playing clubs with professional players, professionalism was not long in venturing into the open. The next year, the Cincinnati Red Stockings became the first openly salaried, and hence fully professional, club in America. Two years earlier, the club had started bringing in professionals to compete with a local rival club, the Buckeyes. Four Red Stockings drew salaries in 1968, while the rest were compensated with a share of the gate receipts. Many club members, however, soon grew disenchanted with the mix of outside professionals and club members and with the club's growing debt ($8,000–$9,000). In a heated debate over whether to eliminate paid outsiders or pursue the very best of them, the club's civic boosters won out. For them, the team was less a money-making venture than an effort to publicize their hometown (Riess 1989). Strong touring teams from both clubs and colleges were beginning to attract national attention. At the time Cincinnati was a young vibrant city of over 200,000 people, still on the periphery of the national landscape. It was in need of an identity to enter the circuit of cities that increasingly were to dominate national life.

The idea of a professional team representing a city originated in the West, sparked by intense rivalries between upstart western cities. "Only a few decades separated small, sleepy trading posts from large, bustling cities . . . local newspapermen, merchants, and manufacturers frequently resorted to strident boosterism" in promoting this transformation (Rader 1992, p. 25). Soon after the Cincinnati Red Stockings formed, rival Chicago boosters organized a team of their own. Joseph Modell of the *Chicago Tribune* and Potter Palmer of the Palmer House organized the Chicago White Stockings as a joint stock company. In eastern cities, too many established clubs existed for any to represent its city. Success brought recognition to a club in its rivalry with other clubs, although there was certainly prestige to be gained for any outside club that could beat one of the intracity rivals.

Ignoring the still powerful stigma of professionalism amid the traditional entities of athletic clubs and colleges, civic boosters used professionals to help construct an identity for their city.[6] Only one of the ten members of the all-professional Cincinnati Red Stockings was a local man. At this early stage, all had other professions, including engraving, bookkeeping, piano tuning, insurance, marble cutting, and jewelry making (Lieb 1951). With no pretense to loyalty, the players were paid to gain attention for Cincinnati through winning. The local press helped legitimate the effort by carefully explaining to Cincinnatians that, even though the players might have come from the New York area, their "capital play is mainly to be attributed to their organization, and, as that originated and was perfected in Cincinnati, that city is fully entitled to credit therefore" (quoted in Goldstein 1989, p. 116). In this way the association between professional teams and cities was born.

The Cincinnati Red Stockings attracted considerable attention for "their" city. During their 1869 season, in a 12,000-mile coast-to-coast tour played before 200,000 people, they won fifty-six games, lost none, and tied only once (56–0–1).[7] After beating six of the best New York teams, they were welcomed upon arriving in Washington by President Ulysses S. Grant. But after winning their first twenty-three games of the next season, support for the team on the road waned and then collapsed after the issue of who would be the first to beat them was resolved by the Brooklyn Atlantics (by one run). With players making "exorbitant" salary demands, club members concluded that the team had "failed to live up to expected standards" and disbanded a team that had lost only four games by the end of its second season (Goldstein 1989, p. 118). Although the team had made a profit its first year, it only broke even in 1870. Suddenly amateurism took on renewed appeal for the Cincinnati club members who had remained behind. The press changed its colors, arguing that the paid players were not representatives of the "real club," whose members were back home, but only hired assistants. Professionals kept the real members from becoming skilled players, in a game that suddenly became "sport and recreation" as opposed to a regular trade (Goldstein 1989, p. 120).

As the Cincinnati experience illustrates, amateurism and professionalism were articulated in parallel. From the murky soup of club baseball in the 1860s emerged the two counterposing alternatives. Each was unstable without a larger organization to fit within. Professional leagues and powerful amateur organizations had not yet appeared. Both were to grow as offshoots of the weak NABBP, which was unable to resolve within itself the struggle between amateurism and professionalism. This struggle, entangled with struggles between New York and the periphery and between state associations and the national association, led to the demise of the NABBP by 1874.

As early as 1866, elite athletic clubs formed in New York to promote amateurism. College administrators used these clubs as models in their struggles with student-run college athletic programs. Later these clubs organized into the Amateur Athletic Union (AAU) and colleges organized into the National Collegiate Athletic Association (NCAA), giving strong organizational backing to amateurism.[8] Clubs opting for professionalism, however, were, quicker to organize. This fortuitous development had profound consequences for the future of team sports. Major league baseball was to provide a stable context in which professional athletes and teams could prosper, a feat that was greatly facilitated by the absence of powerful amateur organizations during the start-up years.

Outside a league context, professional teams like the Cincinnati Red Stockings could gain attention but not sustain involvement. People turned out in distant towns to see the new Red Stockings, as they would for any odd and unique phenomenon. But even if the Red Stockings had continued to win, it is doubtful whether return visits would have been met with the same curiosity. Success was predicated on winning, but this required a team to keep moving in search of new challengers. Even Cincinnatians, had the Red Stockings played more of their games at home, would have soon tired from the lack of strong visiting teams. The lack of a home audience later contributed to the demise of the great New York Celtics basketball team shortly after it joined—and dominated—the first major basketball league. Hence the association of the Red Stockings with Cincinnati had meaning primarily outside the team and city. It was not until major leagues emerged that professional teams became securely attached to cities and sustained the enthusiasm of local fans season after season.

Traveling teams good enough to elicit the investment of local boosters could win consistently by playing local teams. Yet traveling teams would also play other traveling teams, mostly in what was downplayed as an "exhibition" game, or strong teams from well-organized local clubs. The importance of winning can be seen from the negative consequences of the unavoidable losses in these games. A few losses proved fatal for the Red Stockings. Independent teams that followed were no more secure. Three-quarters of them failed to survive more than two years (Vincent 1981). And losses brought negative publicity. A Chicago newspaper reported, after a loss to St. Louis in 1875, that "a deep gloom settled over the city. Friends refused to recognize friends, lovers became estranged, and business was suspended. All Chicago went to a funeral, and the time, since then, has dragged wearily along, as though it were no object to live longer in this world" (quoted in Radar 1992, p. 29). If the country's best teams were to start playing each other on a regular basis, losing somehow had to be better accommodated.

By the end of 1870, the groundwork for major leagues in baseball had been laid. Baseball had widespread appeal, both geographically and across the social spectrum. Various players and teams had gained national attention, distinguishing themselves from the mass of grass-roots players and teams. Contentious debates took place over the relative ability of teams, and large crowds turned out to observe decisive matches. Most important, however, professionalism had emerged. Unable to gain a secure footing in interclub or interschool rivalries, professionals found a place for themselves as participants in intercity rivalries. As free-floating opportunists, professional baseball players were enlisted by civic boosters to forge identities for newly emerging cities. As cities were themselves agglomerates of newly arrived persons seeking opportunity, professionals had found a place where they might fit in. The possibility of a lasting attachment between professional teams and cities was the idea around which major leagues first formed.

A Fall College Game

At the same time that baseball was growing in popularity, other team sports began attracting attention as well. Colleges, in particular, became seedbeds of sports activity, first entirely through student initiative and later through the eager participation of administrators, who began to recognize the publicity value of sports. As early as the 1870s, Cornell was charging sports expenses to its advertising budget. President Henry Barnard, in congratulating Columbia's crew after a regatta victory, acknowledged that they had "done more to make Columbia known than all your predecessors[—]because little was known about Columbia one month ago[,] but today wherever the telegraph cable extends, the existence of Columbia College is known and respected" (quoted in Lucas and Smith 1978, p. 218). With summer baseball in the firm control of the major leagues by the mid-1870s, college students and administrators turned to other sports and other seasons for something to rival baseball's success.

Football evolved within elite eastern colleges as a modified combination of English rugby and soccer, and became associated with the fall beginnings of the college year. For a while each college cultivated its own version of the game. A match between Harvard and McGill in 1874 used Harvard (soccer) rules for one half and McGill (rugby) rules for the other. In November 1876, Yale, Harvard, Princeton, and Columbia formed the Intercollegiate Football Association (IFA), but Yale pulled out four hours later after failing to get a desired rule change in the game (Falla 1981). Ultimately Yale's Walter Camp introduced rule changes in 1880 that took hold. The main innovation, giving one side undisputed possession of the ball, forever split American football away from its English predecessors.

College football was immensely popular with spectators from the start, reigning supreme among college sports by the 1890s. At Yale, football receipts accounted for one-eighth of the institution's total income, an amount greater than its expenditures on law and medicine (Gorn and Goldstein 1993). With no professional leagues casting a shadow over the college game, college football and its players became exemplars of the sport. But the college game was often brutal and even fatal for players. Mass plays involved barreling down the field in tight formation around the ball carrier. One play, in which the ball carrier jumped off the back of a fellow-player and flew through the air, was blocked only when a defender did the same, resulting in a mid-air collision. With up to forty-four deaths a season and many more serious injuries, college presidents found themselves caught between these alarming numbers and the alluring revenue and publicity football generated. The need to manage both more carefully was the major impetus for administrative intervention in student-controlled sports programs.

When John Crowell moved from Yale to Trinity to assume its presidency in 1887, football was "a crucial part of his plans to remake sleepy Trinity College into a modern educational institution" (Summer 1990, p. 6). With the help of a student imported from Yale and a 225-pound railroad agent from a nearby town, Trinity pulled off a surprise upset over the University of North Carolina in 1888.[9] In the 1890s the University of Chicago's first president, William Harper, similarly placed sports achievement on a par with scholastic achievement in building a great university. He hired Amos Alonzo Stagg and directed him to "develop teams which we can send around the country and knock out all the colleges. We will give [our varsity players] a palace car and a vacation too" (quoted in Seymour 1990, p. 154). Besides helping a school achieve general visibility, successful sports programs rapidly became prime vehicles for gaining continued support of alumni.

But football fatalities too often put a check on college promotion of the sport. The problem rose all the way to the White House, where President Theodore Roosevelt held a conference with the "Big Three" (Harvard, Yale, and Princeton) on October 9, 1905. The IFA's rules committee, however, requiring a unanimous vote, was unable to agree on rule changes when it met in early December. In this crisis atmosphere, the chancellor of New York University called together representatives of twenty-eight colleges on December 28, 1905. Out of this meeting, the National Collegiate Athletic Association was formed.[10] Significantly, the Big Three were left out, but their (IFA's) rules committee was invited by the newly elected NCAA president Captain Palmer Pierce to join forces with the new NCAA's own rules committee. The NCAA's committee required only a majority vote to adopt a change in the rules. Among its early contributions was the forward pass, which Notre Dame popularized in 1913.[11]

The NCAA's vitality was evident from the start, and soon it could bring resisters into the fold by threatening to exclude nonmembers from competition. Quick to claim jurisdiction over other sports, like basketball in 1907, the NCAA soon became a regulatory body for all college sports. Membership grew from thirty-eight colleges in 1906 to ninety-seven in 1912. Harvard and Columbia joined in 1909, Princeton in 1913, with Yale holding out until 1915. A "clean" reputation was carefully cultivated for college sports and deliberately contrasted with the corruption found in professional baseball. Through eligibility rules, the NCAA tried to prevent college athletes from participating in professional baseball during the summers. Loyalty to one's team, along with the lack of compensation, was underscored in the emerging definition of amateur. Athletes had to have ties to their college—measured in terms of both time enrolled and academic standing—that went beyond the sports program. The image of the committed student-athlete was deliberately contrasted with the play-for-pay reality of professionals.[12]

Sports organizers seeking to promote a professional version of football had to contend with powerful amateur organizations like the

NCAA, the Amateur Athletic Union, and the Olympic Movement, none of which existed at the time professional baseball appeared. Large and loyal college audiences had been cultivated before professional football began, with important college games drawing up to 40,000 spectators. Fans identified with nationally prominent players and teams. College programs aggressively stigmatized professionalism among players (though not among coaches), and the resulting marginality of professional options did much to discourage college players from pursuing football careers. Only much later could the renown of college players be tapped by professional leagues, when it meant more to be a professional ballplayer and less to be a college graduate.[13] At the turn of the century, the prospects for professional football were by no means clear.

Professional football had to develop in the periphery and only later move in on the college-dominated eastern cities. The first professional football player, a ringer, was William Heffelfinger, who played for the Pittsburgh Athletic Club in 1892 under the assumed name of "Stayer." In a rematch, Stayer moved to Pittsburgh's opponent, the Allegheny Athletic Association. This episode raised a furor over professionalism that raged for weeks in the Pittsburgh newspaper. Three years later the Allegheny club was barred from the AAU for signing contracts with three players. The AAU was determined to stop the "evils of professionalism" from spreading beyond baseball (Bennett 1977). After a few efforts at barnstorming, the Allegheny club went bankrupt in 1897.

Football was especially popular among small-town steel- and coal workers, and teams were encouraged and supported by industrialists as an early instance of welfare capitalism. A steel industrialist, W. C. Temple, became the first owner of an all-professional team in 1899 when the club sought his help. Industrialist friends of Temple's, W. E. Corey (the future president of U.S. Steel) and A. C. Dinkey, soon had teams of their own. Players were recruited from among the steelworkers. When Dinkey, however, not only went after a college star but raided Temple's team, Temple was outraged. Temple teamed up with Major League Baseball's Barney Dreyfuss, owner of the Pittsburgh Pirates (a nickname earned from the team's habit of stealing players), and raided back his stolen players to form the new Pittsburgh Professionals. The Professionals were the first football team to openly admit professional status. Owners of the two major league Philadelphia teams followed suit in fielding their own football teams, even using some baseball players on their squads.

But crowds were not large. Professional football teams could not compete with local colleges in arousing spectator interest. Even the first "World Series" in team sports, played indoors at Madison Square Garden in 1902 and again in 1903, failed to garner momentum for professional football. But professional football was to take hold farther west, in Ohio. A state football championship among amateur clubs had been held in Ohio since 1896, when, in 1903, the Massillon Tigers imported professionals from the Pittsburgh Athletic Club and beat the reigning state champion 12–0. By the next year, there were eight professional teams in Ohio. Enthusiasm for professional football declined after 1906, however, when Blondy Wallace, coach of the Canton team, was accused of throwing two games for betting purposes. Canton disbanded, not to return until 1911. It was not until 1915, when Canton signed Jim Thorpe, hero of the 1912 Olympics, that interest in professional football was revived in Ohio. Five years later, the National Football League was launched from a Canton car dealership.

It took twenty-eight years from the time that the first professional appeared in football for a professional league to form that could eventually penetrate the large eastern cities. Baseball accomplished this transition in less than ten years, and had highly successful major leagues in operation throughout professional football's early development. As we have seen, baseball owners (and players) had an interest in developing professional football. Yet getting a second professional sport started proved more difficult than the first, owing to the rise of powerful amateur organizations. They effectively marginalized the professional version of football, in much the same way that professional baseball marginalized college baseball. It was only much later, in the modern era of televised sport, that college and professional versions became complementary.

An Inner-City Game

With baseball filling the spring and summer months and football occupying the fall, winter became conspicuous for its lack of a team sport. This presented a problem for a Massachusetts physical education instructor, James Naismith, who needed to find a winter diversion for the restless YMCA youths in his charge. Using peach baskets and a leather-laced ball, Naismith organized the first game of basketball in 1891. Although Naismith sought to emphasize skill over force, his rules and penalties proved insufficient to prevent roughness and outright melees. With the innovations of dribbling and jump shots still far off, and as many as eighty men on variably sized courts, getting a shot off was a rare event (and there was no time limit on possession). Robert Peterson (1990, p. 23) gives a participant's account of a 1892 YMCA game played in Trenton, New Jersey:

> Very few of the eighty who started in with nice new gym uniforms came out with their shirts on their backs, and most of us were artistically tattooed with fingernail scratches. Frequently there were twenty or more fairly good wrestling matches going on simultaneously, and occasional scientific sparring exhibitions took place without in any slightest way interfering with the progress of the game. I cannot recall the scoring of any goals because the defensive work was so remarkable that not one of the eighty players engaged secured on open shot for the bushel basket. If any player did get his hands on the ball it took several minutes to dig him out from under the mob that immediately hopped him.

With free throws not yet introduced, few teams exceeded ten baskets unless the game was very lopsided. The absence of a backboard (later introduced to keep balcony fans from interfering) did not help matters. The numerous changes that made the modern high-scoring contest possible were the result of a struggle among those who sought control over the game.

Yet even in its earliest version, basketball had an immediate appeal. The game spread rapidly among inner-city ethnic groups who frequented the numerous settlement houses central to their community life (Riess 1989, p. 107). Basketball games followed by dances became a respectable way for young men and women to intermingle. The popularity of basketball actually became a problem for many YMCA directors, who watched the rough game squeeze out virtually all other YMCA activities. Some put limits on the use of YMCA facilities for basketball, prompting many young men to look elsewhere for a place to play the game. Armories and dance halls became popular basketball sites. To cover rental and equipment costs, the teams cast off by the YMCA started to charge admission to games (often followed by dances). The first documented case in which players received a share of the proceeds is an 1896 game played in Trenton. The Trenton team played twenty games that season, against high school, college, and

YMCA teams (though the Trenton YMCA director forbade play against professionals), accumulating a 19–1 record. Soon there were many professional teams.

As in football, however, professionalism provoked considerable opposition. Adopting YMCA rules, the AAU had been quick to claim jurisdiction over the game. The YMCA and numerous other clubs and associations aligned themselves with the AAU, which sponsored interclub matches and tournaments. A national basketball championship organized by the AAU—involving twelve teams, mostly from New York—was first held in 1897 in New York City. Resisting the "evils of professionalism" was high on the AAU's agenda, although rules in this area were hard to enforce. In 1899 the AAU conceded that an amateur team could play a professional team as long as the latter registered itself as such (to prevent it from also playing as an amateur team). One team that innocently registered found itself thrown out of the YMCA facilities it practiced in.

High schools and colleges were also quick to adopt, and claim jurisdiction over, basketball. Second only to football, the school game soon exceeded baseball and track in popularity. The first intercollegiate game was played on February 9, 1895. By 1901 Harvard, Columbia, Princeton, Cornell, and Yale organized the Eastern League, and Dartmouth, Holy Cross, Amherst, and Williams formed the New England League. Women's colleges were in the forefront, with Vassar and Smith adding basketball to their sports programs as early as 1892 (Falla 1981). When the young NCAA incorporated the Ivy-dominated Basketball Rules Committee into its own rules committee in 1907, it thereby assumed control over college basketball. Small differences between the AAU and the college game emerged, and were nurtured as a part of the NCAA and AAU's struggle for jurisdiction over the game.

Sports organizers had to contend with this backdrop of grass-roots professionals and powerful amateur organizations. For a glimpse into the early era, consider the Flip Dowling story (Peterson 1990, pp. 6–7). An Albany, New York, group that ran dances in the Catholic Union Hall, which had been an armory, started a basketball team and asked Dowling to join. Every Friday night the group held a basketball game followed by a dance. On other nights, the organizers looked for games in the small towns around Albany. But after having its receipts stolen one night, the group dropped the team. An alderman and saloon owner by the name of Dolan became the new backer, with the team playing under the name of the Dolans. By this time Dowling was in college, so he had to play for the Dolans under an assumed name to keep his NCAA eligibility. When World War I ended, a returning army team led by Brownie Hepinstall provided the Dolans with a rivalry that filled the house. Hepinstall later became manager of the Dolans, and reorganized the New York State League. Dowling played for this league, and later became a referee and high school basketball and football coach.

As the story indicates, professional basketball came in the form of both independent teams and regional leagues. Leagues first appeared in 1898, only two years after the first independent teams. Unlike either baseball or football, the struggle between the two forms of organization in basketball weighed heavily in favor of independent teams, and did so for nearly fifty years. Leagues remained regional until after World War II, except for a short-lived American Basketball League that fell victim to the Depression. Independent teams, however, could capture more widespread attention as they wandered throughout the country (mostly the Northeast) looking for games. After being thrown out of the YMCA, the newly christened New York Wanderers played for years without a home court. Another renowned team was the Buffalo Germans, formed at the Buffalo YMCA in 1895 when its members were fourteen-year-olds and venturing out a few years later as a touring professional club. At one point racking up 111 consecutive victories, the team produced a 792–86 record over two decades of play. Not well supported at home, the Germans played over 80 percent of their games on the road. Another great touring club was Frank Basloe's Oswego Indians, which went 121–6 in 1914–15. A flamboyant promoter, Basloe one year had his team playing under two identities (using reversible jerseys) when a neighboring army company had trouble fielding a team (Peterson 1990).

Unlike baseball, basketball players were and still are drawn from urban, primarily inner-city, populations. Before 1940, 90 percent of professional basketball players were urban, one-third of them from New York City. In the 1990s the percentage of professionals from urban backgrounds remains the same, but now blacks constitute almost 80 percent of the professionals. This change in ethnic composition mirrors the changes taking place within urban areas since the 1940s. As blacks filled the inner city, they inherited the game of basketball from the groups they displaced.

Early independent basketball teams were invariably associated with ethnic groups and became an important source of ethnic community pride. Three-quarters of the prominent early players were German, Jewish, or Irish (Riess 1989). In 1912 the New York Celtics were formed from the Irish community. A decade later, the "Original Celtics"—now containing some Jewish players—were assembled by Jim Furey and quickly became the leading professional team. The Polish Detroit Pulaskis enjoyed a large measure of regional success. A black team, the Harlem Rens, was founded in 1922 and later became a dominant team despite the numerous racial barriers it encountered on the road.

Most independent teams—like the Dolans—failed to achieve fame. Few could afford to travel farther from their home base than an evening's return trip. Most professional players held regular jobs that they had to come back for, and few could afford overnight accommodations. Only teams that could command high guarantees ventured far from home, on barnstorming tours. Teams like the Original Celtics and the Rens gained national fame by barnstorming across regions and beating locally dominant teams, including college teams and informal teams made up of college players. During the Depression the Celtics required a guarantee of $125 a game, with an option of 60 percent of the gate receipts. Unlike the Buffalo Germans, the Celtics did not run up the score on overmatched teams. This restraint "made good business sense because it assured that the Celtics would be welcomed back when next they wandered into that territory" (Peterson 1990, p. 76). When playing two games in a town, the first was often deliberately kept close to stir enthusiasm for the second. Always on the road, however, traveling teams lacked the opportunity to build local support. The very best became national teams, yet without television they had to depend on local populations for survival.

Many barnstorming teams played up the novelty aspect. One team grew beards and traveled as the House of Davids. A Swede, Ole Olson, who shot free throws overhead with his back to the basket, organized and played with Olson's Terrible Swedes. After his playing days were over, Olson put together an all-women road team—the All-American Red Heads. The Red Heads played mostly amateur men's teams, with a success rate over 50 percent and in some years as high as 85 or 90 percent. The team was so successful that in the latter half of its forty-year stint, there were two or three Red Head teams on the road at the same time. The most famous and enduring basketball road show is the

Harlem Globetrotters, in operation since 1927. Starting as a serious and talented black team, the Globetrotters began introducing show routines to relieve the tedium of one-sided games. When a team performed purely as entertainment, won-lost records and even game scores ceased to be important or even attended to. But the drawback was that teams could not return often to any site, as the attention that novelty attracts was short-lived.

Traveling teams played an important role in diffusing techniques of play, and from their ranks they provided numerous college coaches (Isaacs 1984). High school and college teams would travel great distances to watch these teams play. The members of Furey's Original Celtics were the first to be put on straight salary and to develop an identity as a team. This gave them the opportunity to make innovations in teamwork, such as the pivot play. But this kind of independence was something that only a small number of teams could afford to sustain. League play stood as a less glamorous alternative. Most independent teams (and players) were part of a league at one time or another.

Professional leagues long consisted of only loosely structured and short-lived regional alliances. Such was the first league, a six-team National Basketball League formed in 1898 to protect players against unscrupulous promoters (Hollander 1981). It consisted of teams in Trenton and Camden and the Milville Pennsylvania Bicycle, Hancock Athletic, and Germantown clubs, and survived for five years. When it folded, many of its players joined the Philadelphia League, which soon expanded into the Eastern League (1909–1923). Other short-lived leagues included the Central League, the Tri-county League, and the New York State League. In terms of demographics, none of these leagues approached major league status.

One problem these leagues faced was that players were not bound by contracts and were constantly switching teams. A future Celtics star, Joe Lapchick, bargained with team managers over every game he played. Offering more prestige and financial reward, top traveling teams skimmed off talented players like Lapchick as soon as they aroused local fan interest. Although most early leagues had rules that restricted player mobility, akin to baseball's reserve clause, the rules were nearly impossible to enforce with all the other leagues and independent teams that fell outside their jurisdiction. Some players played for as many as five teams a season. A manager in New Jersey noted that just twenty men represented the ten teams he had booked for home games in the 1908 season (Peterson 1990).

In 1920 the presidents of the four existing professional leagues met and agreed to set up a three-man National Commission to make rules and settle disputes among leagues. The presidents' main aims were to restrict players to one league, forbid exhibition games with independent teams, and set up a world series. But despite the fanfare, the National Commission was unable to prevent players from jumping teams or team owners from coveting the talent of other teams. Even the world series proved unworkable when it was discovered that several of the same players played for the champions of both the Eastern and the Penn State leagues. The National Commission died soon after it was born.

Up to the mid-1920s, professional basketball was something that most people equated with barnstorming teams that would sporadically pass through town. Regional leagues received no attention in the press outside of their home cities, which were mostly small towns. These leagues operated in the shadows of barnstorming teams and school teams, which were thriving. By the mid-1920s, 93 percent of high schools had basketball teams, as did virtually every major college. Establishing a major league in basketball entailed a battle on two fronts. As in football, college efforts to marginalize the professional version had to be overcome. But unlike in football, popular barnstorming teams also posed a direct challenge to a major league.

In the early 1920s some sports organizers began to question the emphasis on force over skill in the professional version of basketball. Under the leadership of the NCAA, college basketball had modified Naismith's rough-and-tumble game in many significant ways. It prohibited the two-handed dribble, which allowed a player to bull his way through opposition instead of passing the ball. Naismith's rule that the first team to retrieve an out-of-bounds ball could bring it inbounds was also changed. This rule motivated dangerous dashes of players through crowds of spectators, prompting the first professional leagues to place wire or rope cages around the court to keep the ball and players inbounds. Besides being the source of many lacerations, the cages carried connotations that reinforced the rough image of the game. College basketball, however, simply awarded the out-of-bounds ball to the team that had not touched it last.

Rule changes helped broaden the appeal of league basketball, although it would be decades before it could rival the college game in popularity. The struggle to displace independent professional teams, related in Chapter 4, also was slow in yielding results. By attaching themselves to ethnic groups, the independent teams encouraged a division of fans along ethnic lines. Major league efforts to attach professional teams to large cities, composed of a mix of ethnic groups, were impeded by these ethnic loyalties. The problem has never been wholly resolved. With players 80 percent black in today's National Basketball Association, owners must worry about the depth of identification of some white fans with "their" team.[14]

A Winter Game

Ice hockey originated and underwent considerable development in Canada before it came to the United States. First mentioned as a pastime of English soldiers serving with the Royal Canadian Rifles in 1855, ice hockey evolved from field hockey (devised in Persia around 2000 B.C.), lacrosse, and rugby adapted to ice (Brasch 1970). The earliest record of an ice hockey match dates back to 1875, taking place at McGill University. In 1879 a McGill student wrote the first code of rules. In regard to timing and university origins, hockey parallels American football almost exactly. It was not until the 1890s, however, that ice hockey entered the United States, thus sharing its United States debut, its winter season, and many of its facilities with basketball.[15]

Hockey's long incubation in Canada left many distinctive features that persist to this day. Unlike in the United States, the struggle between amateurism and professionalism produced a single hierarchy dominated by the professional version. Thus a prized trophy, the Stanley Cup, could pass from the possession of amateur leagues to a premier professional league in a way that would be inconceivable in the United States, where amateur and professional sports maintain separate hierarchies. While hockey's fight against professionalism was bitter, once the battle was resolved in the latter's favor, hockey was the quickest of all sports in producing a stable major league (see Figure I.1). In escaping the control of powerful amateur organizations, hockey bears many resemblances to baseball.

Hockey rapidly gained popularity in Canada. Amateur hockey clubs sprang up in nearly all the major cities and formed into associations on a regional basis. A group of hockey lovers formed the Amateur Hockey Association of Canada to refine the rules further, lowering team size from McGill's nine to seven. This organization was analogous to the

NABBP in baseball, seeking to encourage rather than to restrict the inclusion of clubs. The first exclusionary amateur league formed in Kingston in 1885 with four teams, two associated with universities. By the mid-1890s the game was so popular that the governor general of Canada donated a cup, the Stanley Cup, to be presented annually to the champion team of Canada. Before the professional National Hockey League gained exclusive control over the cup in 1926, seventeen amateur leagues challenged for the cup at one point or another. Much of the history of hockey in Canada revolves around the struggle over the Stanley Cup.

Early hockey associations, like the Ontario Hockey Association (the OHA, formed in 1890), were vigilantly against professionalism, expelling any team with a player who was paid, or even any team who played a team with a professional player. The OHA's position on professionalism was adopted by the AAU of Canada and later by the Canadian Amateur Hockey Association, many of whose executives came from the OHA (Metcalfe 1992). Amateur certification by the OHA was made mandatory in 1905, with additional certification by the AAU of Canada becoming required in 1919. Corporate teams and their players were banned from these amateur organizations in 1912.

Such vigilance was prompted, however, by the widespread practice of paying players. Professionalism first came into the open in the United States, where professional versions of three team sports had already developed. The first professional hockey league was created in 1904 by a U.S. dentist and was centered in the copper-mining town of Houghton, Michigan. Starting a long tradition in U.S. hockey, players were imported from Canada. (The first American-born players were not recruited until the 1930s, and they still constitute a minority in professional hockey.) Some of the best Canadian players were lured by pay as high as $500 a game. Soon after the league began, a Canadian team from Sault Ste. Marie, Ontario, joined, giving justification for the name International Professional Hockey League (IPHL). But ultimately the IPHL was both regional and short-lived, failing to dent the prestige of the Stanley Cup in amateur hockey.

The battle between amateurism and professionalism surfaced in Canada in 1907, when the Eastern Canada Amateur Hockey Association decreed that players could be paid to play, but that clubs must publish a list of their paid players in the newspaper. By 1908, winning teams were the ones that paid their players. In the same year the first Canadian professional league was started (the Ontario Professional League), consisting of teams from Toronto, Berlin, Brantford, and Guelph. A six-team National Hockey Association (NHA) formed in 1910, centering around the booming mining towns in northern Ontario, where "the miners wanted the best hockey money could buy" (McFarlane 1989, p. 8). But two of the smaller towns proved unable to support major league hockey and dropped out the next year, while the remaining teams unsuccessfully tried to impose a team salary cap of $5,000. A merger with the East Canada Hockey Association, a weak league also hard hit by World War I, made the NHA again a six-team circuit. But they soon lost an army team, the Northern Fusiliers, to the war in Europe.

A strong Pacific Coast Hockey Association (PCHA) was formed in 1911 by two star NHA players, brothers Frank and Lester Patrick. PCHA teams played in larger and more modern arenas than those of the NHA, including the first artificial ice rinks in Canada, but lacked large population bases. The two leagues raided each other's players, driving up salaries, and disputed with each other over rules. An agreement between the NHA and the PCHA was reached in 1914 for an annual Stanley Cup series, squeezing out amateur leagues in the competition for the cup. Professional hockey came back to the United States when the PCHA transferred its New Westminster franchise to Portland, Oregon, in 1915. The next year saw the addition of a franchise in Seattle, which surprised and unsettled Canadian organizers by winning the Stanley Cup in a match with the NHA's Montreal Canadiens. Only two years after this prized Canadian possession had come into the grip of professional leagues, it had slipped into the hands of an American team. Professional leagues can make the unthinkable possible, with amazing quickness.

With interest in hockey growing in American cities and an abundance of hockey talent being produced in Canada, the groundwork was laid for a major league to emerge in hockey. Although the East-West rivalry would later be an important feature of major league sports, without air travel (or divisions within leagues) it could not be incorporated within a single league. Ultimately the PCHA's small population bases proved the undoing of this western league, which sold out to a reorganized version of the NHA, the National Hockey League, as it expanded into the large eastern U.S. cities. As in football, a truly major league grew slowly out of the expansion of a regional league.

On the Eve of Major Leagues

The groundwork for major leagues was first laid in baseball, and then relaid in three subsequent sports. Without the aid of a major league, widespread interest in each sport was cultivated, and professionalism in each gained a foothold. Athletic clubs and associations played pivotal roles in diffusing each sport, and the rivalries that developed between them led to the hiring of the first professionals, or ringers. The appearance of free-floating professionals, bound by no affiliations or loyalties, opened up endless new possibilities for the organization of sporting competition. Soon there were all-professional teams touring the country and—outside of baseball, where the first league was a major league—less conspicuous regional professional leagues providing a more regular venue of sporting events for given locales. Out of these beginnings, major leagues emerged.

Why, one might ask, was the rise of major leagues such a significant event once so much had already been accomplished? To start, major leagues became vehicles for controlling player movement. While the free-floating nature of professionals made their activities amenable to design, before major leagues no vehicle existed that was capable of imposing a design. The constant flux of players hindered the development of strong fan attachments. Only after major league play had superseded the independents in appeal and extended its reach across the entire opportunity spectrum for players, could player movement be controlled. Major leagues brought about these necessary qualitative and quantitative changes.

In addition, major leagues upped the ante in the costs of producing competition, which motivated innovations in the way sports publics were mobilized. The national tours of independent teams were expensive affairs, and only the very top teams undertook them. Losing teams did not trace the same paths as winning teams, as became the case in major league play. For major leagues, mobilizing the ongoing support of the largest cities was essential. Here getting noticed was always problematic, and particularly so for losing teams. Major leagues had to figure out how to attach teams to cities, with bonds so strong that losing could be accommodated.

By superseding independent teams and later subordinating regional leagues into minor leagues, major leagues provided a center to a system that had none. This carried both larger opportunities and larger risks than had ever appeared in sports of any kind. Before major leagues appeared, a large number of teams could claim to be champions, because there was no clear way of resolving the issue. Major leagues eliminated the contentions of would-be champions by staging carefully constructed and closely watched pennant races among the nation's very best teams. Herein lies the risk. Although audiences had thus far been formed on the basis of unresolved contentions, major leagues eliminated the multitude of unresolvable claims and created a single arena where contentions were to be seemingly resolved.

On the eve of the first major leagues, only persons with the boldest of visions could have remotely anticipated what was to come. Although major leagues could not themselves first popularize a sport or establish professionalism in it, they extended involvement and enhanced the stature of professionals in remarkable ways. To these accomplishments, we now turn.

2

· · ·

Getting Established

From their very beginnings, professional team sports were an urban phenomenon. The concentration of people in towns and cities made it possible for sports organizers to mobilize large crowds of spectators for sporting events on a regular basis. In more rural areas, no sports organizer could overcome the obstacle of sparse population and poor transportation.[1] Nowhere is the importance of population concentration more evident than in the South, which lagged behind the Northeast in organizing professional sports, not for lack of interest, but simply because it was slower to urbanize and hence offered fewer opportunities for sports organizers (Guttman 1988, p. 49). Even within large cities, the logistics of getting people to the ballparks could be complex. Conveniently located sites required considerable economic and political clout to secure, and even then adequate streetcar service, parking, and security had to be provided.

Although sporting events had to be staged in urban areas to be commercially viable, the attachment of teams to cities in the perception of fans was by no means inevitable. In most European countries professional teams are attached to athletic clubs, and rivalries are interclub rather than intercity. Alternatively, professional teams can be attached to commercial enterprises, as in the case of Indian cricket and a number of early American professional football and basketball teams. Corporate sponsors long held an advantage in enticing the most talented players by offering them managerial positions after their athletic careers were over. And teams can be attached to colleges, of course, an alliance that dominates amateur sport in the United States but is absent from Europe. Despite these viable alternatives, professional sports teams came

55

under private ownership in America and became attached to cities in the perception of fans.

The attachment of professional teams to large cities was the first great achievement of the major leagues. It took considerable time, energy, and creativity to pull off. Control had to be wrested from players. Owners had to band together into alliances called leagues to defend exclusive claims to cities, against both independent teams and rival leagues. In the background were businessmen and politicians who stood to gain from the revenues and publicity that professional teams would bring the city. To develop the simple love of a city for its team, many interests had to crystallize and much organization had to be built up.

This chapter traces the attachment of professional teams to large cities in baseball. Baseball was the first and by far the most successful team sport in attaching a set of professional teams to a stable set of large cities, eventually producing a pair of major leagues whose composition did not change for over fifty years. Stability did not come easy for aspiring major leagues, however. Getting established involved difficult tradeoffs among population bases, travel distances, and site competition. Large cities were coveted sites, but the distance between some of them, like Chicago and New York, exacerbated travel costs. The large proximate cities of the Northeast offered a degree of relief from this tradeoff, a fact that often triggered fierce site competition among rival leagues.[2] The struggle for exclusive control over a set of large, conveniently located cities is central to the story of establishing viable major leagues.

But securing sites is only one side of the story. For early major leagues to survive, they also had to secure the continuing broad-based support of local publics. Professional teams had to become city teams in the perception of local residents, and attachments had to form that could endure the tremendous amount of losing that closed circuits of competition produce. At the time the first major league formed, the idea that the status of professional players and teams could be high even though they collectively lost half of all games they played would have seemed far-fetched. Bold ideas were needed to get cities to attach to professional teams.

The First Major League

Only one year after the Cincinnati Red Stockings took to the road as baseball's first openly professional team, there were twenty professional teams in operation.[3] Through a deft use of proxies, the professional teams succeeded in dominating the 1870 NABBP convention, attended by over one hundred amateur clubs. Although this strategy ensured that the professionals could continue to play NABBP teams, the 1870 season was marked by escalating disputes over the professional teams' relative standings. To avoid losing, professional teams either tended to seek out weaker teams or played strong teams in "exhibition" games that did not count in calculating the standings. At the end of the season, the Brooklyn Atlantics claimed the title as the first team to beat the Red Stockings. Yet the Red Stockings had been beaten three more times after this loss. The Philadelphia Athletics and the New York Mutuals each claimed the championship on the basis of having "about the best record" and losing "the fewest regular match games," respectively (Ryczek 1992). Faced with the task of sorting through these contentions for their readers, sportswriters like Harry Chadwick were among the first advocates of a framework to resolve them, a major league.

Outmaneuvered at the 1870 convention and eclipsed on the playing field, amateur clubs held their own convention in March 1871 at the headquarters of the Brooklyn Excelsiors and proceeded to place a strict ban on professional teams. Led by elite clubs (including the Knicker-bockers) from New York, the self-proclaimed "seat of baseball virtue," the amateur clubs banned future meetings outside of New York in order to avoid exposure to lurking professional forces. But in its efforts to reconstruct a past that had never really existed in baseball, the group succeeded only in forcing professional teams to construct a new future.[4]

Representatives from professional teams had also arrived in New York City for the 1871 NABBP convention. A day after the amateurs had preempted them, ten professional clubs from New York, Phila-delphia, Boston, Troy, Cleveland, Fort Wayne, Rockford, Chicago, and Washington, D.C., met at Collier's, a Broadway barroom. The ease with which they agreed on establishing a new association, the National Association of Professional Base Ball Players (soon called the National Association), grew out of a willingness to ignore critical issues. Without having the NABBP rules at hand, they adopted them wholesale and asked Washington's Nicholas Young to write the old NABBP for a copy. Besides electing Philadelphia's James Kearns as president, a large portion of the meeting was consumed as "teams scurried about to gar-ner the choicest dates" to play (Pietrusza 1991, p. 8). The idea of a fixed schedule was not even discussed. As a consequence, for example, Troy and Chicago did not schedule any games with each other because their management was not on friendly terms.

A fight was waged over setting an admission price for spectators, but since no agreement was reached the amount was left for each team to decide. This issue was connected to the even more troublesome (and therefore unresolved) issue of gate sharing—the division of game receipts between home and visiting teams. New York and Philadelphia teams, with their potentially larger audiences, were opposed to giving any share of gate receipts to visiting teams. This practice would create a serious economic disadvantage for smaller-city teams. Without a fixed schedule, ensuring a balance of home and away games, the lack of gate sharing added to the difficulty of enticing a large-city team to play an away game.[5] It also later led the New York Mutuals to refuse to go to the Philadelphia Pearls' homesite, after having garnered the receipts from games played with the Pearls in New York. In short, National Association teams were left to face the same economic problems they had faced as independents.

The National Association has been ignored or at best regarded with scorn in the baseball literature. In the words of one of the few scholars to take it seriously, "Everyone seemed embarrassed to tell the tale" (Ryczek 1992).[6] Though distinguished, and ultimately condemned, for its lack of new ideas, the National Association half-heartedly introduced several fundamental innovations that redirected the course of professional sports. In excluding amateur clubs and even some weaker professional teams, the National Association became the first group to admit teams on the basis of their superior playing ability. Only potential contenders for the championship title were admitted. No attention was directed, however, to playing ability after admittance. As will soon be clear, many teams quickly dropped out of contention, and out of the National Association altogether, owing to the absence of mechanisms to keep them in contention.

A second half-hearted innovation was the pennant race. Nicholas Young proposed a process for determining the champion, open to any National Association team willing to pay a special $10 assessment (in addition to regular dues of $10) for the championship banner. A five-game match between each pair of entrants was to be played, with the championship going to the team winning the most match games. This team would receive the championship banner to display at its home ballpark for the season. One team, the Brooklyn Eckfords, declined to enter this optional race, a striking reminder that at the time games and matches, and not pennant races, were the primary "product" of professional sports. Most sports organizers were still thinking in terms of gathering crowds rather than creating publics.

But by closing the circuit of competition (and failing to work out gate sharing), the National Association made teams ultimately dependent on "their" cities for support. The attachment of professional teams to cities could no longer be in name only, as was the case for the Cincinnati Red Stockings. Local publics, consisting of people willing to watch the same team play a set of other teams over and over, had to be mobilized. The baseball fan was to be someone who, "carried away by fervid partisanship and imaginary ownership [in 'his' city team], . . . would forget he paid money to watch professionals play for money in the interests of promoters" (Seymour 1971, p. 38). Unfortunately for the National Association, it never succeeded in cultivating this peculiar attachment of cities to their teams.

The National Association was lacking in both rules and the authority to enforce them. At the end of the 1871 season, Young's rules for determining a champion left so much latitude that three teams claimed the title. When Boston was found to have used an ineligible player and Chicago did not send a representative to the meeting to resolve the issue, Philadelphia was awarded the championship banner. At the second annual convention, Kearns could not find the time to show up, and the player-manager Bob Ferguson (whose nickname was "Death to Flying Things") was elected president. Yet the association's new leader was concerned mainly with catching fly balls from third base, and "there is little record of [his] taking any interest whatsoever in the affairs of the governing body" (Ryczek 1992, p. 73). Following in Kearns's footsteps, Ferguson did not even attend the 1874 convention. By then, however, the National Association was so weak that this dereliction created no pretext for removing him from office.

As a consequence of the National Association's lack of regulatory attention, there was increasing inequality across seasons in the playing strength and resources of National Association teams. In its first year, the inequality in season performances across teams was 1.96 times what it would have been if every team had had an equal chance of winning each game.[7] Philadelphia won with a 22–7 record, and Rockford finished last at 6–21. By 1875 performance inequality had increased to 3.58 times what competitive equality would yield, with the first-place

Boston team finishing at 71–8 and the last-place Brooklyn team at 2–42. Financially stronger clubs stripped the weaker clubs of their better players, producing some extremely lopsided games. After Philadelphia's 1871 pennant victory, the Boston Red Stockings won four consecutive pennants with the help of player-manager Harry Wright from the dis-banded Cincinnati Red Stockings. Although winning had been essential for the Cincinnati team, the success of the Boston team was a substantial factor in destroying the National Association. As organizers would soon learn, the domination of league competition by a single team, partic-ularly a small-city team, is a prescription for trouble.

Initially, winning teams tended to be located in the larger cities. Phil-adelphia and Chicago finished at the top the first year, while Fort Wayne and Rockford finished at the bottom. Only New York, finishing sixth, substantially deviating from the clear ordering of team perfor-mance by the population size of the host city. A measure of the degree of this ordering, Kendall's tau (ranging from 1 when larger cities have better teams and −1 when smaller cities have better teams; see also Appendix B), yielded a .67 for the National Association's 1871 season. As teams depended entirely on local audiences for support, this strong ordering of performance by host city size was beneficial from a league standpoint. Winners in large cities could draw many more fans than winners in small cities, just as they could lose more fans by not winning. With winners in small cities and losers in large ones, overall attendance was threatened by the separation of winners from potential fans. This separation began materializing in the National Association as the or-dering began eroding after the first season. Figure 2.1 shows a dis-couraging relation between increasing disorder and performance in-equality across seasons in the National Association. By 1875, small cities were doing better than large cities in runaway pennant races.

Under these conditions, even winners could lose money (as the Boston Red Stockings did in 1872). With flagging fan interest and sub-stantial geographical dispersion, many teams had trouble paying travel expenses and dropped out before the season's end. Of the twenty-five clubs that played in the National Association over five years, eleven survived only one or less than one season and only the Boston Red Stockings, Philadelphia Athletics, and New York Mutuals competed every year. Although the National Association drastically cut average travel distances and boosted average population bases by eliminating western cities and some smaller eastern cities by 1873 (with multiple

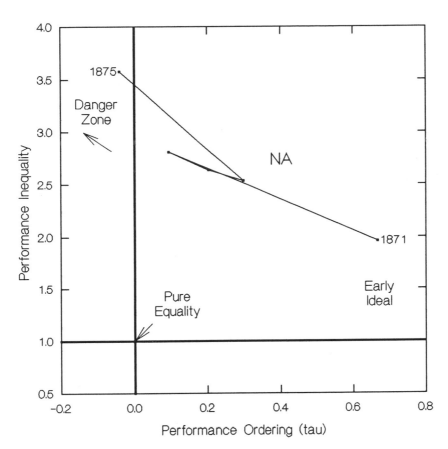

Figure 2.1 Season performance characteristics in the National Association (NA), 1871–1875. Performance inequality is assessed relative to the baseline of competitive balance, and the performance ordering (tau) is the extent of large-city domination of competition. In 1871, for example, large-city teams came out ahead in a relatively close pennant race—an ideal outcome for early leagues. By 1875, the pennant race slightly favored small-city teams and generated over 3.5 times the inequality that would be expected among competitive equals.

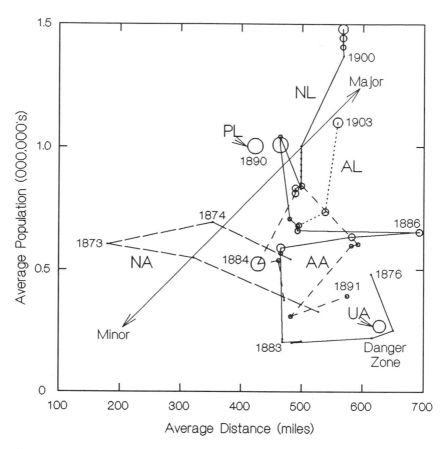

Figure 2.2 Demographic movement of major leagues in baseball, 1871–1903. Lines capture the struggle to find a set of cities with large average populations and small average travel distances, with lateral movement indicating changes in league composition. Site competition drove rival leagues to different solutions, and is indicated by circle size. The 1884 Union Association (UA), for example, faced stiff site competition from the National League (NL) and the American Association (AA) and had the worst demographics, with teams in mostly small, far apart cities. PL = Players League; AL = American League.

teams in remaining cities), the league went back west for new members as it continued to flounder. These changes in average population base and travel distance are charted in Figure 2.2, along with comparable data for the major leagues that were to follow. Clearly no subsequent major league sought to emulate the National Association in its composition. In its final 1875 season, the league had an unwieldy thirteen teams, only seven of which came close to completing their season.

With virtually no leadership, the National Association was unable to handle the series of cancellations, forfeits, and standing disputes that plagued it from its inception. It also could not prevent the infiltration of powerful gambling interests. Corruption in the National Association was "so shameful that the highly respected element of patrons began to drop out of attendance . . . crowds [were] composed exclusively of bettors." Baseball entered its "dark age," with "bribery, contract-breaking, dishonesty, poolroom manipulations, and desertions of players" becoming commonplace (Lieb 1951, p. 59). This is a fitting epitaph for the first major league, which, far from enhancing the stature of professionals and becoming the pride of cities, was something baseball fans have since tried to forget.

Baseball bore some ominous similarities to the two other major professional sports in the mid-nineteenth century, boxing and horse racing. Each was an urban phenomenon, infiltrated with vice, and alluring to young males drawn to the cities by industrial employment. Early baseball owners were largely drawn from sports organizers with substantial financial interests in boxing and horse racing. They were closely tied to urban political machines, as professional politicians, friends or business allies of politicians, or transportation magnates. Philadelphia's Republican machine operated the Athletics from the 1860s to 1892, while Boss Tweed supported the New York Mutuals for all five years of the National Association. Of 1,263 officials and stockholders of major and minor league teams before the turn of the century, there were 50 mayors, 102 state legislators, and numerous judges, councilmen, and police commissioners (Vincent 1981).

In the early 1870s, it was by no means clear that baseball would part company with boxing and horse racing in becoming the national game. Its main advantage, however, was that it did not suffer from the legal constraints that boxing and horse racing labored under. In boxing, "World Championships" often had to be fought in secret locations, and even this did not always stop the fighters from being arrested after local authorities had enjoyed the match (Sammons 1990). But baseball's legal advantage could easily have been lost if the violence and gambling associated with the sport had continued to worsen. To secure its attachment to cities, baseball would have to become a "clean" sport. This would entail purging the game of some of its main constituencies, including gamblers, rowdies, and violent and vulgar players. Owners became somewhat exempt from the purging, and there was often little relation between the moral background of owners and the diligence with which they tried to clean up baseball.

In 1875 William Hulbert, a businessman and officer of the Chicago Baseball Club, violated National Association rules by raiding the champion Boston team of Chicago native Al Spaulding and three fellow-players in mid-season. Threatened with expulsion when the theft was exposed, Hulbert planned a new league before the National Association could take action. In February 1876, Hulbert showed up in New York and called a meeting of East Coast club owners. He locked the irate owners in a conference room and mysteriously converted them to the idea of a new league. Hulbert's appeal was simple. He promised to eliminate inflated salaries, players jumping from team to team during the season, gambling scandals, team imbalance, and incomplete schedules. And then he posed the question: "Why should we be losing money when we represent a game that people love?" (Pietrusza 1991, p. 28). While some owners suspected Hulbert of merely scheming to get a good team in Chicago, the consent he received marked the death of the National Association and the birth of the National League.

Building a Viable League

The National League was, for the first time, an association of owners.[8] To make baseball into a viable business, Hulbert recognized that a select group of teams had to be isolated and regulated to an unprecedented degree. Hulbert insisted that the National League be limited to eight teams, based in cities with populations over 75,000. Louisville and Cincinnati were added to the six other qualifying National Association sites (Boston, Philadelphia, New York, Chicago, Hartford, and St. Louis). Territorial rights were granted to member teams, barring any team from competing with a nonleague team in a league city. Scheduling was put under league control. Each team was to play ten games with each other, five at home and five away. Fifteen cents (roughly 30 percent) of the 50-cent admission price set by the league went to the visiting team, to defray travel expenses and help equalize revenues across teams. Player contracts were to be respected by member clubs, and a blacklist was established to disbar contract jumpers.

A five-man board of directors was to govern the league, with one member chosen from among them to serve as president. As the first of the five owner names drawn from a hat, Morgan Bulkeley of Hartford (whose father founded Aetna Life Insurance) became the first president. Bulkeley agreed to serve as president only one year, and in 1877 the title was bestowed on Hulbert, who retained it until his death in 1882. Bulkeley's good luck and humility earned him a place in baseball's Hall of Fame. The immensely more deserving Hulbert has never been accorded this honor.

Hulbert's organizational innovations were remarkably bold. The ban on games with nonleague teams in league cities was tantamount to a declaration of war on the many excellent independent teams then in operation. In 1876, National League teams "usually won" against independents in nonleague cities, but the next year seventy-two losses were suffered. Only the Hartford team emerging with a winning record against the independents. After 1877 fewer and fewer games were played with nonleague teams. This required considerable discipline, as the matches often provoked considerable public interest that National League owners could tap for short-term profits. But losses to independents, and teams in rival associations, threatened the legitimacy of the National League. By not losing to nonleague teams in league cities, and then seldom playing them anywhere, National League teams could both claim superiority in "their" cities and deprive nonleague teams of prestigious playing partners and prime playing sites. As nonleague teams found it harder to survive, National League teams could more easily become sole claimants to city-team status.

At the same time, league control over scheduling helped focus attention on National League teams by creating orderly and legitimate pennant races. Isolated matches with nonleague teams receded in public importance as rivalries between league teams came to be sustained in these races. With league teams playing half their games in the same "home" site, local populations could for the first time become involved in a team's progress on an ongoing basis. Once a team had settled in and laid claim to a city, this continuing support was essential for team survival. Territories claimed by teams had to be conferred by their residents. While independent teams simply moved on when support waned, fixed schedules made it imperative for teams to keep local interest alive.

As president of the National League, Hulbert tried to broaden the appeal of baseball by reducing rowdiness and corruption. A strong signal was sent out when four Louisville players were suspended from the game for life for gambling. Beer sales were eliminated (Cincinnati was expelled for not complying). The 50-cent admission price, twice the amount that any team had charged in the National Association, enticed "respectable" people in by keeping out their less respectable counterparts. Overtures were made to draw in more women and families. Ladies' Days, when women accompanied by men were admitted for free, were started by many clubs in the 1880s and 1890s. It also became common practice to give free tickets to priests, whose presence at games did much to improve baseball's tarnished image. To give even more assurance to the religious minded and to avoid clashes with state and municipal officials, Sunday baseball was banned.[9]

Players were subjected to fines for uncouth behavior. "The promoters wanted baseball to appeal to the masses by being ruggedly competitive, but at the same time they were anxious that it be sufficiently respectable to attract the 'better classes' . . . ruffianism and uncouth behavior would scare away women and more staid males . . . but if the boys were too well behaved and agreeable, the illusion of an all-out struggle for pennants would become increasingly unreal. Consequently, both extremes were officially ruled out" (Seymour 1971, p. 91). This careful calibration of players to fit the audience may have also been behind the later banning of blacks from Organized Baseball by 1898. Many owners feared that black players would attract black spectators, who would supposedly scare away "respectable" white spectators.[10]

In the long run, however, ongoing support required that a team remain a contender in pennant races. Besides restricting the number and quality of teams admitted into the National League, Hulbert set out to keep teams in contention after they were admitted. Gate sharing marked a first step toward combating the unevenness of support across cities, a problem that had plagued the National Association. In addition, restrictions on player movement (soon extended beyond contracts to whole careers) gave owners control over the allocation of talented players across teams. Even if Hulbert was merely scheming on behalf of his Chicago team (which won the 1876 pennant), the apparatus he created permanently shifted the focus of organizers from building great teams to composing sets of potential contenders.

The new controls over revenue and player movement by no means eliminated the advantage held by large-city teams. The need to field strong large-city teams, in fact, counterbalanced the need to keep teams in contention. Close pennant races, with large-city teams winning in the end, were the desiderata of early leagues. The National Association had veered in the opposition direction, with imbalanced races and a small-city team winning in the end. This was a sign of both the weakness of the National Association and its failure to successfully attach teams to cities. Hulbert recognized that a strong league was needed to keep teams in contention so that local support could be mobilized throughout the league. Widespread local support, however, ensured large-city teams an economic advantage, because they had larger bases of support to draw from and thus could more vigorously pursue talented players. Therefore one sign that a league had successfully attached teams to cities was the consistency with which large-city teams won close pennant races.

Attaching a set of teams to a set of cities, however, proved far from easy for the National League. New York and Philadelphia got themselves expelled the first season for refusing to complete their final road trips (they were over twenty-five games out of contention and still resented Hulbert's coup). Without these two major cities, travel distances were greater and population bases were less than in any of the five years of the National Association. These unfavorable demographics meant that most clubs lost money. Not until 1882 did the National League field the same teams for two consecutive years, and not until 1894 did it do so for three consecutive years. Only Chicago and Boston were to make it to 1900, with twenty-one cities being represented in the National League at one time or another over this period. Small-city teams like those in Troy, Indianapolis, Milwaukee, Providence, Syracuse, and Buffalo came and went. The demographic wandering of the National League is represented in Figure 2.2. When there is stability in team composition, a league's average travel distance does not change across time while its average population base grows steadily, resulting in a vertical line. A striking feature of Figure 2.2 is the lack of team stability in the National League until 1894.

One problem was the fifty professional independent teams that existed as of 1877. Many were reluctant to join the National League, preferring to hold down travel expenses by playing more proximate teams. Others wanted in, but were rebuffed by what Hulbert deemed the impracticability of writing a schedule for more than eight clubs. More than eight would be an "unwieldy body burdened with too many tail enders to the detriment of the box office" (quoted in Seymour 1960, p. 125). Antagonism toward National League teams was heightened by their practice of freely raiding independent teams for players. In the battle for players and spectators that ensued, it was by no means inevitable that the small National League would win out, especially after the expulsion of New York and Philadelphia.

A league alliance was proposed in 1877 that foreshadowed what came to be known as "Organized Baseball." This alliance would have created a group of satellite clubs under National League direction who lacked equal membership in the league, but had their player contracts respected. The proposal prompted seventeen clubs to counter the National League by forming the International Association of Professional Base Ball Players, with the pitcher William Cummings as president. But this association did not limit membership in number or quality, and had trouble sticking together (a subgroup entered into a covenant with the National League on satellite terms). As the National Association had done, it made contention for the championship optional (for $15 in addition to the $10 membership fee). Its best team had a winning record (10–7) against National League teams, and it possessed as many nationally recognized players (Pietrusza 1991). The failure of the International Association in its third season, with just four teams and three contenders remaining, only highlights the importance of organization.

Other alternative leagues were even weaker. The New League (1879) and the Eastern Championship Association (1881), with cheaper admission prices and no fixed schedules, failed within the year they were started. The New England League did much better, surviving from 1877 to 1949, but only by operating as a well-behaved minor league and not encroaching on National League players or playing sites (Sullivan 1990). In all, 278 minor leagues have formed and survived for varying lengths of time since 1871, without ever challenging the major leagues (Filichia 1993).

As new leagues began to challenge the National League in varying degrees and as internal rivalries intensified, competition over players mounted. The freedom players had always enjoyed in moving between teams gave them leverage in salary negotiations. Player salaries typically constituted two-thirds of team expenses, and hence were the central cost concern of owners. At first the National League sought only to restrict player movement for the duration of an annual contract. But management soon began to assert itself. In 1878, negotiations during the season were banned (ostensibly to allay suspicions among fans regarding player loyalty). A year later, the National League began promoting what eventually became the reserve clause. This clause, a source of controversy for the next century, gave clubs a continuing option on the services of players and hence protected their property rights over players.[11] Players lost their freedom of movement, as they were limited to either re-signing with their team or leaving Organized Baseball. In 1879 each team was allowed to reserve five players. No team could play a team that did not honor the reserve clause. By 1887 each team could reserve fourteen players.

The reserve clause had the effect of stabilizing team composition, which helped teams cultivate loyal followings. In putting a damper on player salaries it also helped keep poorer clubs in business. The 1880s saw a rise in revenues and profits. In 1881 Hulbert could boast that there was not a "weak sister" among the eight National League clubs. In an effort to control player salaries further, a lid of $2,000 was imposed, but proved hard to enforce. While coveted players, who could threaten not to play, could command high salaries, most players were not so fortunate. Players had to buy their own uniforms, pay for some travel expenses, and were on their own if injured. Those released from the team after an away game had to pay their own way home. Antagonism arose between players and management over division of the surplus.

Budding success, disgruntled players, and vacancies in New York, Philadelphia, and after 1880, Cincinnati set the stage for the first serious challenge to the National League. By the early 1880s, carefully constructed pennant races had replaced games and matches as the basis for a stable business foundation in professional baseball. In seeking to involve local publics in a protracted race for the national championship, it became essential to forge a single framework that would select potential contenders and fix the terms on which they met. While rival independent teams created opportunities for profitable matches among each other, rival leagues threatened the raison d'être of an established major league. Every challenge triggered a battle, and every battle produced death, absorption, or at best, a formal alliance among challeng-

ers. Nothing better illustrates the exclusionary nature of major league
sports than challenges.

Early Challenges

By 1881, five teams had been expelled from the National League: New
York and Philadelphia for failing to complete their schedules, Cincinnati for selling beer at games, and St. Louis and Louisville for gambling
offenses. These teams continued in operation, often with numerous
games against remaining National League teams. In the late summer
of 1881, the Philadelphia manager and former president of the Cincinnati club, Justus Thorner, sent postcards to the other expelled teams
announcing an October meeting in Pittsburgh. Only Thorner showed
up (the manager had lost his job). With a few sports editors and re-
porters, Thorner went bar hopping and met Al Pratt, bartender and
former pitcher, who advised them to seek out the "crank" H. D.
McKnight, an iron manufacturer who headed the Alleghenys of the
defunct International Association. Together, Thorner and McKnight
schemed to draw in more clubs by wiring them messages implying that
each was the only one missing from the "Liberty for all" meeting. Only
the New York Metropolitans hesitated to come, because of their heavy
schedule with National League teams (Pietrusza 1991). Hulbert, then
president of the National League, had his first heart attack shortly after
hearing news of the meeting.

As an outgrowth of the Pittsburgh meeting, the American Association was formed. The American Association was modeled after the National League, but allowed Sunday baseball, charged only 25 cents admission, allowed liquor sales, and had a permanent staff of umpires.
Unlike the earlier rival leagues run by players, the American Association
was run mostly by brewers and saloon owners who, like Chris Von der
Ahe of St. Louis, became interested in baseball because "he noticed
that baseball fans drank a lot of beer" (Dellinger 1989, p. 566). The
American Association catered to working-class fans, largely shunned by
the National League in its quest for respectability.

The American Association began with six teams, placed in Cincinnati, Philadelphia, Louisville, Pittsburgh, St. Louis, and Baltimore. Although the league did not infringe on National League sites, the population of these six cities outnumbered the eight of the National League
by half a million, with almost the same travel distances. In response to

the American Association's favorable demographics, the National League eliminated Troy and Worcester from its membership in 1883 and moved back into New York and Philadelphia, thereby surpassing American Association cities in population even though the latter also moved into New York (and Columbus) in 1883. At first, the American Association was similarly cautious in raiding National League players, signing only a few who were marginal. But after faring poorly against National League teams in exhibition games, the American Association starting making offers to National League star players (and banned exhibition games).

With its wealthy backers, star players from the National League, and working-class fans, the American Association prospered in its first few years despite the raging trade war between the leagues. By the middle of 1883, the warring leagues were ready to negotiate a peace. The two leagues, and the newly formed minor Northwestern League, met in 1883 and agreed to respect each other's contracts and allow each team to hold eleven players in reserve as part of a National Agreement. In addition, a system of minor leagues was organized and placed under the rule of the National Agreement, to be overseen by a National Board. As part of this agreement, a player draft was established whereby higher-level leagues could draw players from lower-level leagues at a fixed price. Over the years, there were numerous struggles over the draft price, the number of players that could be drafted, and exemptions from the draft for teams or leagues. Paralleling the draft was an option clause, which allowed the majors to send players back to the minors and yet maintain exclusive rights over them. The National Agreement marks the beginning of what is called Organized Baseball, a rigidly hierarchical arrangement in which the control of the majors at the top is the source of endless resentments and aspirations for the multileveled minors below.

The first rebellion against the National Agreement came in 1884 from the Union Association. Aided by very wealthy backers, the Union Association rejected the reserve clause and began freely raiding teams bound by the National Agreement. It also moved into the National League and American Association cities of St. Louis, Cincinnati, Baltimore, Boston, Chicago, Pittsburgh, Philadelphia, and Washington, D.C. (but not New York). As a response, exhibition games with Union Association teams were banned by Organized Baseball under the threat of expulsion. Whole "reserve teams" were formed to keep players out of the Union Association. Players who jumped to the Union Association were blacklisted. But despite the faltering of the Northwestern League, many of whose players and teams went over to the Union Association, the Union Association lost the trade war. In 1884 only five of its original eight teams made it to the end of the season. In all, twelve teams played in the Union Association during 1884, playing anywhere from 8 to 113 games. The teams that survived the season failed to produce a closely contested pennant race. The St. Louis team won with a 94–19 record, followed by Cincinnati, twenty-one games behind with a still impressive 69–36 record. Season performance inequality was 3.18 times what competitive equality would yield.

Yet 1884 season performance inequality was greater in both the National League (3.51) and the American Association (3.22), although their respective first-place teams of Providence and New York finished only 10.5 and 6.5 games ahead of the nearest contender. In terms of the ability to field winners in the largest cities, the Union Association exhibited the strongest ordering of performance by population with a tau of .42, followed by the American Association (.09) and the National League (−.14). Hence on performance grounds, it was the National League that exhibited the most dangerous combination of high performance inequality and large-city weakness. If plotted on Figure 2.1, the National League lies further into the "danger zone" than the National Association moved the year it dissolved. What saved the National League and the American Association, in addition to will, was demographic superiority. In terms of average population bases and travel distances, the Union Association was at a distinct disadvantage to both rivals. It had by far the greatest travel distances and lowest population bases of the three major league contenders, as can be seen in Figure 2.2. Combined with the intense site competition of eight overlaps with National League and American Association cities, the demographics were not sufficient to support major league player salaries.

The Union Association folded after its first season. Competition also took its toll on the American Association, which lost five of its thirteen teams but emerged as a trimmer and demographically more viable league in 1885. Directly competing for fans at only four sites, instead of the eight of the American Association and Union Association, the National League was less shaken up by the 1884 season. Only one team, Cleveland, folded, and it was replaced by the addition of the Union Association's strong St. Louis team.

For the rest of the decade, the National League and the American Association ruled over baseball in an uneasy alliance. The National League's move into St. Louis, where the American Association had one of its strongest teams, created tensions between the two leagues. There were also internal struggles over the division of gate receipts between home and away teams. Some American Association teams, not happy with receiving a fixed amount for away games, threatened to join the National League to gain a percentage of the receipts (30 percent). Weak leadership in both leagues had difficulty handling such routine squabbles.[12] Power was only reluctantly conferred on league presidents by owners who were in the habit of asserting themselves (Seymour 1960).

Each league held steady at eight teams, but franchises continued to change locations. In 1887 the National League moved out of St. Louis, while the next year the American Association left New York (though it stayed in Brooklyn). Thus by the end of the decade, the two leagues directly competed for fans only in Philadelphia and New York (if one includes Brooklyn). National League movements increased its population base and decreased its travel distances, while the American Association strayed dangerously in the opposite direction (as can be seen in Figure 2.2). After the 1889 season, the American Association was particularly damaged when the National League lured away two of its strongest franchises, Brooklyn and Cincinnati. While interleague player raids were strictly prohibited, nothing in the National Agreement prevented whole teams from being enticed across league boundaries.

As the two leagues moved toward the end of the 1880s, they began to diverge on performance measures as well. Season performance inequality was increasing in the American Association while declining in the National League. In addition, the National League achieved an increasingly clear ordering of teams on performance by population size. This is both sign and consequence of a strong attachment of teams to cities. With populations widely mobilized behind "their" teams, population size comes to determine the support and resources available to teams. The American Association never achieved such a stable ordering, as shown in Figure 2.3. Its failure to reach the ideal lower-right zone reflects the league's inability to reduce performance inequalities and the unwillingness of local populations to support American Association teams consistently.

At the start of the new decade, the players revolted in what became

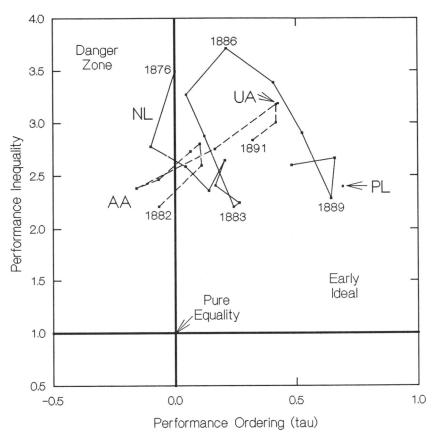

Figure 2.3   Season performance characteristics in baseball major leagues, 1876–1891. Aside from the ill-fated 1890 Players League (PL), the National League (NL) emerged from the contentious 1880s with the most ideal combination of close pennant races won by large-city teams. Three-year moving averages (based on current and prior two seasons) are used to dampen yearly fluctuations. UA = Union Association; AA = American Association.

known as the Brotherhood War of 1890. The players had formed a union in 1885 led by John Ward, a talented pitcher who had earned off-season degrees in law and political science from Columbia College. With owners like Boston's Arthur Soden requiring players to man turnstiles and jump into the stands to retrieve foul balls, the players had no shortage of grievances. What instigated the strike, however, was an 1889 owner scheme to impose salary caps and a classification scheme to standardize pay (Lowenfish 1991, p. 30). Although the reserve system was not directly attacked, players sought to receive some of their sale price and to derail the owners' dreaded blacklist. In what was to be a democratic alliance with capitalists, the Players League was conceived. Each team was governed by four players and four "contributors," and the league by a "senate" of sixteen representatives (two from each club, one chosen by players, one by contributors). The reserve system and classification scheme were rejected, but three-year contracts were required to reduce player mobility. Gate receipts were split 50–50 between home and away teams to remedy the disadvantage of small cities.

With remarkable boldness, the Players League nearly gutted the National League of players and moved seven of its eight teams into National League cities (its eighth was placed in Buffalo instead of Cincinnati). One hundred players jumped to the Players League, of which only twenty-five were lured back by the National League. The National League counterattacked by scheduling its games to conflict with those of the Players League. Attendance at both leagues was less than attendance at the National League the year before. New York was particularly hard hit. The New York team's owner, John Day, sent out a call for help, and by now the other owners realized that New York had to be held on to (Day had threatened to sell out to the Players League). The other owners bailed out Day, but sought a meeting with the Players League to avoid further damage. By most accounts, the Players League had drawn larger crowds than the National League (actual figures were greatly manipulated). Successful in hiding its true weaknesses, the National League succeeded in getting its fellow-capitalists in the Players League to bypass the players and sell out. It was a close call for the National League, and a devastating blow to the players. Their league had survived only one season, and it would be eighty years before players would again seriously confront the major league owners.

Neither demographics nor performance played any role in the quick demise of the Players League. It had nearly the same population base and slightly less travel distance than the National League, differing in only one site. There was a strong ordering of performance and population, with a tau of .69, as well as moderately low performance inequality (2.40). At the same time, the National League's performance position clearly eroded. Performance inequality rose to 3.65, and its ordering of performance by population slipped to .47, a setback from what it had achieved in the late 1880s. Were it not for the fault line between players and capitalists in the Players League that the National League owners shrewdly perceived, the National League could easily have joined the ranks of defunct leagues. Sports had evolved to the point where use of the terms "players and contributors" was not enough to conceal the potential conflicts between "labor and capital." The National League masterfully exploited these conflicts.

Although the players' revolt was clearly aimed at the National League, it was the American Association that in the end fell victim. Turnover of American Association teams reached 50 percent in 1890, with small cities like Toledo, Rochester, and Syracuse joining its ranks. The next year again saw a 50 percent turnover. Although some larger cities came back on board, the American Association was unable to withstand a renewed trade war with the National League over divvying up the players from the disbanded Players League. The trade war broke the American Association. Four of its teams became part of a new twelve-team National League (St. Louis, Baltimore, Louisville, and Washington, D.C.), and the remaining four were bought out by the twelve teams for $130,000, as part of a ten-year "ironclad" agreement (Seymour 1960). To counter rising salaries resulting from recent trade wars, teams were limited to fifteen men, then thirteen, and payrolls were cut 30–40 percent.

The National League was to enjoy relative tranquillity for the rest of the decade. Aside from two failed efforts to revive the American Association, no new major leagues emerged and no changes in National League composition occurred. But beneath the tranquillity were unresolved problems. The twelve-team pennant race was, as Hulbert foresaw before his death in 1882, unwieldy. Winning teams, typically winning more than 70 percent of their games, drew too far ahead of the pack too early in the season to sustain widespread interest. Season performance inequality increased over the decade, from a low of 1.86 in 1891 to a high of 3.52 in 1899. Boston and Baltimore won every race but one. The dominance of these moderately sized cities was part of an overall weakening of the ordering of performance by population. In addition to this dampener on overall attendance, many potential fans were turned away by the National League's high admission charge, alcohol prohibition, and ban on Sunday baseball.

Behind the turmoil and tranquillity of the early years of major league baseball are innumerable political stories. Cities were as active in attaching themselves to teams as teams were in attaching themselves to cities. Every franchise shift and entrenchment had political implications, especially as both baseball and the land and services it required became more valuable. Tammanyite John Day was awarded the New York franchise in 1883. Day later sold the New York Giants to a syndicate of Republican politicians, but Tammany regained control when a friend of Boss Richard Croker, Andrew Freedman, bought a majority share. Freedman ran the team "as if they were an adjunct of the machine, bullying fellow owners into accepting various demands for special treatment and getting into fights with players, umpires and journalists" (Riess 1989, p. 198). In Cincinnati, John Brush was forced to sell to a syndicate of Republican boss George Cox, Water Works Commissioner August Hermann, and Mayor Julius Fleischmann when, Brush claimed, they threatened to cut a street through his ballpark (Riess 1989). Connections brought preferential treatment in municipal services, fees and assessments, and eventually helped legalize Sunday baseball. It was not until the 1920s that political connections became less essential. By then baseball was so well established it had its own independent political clout.

Outside the National League were a host of minor leagues bound by the National Agreement. These leagues were in a constant state of flux. Unlike the majors, the minors were highly sensitive to local and regional economic conditions. They were also sensitive to the actions of the majors. Every new city a major moved into was one where a high minor had thrived, and the entrance of the major often compelled the high minor to invade a lower minor's prime location. When a high minor challenged a major, it would in turn create a chain of vacancies that would draw lower minors up. The same ripple effects occurred when players were sent up to or down from the majors. The National League's right to engage in the unlimited drafting (at $500 per player) and optioning of players left the minors with little control over their own rosters.

In the next chapter, we shall see that this lack of control was the main impetus behind Ban Johnson's bid to pursue major league status for what became the American League—after failing to get the draft fee raised to $1,000. Johnson's efforts produced the most successful challenge of an established league in the entire history of major league sports. After surviving a trade war, the American League joined the National League as equal partners in what has since endured as Major League Baseball. For fifty years, there would not be a single change in the composition of either league. Never in the history of major league sports would the attachment of teams to cities be stronger. Major League Baseball in the first half of the twentieth century became the early prototype for organizing professional team sports.

3

· · ·

The Early Prototype

By the turn of the century, the National League had firmly established itself. Independent professional teams of comparable caliber had virtually disappeared, and college baseball programs were rapidly being eclipsed by programs in the new sports of football and basketball. The composition of the National League had remained stable since 1892, with twelve teams in twelve cities extending from the East Coast to as far west as Chicago and St. Louis and as far south as Louisville and Washington, D.C. In each city, efforts to clean up the game had succeeded in broadening its audience to include "respectable" men, women, and children. Pennant races had greatly extended the involvement of the newly emerging local publics, although with twelve teams in the race too many teams dropped out of contention too early. The idea of using leagues to attach teams to cities was securely in place.

Much, however, was not yet resolved. With the formation of divisions still decades off, the National League had too many teams for a single pennant race. Even with fewer teams, moreover, the National League lacked sufficient mechanisms to ensure close pennant races, ones that tended to be won in the end by larger-city teams. The relatively small cities of Boston and Baltimore dominated competition during the 1890s, winning all but one pennant race. Without winners to support, the potentially more lucrative attachment of fans in large cities like New York, Philadelphia, and Chicago was jeopardized. The fact that smaller cities could dominate league competition indicates that the attachment of teams to cities had not fully developed. Later, the local support of teams throughout the league would give large-city teams, with larger bases for support, a distinct advantage on the field.

Change was forced on the National League by a new challenger, Ban Johnson's American League. A vicious trade war between the two leagues was, in the end, to produce a set of teams that would remain stable for fifty years. Johnson's challenge also introduced a stronger form of leadership in league affairs than even Hulbert could have envisioned. Gradually a prototype for major leagues emerged that the other newly arriving sports aspired toward. This chapter outlines the development of the prototype for early leagues. The next chapter outlines the difficulties the other sports had in emulating the prototype.

A Successful Challenge

As a Cincinnati sportswriter, Ban Johnson had frequently irritated John Brush, then owner of Cincinnati's weak National League team. To get Johnson out of Cincinnati, Brush used his influence in 1894 to win Johnson the presidency of the Western League, a minor league. There Johnson learned several important lessons. In the first year, the pennant was won by the smallest city in the league, Sioux City, Iowa. Paid admissions only numbered 42,000 for the whole season. This was a debacle not only for Sioux City but for the visiting teams, who depended on a share of the gate receipts (particularly when their own home receipts were small owing to their failure to win). Sioux City had to be dropped from the league. In a similar vein, Johnson regarded the defunct Players League's equal division of gate receipts as foolhardy (Lowenfish 1991, p. 58). Johnson would rather abandon small cities than empower them.

Over the next five years, Indianapolis dominated the Western League with three pennant wins and two second places. Owned by none other than John Brush, Indianapolis players were transferred back and forth to the National League team in Cincinnati as the need arose. This made Indianapolis the first farm team, an innovation usually credited to Branch Rickey thirty years later. The other two Western League winners, capable of becoming rivals to Indianapolis, were gutted by National League teams after their winning seasons. The unlimited draft blocked Ban Johnson's efforts to organize competition in a way that maintained fan identification with teams and players. Johnson's ambitions required major league status.

In 1900 Johnson saw an opportunity to move eastward when the National League trimmed its membership back to eight teams, dropping Baltimore, Cleveland, Louisville, and Washington, D.C. Keeping teams in Detroit, Milwaukee, and Minneapolis, Johnson's newly christened American League moved out of Grand Rapids, Kansas City, St. Paul, and Toledo and into Buffalo, Chicago, Cleveland, and Indianapolis. So as not to break with the National Agreement, however, Johnson had to submit to harsh conditions to move into the National League stronghold of Chicago.[1] Well poised for attack, the American League broke out of the National Agreement in the 1901 season. It moved out of Buffalo, Indianapolis, and Minneapolis and into two more of the recently abandoned National League sites, Baltimore and Washington, as well as into two occupied National League sites, Boston and Philadelphia. Although these shifts purged the American League of minor league sites, it still had little more than 60 percent of the population base of the National League. A New York team was needed.

Andrew Freedman blocked the American League from New York City by holding leases on most possible park sites and by threatening to use his power to cut streets through sites he did not control. In 1902 the American League did manage to break into St. Louis, moving in its Milwaukee team to remain within the by now absolute limit of eight teams. By the next season the American League succeeded in entering New York (abandoning Baltimore). To do so, it had to grant the New York Yankee franchise to a Tammany syndicate that could counter Freedman's power. The syndicate was headed by poolroom king Frank Farrell and former police chief William Devery, a corrupt protégé of Tim Sullivan, a race track lord, and Boss Croker. With a secure grip on New York and four other major National League cities (Boston, Philadelphia, St. Louis, and Chicago), the American League had narrowed the population gap to 19 percent.

The battle over sites was accompanied by a trade war over players. Claiming that the reserve clause was illegal, Johnson drew up a list of forty-six National League players in 1901 to be contacted and divided among his newly formed American League teams. "Each team was to receive a fixed number of men, except Chicago and Philadelphia, who were allowed to exceed the number. Since it was believed that the war would be won or lost in those two-club cities, it was essential for them to field the strongest teams" (Murdock 1982, p. 48).[2] From his Sioux City experience, Johnson saw large-city dominance as essential for the fledgling American League. Chicago won the pennant in the American League's first season and Philadelphia won the second season. In its early years, the American League was more successful than the National League both in maintaining the ordering of performance by population and in holding performance inequality to moderate levels. The National Association had failed to do either. And unlike the Players League, the American League was united under the strong leadership of Ban Johnson.

In order to ensure the survival of the American League, Johnson manipulated rosters, blacklisted contract jumpers, and established interlocking ownership of teams to secure cooperation from owners. Johnson kept 51 percent of the stock of each club in his possession as a precaution against clubs deserting the league (Seymour 1971), and Johnson's close friend Charles Somer of Cleveland financed several clubs in the early years. Hence Johnson could maintain considerable control over owners in orchestrating tighter pennant races than found in the National League. Johnson also used his clout to start a new drive to clean up the game, an effort that had lost momentum since Hulbert's death in 1882. This helped draw new audiences to American League games.

Meanwhile, the trade war helped trigger the worst internal feud in National League history. Angered by weak National League leadership, the New York owner and politician Andrew Freedman launched a conspiracy to form a baseball trust in which all clubs would pool their interests and hence be better able to pursue a common interest. Freedman was joined by Soden of Boston, Robison of St. Louis, and Brush of Cincinnati, and was labeled an "insidious, pugnacious troublemaker" by the remaining four National League teams (Lieb 1951, p. 148). Freedman was to get 30 percent of the common stock, with 12 percent to each clique member and a combined 34 percent to the four outsiders. Management would rest in the hands of a five-man Board of Regents, including a president and a treasurer. All team managers would be assigned by the league. When word of Freedman's plans became public, outrage was expressed by sportswriters and fans. At a showdown in December 1901, twenty-five ballots resulted in a 4–4 deadlock before Freedman gave up and shortly after sold his team to Brush.

National League internal leadership problems created opportunities not only for the American League but for the minor leagues as well. In challenging the National League, the American League had rejected the National Agreement. In what *Sporting News* branded a "foolhardy step and asinine departure from the regular," the National League shortly thereafter also abandoned the soon to expire ten-year agreement (quoted in Sullivan 1990a, p. 38). This action prompted the remaining minor leagues to organize. In October 1901, they formed the National Association of Professional Baseball Leagues, consisting of class A, B, C, and D minor leagues. Seeking security rather than independence from the majors, the newly organized minor leagues were quick to draw up a new National Agreement that reestablished the reserve clause and imposed salary limits. Over the next two decades, the minor leagues were successful in forging a more equitable relationship with the major leagues. Among other things, they succeeded in limiting draft privileges and raising the draft price.

By 1903 the American League had firmly established itself and was drawing larger crowds than the National League. With the two-year trade war benefiting only the players, owners from the two leagues worked out a new National Agreement. The National and American Leagues became equal partners, with the National Association of Professional Baseball Leagues as a junior partner. Organized Baseball would be overseen by a National Commission, consisting of the two league presidents and August Hermann, the new Cincinnati owner, as chairman.[3] The commission, however, was at best an uneasy alliance. From the beginning there were fights over players and schedules. In 1904 John Brush refused to let his pennant-winning New York Giants play the "minor league" American League winner, the Boston Red Sox. When Boston swapped a competent hitter with the New York Yankees for an untried infielder, the president of the National League publicly criticized Johnson for trying to build a strong New York rival to the Giants. Whatever side Chairman Hermann took in such squabbles, he was accused of bias by the other side. The National Commission was no match for the strong leadership of Johnson in the American League or the strong tradition of club autonomy in the National League.

Unlike in the American League, the National League president was weak. His decisions could be repealed by a four-member board. According to Harold Seymour (1971, p. 24), his role "was no more than that of a well paid clerk. The real power rested with the club owners, or whatever combination among them was dominant." When President Harry Pulliam suspended the Giants' player-manager John McGraw for abusive language, McGraw took Pulliam to court and won. After

Pulliam's suicide in 1909, club owners elected as acting president John
Heydler, "not a spectacular man," who made the mistake of trying to
enforce some of the owners' own rules (Seymour 1971, p. 30). By the
end of the year, Pittsburgh, Philadelphia, Boston, and Cincinnati
wanted Heydler to remain as president, but the other four owners, led
by Brush, wanted the old Brotherhood Revolt leader John Ward, oddly
enough. After four days of futile balloting, Brush offered as a compromise Thomas Lynch, a former head of the umpires (under the premise
that the president's chief function was to supervise umpires). After
Lynch's short term came John Tener in 1913, a former governor of
Pennsylvania who quickly found himself limited to presiding over
meetings and supervising umpires.

The National League was held together more from below, through
cross-ownership. Shifting ownership patterns were often the basis of
intrigues against the league president. Murphy of Chicago put Fogel
in as one-third owner of Philadelphia in exchange for his help in ousting
Heydler, and later in his struggles with Lynch. Chairman Hermann,
besides being president of Cincinnati, held stock in Philadelphia, St.
Louis, and loaned money to Brooklyn. Dreyfuss owned Pittsburgh and
held stock in Philadelphia, shipping three players to them in one year
to help them out. New York stock was held by the Boston owner, and
later (after 1919), Boston stock was held by the New York owner. Ned
Hanlon managed Cincinnati and held stock in Brooklyn as well as in
the minor league Baltimore club. In addition, loans between owners
became a routine affair. Cross-ownership, until it was outlawed in both
leagues in 1927, was much more interwoven in the National League
than the American League, where cross-team ownership was concentrated in the hands of Ban Johnson's friend Charles Somer.

However difficult a time August Hermann had with the owners, the
new format for competition proved to be immensely popular with fans.
It brought a prosperity to Major League Baseball that few owners were
willing to upset. The old twelve-team National League (with no divisions) was too large, and the effort in 1900 to trim it back to eight teams
excluded too many cities. There was ample room for two major leagues.
Public interest was particularly stirred by the new World Series, which
became an annual event after 1904 (despite McGraw's effort to block
an interleague playoff).[4] In the competition for fans, the American
League did better (by around 10 percent) than the National League.
Seymour (1971, p. 48) attributes its success to the closeness of their
pennant races. Season performance characteristics of the two leagues

can be seen in Figure 3.1. While National League winners often won over 110 of their 154 season games, American League winners rarely won over 95, producing a tighter race. Overall, 5.25 million fans turned out per year for both leagues from 1901 to 1908, and 6.8 million from 1909 to 1913. The New York Giants showed a profit of $500,000 over the 1906–1910 period, while the Chicago White Sox showed $700,000 over 1901–1911. Prosperity fueled, and was then fueled by, a rush to build large concrete and steel ballparks, replacing smaller and more hazardous wooden structures.

Prosperity, however, spawned a new players' union in 1912 (which succeeded only in threatening the first major league strike two years later) as well as new major league challengers. In September of 1910 a St. Louis theatrical producer, Ed Butler, announced a new twelve-team "Burlesquers League." Butler claimed that he had $50 million in backing from leading theatrical personages. But the backers withdrew before a single game was played. Later in the same year, the promoter Daniel Fletcher tried to organize a twelve-game tour using major league stars following the World Series. The baseball owners suspected Fletcher of wanting to start a new league and denied him the use of any stadium in Organized Baseball. They also threatened to blacklist any participating player. After much confident talk, Fletcher quietly disappeared from the scene, leaving behind $200 in unpaid printing bills (Pietrusza 1991).

A slightly more serious challenge came from the United States League, organized by a Pennsylvanian named William Witman in 1912. Teams consisted of named managers, promising young players, and washed-up major leaguers. The May 1 season opener was played before a crowd of 2,000–2,500 people, but attendance quickly dropped to 300–400 per game. Witman started scheduling more games at sites where more spectators were likely to attend, such as Pittsburgh and Richmond, but the glut of games quickly reduced the crowds. On May 27, New York forfeited a game at home when only fifty spectators showed up. A few days later Witman filed for bankruptcy (Pietrusza 1991). An attempt by Witman to reform a new eight-team United States League the next year failed again, on only the third day of the 1913 season.

A more successful challenge grew out of the efforts of John Powers, an organizer of the class D Wisconsin State League. An early attempt in 1912 to form a "Columbian League," with teams placed in Chicago, Cleveland, and St. Louis, failed when an important backer pulled out. Not discouraged, Powers organized the Federal League for the 1914

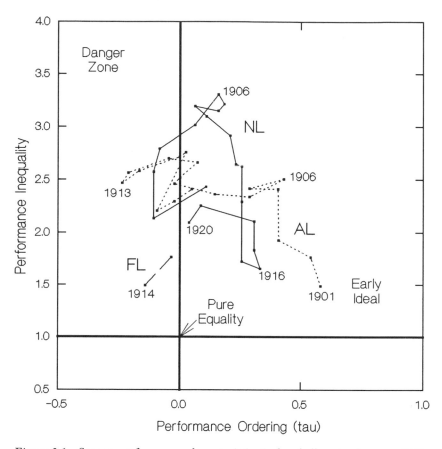

Figure 3.1 Season performance characteristics in baseball major leagues, 1901–1920, using three-year moving averages. Close pennant races led by large-city teams helped the American League (AL) make the most successful challenge in major league history. In the more long term process of attaching teams to cities, however, performance characteristics fluctuated considerably. FL = Federal League; NL = National League.

season. The Federal League did not recognize the reserve clause of organized baseball and initiated a costly trade war. With strong backing, the Federal League posed a serious challenge to the American and National leagues. In all, the Federal League lured eighty-one players from Major League Baseball. Caution was exercised in site competition, however, as only one two-team city (Chicago) and three one-team cities (Brooklyn, Pittsburgh, and St. Louis) were invaded. Other Federal League cities were Indianapolis, Baltimore, Buffalo, and Kansas City. In 1915 the Indianapolis franchise was moved to Newark, giving the league two teams adjacent to New York. With slightly greater travel distances and a substantially smaller population base, the eight Federal League teams faced a difficult struggle.

Federal League owners invested in the league instead of in teams, and thus it lacked the internal division between rich and poor teams that characterized the National League and, to a lesser extent, the American League. Although public outrage had been expressed when the National League toyed with the idea of syndicate baseball in 1900, the underdog Federal League was shown more tolerance. Not surprisingly, the Federal League used its internal cohesion to produce close pennant races, with the crucial city of Chicago in the race each season until the very end (though no overall ordering of performance by population was achieved). Besides fielding strong, evenly matched teams, the Federal League mounted a strong legal case against Major League Baseball for violating antitrust law. Judge Kennesaw Landis, an avid baseball fan and later commissioner of baseball, postponed the decision long enough for the fans to show they were not able or willing to support three leagues. The Federal League dissolved in 1916, dropping its suit in a $700,000 settlement. Aggrieved by the settlement, Baltimore's Federal League owners initiated a new lawsuit that led to baseball's 1922 exemption from antitrust law.

World War I posed another kind of challenge for Major League Baseball, one that affected both its image and its operations. The military draft, striking the various clubs in random fashion, "could well throw the delicate machinery out of balance, destroy competition, and wreck the game," in the words of Ban Johnson (quoted in Murdock 1982). As a patriotic overture, Johnson offered to shut down baseball. But after President Woodrow Wilson decreed that baseball was important for maintaining morale at home and among troops abroad, Johnson sought an exemption from the draft for baseball players. Baseball could be either organized or not played at all. The exemption request drew much criticism.[5]

The difficulty of the war years exacerbated Major League Baseball's leadership problems. In January 1920, Chairman Hermann resigned in the face of mounting pressure. Many National League owners sought to do away with the commission altogether, as wasteful overhead, and successfully blocked refilling the position for a year. Hermann's buddy and primary supporter in leadership, Ban Johnson, faced an insurrection within his own league, but was harder to get rid of. Another commission member, National League president John Tener, had resigned from his baseball posts in 1918, after Philadelphia's owner, Connie Mack, had defied his order to return a player to the Boston Braves. The minor leagues had pulled out of the National Agreement in 1919, angry with the commission's resolution of disputes over players. Always weak, the National Commission simply ceased to function. Major League Baseball had only squabbling owners and an increasingly inebriated Johnson to hold it together.

In this state, the worst scandal in baseball history occurred. Eight Chicago White Sox players were charged with fixing the 1919 World Series, in what became known as the Black Sox Scandal. A great deal of corruption over the past fifty years had been concealed and gone unpunished by the owners. But this scandal came at an opportune time in league politics, taking place alongside efforts to appoint a new chairman and oust Ban Johnson. The ultimate result was an end run around Johnson by the "Insurrectionists" and the old enemies of Hermann in the National League, supporting a previously proposed plan (by a Chicago businessman with 10 percent interest in the Cubs) to have baseball run by a triumvirate with no financial interest in the game. All sixteen owners met November 12, 1920, without league presidents, lawyers, or stenographers present, and unanimously confirmed Judge Landis as commissioner of baseball. The idea of two associate commissioners (along with representation of the minors) was abandoned. The league presidents were to serve in only an advisory capacity to the commissioner. This structure was to prove remarkably durable.

The Landis Years

Landis was an autocrat, refusing to accept the position unless the powers of the commissioner were greatly expanded. A new National Agreement in 1921 gave Landis complete authority to "investigate . . . any act, transaction, or practice suspected to be detrimental to the best interests of baseball . . . and the power to take punitive action against leagues, clubs, officers or players" (Seymour 1971, p. 322). Owners had to waive their right to challenge Landis's decisions in court or in public (and their right to criticize each other in public). With the self-assurance of a judge and the security of a five-year contract, Landis was never intimidated by the owners. J. G. Taylor Spink (1947, p. 74) reported that Landis "mimicked some of the owners, aggravating their lapses of grammar, collogialisms and pronunciations. He always screwed up his face as though he were eating a particularly bitter olive when he referred to them as 'magnates.' "[6] If anything, Landis cowed the owners, who were only able to grab back some of their powers after his death in 1944.

Landis banned the eight Black Sox players from baseball for life, despite their acquittal in court. Some had turned in star performances and had not received payment, but Landis thought bold action was needed to restore the integrity of the game, or at least to secure his position as restorer of this integrity. Later Landis took similar action against a player indicted, but then acquitted, for car theft, because he deemed that the man was probably guilty. Landis's identification with integrity often constrained owners in dealing with his "narrow, arbitrary, and vindictive nature" that would "blandly ignore the law in the interests of what he conceived to be justice" (Seymour 1971, p. 368). The owners had some forewarning in the 1915 Federal League trial, where Landis, serving as judge in the case, declared, "Both sides must understand that any blows at the thing called baseball would be regarded by this court as a blow to a national institution." At another point, Landis cut off an attorney who was discussing the working conditions of players, snapping, "I am shocked because you call playing baseball 'labor' " (Lowenfish 1991, p. 90).

To bolster the security of the sport, in 1922 Landis helped push through Congress a bill that exempted Organized Baseball from the Sherman Antitrust Act. This made territorial monopolies granted teams and restrictions on player movement less vulnerable to legal challenge. With no oppositional player's union, litigious owners, or legal constraints, Major League Baseball was in a strong position to pursue its interests. During the Landis years, there were no challenges to the majors by rival leagues, nor was there any change in major league composition.[7]

Aiding Landis's rise was the prosperity enjoyed by the owners under his tenure. While Landis was commissioner, the attachment of teams to cities reached its fullest maturity. Fifteen of the sixteen clubs showed a profit for the 1920s as a whole, with the New York Yankees making over $3.5 million. Radio broadcasting of baseball began during this decade, as did Sunday baseball. Perhaps the greatest boost to baseball came from the rise of slugger heroes exemplified by Babe Ruth. Ruth's phenomenal twenty-nine home runs in 1919 rose to fifty-four in 1920 with the help of a more resilient baseball (James 1988). The slugger became a prized gate attraction that owners have been cultivating ever since. In 1929, gate receipts made up 87.6 percent of gross major league incomes (with concessions accounting for another 5.5 percent). As perhaps the greatest box office draw in baseball history, Ruth commanded a 1927 salary of $70,000 (the next highest paid player on the championship New York Yankees received $15,000).

An effort to revive the players' union in 1922 died quickly. Landis saw such a union as an affront to his judicial impartiality, and refused to have dealings with it. Landis did rule in favor of players on some occasions, or at least against owners, and was certainly unpredictable enough to keep all his constituencies hopeful of favor. When the players launched a purely charitable organization in 1924 to aid indigent players, the Association of Pro Ball Players, the owners helped out. Welfare capitalism was popular during the period, and with the continuing support of owners, the association still exists.

Another potential source of opposition to Landis, Ban Johnson, was forced out of baseball by 1927. Johnson had called Landis a "wild-eyed crazy nut" over his handling of a 1924 player corruption charge, and had been promptly banned by Landis from the advisory board for the comment. In addition, American League owners had to sign a humiliating document regarding their loyalties. At the time of Landis's reappointment (for seven years), Landis appeased some grumbling American League owners by reappointing Johnson to the advisory board. But Johnson was far from tamed by his two-year ban, and soon publicly attacked Landis over his handling of another gambling charge against two players. This time the American League owners met and relieved Johnson of his duties "for health reasons." Johnson, not one to quit easily, returned the next season, but was forced to resign for good on July 8, 1927 (he died a year later).

In Seymour's (1971, p. 422) summation, Landis made "a significant contribution to Organized Baseball . . . He kept the magnates in line to a greater extent than before . . . or since, for that matter." The popular identification of Landis with the integrity of baseball, and baseball's prosperity, gave Landis a secure foundation. Yet Landis could only enforce rules and not make them. Nowhere was this limitation more apparent than in the only public battle Landis lost with the owners, over the rise of the farm system.

Ever since the distinction between major and minor leagues had emerged, there had been conflict between them. Battle lines were mostly drawn over the draft price—the compensation a major gave a minor for drafting one of its players—and the number of players that could be drafted. The loss of a few star players for inadequate compensation could destroy a minor league team, which depended on a mix of gate receipts and player sales for its revenue.[8] Under the new 1921 National Agreement between the majors and minors, draft prices increased and only one player per season could be drafted from the top two levels of minors ($5,000 for an AA player, $4,000 for an A player). In addition, eight players from each major league team could be optioned—that is, protected from being drafted by other teams. A minor league team could exempt itself from the draft only by giving up its right to draft from lower-level minors.[9] By 1931 the minors had surrendered their special privileges with respect to the draft, but got $7,500 for an AA player and $6,000 for an A player. In addition, AA players with less than four years experience were exempted from the draft (three years for A players).

This struggle itself changed baseball, in prompting some owners to seek control over minors through ownership. Branch Rickey, general manager of the St. Louis team, led the pack in the development of a "farm system," where teams developed instead of purchased their talent. St. Louis owned five farm clubs (of eighteen owned by majors) in 1928, and thirty-two by 1940. Besides being quite lucrative for Rickey (who received a 10 percent commission for each player sold), the farm system allowed a smaller-city team like St. Louis to cultivate the talent it could not afford to buy. Once larger-city teams started copying Rickey's system, however, its function in facilitating a competitive balance was no longer clear. By 1952 the majors controlled 175 of the 319 existing minor league clubs.

Landis openly opposed the farm system from its start, but was hindered by the lack of a rule banning majors from owning minors. He saw the farm system as a device for avoiding roster size limits and as restricting player mobility. Yet he could only fight a rear-guard action, watching for infractions and interceding against the owners case by case. For example, Landis made free agents out of ninety-one St. Louis minor leaguers in 1938, and freed the same number from Detroit two years later. But in the end, his efforts to stop the development of the farm system failed. Ironically, by the 1950s, as television began to erode minor league gate revenues, the farm system the owners fought so valiantly for became a sizable burden for them.

By all accounts, Landis was the strongest commissioner organized baseball ever had. Only death could remove him from office, after he had remained at the helm for almost twenty-four years. Yet it is difficult to identify any real uses of his authority outside of those that fueled his cult of personality. Landis contended with people, not systems, and the havoc he could cause the former often had little impact on the course of the latter. In particular, Landis did nothing to undermine the dominance of large-city teams.[10] Of the forty-eight pennant winners under Landis, the two New York teams supplied twenty-one of them (plus one from Brooklyn). Born under Landis, the New York Yankee dynasty is unrivaled in its domination of baseball, with thirty-three World Series appearances (the New York Giants are second with fourteen appearances). Because there was so much site competition between the two leagues, and no city outside New York could evidently support two top teams, the overall ordering of performance by population fluctuated somewhat. For example, the National League Chicago Cubs sent four teams to the World Series under Landis, but the American League Chicago White Sox sent none. Of the two Philadelphia teams, only the American League Athletics made it to the series—three times. Likewise, only one St. Louis team (the Cardinals) made it—seven times. In Boston, the smallest two-team city, no team made it to the World Series under Landis. Even with the complication of site competition, the ordering of performance by population was the rule in Landis's regime, as evidenced in Figure 3.2.

Despite tendencies for large-city dominance, particularly in the American League, performance inequalities remained stable and moderate under Landis. In the most extreme year, the American League's 1932 season, New York finished sixty-five games ahead of last-place Boston, yielding three times the inequality that chance alone would produce. But for most years the spread between top and bottom was in

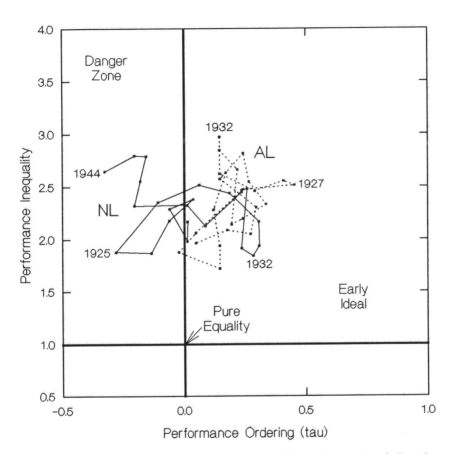

Figure 3.2 Season performance characteristics in Major League Baseball under Commissioner Landis, 1921–1944, using three-year moving averages. Performance characteristics stabilize with teams solidly attached to cities, particularly in the American League (AL). The military draft in World War II and Branch Rickey's St. Louis farm system temporarily benefited smaller-city teams in the National League (NL).

the thirty- to fifty-game range, or slightly over twice what one would expect if all games were decided by a coin toss. Baseball had at last achieved a stable attachment of teams to cities, strong enough to weather world wars and a Great Depression. Most teams remained potential contenders, but the widespread support this generated gave an advantage to the largest-city teams with the most potential support (with the exception of "second" teams in cities outside New York). Large-city dominance that does not unravel widespread contentions is the hallmark of the early prototype, exemplified by Major League Baseball under Landis.

Not long after Landis's death, this stable system was to fall apart. Second teams in two-team cities were the first to abandon the old order. Opportunities for dominance became no longer as dependent on local population size. As site competition—once a complication to the ordering of performance by population—diminished, the ordering of performance by population grew weaker, not stronger. But unlike the early National Association, this condition was associated with a decrease in performance inequalities. To account for this strange development, the attachment of teams to cities has to be abandoned as the basis for organizing league sports. But to get to this point, Major League Baseball ceases to be the most useful path to follow.

Overview of a Successful Prototype

Up close, the emergence of Major League Baseball can easily seem to consist of an endless series of struggles. Owners had to wrestle control away from players, and then contend with each other and local politicians. There was plenty of betrayal and loyalty, machination and thoughtlessness, luck and misfortune. Yet such an accounting skirts the issue of how something as rock solid as Major League Baseball came about. A step back allows us to see how the practically infinite number of threads in the story came together into three large strands. The way these strands came together made Major League Baseball a prototype for other league sports to emulate.

The first strand was demographic, and was laid out in Figure 2.2. Each line represents a major league. Too much site competition—big circles—invariably led to the demise of a contending league, or the end of a line. Moving into the lower-right region of the figure, with large travel distances and small population bases, also put severe survival pressures on leagues. The upper-left region would be ideal, but unfortunately for sports organizers large cities are not all close together. Along the remaining diagonal axis lies the realistic trade-off that entrepreneurs face. Moving to the lower left entailed minor league status—a hard lot but for a long time survivable when the economy, and relations with the majors, were good. The focus of this chapter, however, has been on the upper right—the route to major league status.

By 1903 the National and American leagues had secured major league upper-right-corner niches that remained stable for the next fifty years, affected only by population growth in host cities. League size had been de facto limited to eight teams, a huge constraint on further movement in Figure 2.2. The earlier comings and goings of small-city teams in leagues—invariably more geographically proximate—produced large movements in the population-distance space. But when large cities were occupied and mobilized to provide the support necessary to sustain the high salaries and travel expenses of major league teams, movement in Figure 2.2 ended. At least from a demographic standpoint, baseball was organized in a sustainable way. The only blemish was the high site competition between the National and American leagues. In the 1950s this helped reopen demographic movement, but only after the role of host population and travel distance had been fundamentally changed by television and air travel.

A second strand hinged on performance, and was depicted in Figures 2.1, 2.3, 3.1, and 3.2. Early league organizers were quite aware of the importance of competitive balance, yet they also sought to place winning teams in the largest cities. Pursuing these conflicting goals entailed moving to the lower-right side of the figure. A close pennant race that in the end yielded a consistent ordering of performance by population size was ideal. Because teams were so dependent on local populations for support, this ordering can itself be taken as an indicator of the attachment of teams to cities. With teams throughout the league attached to cities, and hence mobilizing their populations, larger cities received more support and hence had an edge in pursuing the best player and managerial talent. Yet while widespread attachment generated performance inequalities, it also depended on some degree of competitive balance: smaller cities had to believe that their team had some chance for a pennant. The conflicting goals of the organizer were thus firmly rooted in the nature of the attachment of teams to cities.

The basis for a third strand can be seen in the curious upper left–

lower right diagonal movements in the performance figures. Somehow a strong ordering of performance by population is associated with low performance inequality. This suggests that the conflict between organizers' two performance goals was being resolved. Yet a lack of ordering—a necessary property of competitive balance, where small-city teams are just as likely to be winners as large-city teams—is associated with high performance inequality. Neither of the organizers' goals was satisfied, and, as expected, league existence was threatened. Hence the trade-off implied in the conflicting goals was somehow being suppressed in these diagonal movements. A third strand, league organization, accounts for the curious observed consistency between the conflicting goals. When leagues are well organized, attachments between teams and cities are nurtured through performance equalities and in turn provide the basis for ordered inequalities. Without effective league organization, an unordered inequality appears—both indicating and inducing a lack of attachment between teams and cities.[11]

Unfortunately, the organization strand cannot be as neatly represented as the other two. It is best seen as an anchor for the other strands. Without organization, a small number of teams could not maintain a stable attachment to the largest cities in the nation, an attachment central to both the demographic and the performance strands. Yet organization is difficult to observe directly. The only clear markers arise from failures in otherwise endless struggles for control (White 1992). Rules are one such marker. Every rule marks some momentary success of one constituency over another, yet can be undermined should underlying relations change. The reserve system, for example, marked a triumph of owners over players, just as the National Agreements after 1877 marked a triumph of the majors over the minors. Yet neither was immutable. A minor league draft, revenue sharing, and centralized scheduling were additional innovations spun out of struggles internal to the leagues.

Organization charts, as a compilation of rules concerning divisions of responsibility and authority, are perhaps the most widely used marker for organization. From a formal standpoint, the American League had a stronger president than the National League, and this undoubtedly helped the American League in getting established so quickly and successfully. Earlier, the Players League—with both strong demographic and performance measures—failed owing to a flaw in its organization that stemmed from the awkward alliance between players and contributors. The organizational design that proved most able to sustain itself came with Landis. The fact that this design has since accommodated such a variety of commissioners indicates its flexibility with respect to adjustments based on informal power realities.

People came and went within the major leagues. Immensely powerful persons like Andrew Freedman disappeared from the sport only weeks after coming within one vote of controlling 30 percent of a syndicated National League. The only force that was irresistible was the attachment of teams to cities. Anyone standing in the way of this attachment could not last long, or his league could not last long. Successful organization was organization consistent with this attachment. The prerogatives of large-city teams in fielding the strongest teams had to be respected, as did those keeping smaller-city teams from falling hopelessly behind: hence the emergence of partial institutions, like limited revenue sharing and a minor league draft full of loopholes. These were consonant with an attachment of teams to cities that gave every team its strength, but larger-city teams more of it.

By successfully interweaving the three strands of demographics, performance, and organization, Major League Baseball became the prototype for league sports. None of the sports that followed could ignore the apparent limit of eight-team pennant races or the importance of attaching teams to large cities. With the reserve clause, player drafts and options, and blacklisting, the apparatus for player development and control was largely fine tuned. Rules that addressed competitive balance, like gate sharing and roster size limits, were also well established. Numerous devices for broadening appeal had emerged, from stadium location and construction to special promotions to player codes of behavior. With so much proven success available, why did the team sports that followed baseball fail to emulate the prototype? And how did a new prototype emerge from one failure, that of football, when the attachment of teams to cities was no longer the most secure foundation for building successful leagues? These questions are taken up over the next three chapters.

4

• • •

Attachment Failures

Opportunities for additional league sports became increasingly apparent as the twentieth century neared. America was becoming more urban and affluent, creating ever-larger potential publics for sporting events. Widespread acceptance of organized sports among work, community, educational, and even religious institutions was rapidly broadening the base of both participants and spectators. Baseball dominated the summer, but left the remaining seasons open.[1] Invention of the electric light in 1879, along with new steel and concrete construction methods, opened the winter to indoor sports. As other sports came on the scene, many people were attracted to them by features that baseball lacked. Football provided sanctioned violence, while basketball and ice hockey provided continuous action. These sports quickly became immensely popular in their amateur versions, and professionals soon appeared in each. For sports organizers, the challenge was to emulate baseball in establishing major league versions of these new team sports.

Yet despite the visible prototype of Major League Baseball and the apparent opportunities, enormous difficulties were encountered in organizing major league versions of the new team sports. Only hockey succeeded in attaching itself to a set of cities. Even so, just four of these were in the United States, and player development long remained an entirely Canadian affair. In football, it took twenty-eight years after the first professionals appeared for a "major" league to emerge—in and around Ohio—and another sixteen years for the league to field the same teams for two consecutive seasons. Basketball had an even more difficult time, taking almost thirty years after professionals appeared to form a major league and another twenty-seven years to achieve two years of stability. Attaching professional teams to cities proved enormously problematic.

This chapter chronicles the development of major leagues in football, basketball, and hockey using the prototype of Major League Baseball as a benchmark. These sports failed, in varying degrees, to achieve the stability and success of Major League Baseball in attaching teams to a set of cities, largely because of the work of powerful amateur organizations that formed as a reaction to professional baseball as it forged ahead. This very failure, however, facilitated later successes in exploiting the opportunities of the modern era of televised sport, when the relation between amateur and professional organization suddenly became complementary. But this distant future provided little consolation for the early organizers, who could hardly have envisioned the magnitude of their future success amid their more immediate difficulties.

Out of Canton

It was no accident that the first professional football league appeared in Ohio, far from the center of "amateur virtue." Football had first emerged within elite eastern colleges, and was rapidly popularized as a college game. The professional version was actively marginalized by college programs, and had to take hold outside their reach in terms of both social class and geography. Professional football appealed predominantly to working-class men, in small company towns far removed from the eastern seaboard. The task of building a major league, which at the time meant attaching professional teams to large eastern cities, proved to be a formidable one.

In the fall of 1920, teams from five states met at a car dealership in Canton to form the American Professional Football Association, renamed the National Football League (NFL) a year later. Jim Thorpe, still active as a player, was named league president. A $100 membership fee was set, but never collected. Scheduling was left to the teams, who ended up playing varying numbers of games with as many nonmembers as members. Although a silver loving cup was to be awarded to the league champion, the latter was determined as much off the field as on as teams came and went, games were and were not counted, and the season was blurred with the pre- and postseason. It became evident to all that Thorpe was a better athlete than organizer, and Joe Carr was named president after the first season, remaining in that position until his death in 1939. Carr had been a minor league baseball executive and was soon to be president of the first major professional basketball league, as well.

The number of NFL teams grew to twenty-two by 1926, but dropped to ten by 1928 and eight by 1932. It was not until 1936 that the same set of teams competed for two consecutive seasons and played the same number of games. A Kansas City team played no home games, while the Los Angeles Buccaneers and the Louisville Colonels were actually road teams based in Chicago. The Canton team, dominating the early years of the league, moved to Cleveland in 1924 in search of a larger audience. The league did little to assert itself as teams came, went, moved, and struggled for their own survival. The marginality of the professional game and the weakness of the league served to reinforce each other.

The early demographics of the NFL would hardly have qualified it as a top minor league in baseball. In 1920 baseball's National League had an average population base of 1,654,000; the NFL had only 631,400. While National League teams traveled an average of 566 miles for away games, the NFL had a more regional 318 miles to travel. Early demographic instability is captured in Figure 4.1, with horizontal movements indicating changes in league composition. Early locations included such now-forgotten sports towns as Rock Island, Evansville, Hammond, Muncie, Marion, Duluth, Kenosha, Racine, and Pottsville. Outside of these small franchise cities, most people were not even aware that the NFL existed.

To remedy this situation, NFL teams tried to recruit college stars to gain both prestige and visibility. College coaches, however, actively condemned professional football and helped maintain a stigma on the game not so different from that attached to professional wrestling today. At the University of Chicago, coach Alonso Stagg took back players' varsity letters if they turned professional. Lured by the promise of $100,000 for a national barnstorming tour with the Chicago Bears, however, the college superstar Red Grange turned professional in 1925. Grange's tour did much to give the professional game positive national exposure.

It was only after the large eastern cities began noticing professional football that the NFL could improve its demographics. Entry was by no means unproblematic, however. In 1927 the NFL entered New York

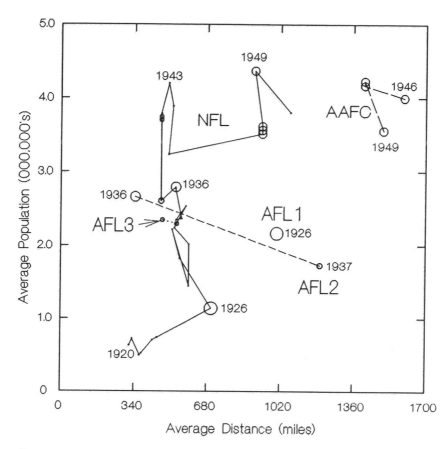

Figure 4.1 Demographic movement in major league football, 1920–1950. As the National Football League (NFL) slowly worked its way into major league cities, four rival leagues formed around NFL weaknesses (with circle size indicating the extent of site competition with the NFL). These challenges prompted the NFL first to enter large northeastern cities, and later to move to the West Coast. Travel distance measures for the first two American Football Leagues (AFL) included a Los Angeles team that played no home games, and thus do not accurately reflect actual travel. AAFC = All American Football Conference.

with a team named the "New York Yankees," but baseball's 1927 Yankees with Babe Ruth and Lou Gehrig were a hard act to follow. In their two years of existence, the NFL's Yankees went 11–16–2 and played most of their games on the road. New York's huge population base provided less assured support than a small town like Pottsville. And costs were much higher. In 1933 the NFL entered Philadelphia. By 1935, the NFL had nearly the same demographics as the National League, with every team located in a major league baseball city except the Packers, in Green Bay. Two teams were located in Chicago, and one each in New York, Brooklyn, Boston, Philadelphia, Pittsburgh, and Detroit. Figure 4.1 indicates the rapid improvement in NFL demographics by the mid-1930s. The challenge facing the NFL was somehow to tap the potential of these favorable demographics, before it was dragged down by high costs.

In the mid-1930s there was a belief among football fans in the superiority of strong college teams. To combat this belief, an annual game between the NFL champion and a team of college all-stars was initiated in 1934. Results were split through the first decade (2–2–2) and leaned toward the NFL in the next two decades (7–3, 7–3). The last college victory was in 1963, and the contest was discontinued after 1976. Although on competitive grounds professional football did not deserve the scorn it received, it was slow in establishing its superiority. Only after the best college players regularly started turning professional was NFL superiority established in the minds of fans.

The early marginality of major league football had peculiar consequences. Small towns could often generate more interest in home teams than could larger cities, particularly when the latter had strong college teams in residence. Canton was the home of the NFL's best early team. In the mid-1920s the Pottsville (Pa.) Maroons galvanized the population of 21,876 to such a degree that many larger-city teams (including New York City teams) agreed to give up their home field advantage for the guaranteed crowd, averaging 8,000, in Pottsville (Gudelunas and Couch 1982, p. 53). Such fan loyalty was gained through a mix of nationally known college stars (paid up to $150 per game) and local players (paid up to $25 per game). But even with a winning team, to steer through the club's financial difficulties required backing from a local surgeon.[2] By 1929 the team was sold to a Boston concern, and eventually landed in Washington, D.C., as the Redskins, under George Preston Marshall.

In the first fifteen years of the NFL, there was no tendency for larger-city teams to perform better than smaller-city teams. While a town like Pottsville might mobilize behind its team, a team in New York or Philadelphia could receive scant attention. Indeed, teams could depend largely or entirely (as in the case of road teams) on away games for support, and hence it is not surprising that their home population had little to do with their success. Unlike in the earliest baseball leagues, however, the failure to attach to cities was not associated with large performance differences among teams. Early NFL season performance inequality remained fairly stable, varying between 1.18 and 1.77 times what one would expect on the basis of competitive equality. Figure 4.2 depicts the relation between the ordering of performance and host population (tau) and season performance inequality. The main reason why the NFL did not experience high performance inequality, and early baseball leagues did, was the liberal revenue-sharing policies adopted by the NFL. The revenue sharing may also, however, have impeded the attachment of teams to cities (reflected in the near zero tau).

Early uncertainties in local support fostered football's generous 60–40 home-away team sharing of gate receipts. Large-city teams, often competing for fans with established college football teams as well as other professional teams, could not be certain of support. Sometimes small, one-sport towns like Pottsville could generate larger crowds. Revenue sharing served as a hedge against this financial uncertainty. Teams could set their own schedules, playing games at whichever site was most likely to draw the largest audience. Generous revenue sharing allowed teams to work out mutually advantageous schedules, bringing football to wherever it might attract large audiences. Under this arrangement, some teams survived exclusively on the basis of away-game receipts, competing as traveling teams with no home location. Scheduling uniformity is as much an outgrowth of a stable attachment to cities as a precondition for it. Support must be spread throughout the league, so that teams can survive playing half their games at home. Until this widespread attachment existed, the NFL was in no position to emulate baseball's even split between home and away games. And without this even split, the league had difficulties cultivating a stable and widespread attachment.

In an agreement forged at the start of baseball's National League, when support was uncertain, 15 cents of every 50-cent admission went to the away team. Framed in terms of cents and not percentages, the

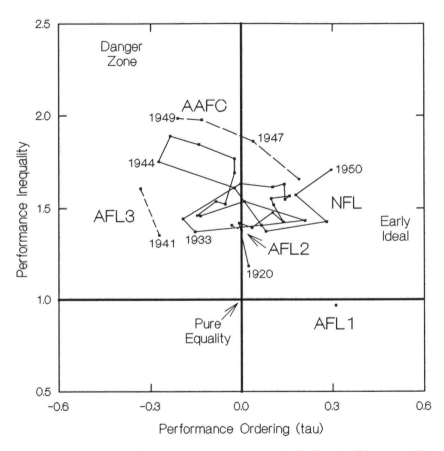

Figure 4.2 Season performance characteristics in football major leagues, 1920–1950, using three-year moving averages. Failure to strongly attach teams to cities underlay the absence of a performance ordering, or large-city domination, in major league football. AAFC = All American Football Conference; AFL = American Football League; NFL = National Football League.

home-away split was allowed to erode through inflation all the way to 1965. As the attachment of teams to cities became secure, large-city teams that enjoyed superior support successfully blocked change throughout the first half of the twentieth century. When change came, it was conservative (90–10 percent for the National League, 80–20 percent for the American League). With such a conservative split, "sharing" had to come through more centralized league control over scheduling that ensured teams a mix of home and away games. Rather than moving to where audiences are expected, the location of sporting events becomes fixed—making team locations more crucial to the survival of a league. Inequalities are built into the system and carefully guarded by prosperous teams, who potentially draw larger home audiences and thus whose advantages in hoarding home receipts far outweigh their disadvantages in giving up away receipts.

Hence it was marginality, not prescience, that led to a policy of revenue sharing that would serve the NFL well in the future, particularly with the advent of television revenues. Conversely, the security of baseball's attachment to cities led it toward a conservatism that was to impede its transition into the modern era of sports. Reluctance to share gate receipts was carried over to broadcast revenues, helping to maintain a large-city dynasty like the New York Yankees long after dynasties had lost their value from a league standpoint.

Marginality also played an important role in forging the NFL's relationship with college football programs. College stars lent badly needed prestige to professional teams, but were strongly discouraged from playing professional football both by college coaches and by the general stigma attached to the professional version of the game.[3] In an effort to allay colleges' fears over losing their best players before graduation, the NFL early on prohibited the use of college players before their class had graduated. Teams were harshly disciplined for using college players under assumed names (one manager was suspended for life for using four high school players). The NFL's efforts to maintain good relations with colleges, born of necessity, were to reap great rewards in the future.

Major League Baseball, by contrast, had always shown contempt for college programs and efforts to preserve the amateur status of athletes. Baseball owners stated outright that they were going to sign any college players they could. In response to the University of Chicago's complaint over a signing, the White Sox owner Harry Grabiner retorted,

"Both the boy and his father signed the contract with us willingly, and we can't see what the university can do about it" (quoted in Seymour 1991, p. 184). Landis, who saw no reason why high school boys should be denied entry into the baseball profession, supported the owners. For recruits seeking to retain college eligibility, Major League Baseball concealed signings, often with the complicity of college coaches. Some colleges, unable to deal with the problem of collegians playing professional baseball in the summer, dropped their baseball programs in the 1920s and 1930s. Major League Baseball's disregard for the integrity of college programs came back to haunt it when minor leagues started collapsing in the 1950s. Baseball had to start subsidizing the training of players who were far from stardom, whereas colleges began supplying ready-made stars for professional football and basketball.

In May 1935 Bert Bell, owner of the cellar-dwelling Philadelphia football team (and future commissioner), conceived the idea of a reverse order college draft. Such drafts help weaker teams by giving them first pick of top college players.[4] They also help prevent unchecked bidding for top recruits by giving teams exclusive rights in negotiations with selected players. Bell had just come out of a bidding war to sign a college fullback that had landed the rookie a salary ($5,000) equal to that paid the top player in the league. In baseball, large-city teams blocked an amateur draft until 1965 as they maintained their dominance through outbidding smaller-city teams. In football, with little attachment between teams and cities, large-city owners had to be concerned with holding bidding costs down. An initial nine-round draft was held in Philadelphia early in 1936. But the top pick, selected by Philadelphia, never signed with the team, nor did he sign with the Chicago Bears after they traded for his rights (Riffenburgh 1986). Largely because of such difficulties in securing college players, the draft was increased to twenty rounds by 1939 and thirty rounds by 1942, when the war compounded draft uncertainties. By 1977 college stars were eager to sign with NFL teams, and the draft was back down to twelve rounds.

Only players whose class had graduated were eligible for the draft. Until 1967 players with remaining college eligibility could be selected as "future picks," but could not be signed. With colleges providing star players, NFL deference to college programs offered enormous returns. By contrast, Major League Baseball's past contempt for college programs contributed to its failure to develop star players. When baseball got around to establishing an amateur draft in 1965, some thirty years after football, high school players were not only included but were the preferred choice for the first twelve years. College players could be drafted after their junior year. Baseball training in college was regarded as inferior to experience in the minor leagues, and few college players ever went straight to the majors.[5]

By 1935 many of the pieces were in place for the NFL's future success. No longer located on the nation's periphery, the NFL had solid major league demographics. Except for a 1937 expansion into Washington, D.C., and Cleveland, and an exodus from Boston, the NFL's membership remained stable until World War II forced retrenchments in 1943.[6] Teams began playing the same number of games, and these could be split between home and away as the NFL found its stable set of sufficiently supportive cities. NFL policies of revenue sharing and a reverse amateur draft were in place, but their full impact would not be felt until marginality was fully shed. A game between the NFL champion and college all-stars was in place to help the NFL prove itself. But the main vehicle for dispelling professional football's marginality, television, had yet to be harnessed.

During the NFL's first fifteen years, there was only one challenge by a rival league. In 1926, the NFL had a sprawling twenty-two teams, but weak representation in major eastern cities. Red Grange, after failing to work out a gate-sharing arrangement with the Bears, petitioned the NFL for a New York franchise. Blocked by the veto of a single owner, Grange and his manager, "Cash and Carry" Pyle, put together a trim nine-team American Football League with teams in the eastern cities of Philadelphia, New York, Brooklyn, Newark, and Boston, along with teams in Cleveland, Rock Island, Chicago, and Los Angeles (a road team). Though with good demographics on paper—an average population base almost twice that of the NFL—this first challenger barely survived its first season. Three teams played fourteen games, but four did not play more than six games. Grange's New York team made it through the season, but an injury to Grange near the end ensured that the team lost both money and the championship. Although team performances were ordered by host population size and performance inequality was low, there was simply not enough enthusiasm for professional football in the East, and not enough anywhere for two major leagues.

As the NFL stabilized and began attracting favorable attention to professional football, two new versions of the American Football

League made fresh challenges. A six-team American Football League formed in 1936, with teams in Boston, Cleveland, New York, Pittsburgh, Rochester, and Brooklyn. While its winning Boston team drove the NFL's team out of that city the next year, its second-place Cleveland team moved to the NFL its second season. For the 1937 season, two new teams in Cincinnati and a Los Angeles road team were added, and the prior season's last-place Brooklyn team folded. But the second American Football League shut down during its second season before any team had played more than eight games. A third American Football League formed with six teams in 1940 and also survived only two seasons (fielding only five teams its second season). Not helped by the fact that the team in its smallest city, Columbus, won both pennants, the rival league was far too weak to survive the onset of World War II.

A more serious challenge to the NFL came right after the war. Capitalizing on the postwar sports boom, a well-placed eight-team All American Football Conference (AAFC) formed in 1946. With teams in both Los Angeles and San Francisco as well as Chicago, New York, and Miami, the All American Football Conference could boast of truly national coverage. Commercial air travel had only recently made such a league possible, and was soon to eliminate travel distance as a constraining factor in league composition. In response to the new rival, the NFL became the first established major league to place a team on the West Coast when it set up a Los Angeles franchise in 1946. As major leagues started expanding and aiming for national coverage (and soon national television audiences), local population bases on average declined. The average population of AAFC cities was only about 5 percent below that of the NFL, a deficit more than compensated for by its penetration of the South and West.

But performance inequality was substantially higher in the All American Football Conference, and one team, Cleveland, finished with the best record each of the league's four seasons (losing only four out of fifty-four games played). Overall, smaller-city teams tended to perform better after the first season (see Figure 4.2). In the end, the All American Football Conference succumbed to a vigorous trade war with the NFL and agreed to merge for the 1950 season. Three AAFC teams—San Francisco, Cleveland, and New York—joined the NFL, and a special draft was held for the remaining players. This left the NFL with twelve teams, divided into two conferences. Conference winners met in a championship game at the end of each season.

Although weakened by the trade war, the NFL was to prove remarkably adept at exploiting the opportunities opening up in the 1950s. The league was well positioned in cities across the entire nation. Unlike baseball, it had never been dominated by the teams in its largest cities, on or off the playing field. On the field, a reverse ordering of performance by population had predominated since the NFL began to stabilize in 1935 (see Figure 4.2). Off the field, the lack of large-city domination had facilitated cooperative arrangements. The NFL had pursued good relations with college programs, a reverse draft, and liberal revenue sharing. As we shall see in the next chapter, its aggressive bonding with the new television media helped it overcome the stigma under which it had long labored. With remarkable rapidity, the NFL attached itself to the nation while baseball clung to its increasingly antiquated attachment to cities.

Into the Midwest

The groundwork for the majors was laid the most quickly in basketball, yet no sport underwent more difficulties in establishing major leagues. In less than a decade after the game was invented, basketball had become very popular, and professionals had appeared on the scene. Yet obstacles had also arisen that hindered prospective major leagues from harnessing this popularity and professionalism. Although basketball had not originated in colleges, its rapid adoption and popularization as a college game gave rise to efforts, as in football, to stigmatize the professional game. Moreover, basketball's roots among inner-city ethnic groups had spawned a tradition of independent traveling teams that posed a direct barrier to any major league efforts to attach teams to cities. Besides associating professional teams with ethnic groups, these independent teams had themselves stigmatized league play by their superordinate relations to the unstable system of regional leagues they fed upon. Hence prospective major leagues in basketball had to contend with both amateur and professional organization in getting established.

The first basketball league with more than regional aspirations was the American Basketball League, founded in 1925. This league was organized and backed by a number of NFL owners, and the NFL's president, Joe Carr, served as its first president. To end incessant roster jumping that drove up salaries and undermined the identity of teams in regional leagues, the American Basketball League instigated exclusive written player contracts. It also banned the use of a cage around courts and the two-handed dribble, eliminating some of the slowness and roughness of the professional game. These rule changes were designed to open the game to college players, who, as in the NFL, lent prestige to major league teams. At the time that the American Basketball League formed, few professionals had college experience, coming as they did from inner-city YMCA and settlement house backgrounds. To allay the fears of college coaches, Carr pledged heavy fines for any club that signed a player before his college eligibility had expired.

American Basketball League teams were initially located in Washington, D.C., Boston, Rochester, Brooklyn, Fort Wayne, Detroit, Buffalo, Chicago, and Cleveland. Although clearly not a regional league, the American Basketball League had only 75 percent of the travel distance and 66 percent of the average population of baseball's National League at the time. A New York team was needed, but the champion New York Celtics preferred independence over league play. During the first year of the American Basketball League, the Celtics regularly beat league teams and made more money as well. Only after the American Basketball League teams prohibited its teams from playing the Celtics did they join the league in 1926. The Celtics then dominated league play for two years, whereupon they were disbanded by the league and their players were distributed to the other clubs. This was done not only to address the competitive imbalance but also because Madison Square Garden had threatened to evict the Celtics, who had never drawn large crowds at home (Hollander 1989).[7] Consistent local support of even a champion team rested on an attachment of teams to cities that had not yet been established in basketball.

Despite the rule changes and the addition of a New York team, few American Basketball League teams made money. Boston dropped out at the first half of a split season, and Buffalo did not return for the second season. Every year teams came and went, with no two years seeing the same league membership. Carr resigned as president in 1928. For the 1930–31 season, the next president—John O'Brien, leader of three early regional leagues—required that each team have at least two rookies drawn principally from the college ranks, and that one be on the court at all times. Another rule, restricting the pivot man from holding the foul lane for more than three seconds, was designed to cut down on roughness. But the American Basketball League collapsed the next year, a victim of the Great Depression. Once again professional basketball devolved into regional associations (including a reformed American Basketball League that survived until 1953) with traveling independent teams setting the standards of the game.

The South Philadelphia Hebrew Association (SPHA) team provides a glimpse into the turbulence of early league basketball (Hollander 1989). Formed in 1918, the SPHAs joined the Philadelphia League and won the last two championships of the league's existence. Along with other surviving teams, the SPHAs joined the Eastern League. But this league went out of business its first season. Independent once again, the SPHAs started booking games with teams in the newly formed American Basketball League and with the still independent Celtics. When the American Basketball League set up a Philadelphia team in 1927, two star SPHA players jumped to it. In 1929, the SPHAs were rebuilt from former college stars and joined the third edition of the Eastern League, winning three consecutive championships before jumping to the reformed regional version of the American Basketball League. All teams were within an afternoon's driving distance, and no arena had more than a 3,000-fan capacity. Here the SPHAs played out the last fifteen years of their existence, winning seven championships.

A loose coalition of professional and quasi-amateur teams formed the Midwest Basketball Conference in 1935. Each team booked its own games, and restrictions on the resulting schedules were few. With college basketball enormously popular in the Midwest, the new league adopted intercollegiate rules with only a few exceptions. Strong corporate backing also gave the league an advantage during the Depression years. Goodyear, Firestone, and General Electric entered company teams. Other teams, some operated by basketball men and others by businessmen, were named after the businessmen who backed them. Only a few teams were independent of a business association. College rules and corporate sponsorship also gave the Midwest Basketball Conference an advantage in recruiting college players. With professional basketball marginal, unstable, and, for players, short-lived, the promise of a corporate position once one's playing days were over was a powerful lure.

Successful in recruiting talent on a national level, the Midwest Basketball League changed its name to the National Basketball League in 1937. But while the National Basketball League was "major" with respect to talent, it was not a major league demographically (see Figure 4.3). Teams were located in six states, with half the average travel dis-

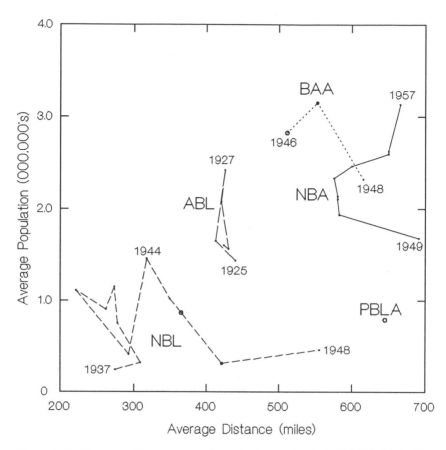

Figure 4.3 Demographic movement in major league basketball, 1925–1957. The National Basketball League (NBL) had minor league demographics and major league talent, while the Basketball Association of America (BAA) had the converse. The smallness of the circles indicating site competition shows that the two leagues competed in almost no sites. When they merged into the National Basketball Association (NBA) in 1949, the best characteristics of each were (gradually) combined. ABL = American Basketball League; PBLA = Professional Basketball League of America.

tance of baseball's National League. Average population was only 243,600, compared with the National League's 2,078,200. In addition, at the start scheduling and even some rules were left to the teams to determine on a game-by-game basis. For example, the home team could abolish the center jump after each basket. Teams did not play the same number of games or the same teams, making the determination of a league champion ambiguous. The looseness of the National Basketball League's first season is summed up in the statement of the player Gene Scholz: "I didn't even know we were in a league. I didn't know what was going on. I was just picking up a few bucks on the side playing basketball" (quoted in Peterson 1990, p. 125).

By its second season, the National Basketball League had asserted control over scheduling and game rules. But the financial difficulties of teams without corporate sponsorship, soon to be compounded by World War II, led to attrition and instability. No two years saw the same membership, with turnover as high as 69 percent across seasons. Only five teams played during the 1942–43 season. Consider, for example, the fate of the Warren Penns. They played home games in the Beaty Junior High School gym, with 900 seats that were rarely filled. Midway through the National Basketball League's second season, the franchise owner Gerry Archibald moved his Penns to Cleveland after he got the backing of a local car dealership, White Horse Motors. The team was duly rechristened the Cleveland White Horses. But when the National Basketball League reduced its schedule from forty-two to twenty-eight games, Archibald had to book outside games to meet the payroll. His problems were solved when he was invited to represent Elmira, New York, in another regional league. For the 1938–39 season, the Cleveland White Horses–Elmira Colonels played in two leagues. The next season, Archibald moved his team to Detroit, where they became the Detroit Eagles. After one season, he sold his franchise to a cigar manufacturer in Detroit, who kept the team together for only one more year. Despite a second-place finish and a tie for the division title, Archibald lost $1,000 to $1,500 each of his years in the National Basketball League (Peterson 1990).

It was simply not clear, war or no war, whether a major league could establish and sustain itself. Some teams had prospered for a time by wandering away from their home base, but no set of teams had yet been able to attach themselves to these home bases within the context of a major league. The failure of both the American and the National

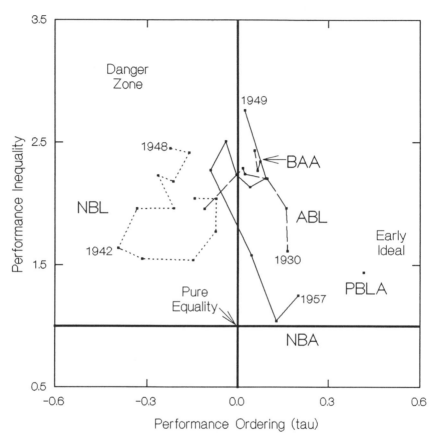

Figure 4.4 Season performance characteristics in major league basketball, 1925–1957, using three-year moving averages. As in football, the failure to strongly attach teams to cities underlay the lack of large-city dominance in early major league basketball. Only the Professional Basketball League of America (PBLA), owned by a single person, exhibited the ideal of a close pennant race led by larger-city teams in its one month of operation. ABL = American Basketball League; BAA = Basketball Association of America; NBA = National Basketball Association; NBL = National Basketball League.

Basketball leagues to attach teams to cities can be seen in the lack of any relation between team performance and city population. Although there was a weak tendency for larger cities to have better teams in the American Basketball League, the National Basketball League was plagued by small-city dominance in ten of its twelve seasons (see Figure 4.4). The three most solid teams in the National Basketball League were the Oshkosh All-Stars, Sheboygan Redskins, and Fort Wayne Zollner Pistons. These small towns supported their teams, while most larger-city residents paid little attention to major league basketball. Football shared the same failure to forge a leaguewide attachment of teams to cities.

From 1939 to 1948, the *Chicago Herald-American* sponsored a World Tournament open to the top league and independent teams, including two all-black independents, the Rens and the Globetrotters. The first two years these black independent teams each won a championship. But as a sign of events to come, National Basketball League teams won the following eight championships. A league had finally managed to acquire and retain some of the best players in the country, ending the dominance of independent teams.[8] Yet the National Basketball League functioned largely outside the nation's major cities, and this hindered its ability to reach the larger audience necessary for financial stability. In its first season after World War II, the eight-team league occupied only the major cities of Chicago, Cleveland, and Indianapolis, and in all of these cities teams were named after corporations or businessmen. As a small gesture to its national claims, the league added a team as far east as Rochester, New York.

Amid the surge in sports interest that followed World War II, a new league with impressive demographics—the Basketball Association of America—was organized by members of the Arena Managers Association of America (on the prompting of a sports editor). All but one of the eleven new franchise owners had hockey teams as their principal sports properties and tenants for their arenas. The first president of the Basketball Association of America was Maurice Podoloff, a New Haven lawyer, arena owner, and president of the American Hockey League (a top minor league). Podoloff knew little about hockey and less about basketball, but he was an experienced executive. Nor were any of the other franchise owners basketball men. But with the exception of teams in Providence and Toronto, all of their basketball teams were located in Major League Baseball cities. This gave the new league a powerful demographic advantage over the National Basketball League, as seen in Figure 4.3. The Basketball Association of America was self-consciously a major league from the start, with teams named after cities, not corporations.

Initially the new major league refrained from raiding the superior talent of the National Basketball League. Player rosters were a mix of old pros, college stars, and men who had played in the military services during World War II, while coaches were drawn from high schools and colleges (Peterson 1990). Perhaps to conceal the league's talent deficit, exhibition games were forbidden during the first season. A centrally organized sixty-game schedule was to be followed by an intricate playoff system for the league championship, modeled, not surprisingly, on the one used in hockey.

Although the schedule was faithfully executed, the first season proved a financial disaster. Attendance averaged only 3,000 per game, a figure that included the beneficiaries of buckets of complimentary tickets. Four teams, not earning enough to cover player salaries, dropped out at the end of the season. Only two teams, New York and Philadelphia, sold more than 100,000 tickets for their thirty home games, yielding revenues over four times those of the departing teams. National Basketball League teams, mainly because of their superior talent and lower travel costs, did much better despite their inferior locations. As was true in football, large population bases meant little—besides higher operating costs—in the absence of strong attachments between teams and cities.

The two leagues met at the end of the first season and worked out an interleague agreement covering uniform player contracts, a joint college draft, player trades, and a possible world series between league champions. But the cordial relations between the two leagues grew more strained as Basketball Association of America teams continued to lose money in their second season. The National Basketball League also had problems when Maurice White, the owner of its champion and best-drawing team—Chicago's American Gears, with the first highly skilled big man in basketball, George Mikan—withdrew his team to start his own sixteen-team league in the Midwest and South. White lost $600,000 when his Professional Basketball League of America died within a month of its initiation.[9] His Gears ceased to be, and its players were distributed across other league teams (sending Mikan to the Minneapolis Lakers).

Around the middle of the second season, Podoloff raised the possibility of a merger to consolidate the National Basketball League's playing talent with the Basketball Association of America's major city locations. This proposal created a rift within the National Basketball League. At the end of the season, four strong teams, including the president's team and both division champions, defected to the Basketball Association of America. Although determined to fight, the rest of the National Basketball League held out only one more season. By both demographic and performance criteria, the league was in serious trouble. In its final year, the National Basketball League faced both its largest travel distances, with a population base only one-ninth as large as that of baseball's National League, and high performance inequality, with its smallest cities dominating. Before its next season, the National Basketball League caved in and merged with the Basketball Association of America to become the National Basketball Association (NBA).[10]

Playing its first season in 1949–50, the NBA had an unbalanced assortment of seventeen teams in three divisions. By the next season, the NBA had lost six smaller-city teams (and one division). Three of the teams that dropped out tried to revive the National Basketball League as a midwestern league. But with colleges taking over player development and television soon providing ample sports and nonsports entertainment, there was less room than ever for regional leagues in basketball. And while this revival was failing to receive sufficient support in small- and mid-sized cities, the NBA was continuing to improve its demographics. In almost doubling its average population base by 1957, it at last achieved major league demographics with major league playing talent. This achievement occurred over sixty years since the first professionals had appeared in basketball, and took place at a time when the model for organizing sports was already undergoing a fundamental change.

Robert Peterson (1990) argues that the modern era in professional basketball was ushered in by two rule changes that emerged from the NBA Board of Governors meeting on April 23, 1954. The first limited each team to six personal fouls per quarter. For all subsequent fouls, an additional free throw would be given to the other side. This extra free throw eliminated the incentive for deliberate fouls aimed at getting possession of the ball. The second rule required a team to make a scoring attempt within 24 seconds of gaining possession of the ball. With this one stroke, stalling became impossible, and the focus of strategy shifted from possession to scoring. Major league basketball had finally seized the initiative from colleges in making the game less rough and more fast moving. Though radically different from Naismith's game, basketball was at last consistent with Naismith's intentions.

On the surface, major league basketball and football bore some similarities as they moved into the 1950s. Both had been dwarfed by the college game, although both had produced barnstorming teams that had attracted national attention. Both had enjoyed a surge of postwar popularity, with new leagues forming and consolidating by 1950. Yet major league basketball had no sharing of gate revenues. Nor were its relations with college programs as good. And the NBA was not nearly as well placed nationally as the NFL, not moving west until 1960—two years after baseball's major leagues moved. And although both football and basketball had overcome most of the difficulties in attaching teams to cities, major league basketball was not nearly as well positioned to exploit the opportunities that distinguished the coming modern era of organized sport.

Across the Border

A major league by Canadian standards is a minor league by U.S. standards. In this respect, the rise of "major" leagues in hockey (by U.S. standards) hinged on the diffusion of the highly popular Canadian game into large American cities. Hockey underwent considerable development before it crossed the border, although this growth was influenced by the rise of professional sports in the United States. Two professional leagues, one in the West and one in the East, had firmly rooted themselves in Canadian cities. Although the Pacific Coast Hockey Association was the first to enter the United States, with teams in Portland and Seattle, it was the proximity of National Hockey Association Canadian cities to large eastern U.S. cities that gave the latter league the edge in pursuing U.S. major league status.

In November of 1917, the National Hockey Association owners squeezed out a troublesome member from their ranks by forming a new league, the National Hockey League (NHL). One owner commented: "Livingstone [the excluded Toronto owner] was always arguing. Without him we can get down to the business of making money" (quoted in McFarlane 1989, p. 13). Frank Calder was named president, and remained in the position until 1943. But in its initial season, the NHL operated with only three teams—Montreal, Ottawa, and Toronto—as one team dropped out and another sat out because its stadium had burned down. By U.S. standards the NHL had minor league demographics its first years, with less than half the travel distance and one-quarter of the average population of baseball's National League.

A Western Canada Hockey League formed in 1921 and lasted four seasons, pitting its champion against the Pacific Coast Hockey Association champion with the winner playing the NHL champion. But as the NHL moved out of Hamilton in 1924 and began moving into the major U.S. cities of Boston, New York, Detroit, and Chicago, it became the premier league in hockey. By 1926 the NHL had an average population base of 1,507,500 (compared with 1,835,600 for the National League) and an average travel distance of 440 miles (compared with 556 miles for the National League). Figure 4.5 shows the dramatic improvement of NHL demographics. Rather than lose players through raids by the new talent-hungry NHL franchises, the two western leagues began selling off players and even whole teams as they phased out of operation by 1926. These sales allowed the U.S. NHL franchises to be competitive from the start. With ten teams in two divisions, the NHL gained exclusive possession of the Stanley Cup in 1926.

The NHL's move into the United States was to produce a stable six-team league with teams in Boston, Chicago, Detroit, New York, Montreal, and Toronto, after efforts to establish franchises in Philadelphia, Pittsburgh, and St. Louis failed. Straddling national borders gave rise to various peculiarities in hockey's performance as well as its organization. Up until its entry into the United States, season performance inequality was relatively low. In only one year was it more than 1.45 times what chance variation would make it if all the teams were equally strong. There was, however, no clear ordering of performance by population. Because hockey's Canadian cities varied relatively little in size, this lack of ordering is not surprising, even with a strong attachment of teams to cities. The move into the United States complicated this picture considerably. Thirty-five out of forty-one years after moving into the United States saw a reverse ordering of performance by population, indicating that smaller-city teams performed better (see Figure 4.6). Among only Canadian teams, however (and pooling decades), there was a positive ordering except for the 1920s. For only U.S. teams, the reverse ordering persists (Leifer 1990a). These results underscore a difference in the attachment of teams to cities between the two

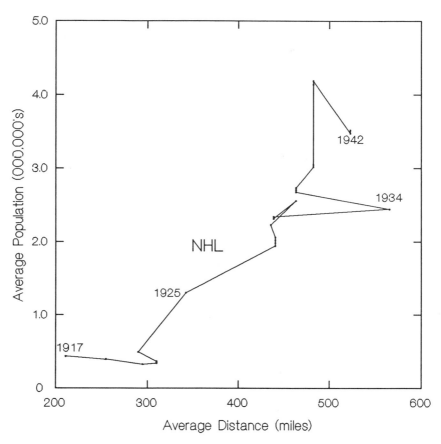

Figure 4.5 Demographic movement in the National Hockey League, 1917–1943. The move into the United States in the mid-1920s gave the NHL major league demographics. After 1942, league composition remained stable until 1967.

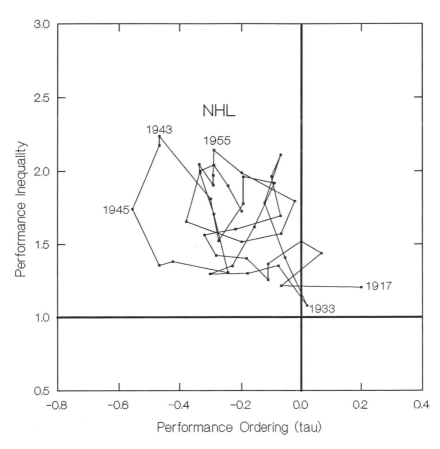

Figure 4.6 Season performance characteristics in the National Hockey League, 1917–1965, using three-year moving averages. Since Canadian cities were mostly smaller than U.S. cities, the early dominance of Canadian teams (which strongly attached to cities) produced an overall negative performance ordering where smaller-city teams consistently did better than larger-city teams.

countries. With strong home support, small Canadian cities can out-perform larger U.S. cities. Because of the strong attachment in Canada, size translates closely into support. In the United States, however, attachment is weaker and less uniform, so smaller U.S. cities tend to offer more support than larger ones (as was the case in football's early period).

As professional hockey became a lucrative export industry in Canada, rifts among Canadian amateur organizations emerged over the appropriate stance toward professionalism. The Canadian Amateur Hockey Association, largely controlled by the Ontario Hockey Association, had since its founding around the turn of the century banned corporate teams and professional players. But it lifted its ban on corporate teams in 1927 (with six of the original eleven-member executive committee still serving), doubling its membership but also causing a formal break with the Amateur Athletic Union of Canada. By 1929 the Ontario Hockey Association started reinstating professionals and the next year allowed amateur teams to play against professionals for charity purposes. A few years later, amateurs were permitted to try out for professional teams and could concurrently be professionals in other sports. "The more popular hockey became, the more difficult became the task of the Ontario Hockey Association in maintaining control over amateur hockey" (Metcalfe 1992).

Gradually amateur and professional leagues became part of a single hierarchy in Canada, with the professional leagues at the top in both skill and control over the sport. In this respect hockey resembles baseball, with its single hierarchy encompassing major and minor leagues. Thus it was that the Stanley Cup quietly became a professional trophy, whereas it remains inconceivable that professional teams could claim the most coveted trophies of college football and college basketball.

In none of the other sports did professional leagues come to so dominate amateur leagues. Starting as early as the 1890s, hockey farm systems had emerged that allowed dominant league teams to control players' careers from the age of seven onwards. But amateur hockey's first official agreement with the NHL was not formulated until the mid-1930s. In it, amateur hockey had to abide by all NHL playing rules, including bodychecking, which had previously been banned by the Ontario Hockey Association as inappropriately violent for children's leagues.[11] Although no compensation was offered for raiding a player (it took thirty more years to work out a satisfactory compensation provision), the NHL agreed not to touch a junior player unless his club consented. But this last clause was viewed as a farce, because "there's no club in Canada that would stand in a player's way if he had a chance to sign with an NHL team" (Young 1989, p. 236).

If an NHL scout spotted a talented player of any age anywhere in the United States or Canada, he could put the player's name on his team's negotiation list without even informing the player. Placing a player on a negotiation list gave the club exclusive bargaining rights with him. When the club decided to exercise this right, it did so through a C-form, a tryout contract accompanied by a small payment (around $100) that bound the player to the team until he was found not good enough and was released, or was traded or sold. If a player refused to sign, he could be left on the negotiation list until he relented. The only restriction on teams, not established until the late 1940s, was that each club's negotiation list was restricted to four players.

Scott Young (1989) illustrates this system with the story of Bobby Hull, a hockey superstar in the 1960s and 1970s. Spotted at age eleven by a Chicago Black Hawk scout during warm-ups before a junior game, Hull's name was placed on the negotiation list (after a few inquiries) with a telegram to NHL headquarters before the game even began. During the game the scout found Hull's father, who approved of the scout's action but asked the scout not to tell Bobby, since it "might give him a big head." Bobby did not learn of his status until age thirteen, when the scout wanted Bobby to move from his home in Belleville to a junior team and boarding house in Hespeler. A year later, Chicago moved Bobby to its junior B team at Woodstock, which accepted players up to age twenty. For the next two years, Bobby played for St. Catherines's junior A team before trying out for and then joining the Black Hawks at the age of eighteen. The NHL cast a long shadow on hockey players and teams.

With a firm grip on all levels of the sport, hockey remained remarkably immune to change in moving into the modern period. For the years 1948 to 1967, transformative ones for major league football, Charles Coleman (1972) reports that "business was routine" at NHL meetings. Expansion did not come until 1967, when the NHL doubled in size in going from six to twelve teams (by adding a new division). Until that year, the league's average travel distance was less than that for the 1871 National Association in baseball. Slow in exploiting the possibilities opened up by air travel, the NHL was even slower to exploit television opportunities (see Chapter 6). There is in this respect a similarity between the transition difficulties of major league baseball and hockey, owing to rigidities each developed through its stable attachment to a set of cities and its strong control over player development.

Like basketball, hockey had no policy of gate sharing. Home teams kept all the gate receipts, and schedules were divided evenly between home and away games. Football's liberal tradition of gate sharing facilitated its cohesion in dealing with television networks and agreeing on the equal sharing of television revenues among teams. Also like basketball, hockey was a continuous-action sport that, without major rule changes, provided no clear opportunity for television commercial breaks. Considering that hockey shares the major liabilities of each of the other sports, it is no surprise that it has been the slowest in adapting to the modern era in sports.

Failure Reconsidered

The attachment of teams to cities was the remarkable accomplishment of Major League Baseball. In the midst of the increasing stigmatization of professionals as they intruded into club and college play, the attachment of all professional teams to cities redefined the identity of both professional teams and cities. As a result of the attachment, professionals came to be loved instead of loathed, and cities acquired distinct identities in the national landscape. The same set of teams could play each other over and over, season after season, tallying up as many losses as wins without jeopardizing the attachment.

Yet with professionalism out in the open, amateur sport could better articulate itself and grow stronger through organizations such as the Amateur Athletic Union and the National Collegiate Athletic Association. Unable to encroach on professional baseball's grip on cities, amateur sport solidified itself at the club and school level as well as the international level, through the Olympic movement. For the sports that followed baseball, the strength and popularity of amateur sport proved to be a major obstacle to establishing professional versions of the game. College football and basketball were immensely popular, and actively stigmatized professional versions of their sports to retain both their fans and players. The Amateur Athletic Union sponsored numerous tournaments for the benefit of both participants and spectators. Professional football could take hold initially only in the periphery, catering to the working class in small towns who remained remote from the circuit of clubs and colleges. Professional basketball began as (and remains) an inner-city sport, growing out of amateur club cast-offs, but had to travel away from the big eastern cities to find its most consistent support. Professional hockey encountered the least opposition from amateur sport, escaping the jurisdiction of American amateur organizations and maintaining control over player development (like baseball). Outside of baseball, it was most successful in attaching itself to limited but loyal publics in major cities.

Professional football began moving into the major eastern cities in response to a rival league that tried but failed within its first season. After the failed American Basketball League effort, major league basketball made its entry by slipping in under the cover of hockey arena owners. For some time after both these inauspicious entries, large-city teams had trouble succeeding both financially and competitively. With support sometimes greater in smaller cities and costs invariably higher in larger ones, large population bases could be more of a liability than an asset. All three sports outside of baseball simply failed to achieve a leaguewide attachment of teams to cities, one that fully mobilized local publics in support of local teams. None achieved the key sign of this attachment, an ordering of team performance by host population size. As will soon be evident, this failure of large-city dominance to develop, both on and off the playing field, was to prove useful in adapting to the requirements of the modern era of televised sport.

The modern era fundamentally changed major league sports. What had once been assets became liabilities, and vice versa. Major League Baseball's powerful attachment of teams to cities hindered its ability to cultivate national publics, the new source of vast opportunities in the modern era of televised sports. The strong college football and basketball programs that had marginalized major leagues in these sports became a rich source of ready-made stars in the new era. These changes set up the shift from baseball to football as the prototype for organizing league sports in the quest for national publics.

5

...

The Modern Prototype

By the middle of the twentieth century, the major leagues had achieved a good measure of success and sophistication. In Major League Baseball, opportunities created by the growth of cities had been skillfully exploited. The attachment of teams to cities had survived two world wars and the Great Depression, and was yielding record crowds in both the minor and the major leagues during the last years of the 1940s. In the largest cities of America, major league teams had earned the broad-based support of fans across innings, games, and seasons, with the same set of teams playing the same game over and over in highly regular schedules. The enduring attachments between major league teams and cities, reaffirmed with such regularity, had come to define both the character of the sport and even the cities themselves.

But the attachment between teams and cities was not without vulnerabilities. Cities were uneven in their ability and willingness to support teams. Winning was the most reliable way to mobilize support, but in a closed circuit a win for one team was a loss for another. Larger cities offered more potential support for winning teams, while smaller cities sometimes proved unable or unwilling to support teams that tended to lose more. The pursuit of competitive balance, or interchangeability, was limited by a league's desire to place the strongest teams in the largest cities. As a result, weak smaller-city franchises became a structural feature of the most successful leagues, as exemplified by Major League Baseball. Success made it possible to subsidize weak franchises. In early football and basketball leagues, however, weak franchises simply perished. The resulting instability in league composition itself became an obstacle to forging an attachment between teams and cities.

By the 1950s, convenient air travel and national television broadcasting were creating opportunities for major league teams to move beyond their attachment to cities. Publics for sporting events were no longer constrained by geographic barriers as television brought sporting events to viewers in their own homes. National publics for single events became a vast new source of opportunity. Air travel, furthermore, eliminated constraints on team location. To engage the entire nation, major league teams began to move west and south. Truly national leagues emerged that sought to capture the involvement of national publics. Because these publics were potentially the same for all teams, the unevenness of cities gradually ceased to be a crucial factor in league organization. Competitive balance, for the first time, became something worth seriously pursuing.

No sport has been more successful at exploiting the new opportunities than football. Quickly shedding its marginality, professional football surpassed both college football and Major League Baseball in popularity, becoming the modern prototype in organizing for the involvement of national publics. Ironically, football's failure to attach to cities facilitated this rapid ascension. Conversely, as we shall see in the next chapter, the success of baseball in attaching to cities made it slow in recognizing and exploiting the new opportunities.

Television and the NFL

As a technology, television has been around almost as long as radio. Yet it was much slower in gaining commercial popularity. Early televisions were expensive, reception was poor, programming was sporadic and of low quality, and the passivity television required took some time gaining acceptance. With few sets in operation, there was little incentive to improve programming, and this in turn did little to increase the number of televisions. Television did not escape this cycle until after World War II. Still lacking the capacity to produce programs, emerging television networks turned to sporting events to fill airtime. "What some people forget," reminisces a retired NBC director, "is that television got off the ground because of sports. Today, maybe, sports need television to survive, but it was just the opposite when it first started" (quoted in Neal-Luneford 1992, p. 64). Although the first boxing match was televised in 1932 and the first football game in 1939, it was not until after World War II that the synergies between television and sport were exploited. The postwar surge of interest in sports fueled, and was soon fueled by, exponential growth in television sales.

Before the advent of television, professional football labored in the shadow of the college game. Teams rarely made money before the 1950s, and forty franchises had come and gone since the NFL started in 1920. The audience for professional football was largely confined to blue-collar workers. Owing to the low salaries, many great college players declined NFL offers, and almost all professional players held off-season jobs (Patton 1984). Entrepreneurial success came less from stable league competition than from showcasing stars like Red Grange on barnstorming tours. Many league teams depended on corporate sponsorship for survival, like the Green Bay Packers (whose patron was a meat packer) and the Decatur Staleys (a starch manufacturer), continuing a tradition extending back to the first professional teams. In short, the prospects for a successful major league with teams supported by large cities were by no means clear.

Unlike baseball owners, who saw television as a sort of knothole through which fans could see the game for free, football owners had less to lose from experimenting with the new media. George Halas received $5,400 for televising six road games of his Chicago Bears in 1947. In 1948, the final game with his cross-town rival (the Chicago Cardinals) brought $5,000 for broadcast rights. By 1950 Halas had developed a regional network that reached fifteen cities by 1951 and reached Florida by 1955. George Marshall, owner of the Washington Redskins, built his own television network in the South; his venture was strengthened by his refusal to hire black players (Patton 1984). The New York Giants built a network in the Northeast, and the Los Angeles Rams built one in the West.

Football proved well adapted for television. Breaks between plays, absent from basketball and ice hockey, proved ideal for commercials. Action was spatially concentrated, allowing the cameras to follow plays close-up, while panoramic shots could neatly fit the whole field into the shape of the television screen. In addition, major league football was neither regional, like college football, whose conferences are drawn along geographic lines, nor as unstable in personnel—its players did not change as frequently as college players did. Both factors made major league football more suited for a less sophisticated and more widespread national public than college football. Yet in the beginning, major league football broadcasts were entirely local, or at most regional, in nature. As with radio, most television broadcasts merely brought away games to a home audience. Pursuing a national public required a bolder vision than had yet emerged in either major league sports or television. Teams could not merely be attached to cities, and television could not merely follow the developmental path of radio. The rise of network television was closely tied to the rise of a new prototype for organizing major league sports.

As the regional networks spread, sensitive issues arose. Could, for example, one team broadcast its game in a city where another was playing a home game? Most troubling were the early declines in attendance when home games were televised. In Los Angeles, attendance declined by 40 percent the first year of broadcasting, although the broadcaster had promised to reimburse the team for any decrease in gate receipts. Blackouts of local games were instigated. By 1952 Commissioner Bell had decided that unlimited television was a threat to the league and rammed through bylaws that gave him virtually complete control over NFL television rights (Klatell and Marcus 1988). It is hard to imagine the baseball owners ceding such control to a commissioner. But in the case of football it was the U.S. Justice Department that resisted. Football lacked baseball's antitrust exemption. An antitrust suit was filed that prohibited the NFL from selling television rights to any one network as a single package. It would take eight years and a new commissioner before football was granted the limited antitrust exemption it needed.

In 1951 rights for broadcasting the NFL championship game nationwide were purchased from the league for $75,000 by Allen B. Du Mont's network (later absorbed by NBC). But it was not until 1956 that CBS contracted to carry selected regular NFL season games nationally, a venture that struck many as highly risky at a time when teams were still seen as attached mainly to cities. This venture was, however, crucial in building a broader audience for major league football. After the first two telecast championships had ended in 47–7 and 50–14 routs, the NFL received the boost it needed when its 1958 championship game between the Baltimore Colts and the New York Giants went into extended overtime. By its end, the game purchased by NBC for $100,000 had attracted 30 million viewers and made the Colts quarterback Johnny Unitas, who three years earlier had been a semi-pro playing for $6 a game, a national figure. By 1960 only four NFL teams would have made money without their television revenues. The inter-dependencies between football and television were quickly becoming irreversible.

Long-time commissioner Bell died of heart failure at a football game in 1959. After considerable haggling over who should replace him, the owners selected Pete Rozelle as a compromise candidate. Rozelle was a youthful thirty-three-year-old director of public relations for the Los Angeles Rams. The selection was prescient. Rozelle's talent for esca-lating television revenues and lobbying Congress served the NFL well and kept Rozelle at the helm for almost thirty years. The league's in-creasingly national focus meant that national politics and the major networks edged out local politicians and civic leaders as the ties that mattered.

At the time Rozelle took office, NFL teams had been on their own in negotiating rights to regular season games with television networks and had been having variable success. Only the championship game was controlled by the league office. In 1959, for example, Green Bay earned $30,000 from television revenues while the New York Giants earned $200,000. Rozelle was a strong advocate of a single contract between the league and television networks, with the revenues to be equally shared among teams. Immediately upon assuming the commissioner-ship, Rozelle began lobbying Congress for a limited antitrust exemp-tion, making good use of connections between the Kennedy family and the NFL. Rozelle succeeded in September of 1961, when Congress extended baseball's antitrust exemption to football, basketball, and ice hockey for the limited purpose of pooling individual franchise broad-casting rights. In return, Rozelle agreed not to compete with Friday night high school or Saturday college games in the league's broadcast-ing (Klatell and Marcus 1988).

The importance of centralizing control over broadcasting rights is a lesson relearned many times since. Without league control, individual teams flood the networks, and more recently cable television, with games. As the sport's audience starts spreading itself thinly across events, the games lose economic value. Television cannot afford to use its limited airtime for programs that fall below a certain rating level. When old movies or rerun series start drawing as many viewers as live sporting events, television drops sports quickly. Major League Baseball, the NBA, and the NCAA each learned this lesson in the 1960s and 1970s.

After succeeding with Congress, Rozelle had a surprisingly easy time persuading the NFL owners to go along with his revenue-sharing proposal. Phil Patton (1984, p. 54) notes that the football owners "had a greater sense of cooperation among them" than baseball owners. NFL owners were a small group, most of whose tenure in the game extended back to the Depression, which they had helped each other through. Football had the most generous gate-sharing arrangement, giving 40 percent of gate receipts to the visiting team, and had instigated a college reverse draft in 1935 to help weaker teams. But the size of the deal Rozelle was able to work out with CBS also helped sway the larger-city owners. On January 10, 1962, CBS purchased the rights to all regular 1962–63 season NFL games for $4,650,000, or $350,000 per team under Rozelle's equal-sharing arrangement.[1]

The opportunities opening up through television motivated the formation of the American Football League (AFL), which stunned sports and media insiders by securing an $8.5 million five-year contract with ABC—then a fledgling network hoping to build a niche for itself through sports broadcasting under the leadership of Roone Arledge. Numerous innovations were spawned from the ABC-AFL relationship in both the sport and the media. Coaches were instructed to open up the game with more passing. Two-point conversions were introduced to add an element of risk taking. Unlike the NFL, player fights were used to enhance the game's entertainment value, as had long been the tradition in ice hockey. On the media side, field mikes, end-zone cameras, and the zoom lens were introduced, allowing the fan to see the game better on television than in person. "Honey" shots of women in the stands and cheerleaders were added. The instant replay, often from multiple camera angles, gave the television viewer a better vantage point than referees in making close calls.[2] Watching football on television became the preferred way to view the sport, particularly for games played in harsh winter climates.

New fans were brought under the football spell by these sports and media innovations. Most knew little of the traditions of major league football, but rather tuned in purely for the entertainment value.[3] While AFL games quickly became media events, attendance at the stadium was sometimes quite low. Camera crews were instructed not to follow punts in the air to avoid showing television fans the empty stadiums. Later, in the 1980s, the United States Football League was to become even more blatantly a "television league," producing games for cable television that lacked a local element almost entirely.

When the NFL television contract came up for negotiation for the 1964 season, Tom Moore of ABC had a bold idea that might allow ABC to outbid NBC. Moore conceived the double header, an East Coast game followed by a West Coast game to exploit the time differences between the coasts. Patton (1984, p. 89) comments, "For both leagues, the double header helped build national followings for teams. Each local market might see its own team playing away from home, and two other teams in the second game." What had previously been presumed to exist only for championships—interest not rooted in locale—was here extended into the regular season. Fans were being lured into following not just "their" team but other teams as well.

ABC's startling $26.1 million two-year contract bid (one million per team per year) exceeded NBC's bid by $5.5 million, but fell suspiciously short of CBS's $27.2 million last announced bid. When the AFL's contract opened up in 1965, the show business agent and owner of the AFL's New York Jets, Sonny Werblin, acting on behalf of the league, secretly orchestrated a deal with NBC for $42 million over five years ($850,000 per team per year). NBC ended up losing about $1 million a year on the deal, but set up a long-term relationship that has for the most part been lucrative.

Such contracts amply demonstrated the viability of two leagues. Rather than cutting into the NFL's audience, the AFL had created a new audience attracted more by showmanship than by sportsmanship. Werblin's marketing of "Broadway Joe" Namath was true to the spirit of the new league. Teams could now cultivate national publics, with the help of league and network collaboration. When the NFL and AFL worked out a merger arrangement in 1966, the merged audiences became available to any given team. As part of the merger, the "Super Bowl" was initiated and became the first sports championship event staged primarily for national television. Played at neither team's homesite, it downplays the antiquated attachment of teams to cities. Promoted by television for weeks in advance, it has become the most popular event of any sport (with the U.S. audience exceeding 130 million people).

In the early 1970s, ABC was brought back into major league football with its popular Monday Night Football broadcasts, completing a "marriage contract" between the three major networks and the NFL that remained remarkably stable until 1994. Entry into prime-time network television was a major step for the NFL, and was something that

Rozelle pursued despite a higher bid from a new Sports Network Incorporated started by Howard Hughes.[4] Monday Night Football boldly offered a carefully selected regular season game for national viewership. At the same time, it drew many women and families into the football audience. Earning a 31 percent market share its first season, the show found that 36 percent of its viewers were women. The announcers Frank Gifford, Don Meredith, and Howard Cosell were carefully selected to please a diverse audience.

While relations between the NFL and the networks have remained stable, television revenues have escalated. The 1974 contract brought $2.5 million to each team per year, and by 1978, each team was receiving $5.5 million per year. Annual television revenues increased to $15 million per team in 1982, when the contract was renewed for four more years. This dramatic escalation halted, however, when television ratings sank after a 1982 player strike. In addition, advertisers were cooling toward football as purchasing power shifted toward younger and more female audiences that had little interest in the game. In 1983 Rozelle unilaterally allowed the networks to increase their ad space from 24 to 25 minutes a game to help reduce their losses. Later the NFL unilaterally extended its season to eighteen weeks to give the networks two more broadcasts for which to sell advertising. By the time a new contract was negotiated in 1986, many owners were relieved that they only had to take a $500,000 cut in annual revenues in a now shorter three-year contract.

But 1989 brought a surprising increase to $3.6 billion for four years from CBS, NBC, ABC, and cable's TNT (owned by Ted Turner) and ESPN (majority owned by ABC), or over $30 million per team each year. Just as cities had come to need major league franchises to gain a place in the national landscape, networks had come to need an NFL contract to retain their prominence amid proliferating cable channels. And like many cities, the networks had become willing to lose money on NFL games in the hope that the presence of the broadcasts would draw football viewers to their other programming. An estimated $300 million was lost by the networks on the 1989 contract. In January of 1994 Fox became a major network virtually overnight when it outbid CBS for the rights to broadcast NFL's National Football Conference games at the cost of $1.58 billion (NBC retained American Football Conference games for $868 million). Fox became "Home of the NFL," while the NFL secured $4.38 billion over four years for its combined television package. Although it is obviously difficult to predict when rights fees will stop increasing, there is a general sense on both sides that saturation in terms of actual viewership has been reached on the domestic front.[5] The focus for expansion has shifted overseas, as we shall see in Chapter 9.

With the 1978 contract, broadcast revenues exceeded gate revenues. After 1982, almost 70 percent of total team revenues came from the equally shared network television contracts. Combined with the generous 60–40 split of gate receipts, the degree of revenue sharing in football far exceeds that in other sports. The NFL is the only sport in which teams have no control over local television broadcasting, outside of the small area of preseason game broadcasts. The relatively minor variation in total team revenue that remains is not clearly related to city size (Berry and Wong 1986).[6] Nor is revenue variation even related to winning, although the publicity and prestige accorded winners may serve as a powerful motivation for owners.

Residents of cities, of course, remain attached to "their" teams, and winning brings much favorable publicity and revenues to home cities. But home crowds are now just a tiny portion of the potential audience, and are themselves audiences for other teams as well. Walk down any street in America and observe the diversity of team logos on caps, t-shirts, and bumper stickers. Fans for any team can turn up anywhere, and they contribute to the support of "their" teams not just by purchasing team paraphernalia but by uniting in front of the television. In the last decade, a number of teams have begun associating themselves with states and even regions instead of cities, extending their claims to special loyalty based on proximity. But even here television becomes the actual basis of closeness for most of the newly claimed fans. The 1992 Super Bowl dramatically demonstrated the diminishing importance of local audiences. Teams from Buffalo and Washington played in Minnesota, and those who braved their way through harsh weather to the indoor stadium had to see a kickoff replayed because it had been interrupted by a commercial break.

As a new medium, television could have served simply as a vehicle for bringing road games to home audiences, as radio mostly did, and hence merely reinforced the attachment of teams to cities. As it did in the 1950s, television could have only exacerbated problems stemming from the unevenness of city sizes. But it held out greater opportunities that organizers in both sports and television gradually recognized.

These opportunities, however, carried with them fundamental shifts in control over the sport. With the pooling of individual broadcasting rights, essential to exploiting the opportunities available, the commissioner came to assume considerable autonomy from the owners in controlling the league's dealings with networks. Television revenue flowed through the league office, and with revenue came control. With the equal sharing of television revenue, it was the league and the networks that had the incentive to create national publics. For teams, who this public tuned in to see was more a matter of pride than of economics.

The cultivation of a national public has made the location of winning teams of less importance to overall league success. Television has allowed the audience to shift its attention anywhere. Although the networks remain concerned with major television markets, such as New York, Chicago, and Los Angeles, they also have to worry about the larger national audience.[7] Competitive balance increased in importance as a property essential in sustaining the involvement of a national public. And television put the commissioner in a position to pursue a competitive balance, once control over contracting was gained. The intricacies of this pursuit will be investigated shortly. But first, the difficulties facing rival leagues are examined to underscore the shift in opportunities of the modern period.

Problems Facing Rival Leagues

In the early days of major league sports, leagues sought to attach teams to a set of supportive cities that were as large and proximate as possible. Because the number of such cities was limited, a rival league invariably had to challenge an established league for control over certain key cities. Leagues that came to be viewed as "major" were the ones that gained monopoly rights over the largest cities proximate enough to keep travel time and costs manageable—major northeastern cities. With the changing opportunities of the modern period, the struggle shifted from teams and cities to leagues and networks. City size and travel distance lost some of their importance in determining the viability of a league. A city left without a franchise was less of a nucleus for the formation of a rival league than a television network without a league contract. The NFL's success in preventing or fending off challenges since the 1960s has come from its ability to contract with the three major networks. The growth of cable television and upstart networks has raised new opportunities, but as yet has not provided the basis for a successful rival.

From 1946 to 1949, the All-American Football Conference represented a serious challenge to the NFL (see Chapter 4). Yet at the time neither professional football nor television had gained enough acceptance to support two major leagues. By 1960, however, the opportunities presented by television were becoming readily apparent. After having been denied a franchise in the NFL, the wealthy Texas oilman Lamar Hunt called a meeting of potential sponsors for a new American Football League (AFL) in August 1959. Joe Foss, a former governor of South Dakota and World War II ace, was selected to lead the new league. Sonny Werblin represented the league in negotiations with the networks. His remarkably successful $8.5 million dollar contract, negotiated before Rozelle's commissionership and football's limited antitrust exemption, certainly influenced the NFL owners' selection of a public relations man as their league's next commissioner. They sought someone who could deal with both Congress and television.[8]

The advent of television as a new source of audience and revenue meant that the size of franchise cities became less crucial for league survival. After its Los Angeles team moved to San Diego at the end of the first season, the AFL had an average population base of 2,702,300, compared with 3,369,500 for the NFL. Nor was travel distance a crucial factor, with convenient air travel available. The AFL's average travel distance was 1,656 miles, compared with the NFL's 1,130 miles. Together, these less favorable demographics—displayed in Figure 5.1— would have put the AFL at a serious disadvantage in an earlier period. Undaunted by its often low attendance at games—averaging only 16,538 fans per game in 1960 compared with the NFL's 40,106, for example—the AFL-ABC alliance focused on aggressively expanding its television audience. At the same time, it avoided challenging the NFL at the gate with site competition. Only in New York did it sustain a franchise along with the NFL. In Dallas, the AFL competed with a new NFL franchise for three years before moving to the open site of Kansas City. In all the AFL's other sites—Boston, Buffalo, Denver, Houston, Oakland, and San Diego (after the first season)—the NFL had no team.

In its first years, the AFL also avoided a trade war by not raiding the NFL for players. Because of the short playing life of football players and the ample supply of excellent college talent, such raids were less tempting in football than they had traditionally been in baseball. In the

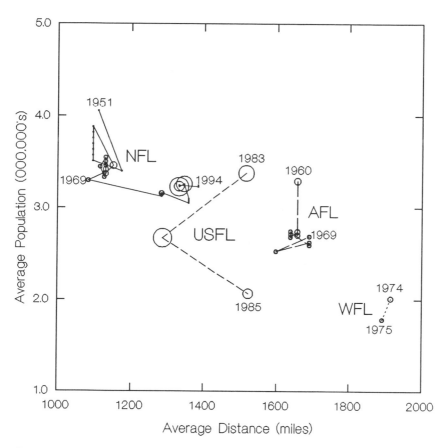

Figure 5.1   Demographic movement in major league football, 1951–1993. Pursuit of national coverage in the modern era led to a reversal in the early direction of demographic movement. Average population bases decreased and travel distances increased as leagues expanded in both size and geographic coverage. Rival leagues continued to lead the way in this new demographic direction but varied in the degree (indicated in circle sizes) to which they competed with the NFL for sites. AFL = American Football League; NFL = National Football League; USFL = United States Football League; WFL = World Football League.

competition for nationally prominent college players, the AFL was able to secure a sufficient number of star players to claim major league status. Threatened by the growing television popularity of the AFL, the NFL broke the informal truce against raids in 1966, when the NFL's New York Giants lured the kicker Pete Gogalak from the AFL's Buffalo Bills (after he had played out his option). Al Davis was made AFL commissioner and given a mandate to pursue a trade war aggressively. He formed a league fund to go after NFL quarterbacks, and quickly got commitments from seven NFL stars to defect.

But the trade war had barely started when the owners surprised the sports world, and Al Davis, with the announcement of a merger that would be phased in over the next three years. Rozelle was to remain commissioner of the new NFL. He returned to Congress to get permission for the merger, using the promise of a new franchise for New Orleans to sway a key Louisiana senator. Working out details for parity was arduous, as the NFL had franchises in each of the top twelve television markets while the AFL had only one (New York). Despite much reluctance, three NFL teams were transferred into what became the American Football Conference in 1970, while the remaining teams made up the new National Football Conference. Both conferences, each divided into three divisions, were part of the newly constituted NFL.

Next to baseball's American League challenge in 1900, the AFL challenge has been the only other clearly successful challenge in the history of major league sports. Rather than a direct challenge, the AFL exploited as yet unrecognized opportunities to gain a foothold and, in the process, greatly expanded the size of the total market. As a challenger league, it could more easily risk violating antitrust restrictions on pooling team broadcasting rights than could the established NFL (which had been stopped from doing so in 1952). With its eye on a television audience, the AFL could avoid site competition with the NFL. And it could avoid raiding the NFL for players by making use of the ample supply of college talent. By 1966 it was clear that there was a lot more room at the top than anyone could have imagined a decade earlier. The merger preserved every one of the existing teams and initiated the most popular event in sports, the Super Bowl. Far from cutting into each team's audience, the merger expanded audiences—as escalating television contracts were soon to indicate.

With the NFL-AFL merger and the introduction of Monday Night

Football on ABC, the new NFL had twenty-six teams and contracts with all three major television networks. For a time, these contracts effectively foreclosed any opportunity to seriously challenge the new NFL. The first attempt, the World Football League, was announced in October of 1973 and began operations in the fall of 1974 with twelve American teams (an international division was part of the initial five-year plan). Of the rival leagues in three sports started by Gary Davidson, the World Football League was the most short-lived. It survived only two seasons (whereas his World Hockey League survived seven seasons in a much less popular sport). Like the AFL, the World Football League avoided site competition by locating in smaller cities that lacked NFL teams. It also conceded the weekend to the NFL, scheduling games on Wednesdays. Only in Chicago, Detroit, and Philadelphia were site challenges made, and none of these World Football League franchises achieved a winning record. The new league's average population was 2,014,700 its first year and dropped to 1,782,000 its next and final year, compared with the NFL's 3,160,000 in 1974. Spread throughout the United States, and particularly making inroads into the South, the league had an average travel distance of over 1,900 miles both years (for the NFL, it was 1,284 miles). But unlike the AFL, the World Football League failed to gain a place on the major television networks.

A second challenge was initiated for the 1983 season by David Dixon, a New Orleans lawyer and entrepreneur who had been instrumental in getting the Louisiana Superdome built. Dixon introduced a number of new ideas to keep from sharing the World Football League's fate. To avoid direct competition with the NFL, Dixon set a spring schedule for his United States Football League. This facilitated entry into large NFL cities, whose populations and publicly financed stadiums were underutilized in the spring (Major League Baseball was by then a less intimidating rival than the NFL). During its first year of operation in 1983, the twelve-team United States Football League was to have a larger average population base than the NFL (3,377,000 versus 3,259,100). The large-city sites made the new challenger more appealing to television networks than the World Football League had been. Before any players were secured, the United States Football League signed a $9,000,000 contract with ABC and a $4,000,000 contract with ESPN, a cable sports network whose president, Chet Simmons (former head of NBC Sports), became the first commissioner of the new league in June of 1982.

Like earlier rival league architects, Dixon sought to build fan appeal by hiring well-known coaches. Coaches have long occupational lives but short job tenure, so they are often available for reasonable rates. Among the NFL coaches signed by the United States Football League were John Ralston and George Allen. Later, Donald Trump's New Jersey team courted Don Shula of the Miami Dolphins, but in a bit of blatant cross-promotion Trump claimed to have called off the deal when Shula insisted on an apartment in the Trump Towers (Byrne 1986). For players, still the major component in team expenditures, Dixon sought both to eliminate competitive bidding and to cater to anachronistic fan localisms by having United States Football League teams draw from "local area" colleges. In practice, Oklahoma became an "area" university for the New Jersey team, while the University of Nebraska was designated for the Boston team. Yet the first player draft, held in January of 1983, went smoothly, much to the consternation of the NFL. In signing the drafted players, teams were constrained by an overall salary cap of $1.3 million for thirty-eight players and $1.8 million for forty (allowing for two "glamorous" players for fan appeal).

Before the first season began, however, serious internal rifts emerged. With ABC and ESPN involved from the start, the United States Football League became the first "television league." There was, for example, no provision for the blackout of home games to motivate live attendance. Yet the interests of network and cable television were far from unified. ABC sought broad flexibility in selecting up to three weekly games to broadcast, even to the point of changing the day of a scheduled game. This upset Simmons, whose ESPN cable station sought to be a regular provider of specific teams to targeted audiences. Television's requirements made Simmons's task of scheduling games nearly impossible when, in addition, ABC called for a twenty-game schedule played over eighteen weeks (Byrne 1986, p. 25).

Rifts also arose among owners over violations of the salary cap. The problem started when Jerry Argovitz, a dentist turned player agent, showed up at the United States Football League headquarters seeking a contract for the Heisman Trophy winner Herschel Walker a year before his college eligibility expired. Although wary of the unchecked scramble for stars that signing Walker might trigger (and the potential breach with college programs), Simmons was finally persuaded to assign Walker to the New Jersey Generals by the threat of an antitrust suit accusing the league of denying Walker the "right to earn a livelihood" (Byrne 1986). New Jersey signed Walker for $1.2 million per year plus a $1 million signing bonus.[9] This action triggered numerous other breaches of the salary cap: in the first year alone, United States Football League teams raided the NFL of forty-eight players and secured seventeen college players highly sought after by the NFL (Carlson 1986).

The debut of the United States Football League was a success, with an average attendance of 39,170 and a television share of 14.2 percent (33 percent of viewers). But a combination of poor performances, bad weather, and the loss of novelty led these figures to erode quickly. Shortly after the season began Dixon bailed out, selling his rights to a franchise to a group that included Jerry Argovitz. By the fifteenth week, most games drew less than 10,000 spectators and television ratings had slipped to 3.3 percent. At season's end, the United States Football League had lost $30 million. ABC, nevertheless, made a profit of $9–12 million, because the league's average television rating of 6 percent was higher than the 5 percent the network had expected.

Most of the owners linked their financial problems to the breakdown of the team salary cap, and readily agreed to a new cap of $1.7 million for thirty-six players with no restriction on salaries for four additional star players. Ironically, this proposal was put forward by Argovitz and his main partner. The cap did not survive long, however. The real estate magnate Donald Trump entered the league after the 1983 season with the purchase of the New Jersey Generals, and he vehemently opposed any retrenching that would lead to "minor league" status. He openly courted NFL players, and boasted that the United States Football League played better football than the NFL. In two months, Trump signed six NFL veterans. In justification of his brazen disregard for the salary cap, Trump insisted that "when you're in New York, you have to win," to which the other owners responded, "You have to win every-place" (Byrne 1986, p. 103).

Increases in the 1984 television contracts for the United States Football League did not begin to cover the escalating salary costs. ABC paid $14 million and ESPN paid $7 million for 1984 broadcasting rights. The 1984 season opener drew only an 8.0 percent television share, and an average of 32,995 spectators attended the opening games of the expanded eighteen-team league. As in the first season, these numbers steadily tapered off. By the end of the 1984 season, the United States Football League had lost $100,000,000 in its first two years of operation. The disastrous combination of escalating payrolls and declining fan interest carried into the 1985 season, with increasing turnover among owners. In 1985, for example, Los Angeles averaged fewer than 13,000 spectators per game and had the highest payroll ($9,000,000), necessitating a levy of $520,000 on every team to keep the Los Angeles franchise afloat.

Unable to survive in the spring, the United States Football League announced that it would move to the fall in 1986, even though it was unable to get a television contract; all the networks were tied up with the NFL. Its actual competition with the NFL took place in the courts, however, where it claimed that the NFL television contracts were illegal and had cost it $440,000,000 in lost opportunities (subject to treble damages). In a bizarre trial, the NFL owner Al Davis testified against his own league (he had been excluded from the suit as another "victim of the NFL"). The jury found the NFL guilty of monopolizing, but awarded the United States Football League only $1 (trebled to $3), wrongly thinking that the ridiculous award would prompt the judge to fix the amount. But judges can only lower amounts set by juries. So ended the United States Football League.

The late 1980s and early 1990s saw no further challenges mounted against the NFL. But as the major networks gradually lose market share to a profusion of cable alternatives in the mid-1990s, the NFL's position may be more vulnerable than it has been since the early 1970s. It is obviously no longer possible to tie up all broadcasting outlets, and selecting among them can be a delicate issue—as was seen in National Football Conference's 1994 move from CBS to the new Fox Broadcasting network. In an effort to foreclose international opportunities, the NFL sponsored a World League of American Football in 1990. Teams were split evenly between U.S. and international sites (Davidson's initial plan for the World Football League), and direct competition with the NFL was avoided through a spring and early summer schedule (as in the United States Football League). Operations were suspended after two seasons, although plans were being made to restart the league entirely in European sites for 1995. In Chapter 9, we will look closely at the NFL and other major league efforts to cultivate an international public. Bolder ideas are needed than have been tried to date, for every major expansion of publics has required a fundamental reorganization of competition. Below, we look at the innovations that ushered in the shift from local to national publics.

Organizational Innovations

Major league football redefined success in its shift from local to national publics. No sport was more innovative in using television to expand its audience, nor more adept at closing opportunities for rival leagues to form after the success of the AFL. Behind the NFL's success, however, have also been changes in the product being produced. Although it is undoubtedly true that many sports, like wrist wrestling on ABC's Wide World of Sports, have been watched simply because they were on television, something more is required for fans to tune in week after week, season after season. Wrist wrestling attracted attention as an oddity; NFL football has elicited involvement as a repetitive routine. Inside the NFL there has been great energy invested in ensuring uniformity of the product. It is this element, and not oddity, that has allowed the NFL to so successfully exploit the opportunities air travel and television made possible.

As we have seen, some crucial aspects of organization were securely in place long before the 1950s. The NFL was the first (in 1933) league to form divisions, allowing expansions within the confines of a league without creating unwieldy pennant races. It was also the first (in 1946) to move west, achieving national coverage. From its beginning, the NFL had the most liberal (60–40) sharing of gate receipts, a tradition that was to help Rozelle push through equal sharing of television revenues. In addition, the NFL adopted the first (in 1935) reverse order college draft, aiding weaker teams on the field and all teams by eliminating competitive bidding over college players. By carefully regulating the induction of college players, the NFL was slowly able to build goodwill among college programs.

As major league football began to shed its marginality in the 1950s, a potential arose for serious revenue inequalities based on the unevenness of local and regional broadcasting rights. Yet these possible consequences of television were redirected by changing the institutions through which television viewership and revenues were channeled. Following the AFL's lead, Rozelle assumed control over television contracting and instigated equal sharing of television revenues. Instead of only local broadcasts of games involving a local team, a limited number of games were nationally broadcast. In this way, a national public began to follow major league football rather than local publics following local teams. Within the NFL there continued to be no clear ordering be-

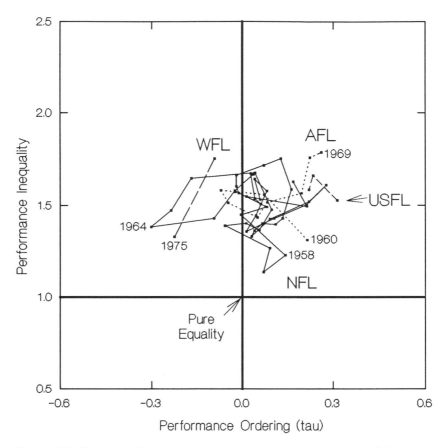

Figure 5.2 Season performance characteristics in major league football, 1951–1993, using three-year moving averages. Outside the height of the American Football League (AFL) challenge, performance characteristics of the National Football League (NFL) modern prototype converge on mild inequality and only a weak tendency for large-city teams to come out ahead. USFL = United States Football League; WFL = World Football League.

tween team performance and host population size, as is shown along the horizontal axis in Figure 5.2. This lack of ordering is, however, no longer attributable to marginality. With national publics and shared revenues, the location of winners is no longer as important or as predictable. Nor is this lack of ordering associated with increasing performance inequalities within seasons, as occurred for weak leagues in baseball. Figure 5.2, along the vertical axis, shows relatively low and stable performance inequality for both the NFL and the AFL.

Rozelle's passion for uniformity extended well beyond equal sharing of television revenues. He "became known for advocating short hair in the locker room and for behaving sternly on such 'issues' as players' socks. They had to be knee length, he said, and pulled up, so that the league presented a 'standard uniform product'" (Patton 1984, p. 51). While Commissioner Bell simply had not liked the sight of players' legs, Rozelle had a more positive motivation for legislating on socks. Creating a "standard uniform product" was central to Rozelle's efforts to broaden involvement. The more uniform the product became, the greater role publics could play in reading differences into the setting.

A more serious quest for uniformity can be found in NFL control over scheduling. For quite some time the NFL had gotten teams to play the same number of games and to divide home and away games evenly. More of a challenge, however, were the NFL's efforts to alternate home and away games. This bit of uniformity in schedules both extends home fan interest across the entire season and ensures that every team faces a similar sequence of home-away games, should any particular sequence give a team an advantage.[10] The amount of home-away game alternation after Rozelle became commissioner steadily increased up to the expansion of the NFL in 1970 (through merger), whereupon it started increasing again up to a threshold reached in 1977 (see Figure 5.3). In an analysis of the difficulty of attaining home-away alternation, it was found that league size greatly increases scheduling difficulties, which accounts for the 1970 setback (Leifer 1990b).

The analysis of scheduling difficulty also revealed that reaching the 1977 threshold from the early 1960s levels entailed a twofold increase in difficulty, while exceeding it would entail a sevenfold increase. Thus the 1977 threshold marked a point beyond which NFL schedulers (who constructed schedules without the aid of a computer) could not progress.[11] Perhaps not coincidentally, 1977 marked the year when the NFL started to use scheduling to promote performance uniformity by

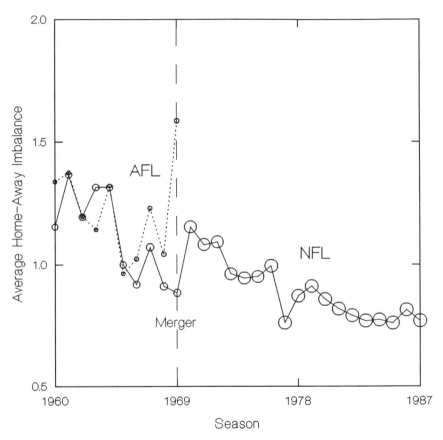

Figure 5.3   The pursuit of scheduling uniformity in the NFL, 1960–1987. Scheduling uniformity is measured by the average imbalance between home and away games at each week in the season, for each team. Since on odd-numbered weeks teams could not have played the same number of home and away games (and on even weeks they could), maximum uniformity is 0.5. Circle sizes are proportional to league size, which affects the technical difficulty of achieving scheduling uniformity.

deliberately pitting the past season's best-performing teams against each other.

Institutionally imposed uniformities have effectively limited the competition for playing talent. Unlike in baseball, the advent of free agency in football in the early 1970s had little impact on player salaries; owners simply refrained from competitive bidding. Propping up this cooperation was the Rozelle Rule, which allowed the commissioner to set a high level of compensation for any team losing a free agent (paid by the receiving team). Although the Rozelle Rule was voided by the courts, it was regained through collective bargaining in 1977, and again in 1982 in modified form. A complex formula for compensation was to be used, with one or more first- or second-round draft choices serving as compensation. Given the short playing careers of professionals and the high level of proficiency of college stars, draft choices are too valuable to be surrendered lightly.

If NFL policies undermine the owners' economic incentive or ability to field superior teams, what happens to the traditional emphasis on winning? In a closed system where every game produces a winner and loser, one might wonder what difference it would make if all teams were indifferent to winning or if all were obsessed by winning. In either case, there would be an equal number of wins and losses for the league as a whole. Indifference, however, would undermine the absolute quality of play and make college football or a new rival major league more attractive to fans.[12] Hence it becomes imperative, in the quest for uniformity, to ensure that all teams want to win and make every effort to ensure a high quality of play.

When revenue is not clearly related to winning, the "profit maximization" motive of economists might seem irrelevant for understanding NFL owners. Yet ironically, there are large profits to be made as long as rich persons seeking NFL franchises continue to escalate the sale price far beyond what the earnings of franchises can possibly justify. They are buying in not for the earnings but for the prestige and publicity that come with franchise ownership (which can be resold). Those buying sports franchises quickly discover, however, that there is good publicity and bad publicity. Winning brings celebrity standing, but losing brings only disparagement and criticism.

The heightened public focus on winning brought by uniformity makes the emphasis on winning among owners all the more intense in their efforts to maximize "publicity." Gene Klein, owner of the San

Diego Chargers, described all twenty-six owners who represented their teams at league meetings (in 1974) as "obsessed with the need to win" (Harris 1987, p. 20).[13] Art Modell, owner of the Cleveland Browns, was viewed as a carpetbagger from New York until "winning change[d] everything" (ibid., p. 33). For Leonard Tose, owner of the Philadelphia Eagles, winning changed him from someone who "couldn't even talk at the [league] meetings" to "one of the leading guys getting respect" (ibid., p. 422). Al Davis, owner of the Oakland Raiders, titled his autobiography *Win, Just Win.*

League success rests on the ability to maintain the inconsistencies between institutionally induced uniformity and the personal quest for distinction among owners (and players). Collectively, the owners set up rules that foreclose any ability to make more football revenues, raid each other's star players, accumulate a surplus of college talent, or obtain an advantageous schedule. But having safely foreclosed any real basis for getting an edge on winning, they engage in vicious battles on largely ceremonial fronts. In the midst of one losing streak, Klein hired a psychiatrist for his team. Leonard Tose refused to sit in a classroom chair at a league meeting, requiring his general manager to go out and purchase an executive chair. Al Davis made frequent use of the courts against both the league and the other owners. Such antics fill David Harris's (1987) look inside the NFL. He portrays "league think" as something that seemed always on the verge of breaking down from the shifting enmities within the league.

Rozelle, most of the time, held a more sanguine view than Harris: "I found out early on that you're not going to make everybody happy. There were many times . . . that as many as ten or twelve clubs might be upset with me. Fortunately, there's a turnover on it all the time. You make up with someone and then someone else gets mad at you" (quoted in Harris 1987, p. 17). Being on the verge of breakdown is part of promoting uniformities while cultivating egotism. The commissioner must carefully manage the countervailing forces. Indifference among owners over who wins, as syndicates or revenue sharing make possible, could quickly work its way down to the playing field. Scheming among owners is a healthy sign of a will to win. For scheming to continue, institutionally induced uniformities are needed to maintain a level playing field among owners. On this field, the commissioner ensures essential "turnover" by providing a constantly moving target. Owners can be brought together and divided on the basis of who happens to be mad at the commissioner at any given time.

The intense involvement of both owners and fans in NFL competition rests on inconsistencies. Fans are drawn into the competition by the interchangeability of teams, but this only serves to arouse their search for winners and losers. Likewise, owners endlessly scheme for advantage when institutionally induced uniformities have removed any obvious means for advantage. For the NFL to keep the involvements alive, the searching and scheming cannot undermine the conditions that bring it into being. Organizing for sustained involvement entails building inconsistencies into the system. Nowhere has this been better achieved than in the NFL.

Persisting Performance Inequality

The NFL has been phenomenally successful in cultivating national publics for regular season games. Instead of using television to reinforce the attachment of teams to cities, television was used to involve a nation of fans in leaguewide competition. With fans searching across an entire league for winners and losers, the potential audience for televised games became the composite of fans everywhere. While NFL teams are still primarily attached to cities in name, each aspires to be watched by the nation. In the course of this achievement, the league has come to serve as a new prototype for organizing sporting competition.

As in the early prototype, some limitations of the modern prototype have appeared. Major League Baseball, in successfully attaching teams to cities, became the early prototype for organizing competition. But within this early prototype, there was a built-in tendency for smaller cities to have chronically weak teams that often required subsidization from the others to survive. The modern prototype has made it possible for smaller cities to possess winning teams by giving them access to national publics and an equal share of the television revenues these publics generate. Yet in practice, local publics have persisted and continue to exert influence on the basis of their size. As long as this continues, there is still some advantage in placing the strongest teams in the largest cities. Networks are reluctant to risk the sure loss of, say, locally attached New York fans with a weak New York team for an uncertain increase in scattered rural and smaller-city fans that may come from heightened competitive balance.[14]

Despite the network television pressure, however, there has been only a weak tendency for larger-city teams to win in the NFL (see Figure 5.2). One complication, fast becoming a second limitation of the

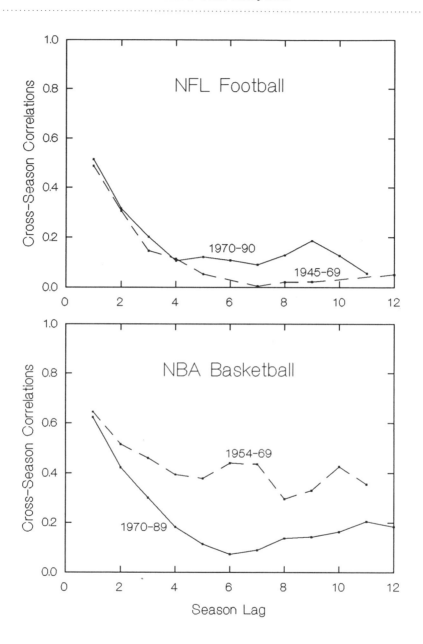

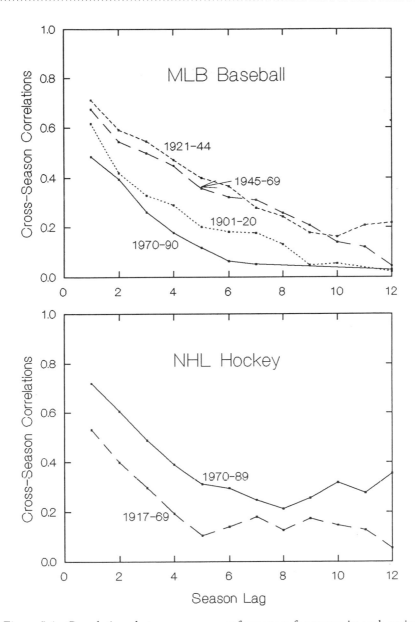

Figure 5.4 Correlations between season performances for teams in each major league sport. In football, for example, there is a strong tendency (*r* = .5) for a winning team to win in its next season, but this tendency has almost disappeared (*r* = .09) four seasons later. Only data for currently existing major leagues (plus the AFL) were used, and only after league composition had stabilized. Performances were not correlated across periods where teams had moved.

modern prototype, is that the networks themselves are growing weaker in the face of strong competition from cable, satellite, and pay-per-view television. Only network television has been capable of mobilizing national publics, and hence is essential for the modern prototype. The new rivals are in the process of carving out a patchwork of publics, by no means coterminous with city or even national boundaries. Implications of this development are pursued in Chapter 9. For now, it is important only to note how squeezed the modern prototype is between the lingering attachments of the past and the uncertain basis for future publics. On the narrow ground of the present, the NFL has gone further than any other major league in building the formal and informal mechanisms needed to sustain interchangeability among its teams.

This claim, however, seems directly at odds with the fact of persisting season performance inequality (see Figure 5.2). The emergence of the modern prototype did not decrease the season performance inequality across NFL teams, which has wavered around 1.5 times what one would expect on a random basis since the league began in 1920. A similar conclusion emerges when we look at the relation of team performances across seasons (see Figure 5.4). Correlations measure the extent to which winners in one season tend to win in subsequent seasons, and the extent to which losers tend to continue losing, with "0" indicating no relation and "1" a perfect positive relation. Entry into the modern period did not substantially change the persistence of winners and losers in the NFL. Winners in any given season tend to continue winning, and losers continue losing, for at least four seasons. If the modern NFL achieved competitive balance, or the interchangeability of teams, shouldn't there be no systematic relation between a team's performance across seasons?

In the next chapter, we examine the extent to which the other major league sports have adopted the modern prototype. Figure 5.4 indicates a dramatic reduction in the stability of winner and loser roles in both Major League Baseball and the National Basketball Association, to levels similar to those of the NFL. Only the National Hockey League is failing to converge, and we will see that it is the most laggard in adopting the modern prototype. In every major league sport, however, there is a clear persistence of winner and loser roles for at least four seasons into the future from any given season. Yet, as the next chapter shows, there are at best only weak tendencies for winners to be large-city teams in any modern major league sport. Hence stable winners and losers persist even after the mechanisms for maintaining large-city dominance have been seriously eroded.

In what sense is interchangeability an accomplishment of the modern prototype, if performance inequality persists even as a sport approaches, and achieves, this prototype? Every fan is aware that some teams do better than others, and often continue to do so for many seasons. To fans, this is proof enough that teams are not interchangeable, and justification for the distinct identities teams acquire. Yet we will see, in Chapter 8, that performance inequality can persist among interchangeable teams. There we look at the role local and national publics play in generating and sustaining performance inequality among interchangeable teams. Only then will the full accomplishment of the NFL be apparent. Only the NFL has succeeded in transferring full control over performance inequality to its publics.

Success in exploiting opportunities in one setting, however, can quickly become a limitation in adapting to a new setting. This is illustrated by the difficulties Major League Baseball encountered in adopting the modern prototype, discussed in Chapter 6. With the potential of international publics looming on the horizon, the modern success of the NFL is currently becoming an obstacle to adapting to the vast new opportunities. If marginality again proves itself as an asset, as it did for professional football entering the modern period, then we should keep a close eye on the sports that have so far failed to adopt the modern prototype.

6

• • •

Modernization

During the 1960s, the NFL replaced Major League Baseball in defining standards of success against which the other major leagues were judged. Without the NFL's lead, few people could have remotely imagined the magnitude of the new opportunities. The idea of national interest in regular season games appeared odd to generations accustomed only to the powerful attachment of teams to cities. A team's games and standing in pennant races seemed of local interest only. Yet once the NFL had cultivated national publics, the path for others to follow became clearly defined. To what extent have the other major league sports emulated football's success in their own respective seasons? The machinery exists for year-round sports involvement, both in the space and time given over to sports in the media and in the lives of fans. Yet the extent to which national publics have so far been cultivated in the other sports varies considerably.

The first prototype for organizing sport, Major League Baseball, proved extremely difficult to emulate. Major League Baseball's very success changed the setting in which the other sports had to contend. Powerful amateur organizations emerged as a reaction to the extension of professionalism, and effectively marginalized professional versions of the sports that came after baseball. If we look for a comparable reaction to the emergence of the new modern prototype, however, nothing appears. College programs no longer try to marginalize major league sports. Instead, they use the promise of glamorous professional careers to extract prodigious efforts from unpaid college athletes. Nor is the media likely to stop glorifying major league sports and professional athletes. Twenty-five percent of network television revenues are derived from sports broadcasting, and nearly 33 percent of the space in some daily newspapers is given over to sports news. Only conservative economists, still unwilling to forgive the leagues for granting teams territorial monopolies decades after the attachment of teams to cities has lost its economic centrality, stand ready to battle the majors.[1]

All four major league sports have their league offices within a few blocks of each other in midtown Manhattan. A few blocks away are the offices of the major television networks. Owners are businessmen, commissioners are lawyers and public relations experts, and players are represented by agents and unions. Unconstrained by sentimental attachments to the past, all are in the business of exploiting new opportunities. Even if the owners were not inclined to mimic each other's effective institutions, parallel pressure from media executives and player unions would bring about much uniformity. Institutions like free agency spread, regardless of differing legal constraints, from pressure by players' unions, which watch each other closely. Protection of college programs from major league poaching came from network television, interested in maintaining the high ratings of both college and major league broadcasts. What, then, stood (or stands) in the way of emulating the NFL's success in cultivating national publics for the other major league sports?

In this chapter, the progress in cultivating national publics is evaluated for major league baseball, basketball, and hockey. Each of these sports has encountered serious obstacles, both from within and without, in adapting to changing opportunities. As prospects for cultivating international publics begin to open up, however, the possibility arises that the very failure to emulate the NFL may provide the basis of success in cultivating this new kind of public. Hence while the modern prototype of the NFL provides a metric for assessing other sports, we cannot forget that this metric may itself change in the near future.

Reluctant Modernization

Major League Baseball backed into the modern era, looking at the fifty years of stability behind it rather than at the new opportunities ahead. Teams were attached to cities that had mostly proved able to support them. As the soldiers returned from World War II and sports interest boomed, the owners looked forward to growth through business as usual. The late 1940s were indeed years of record-breaking attendance for both major and minor leagues. On the strength of these years, decade attendance for the majors rose from 81 million in the 1930s (after falling from 93 million in the 1920s) to 135 million in the 1940s. Annual attendance exceeded 20 million by the end of the decade. In the minors, fifty-nine leagues drew almost 42 million people in 1949 alone. Local support throughout Organized Baseball had never seemed more solid.

Prosperity brought new challengers, however. In Mexico, a syndicated league operated by the Pasquel brothers initiated a concerted effort to lure Major League Baseball players in February of 1946. Sons of a cigar factory owner, the brothers had amassed a great fortune ($30,000,000) after one married the daughter of Mexico's president and was appointed customs broker. Earlier, in 1940, their Mexican League had begun seeking out black and Cuban players. By 1946 the Pasquel brothers were courting major league stars with bonuses and salaries that were up to five times what the majors were paying. But white players who jumped to the Mexican League quickly became disillusioned. Many found themselves outclassed by the black players who were as yet still banned from Major League Baseball (Pietrusza 1991). Some refused to cooperate with black players, and antagonisms frequently escalated into violence. Most major league players found the living conditions appalling, discovering in their first excursion outside the United States that the Mexicans "didn't even have screens on the windows" (ibid., p. 274). The Pasquel brothers attempted to prevent players from returning to the United States, but when their salaries were slashed in 1947 they began leaving en masse. By 1948 the threat to Major League Baseball was over.[2] The Mexican League, relinquishing its claims on major league players, still survives as an independent circuit accorded AAA status by organized baseball (Pietrusza 1991).

A more serious threat developed out west, when the AAA Pacific Coast League started escalating its claims for major league status on the basis of its rapidly expanding population base. Tensions between Major League Baseball and the Pacific Coast League had long been high, and were alleviated only slightly in 1950 when the Pacific Coast League was granted a special AAAA status that gave it more autonomy and higher compensation in the draft. Besides the draft, the Pacific Coast League was concerned about major league teams moving west. Plans to move the weakest Major League Baseball team, the St. Louis Browns, to the strongest Pacific Coast league market, Los Angeles, had been made as early as 1941 but were set aside due to the war. In 1945, to placate the Pacific Coast League, the baseball owners agreed to pay the it an indemnity if any Major League Baseball team moved into its territory. This indemnity was one reason why the St. Louis Browns, and other weak teams, did not move west in the 1950s, and why only the strong Brooklyn and New York teams managed to do so in 1958 (Sullivan 1990a).

Even closer to home, Robert Murphy, a Harvard-trained labor relations man and baseball outsider, began actively recruiting players into his American Baseball Guild during 1946 spring training, held by most teams in Florida. Murphy advocated basic reforms, such as a minimum salary of $6,500, impartial arbitration in disputes involving both salaries and labor conditions, compensation for players when sold or traded, and a weakening of the reserve clause. He saw these reforms as necessary for the owners to avoid losing players to the Mexican League and, potentially, the Pacific Coast League. But the owners moved quickly on their own to defuse player activism by granting some concessions: $25/week for spring training expenses, a minimum salary of $5,500, and baseb·'i's first pension fund. After the Pittsburgh players voted 15–3 against using the Guild as a collective bargaining agent, Murphy disappeared from baseball (Lowenfish 1991, p. 150).

Within Major League Baseball, the only urge for change among the owners was regressive. Many had come to resent the arbitrary power Landis wielded, and viewed the commissioner more as their competitor than their leader. When Landis died in November of 1944, the owners rose up to reassert themselves. They changed the voting requirements to elect a commissioner from a simple majority to three-quarters' support in each league. They reclaimed their right to challenge a commissioner's decisions in court. And they emasculated the "detrimental to baseball" clause that Landis had insisted upon. "The owners didn't know who they wanted but they knew one thing: they were never again going to have a Commissioner with the absolute power that Landis had demanded, gotten and retained for a quarter of a century" (Barber 1982, p. 65). Once more trying to maintain the public integrity Landis lent the game, but this time without the accompanying discipline, the owners elected a former U.S. senator, Albert (Happy) Chandler, to the commissionership.

Chandler, however, had a will of his own. His initiatives included opening baseball to black players, suspending the colorful Brooklyn manager Leo Durocher for associating with gamblers, imposing five-year suspensions on players who had jumped to the Mexican League, and establishing the first pension plan for players. Chandler, pursuing real change rather than parading his power through arbitrary and capricious rulings, seemed bent on using his authority in a way more threatening than Landis. Perhaps most challenging was Chandler's interest in pursuing television contracts. Here owners "operated like little fiefdoms, [being] alternately suspicious of broadcasting and selfish in enjoying its benefits" (Klatell and Marcus 1988, p. 116). Chandler's success in televising the World Series, starting for $60,000 in 1947 and increasing to $800,000 in 1949, only strengthened the owners' resistance to his encroachment on their regular season games. Rozelle's NFL success was still far off. Powerful large-city owners branded as socialism Chandler's push for control of television contracts and the equal sharing of revenues. On this basis they had also rejected the NFL's reverse order amateur draft and liberal revenue-sharing arrangement.

Chandler's initiatives were not what the owners had in mind for post-Landis baseball. At the end of his first six-year term in 1950, Chandler fell short of the 75 percent support he needed for reelection and was rather unceremoniously shuffled out of office. The owners turned back to one of their own, electing Ford Frick, the National League president, as their new commissioner. Frick was a low-key peacemaker type who gave much autonomy to the leagues in running baseball.[3] He served for fifteen years before retiring at age seventy, and his popularity was untouched by the near demise of the minor leagues and the ascension of the NFL. Nothing could better reflect the owners' backward orientation and insensitivity to new opportunities. Out of their past attachment to cities, a small group of large-city owners continued to dominate league politics as their teams continued to dominate league competition. They proceeded ahead with what had worked in the past.

During the 1950s, impetus for change came not from the commissioner but from the effect of changing economic conditions on individual teams. The devastating impact of television on the minor leagues put many major league teams in financial jeopardy, both from their ownership of failed minors and from the rising costs of securing players. Weak second teams in St. Louis, Boston, and Philadelphia were the most severely affected, and they jumped at the opportunity to move into the past minor league strongholds of Baltimore, Milwaukee, and

Kansas City by 1957. Stronger second and third teams in Brooklyn and New York, playing in aging stadiums and decaying neighborhoods, exited for Los Angeles and San Francisco the next year, lured by western population growth and the growth of commercial air travel. The other owners consented to the moves west only after the two teams promised to subsidize visiting teams' travel costs. MacPhail's 1934 Cincinnati team had been the first team to fly during the season, but in 1958, aside from MacPhail's New York team, travel was still by train (Barber 1982).

National expansion came, however, without league expansion, and cities that lost or did not get major league teams began to clamor for them. The two New York vacancies led Mayor Robert Wagner, after failing to lure the Cincinnati and Pittsburgh National League teams to New York, to ask the politically well connected lawyer William Shea to get the National League to place new teams in New York. After realizing that the National League "couldn't have cared less" about New York's problem, Shea turned to Branch Rickey to help him organize a new Continental League in May of 1959. Rickey's superb organizing abilities prompted Major League Baseball owners to begin a series of conciliatory but delaying actions. The Continental League threat was finally buried when the National and American leagues announced expansion plans in August of 1960 (without conferring with Commissioner Frick), enticing Continental League backers to scramble for the open slots in Major League Baseball instead. Continental League backers were granted National League franchises in New York and Houston, but were double-crossed when the American League awarded its new Los Angeles and Washington, D.C., franchises to backers with no Continental League connections.

With more teams covering a broader geographical area, Major League Baseball demographics approached those of football. Both sports had taken the distinctly modern step of decreasing their average local population base and increasing their average travel distances (see Figures 5.1 and 6.1). But the baseball owners were still not oriented to cultivating a national public through television, outside of their World Series broadcasts. Expansion, for them, meant admitting weak teams in smaller cities that would be a drain on existing teams. It was something they had to be forced into doing by threats from the Pacific Coast and Continental leagues.

Major League Baseball's 154-game season, extended to 162 games with league expansion in 1961, was an outgrowth of its strong attach-

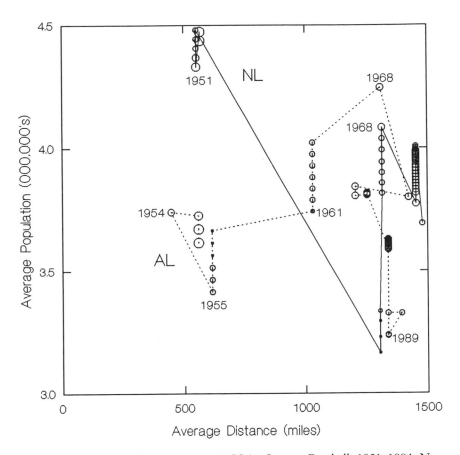

Figure 6.1 Demographic movement in Major League Baseball, 1951–1994. National coverage was achieved through intermittent jolts, particularly in the exit of the New York Giants and the Brooklyn Dodgers for California in 1958 and later league expansions. Circle size indicates the extent of site competition. AL = American League; NL = National League.

ment to cities. This attachment made it possible for a team to play half its games in the same site without losing the support of home audiences. The more games this attachment would sustain, the more revenues and publicity the owners would reap. The addition of nearly 100 games to the season of Major League Baseball since its inception is a remarkable testimony to the growing strength of its attachment to cities. Yet in moving into the modern era of televised sport, baseball's large numbers of games became more of a liability than a strength. With the new emphasis on national publics, broadcasts had to be limited so that base-ball fans *everywhere* would feel compelled to watch *any* baseball broad-cast. The large number of games and the lack of centralized control over broadcasting made it nearly impossible for Major League Baseball to limit broadcasts. In moving into the 1960s with more than ten times the games of the NFL and AFL combined, Major League Baseball was more tied to the past than poised for the future.

Radio coverage of baseball had been around since 1921. Teams had control over the broadcasting of their home and away games over local radio stations. While radio substantially expanded baseball's audience, it had always been viewed as a vehicle for enticing more fans to come to the games. Until the early 1930s, there were no sponsors, and teams earned nothing for radio broadcasts. When television first appeared, however, it was seen as a threat to the extent that it allowed viewers to watch Major League Baseball for free. A few more farsighted owners began to build limited networks for broadcasting their away games, but their efforts were mainly aimed at using television as they had been using radio—to get fans interested enough to come to the ballpark when their teams played at home.

In 1953 Edgar Scherick, a New York advertising man, proposed a television "Game of the Week" to a potential sponsor for the new ABC network, Falstaff Breweries. Although the proposal was met with en-thusiasm, only three baseball owners agreed to sell rights for the broad-casts. The rest pushed through a rule blacking out the games in all major league cities—a substantial part of all television viewership. Re-fusing to let baseball's localism block this first effort to create a national public, Scherick persisted despite this sizable obstacle. Scherick's selec-tion of Dizzy Dean as announcer resonated with small-town and rural America. Dean's colorful mispronunciations and slang were new to television, which at the time had been dominated by highbrows. Even with the blackouts, the show earned an amazing 51 percent market share of viewers.

By the next year the Brooklyn Dodgers and New York Giants joined in, and soon the rest followed. "In the long run, perhaps the most important effect of Dean's broadcasts was to interest viewers in watching games which did not involve their local or favorite team. He helped make possible the later emergence of national teams" (Klatell and Marcus 1988, p. 119). But while the experience helped allay owners' fears about television, it did nothing to convince them to cede some of their authority to the commissioner in contracting with the networks. The ghost of Landis was soon replaced by the shadow of Rozelle as an object of dread and flight for many of the baseball owners.

It was not until the NFL and AFL started signing huge television contracts in the early 1960s that Major League Baseball was stunned into collectively addressing the changes going on. Some had begun to blame declining attendance on the domination of competition by the American League's New York Yankees and, to a more recent extent, the National League's Brooklyn–Los Angeles Dodgers. Because the Yankees were so clearly dominant, little national interest could be aroused in games not including them. CBS weekend national broadcasts invariably involved the Yankees, and without revenue sharing, left the team with the lion's share of national broadcast money. With greater local broadcasting revenues and gate receipts as well, the Yankees had an insurmountable financial advantage in securing the best talent. There was a limit, however, to how long local and national publics were willing to watch the Yankees win so regularly.

Major League Baseball attendance had begun to stagnate by the late 1950s. In 1965, plans were under way to build a league around the world's most popular sport, soccer. Many baseball owners believed that soccer would provide a serious rival to baseball during the summer months, and five bought in as a hedge against their baseball investments (Voigt 1983). In this crisis atmosphere, baseball was ready to borrow ideas from football, whose recent television success had not gone unnoticed. Major League Baseball adopted a comprehensive reverse order amateur draft in 1965 despite vigorous opposition from the large-city teams (Miller 1990). A reverse order minor league draft, in effect since 1919, had been too limited and too easily circumvented to be effective in evening the distribution of talent.[4] Of some three thousand players eligible for the draft in 1959, only a dozen were considered to have major league potential. Baseball's new amateur draft was modeled on the NFL college draft, started in 1935, though high school players were for a long time the most coveted prizes. In addition, Major League Baseball increased the sharing of gate receipts (80–20 for the American League and 90–10 for the National League), but fell short of the NFL's 60–40 split. Finally, an effort was made to extend the pooled national contract with the networks (beyond a "Game of the Week" and the World Series and the All-Star Game). Baseball would vacate its Monday night schedule to showcase a single game on national television. But the networks were not interested, citing the primarily local basis for fan interest in regular season games and the overabundance of baseball games available through local networks. Major League Baseball was advised by the president of ABC "to make itself scarce" on television. An alternative arrangement, based on another Saturday "Game of the Week," failed in its first year with ABC.

Although no immediate effect of the small reforms could be expected, the New York Yankee dynasty curiously collapsed in 1965. A year earlier, the Yankees had been purchased by CBS. In the year of the purchase, the Yankees had a first-place 99–63 record. But the team tumbled to 77–85 in 1965 and then to a last place 70–89 in 1966. Future commissioner Bowie Kuhn claimed that this collapse was the will of the major leagues, a will that was formally expressed in the 1965 policy changes. "We wanted no more dynasties like the Yankees; they would be sacrificed in the interest of competitive balance among our clubs . . . the game would be a lot more attractive to North American fans if we sent to the gallows the old-time patricians of rule by the rich and the few . . . baseball was adopting the spirit of the New Deal" (Kuhn 1987, p. 184). Yet for some of the more powerful owners, who detested Rozelle's "socialism," the reverse draft was more likely seen as a way to eliminate competitive bidding. Since the collapse of the minors in the 1950s and the increasing competition from other sports for athletic talent, the cost of signing amateurs had skyrocketed. In 1961, signing bonuses paid to amateurs cost the majors $12 million. Competitive bidding had greatly contributed to the financial drain that farm systems had become for the owners. With the formation of the centralized Major League Scouting Bureau in 1968, teams also cut back dramatically on the amount they spent searching for amateur talent. From a high of thirty to forty full-time team scouts, by 1981 most teams employed fewer than twenty.

The ambivalence toward change within Major League Baseball was reflected in the selection of a new commissioner when Frick retired in 1965. The choice was William Eckert, a retired air force general who possessed no relevant experience for the job. Eckert quickly learned that discipline among soldiers was of a different sort than could be gotten from baseball owners; his position offered little opportunity for commanding those who paid his salary. Entirely ineffectual, Eckert "resigned" in 1968 after serving only three years of a seven-year contract. Bowie Kuhn, then a young lawyer who represented the leagues, was appointed interim commissioner and soon slipped into the position to stay. Kuhn was the first commissioner steeped in the requirements of the modern position. Kuhn was intent on doing for Major League Baseball what Rozelle had done for the NFL, a mission that by no means received consistent support from the owners.

Kuhn fully recognized the importance of centralizing control over television contracts. Major League Baseball network rights had grown from $3,174,000 in 1960 to $9,600,000 in 1970, but this was extremely sluggish growth compared with the NFL's gains. Owners had persisted in maintaining control over local television broadcasts and revenues. The advent of cable and television superstations in the 1970s only exacerbated this situation, as each team scrambled to control the broadcast of its own games. In 1976 the broadcast tycoon Ted Turner bought the Atlanta Braves, and in 1981 the owners of superstation WGN bought the Chicago Cubs. Despite these obstacles, by 1983 Kuhn had negotiated a $1.2 billion multiyear contract with NBC and ABC ($4 million per team per year) on the condition that local telecasts (and the USA cable network's Thursday night package) opposite network games be eliminated. But key owners resented the attendant centralization of power and constraints on their local television revenues, along with Kuhn's advocacy of a revenue-sharing plan modeled on the NFL. By the end of 1983, Kuhn had lost his job for sounding and behaving too much like Rozelle.[5]

Kuhn had boosted national broadcast revenues to $41,575,000 by 1980, which for the first time surpassed the $38,650,000 earned in local broadcasting revenues. Kuhn's replacement, Peter Ueberroth, was also a strong and active commissioner intent on disciplining the owners for their own good. Under Ueberroth's leadership, national broadcasting revenues grew to $196,500,000 by 1987. Under agreed-upon restrictions, however, clubs retained cable broadcasting rights. The New York

Yankees, for example, signed a cable contract for $500 million for 150 games over twelve years. On the basis of such contracts, local broadcasting revenues soared to $153,350,000 by 1987. In flooding regional television with baseball, the value of national baseball broadcasts was threatened. By the late 1980s, the networks were broadcasting only about 75 games (including playoffs and the World Series) a year though they held the rights to many more, whereas over 1,700 games (of the 2,200 each season) were televised by cable and local television on a regional or pay-per-view basis (Wenner 1989). Even with the networks grumbling over the local broadcasts, Major League Baseball received more rights fees for the 75 games than for the 1,700 cable and local broadcasts combined. With no local television contracts, the NFL received more for its 57 broadcasts than baseball did for its nearly 1,800. Nothing better illustrates the value of a limited stream of national broadcasts.

The consequences of clinging to local and regional attachments were to prove severe. Baseball's four-year $1.06 billion CBS contract (plus $400 million from ESPN), signed in 1989, had cost the network, by some estimates, as much as $500 million in losses. CBS had to drop its "Game of the Week" because of poor ratings, and it cut regular season broadcasts down to twelve games. By the 1993 negotiations, CBS had lost interest in baseball broadcasting, and NBC and ABC could be enticed only by a novel contract that gave Major League Baseball no guaranteed broadcasting rights fees. In effect, Major League Baseball entered into a risk-sharing partnership with the two networks, forming a new corporation to sell advertising for all broadcasts with baseball getting 80 to 90 percent depending on the amount sold (Gorman and Calhoun 1994). Furthermore, only the World Series would be broadcast to the entire country. Even the National and American League playoffs would be regionally broadcast. With less than a yearly $8 million average per team guaranteed from cable and local television contracts, baseball teams could receive a quarter of what football teams make from television after playing ten times and broadcasting thirty times the number of games.

In attempting to emulate the modern prototype, Major League Baseball has a number of handicaps that are rooted in its past success. The powerful attachment it forged between teams and cities continues, as already noted, to constrain its broadcasting strategy. Team owners still think in terms of building loyal followings, although these are increasingly subscribers to particular cable packages rather than city residents. Loyalty allows the owner to make more money by increasing the number of games produced. The long season of Major League Baseball, including eighty-one games in the same home location, is a testimony to its past success in cultivating local followings. But as the NFL has demonstrated, there is much more to be gained from persuading fans from all locales to converge on a small number of televised games. Here, Major League Baseball's large number of games and profusion of local broadcasts have become a serious obstacle.

Another obstacle facing Major League Baseball is that, unlike the NFL, it must still cultivate its own star players. Although by the late 1970s college players constituted over 50 percent of the amateur draft choices, college programs are not strong enough to feed players directly into the major leagues. Most college draftees enter the AA minors, proceeding to a AAA team before getting a chance at the majors. Lately the major leagues have provided more support for college programs, but the years of neglect and disdain are hard to overcome. Because television nearly wiped out the minors in the 1950s, it costs major league teams $1 million a year each to subsidize the minor leagues. Hence Major League Baseball pays dearly for the minors to develop potential stars, while the NFL pays nothing for college programs to develop actual stars. National publics, unlike many loyal local fans, have little patience in waiting for stars to develop. Thus the weakness of college baseball, once an advantage for budding major leagues, has become a liability. The strength of college football programs, once a liability for the NFL, has become a crucial asset.

In part because of the weakness of college programs, Major League Baseball has nurtured the strongest players' union in all of sports. Baseball playing careers are longer than those of any other major league sport, and Organized Baseball controls more of those careers than is the case in any other sport outside of hockey. Players have plenty of time to brood over grievances and to organize on their own behalf. In addition, the unique antitrust exemption of baseball has made it imperative that players use collective bargaining rather than the courts in pursuing their interests. Undermining the reserve system, thus gaining players the right to sell their services to the highest bidder as free agents, became an interest worth pursuing. While the antitrust exemption allowed baseball owners to hold out against free agency longer than in the other sports, the time gained served mainly to convince players of the need for a stronger union. In the end, baseball owners were to become dependent on the approval of the players' union for many of the policies they sought. This was to become another obstacle in pursuing the modern prototype.

A dormant players' union, formed in 1953, was revitalized in 1966 by an aggressive union organizer and lawyer, Marvin Miller. Making the reserve system its central issue, the players' union boycotted spring training in 1969 and organized the first general strike in American sports history in April of 1972. After thirteen days and eighty-six missed games, a settlement was reached. Ten-year veterans who had played for a team for five years could no longer be traded without their permission. In addition, the players gained salary arbitration. By 1975 the players had won the right to become free agents after six years in the majors. The first free agent, Catfish Hunter, was signed by George Steinbrenner's New York Yankees for $3.5 million, marking the start of spiraling salaries.

In order to constrain bidding over free agents, Kuhn advocated a compensation rule modeled after the Rozelle Rule in the NFL. It would give the commissioner wide latitude to "punish" any team purchasing a free agent by setting compensation levels for the team losing the free agent on a case-to-case basis. The compensation issue not only divided the owners, eventually leading to Kuhn's downfall, but also triggered a fifty-day players' strike (714 games) in 1981. In another victory for the players' union, compensation was abandoned. With only self-constraint to rely on in limiting the bidding for free agents, the baseball owners managed only temporary lulls in the salary escalations due to free agency.[6] In this regard, NFL owners have been much more successful. The Rozelle Rule effectively discourages NFL owners from bidding on free agents, because owners are wary of pursuing a veteran with a short NFL future at the risk of losing a draft choice.

Free agency has also forced the owners to offer many more multiyear contracts. These were previously rare, because of the exclusive rights the reserve system gave a team in negotiating with a player once his contract expired. By 1980, 42 percent of all major league players had multiyear contracts. The security of multiyear contracts has led to a slackening of performance among many players. The number of games missed by players on the disabled list, for example, rose sharply after the onset of multiyear contracts, from 489 for all players in 1974 to over 8,000 in 1985. Kenneth Lehn (1982) finds similarly dramatic differences in comparing only players eligible for free agency who did and did not become free agents. By 1985 players no longer active who were still on the payrolls received nearly $40 million. Owners found themselves paying more and getting less as a result of free agency. Any real or perceived decline in the quality of play poses a serious threat to Major League Baseball. But has free agency also affected the relative quality of play, or competitive balance, across teams?

From the inception of the reserve system in 1879, it was argued that free agency would produce large-city dominance as talented players sought out the teams that could pay them the most. In an empirical study of the post–free agency period, Christopher Drahozal (1986) found that the average city size of teams losing 129 top-quality free agents was 2.75 million, while the average size of the cities they went to was 2.72 million. Thus they did not go from small to large cities, as many feared and predicted. Using more inclusive samples, but categorizing market size, D. A. Besanko and D. Simon (1986) and Donald Cymrot (1983) find the opposite results—movement of free agents toward larger markets. Yet they also find that receiving teams tend to be worse performers than the senders. In the next chapter, more current and conclusive findings are offered. A glance at Figure 6.2, however, reveals that the advent of free agency has not led to the dominance of large-city teams. With the collapse of the New York Yankee dynasty, large-city dominance has entirely disappeared from Major League Baseball.[7] During the entire 1980s, only three out of twenty-six major league teams failed to capture at least one of the forty division titles up for grabs. The players' union cannot be blamed for large-city dominance, because such dominance does not exist.

In their most recent effort to thwart the sting of free agency, baseball owners have openly embraced the "socialism" of the NFL. They have proposed direct revenue sharing, under which the eight richest teams subsidize the eight poorest teams. This may or may not impose some restraint on wealthier teams in pursuing free agents, but will definitely allow poorer teams to increase their payrolls. While the players' union is in favor of revenue sharing, it is adamantly opposed to the other half of the owners' proposal, team-level salary caps (successfully imposed in the NFL and NBA). Salary caps were largely responsible for the players' revolt in 1890, and over a hundred years later, in 1994, triggered the eighth players' strike since Marvin Miller and his able successor Donald Fehr came on the scene. In major league sports, history repeats

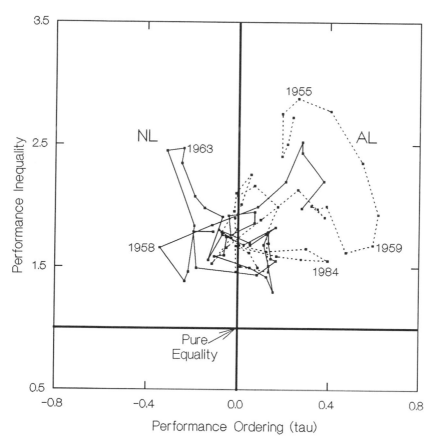

Figure 6.2 Season performance characteristics in Major League Baseball, 1951–1994, using three-year moving averages. Although baseball was slow to enter the modern era, performance characteristics of baseball had converged with those of football by the mid-1960s. Major leagues in both sports exhibited mild performance inequality and little or no tendency for large-city teams to dominate. AL = American League; NL = National League.

itself, but it does not always yield the same winners and losers. The players' union is likely to remain a formidable obstacle in the baseball owners' pursuit of the modern prototype.

Perhaps the most serious obstacle, however, is the reluctance of the baseball owners themselves in ceding authority to the commissioner. Great leaders have always required great followers, and many baseball owners are uncomfortable in the latter role. Crises have rallied the owners behind strong commissioners in baseball's past, but only for a while. Judge Landis was a product of the Black Sox Scandal. But the authority Landis wielded was something that drew only resentment once the crisis had passed. It ultimately drove the owners to seek out one of their own, the very unthreatening Ford Frick.

Kuhn emerged from the decline and turmoil of the late 1960s. While Major League Baseball's popularity rebounded under Kuhn's leadership, however, his standing among owners eroded. Kuhn's pursuit of the NFL's television policy was driving up the value of franchises. As a new franchise in a troubled sport, the New York Mets had sold for $3.75 million in 1962. Under the turnaround engineered by Kuhn, the Mets' resale price rose to $26 million in 1980, and then $100 million in 1986. Yet Kuhn was ousted in 1983, after surviving a number of prior ouster attempts dating back to 1976.

Ueberroth was brought in to save the owners from the players, but the courts did not appreciate the collusion he orchestrated among the owners. After Ueberroth bailed out in 1989, the owners went through two more commissioners in quick succession. Bartlett Giamatti, who as Yale University president had broken the campus union, died of heart failure five months into his tenure. Giamatti's confidant and successor, Fay Vincent, was sacked by the owners in 1992 for not being more aggressive in trying to break the players' union.[8] Since then, the position has been left unfilled in a situation that eerily resembles the years following the dissolution of the National Commission in 1919. Again the owners have fallen back on one of their own, the amiable Bud Selig, to tend to league business.

What is truly puzzling about Major League Baseball is that, despite all the underlying obstacles to its pursuit of the modern prototype, it appears to have achieved all the demographic and performance characteristics of this prototype. In league composition and structure, Major League Baseball and the NFL are remarkably similar. As of 1994, both have thirty teams divided into six divisions. Both are truly national leagues in terms of geographical coverage (with baseball also in Montreal and Toronto). Despite almost forty years of urban population growth, both Major League Baseball and the NFL have smaller average population bases than they did in the early 1950s. Instead of concentrating and even doubling up in the largest cities, to tap the largest local markets, modern major leagues have spread their teams out to capture a national public.

Similarities in the performance statistics are even more remarkable, as they are not something that can be directly imitated. The collapse of the New York Yankee dynasty marked the much broader collapse of large-city dominance in Major League Baseball. In terms of both the lack of an ordering between team performance and host population size and season performance inequality of around 1.5 times what one would expect among perfectly competitive equals, Major League Baseball and the NFL have become strikingly similar. Although Major League Baseball moved toward the NFL in its 1965 reforms, it stopped far short of the NFL's "socialism." With baseball's greater reliance on attendance and local broadcasting, it is hard to account for the disappearance of large-city dominance. The New York Yankees, for example, made over $16 million from local broadcasting in 1988, whereas the Seattle Mariners made less than $3 million. While many idiosyncratic reasons might be given to explain why a particular team with more revenue does not do better than one with less, it is much harder to account for the absence of an overall tendency for this to be the case. In the next two chapters, we probe this issue further by looking at the workings of baseball owners and baseball publics.

Late Modernization

Major league versions of basketball and football shared many features in common at the onset of the modern era of televised sport. Both operated in the shadows of vastly more popular college versions of the two games, and as a result, neither had succeeded in cultivating the attachment of teams to cities that Major League Baseball had pioneered. Yet basketball had not made the adaptations to marginality that were later to prove so useful to football's NFL, such as revenue sharing and a reverse order draft. Instead, major leagues in basketball existed as an appendage to other interests. In the case of the Basketball Association of American, basketball served as a way to better utilize hockey arenas in large cities. For the National Basketball League, most teams served as advertising vehicles for small midwestern businesses. When these two leagues merged in 1949 to form the National Basketball Association, it was not clear what the awkward new league could do for itself.

The newly formed NBA was initially boosted by the scandals that shook college basketball in 1951. Extensive recruiting and gambling violations surfaced, some suspect with the help of the NBA. Most of the recruiting violations had been virtual institutions in Division I basketball. Game fixing had been greatly facilitated in the early 1940s when the point spread was introduced (Figone 1989). Players were more comfortable manipulating a margin of victory, as this need not jeopardize win-loss records. With the college game tarnished, the NBA aggressively promoted its "clean" alternative in an ironic reversal of the relation between professional and amateur sport.

Although the rules that distinguish the modern game were introduced in 1954, the NBA's demographic evolution during the 1950s was firmly rooted in the past. By the end of the decade only eight of the original seventeen franchises remained. Small cities, like Sheboygan, Anderson, Waterloo, Rochester, and Fort Wayne, dropped out. With the exception of Syracuse (which lasted until 1963), by 1960 only major sports cities, concentrated in the East, remained. Average population increased from 1,683,990 to 3,219,760 during the NBA's first decade, with average travel distance actually declining from 691 to 665 miles. This evolution is charted in Figure 6.3. The NBA did not move west until its 1960–61 season, placing a team in Los Angeles.[9] But by its 1966–67 season it still had only two western teams and was only a ten-team league. It looked more like an early National or American League than the new modern prototype already emerging in the NFL.

Until 1967, the NBA made little progress in developing the television market. With meager television revenues, basketball remained largely a way to increase rents from hockey arenas, whose owners dominated the early years of the NBA and, in Maurice Podoloff, controlled the commissionership. A television contract with NBC in the early 1960s had been abandoned by the network after the Nielsen ratings turned out to be "insufficient for reporting." J. Walter Kennedy, who succeeded Podoloff as commissioner in 1963, had slightly better success. Kennedy was an advertising man who had been the first public relations director of the NBA, a background not unlike Rozelle's at the NFL.

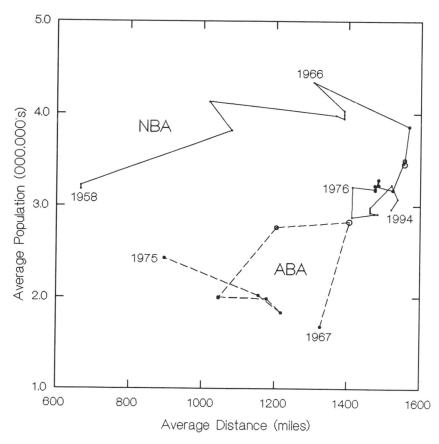

Figure 6.3 Demographic movement in major league basketball, 1958–1994. The National Basketball Association (NBA) maintained demographic superiority to the rival American Basketball Association (ABA), which avoided site competition (indicated by circle size) with the NBA. By the time they merged in 1976, the ABA stood in relation to the NBA much as the NBL had stood with the BAA, with talented players but nearly minor league demographics.

Kennedy cultivated a relationship with Roone Arledge at ABC. A five-year contract was signed in 1965 starting at $600,000 per year for the entire league and increasing by $100,000 each year thereafter. An escape clause was included, allowing ABC to exit if more than one team failed financially.

At a time when the NBA was just beginning to gain national visibility, a rival league appeared on the scene. Gary Davidson and the promoter Dennis Murphy formed the American Basketball Association in 1967, with the legendary player George Mikan serving as commissioner. The challenge triggered intense competition for both cities and television contracts, as well as for players. Although the rival league made few inroads in the larger cities with NBA teams, eventually abandoning Los Angeles, San Francisco, Pittsburgh, and Dallas, it survived nine seasons. American Basketball Association losses totaled $40 million over the entire period, with the NBA not faring much better. The competition over players triggered salary escalations that other sports were to see only after the advent of free agency in the 1970s. The scramble for players also soured the NBA's relation to college programs, when in 1971 it abandoned its rule preventing the signing of college players before their class had graduated. In the end, the American Basketball Association was dissolved through a merger agreement that brought four of its teams into the NBA.

To discourage potential rivals and generate badly needed cash, the NBA began expanding. By 1980 the league had achieved national coverage with twenty-three teams. The value of a franchise had risen from $200,000 in the early 1960s to $1.75 million in 1967, when San Diego and Seattle entered and a national television contract was secured, to $12 million in 1980, when Dallas entered. Besides inflation, the prospect of television revenues and exposure was behind these rises in franchise values. At ABC, Roone Arledge had nurtured the television ratings from 6 (percent of viewing audience) in 1965 to 8.9 in 1969. A new four-year contract escalated television revenues to $6 million for the final year, 1973, when ratings surpassed 10 for the first time.

When the contract came up for renewal in 1973, however, the owners brought in by expansion and resale showed little memory or gratitude for Arledge's efforts. Coveting the Saturday afternoon slot that ABC had committed to college basketball, the owners reneged on a handshake deal with Arledge and shifted to CBS (with a four-year contract paying $13 million to the NBA by the final year). In what became known as "Roone's revenge," Arledge squeezed the NBA out of its new Saturday slot by a massive promotion of college basketball and then moved on the NBA's new Sunday location with a new program called Superstars (dubbed "TrashSports" by *Sports Illustrated*) and a Sunday version of Wide World of Sports (Halberstam 1981). In the course of Roone's revenge, the weaknesses of the NBA were painfully exposed. Ratings fell from 10 to 8.1 in the first year of the CBS contract, and continued to decline steadily for several years thereafter.

Expansion had occurred over a shaky foundation. Talent was diluted by the rapid growth, both from the influx of new players and the redistributions that occurred as each new team was allowed to draft players from existing teams. With more teams spread across greater geographical distances, travel increased and fatigue became a serious problem during the rigorous eighty-two-game season. Compounding the fatigue problem was the introduction of no-cut contracts, which eased the pressure on players to perform at their highest capacity. David Halberstam (1981, p. 15) comments that the "true intensity of old fashioned rivalries in the earlier days of the league" gave way to the "increasing lethargy and indifference of many players in regular-season games, a lethargy and indifference now seen by a largely white audience as at least partially racial in origin."[10] A new commissioner in 1975, Larry O'Brien, did little to improve the NBA's image. O'Brien had earlier served as national chairman of the Democratic Party and postmaster general; his commissionership was plagued by organizational and media problems.

With the regular season failing to attract much national interest, television coverage concentrated on the playoffs. These, in turn, not surprisingly, were extended in the same way that hockey's were. By 1979, only ten of the twenty-two NBA teams were excluded from the playoffs, and only eight of the teams included had winning records in the regular season. CBS started ignoring over two-thirds of the NBA teams during the regular season, in effect creating a large-city version of the NBA, containing six or seven teams, for television consumption. Even the NBA world championship could be slighted, however; in many areas it was shown as a taped rebroadcast after regular programming ended at 11:30 P.M. In the 1977 championship finale between Portland and Philadelphia, CBS switched to a golf tournament the moment the game ended, cutting out the postgame locker room antics that no network would dare cut from its NFL Super Bowl coverage.

Without widespread interest in regular season games, it was crucial that the largest local television markets be effectively mobilized for the broadcasts. For CBS, this meant ensuring that the large cities fielded the best teams. This indeed proved to be the case after the start of CBS's relationship with the NBA. In the 1950s, there had been no systematic relationship between host population size and team performance. This was a symptom of major league basketball's marginality, in failing to attach teams securely to cities. Moving into the 1960s, the relationship actually turned negative. The tendency for small-city teams to perform better than large-city teams helps account for the failure of network contracts during these years. Located in the smaller cities, winners simply could not mobilize enough television viewers to make broadcasting worthwhile. After 1965, however, the televised large-city teams forged ahead in performance every year until 1977. This was not true for the American Basketball Association, which failed to make substantial inroads into television. Season performance inequality remained relatively high, between 2 to 3 times what one would expect among equals (compared with the 1.5 times of the NFL and Major League Baseball). These findings are shown in Figure 6.4. Television evidently functioned to attach teams to cities because its regular season broadcasts were targeted primarily at local publics.

Industry analysts were surprised when CBS signed a new four-year contract for $74 million in 1978. They had expected a figure around $52 million—the $13 million per year paid in the last year of the expiring contract (Halberstam 1981). Nevertheless, the $840,900 each team received per year seemed small compared with the $5.5 million guaranteed in the NFL contract of the same year. In 1982, NBA revenues from its new CBS contract rose to $1.2 million per team per year, growing further behind the NFL's annual $14.5 million per team.[11] Basketball remained a marginal major league sport compared with football and baseball. Only in its playoffs, dominated by rivalry between the Boston Celtics and the Los Angeles Lakers, did the NBA come close to mobilizing a national public.[12]

David Stern assumed the commissionership in 1984. Stern, like Major League Baseball's Bowie Kuhn, was a league attorney. Under the leadership of Stern, the NBA has shown remarkable vitality. Network television contracts are up from $200 million to $600 million for four years. Broadcasts have been limited to fifty games, down from a hundred games, with the elimination of contracts with two cable networks.

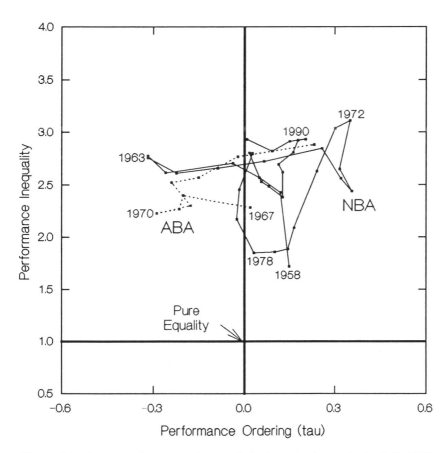

Figure 6.4 Season performance characteristics in major league basketball, 1958–1994, using three-year moving averages. Basketball exhibits more fluctuations in both performance characteristics than football or baseball, and has consistently higher performance inequality. ABA = American Basketball Association; NBA = National Basketball Association.

Thus while the NBA has an eighty-two-game season, it broadcasts fewer games than the NFL with its sixteen-game season. For Stern, this winnowing down of broadcasts was essential: "If you are everywhere, you are nowhere" (from talk at Columbia Business School). A stable positive relation between host population size and team performance emerges, yet smaller than that of the decade before, signifying less reliance on a few large-city markets. As the audience for NBA basketball expanded beyond local markets, it became less important that winners were located in the largest cities.

To stem the financial crises of the early 1980s, a salary cap of 53 percent of gross receipts was agreed upon with the players' union. A cap is designed to bring salaries under control without necessitating informal and illegal collusion among owners. It also checks the conflict between owners and players, although there are numerous complications and exceptions to the seemingly straightforward rule (as the United States Football League demonstrated). In this area, the NBA took the lead in major league sports. The NFL imposed a salary cap in 1992, and Major League Baseball battled the players' union over the issue in 1994 and 1995.

The NBA has also taken the lead in marketing its product internationally, through its NBA Properties Division, which went from twenty-five employees in 1983 to three hundred in 1991. The "NBA" has become a brand that appears on caps, t-shirts, basketballs, videos, and a growing variety of other visible places. The NBA video business alone has increased from $40 million in 1981 to $1 billion in 1991. These enterprises mark a rather blatant shift from cultivating the attachment of teams to cities to creating an international public for stars, teams, and the league as a whole. No major league has been more successful in the marketing of individual players than the NBA, a fact that we shall return to in the concluding chapter.

Currently, NBA teams play in arenas that are on average filled to 90 percent of capacity, and thirteen teams have no more seats to sell. Four-year television contracts with NBC and Turner Network Television starting in 1994 will bring in a total of $1.1 billion, or almost $10 million annually per team. As part of the latter contract, Turner will drop his coverage of Atlanta Hawk games and hence give Stern more control over broadcasting. Although the NFL has demonstrated that there is more room to expand the national television public for the regular season, the time for emulating the NFL's success in this sphere may already be past. A vastly greater international public awaits cultivation. For his leadership in setting out on this path, Stern was ranked the second most powerful person in the sports industry by the *Sporting News*, which stated: "Stern's league remains the standard by which the NFL, Major League Baseball, and the NHL are judged" (January 4, 1993).[13] But while Stern's marketing genius is unrivaled, it will take more than marketing to create an international public. Competition must be fundamentally reorganized. In this area, the verdict is still open on who will lead the way.

Persisting Localism

Major league hockey long remained on the fringe of the modern era in sports. With only six teams (including two Canadian teams) in the NHL circuit until 1967, hockey had limited exposure in the United States for over two decades after World War II. During these years, the growth of television had a negative impact: television only cut into gate receipts by keeping people at home (watching other sports and nonsports programming). It was not until 1958 (and the much heralded beginning of Bobby Hull's hockey career) that NHL hockey appeared on U.S. network television.

In an odd reversal of the economic prediction of large-city dominance, the 1940s and 1950s left some large-city teams (Chicago and New York) perennially in the cellar and some smaller-city teams (Montreal and Detroit) dominating league competition. The Montreal Canadiens, who possessed exclusive rights to sign any French-speaking player, had an abundance of talent. By contrast, the Chicago Black Hawks' hockey and financial performance was so poor that the team had to be rescued by the league. From the end of World War II to the mid-1960s, the league experienced a negative overall relation between host population size and team performance every year except for 1957. In the largest cities, as the least visible major league sport, hockey teams found their success intertwined with the fates of other sports teams. Relatively small hockey cities had fewer franchises in other sports, and hence gave their hockey team more consistent support. The chronic weakness of large-city (that is, U.S.) teams helped ensure the NHL's overall marginality.

With increasing television exposure in the early 1960s and the consequent public awareness of stars like Bobby Hull and Bobby Orr, the popularity of NHL hockey swelled. During the mid-1960s, stadium crowds averaged 90 percent capacity. Expansion became necessary to claim national coverage and thereby thwart the formation of a rival league. Yet even this obvious step toward the modern prototype was heatedly resisted in what became a recurring rift between "traditionalist" and "modernist" owners. When the latter won out in 1967, the NHL doubled its size by admitting six new franchises for $2 million each. With new franchises in Los Angeles and San Francisco, average travel distances increased from 522 to 1,225 miles. Unlike expansions in the other sports, the average population base only declined moderately as, in addition to the populous California locations, a large city like Philadelphia was still available as an expansion site. The impact of expansion on NHL demographics can be seen in Figure 6.5. Only with its most recent expansions into the South did the NHL achieve the high travel distances and relatively low population bases that characterize the modern prototype.

With the 1967 expansion, the professional sponsorship of amateur hockey was abolished to allow the new teams access to hockey talent. A universal amateur draft was adopted, on the model of the other league sports at the time. With compensation given to amateur teams whose players were selected, private businesses eagerly moved in to sponsor amateur teams, and amateur associations like the Ontario Hockey Association thrived with a registration of 132 teams (Young 1989). But as in baseball, amateur and college programs were not adequate to produce ready-made stars. The NFL had to subsidize a network of professional minor leagues to fill its player needs.

Despite the opening up of amateur talent and a special draft of NHL players, the new six-team West division was much weaker than the intact East division. Commissioner Clarence Campbell, in office since 1946, sought to conceal this weakness by scheduling few interdivision games. These games also drew the smallest audiences at East homesites. But the West pressed for scheduling parity, because games at West homesites against East teams drew the largest audiences. In the first expansion year, twenty-four games of a seventy-four-game season were interdivisional (with the West winning a surprising 33 percent of the interdivisional games). By the third year, thirty-six games of a seventy-six-game season were interdivisional (though the West only won 28 percent of the interdivisional games). These changes reflect the complex tensions raised by expansion, as established owners scrambled to

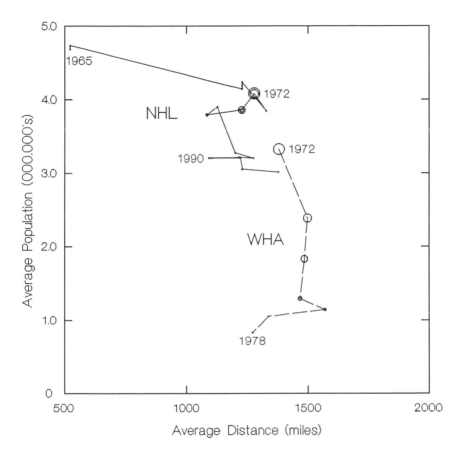

Figure 6.5 Demographic movement in major league hockey, 1965–1994. Expansion in the National Hockey League (NHL) has decreased average population bases and increased travel distances. Although the World Hockey Association (WHA) initially rivaled the NHL in demographics, its demographic deterioration was dramatic. Shrinking circle size indicates a gradual exodus from NHL cities.

protect their prized players yet also sought to escape the drain of weak teams in the league.

The impact of the 1967 changes are easily seen in the performance measures. Smaller cities ceased to dominate league competition. Though mostly weak, the relation between host population size and team performance abruptly turned positive, remaining that way until the mid-1980s. Losing its distinctive trademark of small-city dominance, the NHL came to resemble the other major leagues more. In addition, performance inequality rose to a relatively high level (for hockey) and stabilized around 2.5 times what one would expect on the basis of competitive balance. These findings are shown in Figure 6.6.

Buffalo and Vancouver entered the NHL as East division teams in 1970 for $6 million each. Still resisting expansion, the Chicago Black Hawks owner James Norris quipped, "I don't want a town named Buffalo playing in my building" (Eskenazi 1974, p. 62). Norris's snobbery stemmed from an earlier era, when the local population base was the primary grounds for inclusion in the elite world of major league sports. To accommodate Norris and help balance the divisions, Chicago was moved to the West division (though it had finished last in the prior season).

Despite further NHL expansion to sixteen teams by 1972, a rival league formed in 1972 with twelve teams in major U.S. and Canadian cities. The World Hockey Association (WHA) was organized by, once again, Gary Davidson and Dennis Murphy. Neither had any hockey experience, and few NHL members took the venture seriously until the challenger league began luring away NHL stars like Bernie Parent, Bobby Hull, Derek Sanderson, and others. In all sixty-seven NHL players (and even a referee) jumped to the rival league. After the World Hockey Association survived its first season, complete with an all-star game and a CBS telecast, talks between the two leagues were held, but an agreement was blocked by the NHL old guard and by the threat of a lawsuit from the NHL Players Association. As always, the trade war escalated player salaries. To rival the Stanley Cup, the World Hockey Association persuaded a financial services company, AVCO, to sponsor the AVCO World Trophy.

The World Hockey Association survived seven seasons, going from a high of fourteen teams in its 1974–75 season to seven teams in its final 1978–79 season. A look at the World Hockey Association's demographic and performance measures reveals a fairly clear picture of its

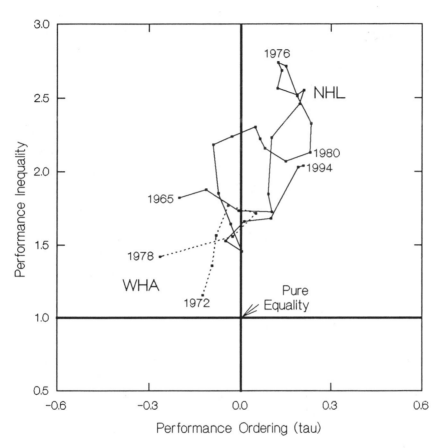

Figure 6.6 Season performance characteristics in major league hockey, 1965–1994, using three-year moving averages. Performance characteristics of the National Hockey League (NHL) resemble those of the NBA, with large fluctuations and generally high performance inequality. WHA = World Hockey Association.

fate. Starting with seven teams in the NHL cities, the rival league had
conceded all these sites to the NHL by its last two seasons. In the
process, its average population base dropped from 3,326,980 to
827,640. With larger-city teams floundering in intra-city rivalries with
NHL teams, there was a slight tendency for small-city teams to perform
better (which did not help in the struggle for large cities). World
Hockey Association teams in New York and Philadelphia, for example,
were in financial trouble after only twenty games—only 790 spectators
turned out for a game between them. With only one overlapping city
remaining in the 1976–77 season, the rival league managed to locate
its winners in the larger of its remaining small cities. It had also, from
the start, exhibited less season performance inequality. But this now
minor league (with major league travel distances) was soon to crumble.
In its final season, the smallest of the small predominated, which allowed a very quiet exit from the hockey scene.

In its competition with the World Hockey Association over playing
sites, the NHL expanded to eighteen teams and four divisions in 1974.
Another four teams were absorbed into the NHL with the collapse of
the World Hockey Association. Subtracting a failed Oakland franchise,
the NHL entered the 1980s with twenty-one teams in four divisions.
Although still the smallest of the major league sports in team composition and geographical coverage, it was no longer far behind. After
three more expansions by the mid-1990s, only the high number of Canadian teams (eight) distinguish it from the other major leagues. The
NHL currently has twenty-six teams spread widely across the United
States and Canada. With two teams in Florida, one in Texas, and three
in California, the winter sport has established a firm presence in the
South and the West. Its demographic expansions over the last two decades have helped give the NHL a national visibility that it had always
lacked.

In terms of performance as well as demographics, the NHL has taken
on the appearance of the modern prototype. During the 1980s, the
ordering of team performance by host population size largely disappeared (see Figure 6.6). Season performance inequality, in addition, fell
by the end of the decade to be remarkably similar to that of the NFL
and Major League Baseball, around 1.5 times what one would expect
among competitive equals. This convergence in characteristics is perhaps hardest to explain in the NHL's case. Among all the major leagues,
the NHL has the smallest amount of shared revenues. As late as 1984,

the NHL depended on attendance for 75 percent of its revenue, and there is no sharing of gate receipts. Until very recently, hockey owners have relied primarily on team-controlled local and cable broadcasting for television revenues. Unshared local broadcasting revenues should give a competitive advantage to large-city franchises, as early broadcasting efforts seemed to do in the late 1960s and 1970s.

In 1985, Philadelphia secured the most lucrative team deal with a $5 million annual television contract. In that same year, however, the NHL signed a three-year $20 million contract with ESPN, a national cable sports network. The latter revenues are equally shared, but amount to little over $300,000 a year for each team (compared with $15 million for NFL teams). Although the NHL signed its first network contract in the late 1960s, it lost it by 1975 because of poor ratings. Not until 1992 did the NHL get another chance with (now weaker) network television, when ABC (and its subsidiary, ESPN) agreed to air three regular season games and three playoff games for $80 million over five years. This contract is far too little and too late to account for the performance convergence with the NFL. In 1995, however, the NHL signed with the Fox network, signaling the rising prospects of both the league and the new network.

The "modern" demographic and performance characteristics are a liability as long as an orientation toward limited, but often intensely loyal, local publics exists. A smaller number of teams in the largest cities, with the strongest teams in the very largest cities, would be preferable. As matters stand, the NHL is poised to enter the modern era, bearing its costs but not yet reaping its rewards. With a recent escalation in star player salaries, to levels comparable with the other major league sports, the sense of readiness became even more pronounced. But as in the case of the NBA, the time to emulate the NFL may already be past. In the last few years, the NHL has shown much of the same dynamism as the NBA in aggressively pursuing international opportunities.

The situation of the NHL is reflected in an episode related in a National Public Radio news broadcast in November 1993. A new NHL commissioner, Gary Bettman, had issued a twenty-one-game suspension ($150,000 in lost salary) to a player for blindsiding an opponent so hard that he separated his shoulder. Under criticism for punishing such a common occurrence so harshly, the commissioner justified his action by pointing out that the NHL had just gotten a network television contract for its playoffs and was trying to "broaden its audience" by reducing violence levels. This was Hulbert's mission in 1876, in seeking to attach National League teams to a broad spectrum of city dwellers. Both Hulbert and Bettman risked alienating small but loyal publics, drawn by the violence, in the uncertain pursuit of larger and more diffuse publics.

Bettman was special counsel to the NBA before replacing the NHL league president John Ziegler as the first NHL commissioner at the end of 1992. Bettman's ambitions for the NHL are far greater than anything Hulbert could have envisioned. In response to a reporter from the *Sporting News*, Bettman insisted: "We're going to dispel the myth that this is a regional sport" (January 1, 1993). Besides pushing the adoption of many NBA policies, including its playoff structure, draft lottery, and player salary cap, Bettman has reached out to the International Ice Hockey Federation and the International Olympic Committee in an effort to get more international exposure for the NHL and its players. But like his mentor, NBA commissioner David Stern, Bettman has not moved far enough beyond the field of marketing in the pursuit of international publics. Without the liability of having become a successful prototype, both the NBA and the NHL are in an advantageous position to forge an altogether new prototype to serve international publics.[14]

Where They Stand

Major leagues evolved from the efforts of sports organizers to exploit new opportunities to concentrate publics. First these opportunities were tied to the growth of cities, or local publics, but then shifted with the advent of network television to the cultivation of national publics. Efforts to exploit the changing opportunities entailed considerable trial and error and consequently met with variable success. Table 6.1 provides an overview of characteristics tied to success in cultivating local versus national publics. It is clear that difficult changes were required in making the transition from local to national publics. Characteristics associated with success in exploiting local publics could be the basis of failure in the pursuit of national publics. These strange reversals have profound implications for understanding the current situation in major league sports.

I argued, for example, that Major League Baseball's success in exploiting local publics actually hindered its adaptation to the modern era

Table 6.1 Overview of the conditions for the cultivation of local versus national publics

Aspects	Local publics	National publics
Performance	Ordering winners by city size more important than competitive balance.	Competitive balance more important than ordering winners by city size.
Demographics	Large proximate cities make site competition unavoidable.	Large geographically dispersed cities make site competition avoidable.
Formal organization	Low revenue sharing. Limited league intervention. ¾ rule change approval.	Revenue sharing. Reverse order drafts. Majority rule.
Informal organization	Large-city domination of league politics.	Strong commissioners with shifting alliances among owners.

of televised sport. The marginality of the NFL in its early history, by contrast, allowed it to recognize and exploit modern opportunities quickly. In this chapter, we have also seen how the NBA and NHL have not fully succeeded in adopting either the early or the modern prototype. This is reflected in their season lengths. The NBA and the NHL have 82- and 80-game seasons, respectively, while the NFL has a 16-game season and Major League Baseball a 162-game season. National publics form around a limited number of nationally broadcast games. Local publics are sustained by, and support, a large number of home games. One way that the NBA and NHL have tried catering to both local and national publics is by creating shorter mini-seasons in the playoffs. With the long regular season fully utilizing the local arena, a nearly separate short season is crafted for television. The risk is, however, that this may alienate both local and national publics.[15]

The fact that cultivating local publics is not part of a natural progression toward cultivating national publics, but moves in an opposite direction, has raised some difficult dilemmas for major leagues in baseball, basketball, and hockey. Without a well-developed national public, broadcasters focus on the largest local markets by broadcasting only games of large-city teams on a local or regional basis. This creates pressures for large-city domination to persist into the modern era of televised sport, which then stands in the way of cultivating a truly national public. In 1965, the collapse of the New York Yankees, then drawing the most television coverage, could hardly have appeared as the harbinger of better times to come. Likewise, the intense rivalry between the NBA's Boston Celtics and Los Angeles Lakers helped mobilize a large national audience, but only for the NBA playoffs. During the regular season, few fans felt a compulsion to scour the entire NBA looking for potential winners. By hanging on to or continuing to cultivate local attachments, these major leagues have at some points hindered the mobilization of a national public.

Yet there are huge risks in alienating a loyal constituency for the uncertain gain of a much larger one. Major League Baseball had the most to lose in abandoning the early prototype, and was often the most reluctant to do so. On a smaller scale, the NHL has also held loyal local constituencies (sometimes largest in smaller cities) that cannot easily be denied. Outside of the NFL, the NBA had the least to lose as it failed to solidly attach teams to cities. These sure risks and uncertain gains have been central in battles waged within leagues, between commissioners seeking power through leveling teams and dominant owners seeking to protect their own standing, in league politics and competition.

What has resulted are varying degrees of limbo for the different major leagues. Even the security of the NFL has recently been threatened, as the television networks it built itself around are themselves threatened by the recent explosion of cable, satellite, and pay-per-view television options.[16] Instead of powerful television networks buoying the strength of commissioners by centralizing contracts and limiting broadcasts, the myriad new television alternatives entice team owners to cut their own deals and hence proliferate broadcasts. Major League Baseball is teetering on the edge of a new localism, defined no longer around cities but around the cable channels that carry the games of individual teams. The NHL has only recently begun looking beyond a limited localism, under which teams strove to mobilize core followings in their own cities or at most regions. The NBA has neither localism to fall back on nor the modern prototype to aspire toward. Having failed to emulate either early Major League Baseball or the modern NFL, the NBA is perhaps best poised to establish a new prototype formed around international publics.

The fact that the major league sports outside of football are converging on the demographic and performance characteristics of the modern prototype, without adopting all of its organizational characteristics, is the most dramatic evidence for their peculiar situation. Despite their continuing dependence on local publics, leagues' expansion in the quest for national coverage has diminished their average local population bases. Nor do teams in the largest cities tend to perform better, which puts the involvement of the largest of these bases in jeopardy. Large-city dominance has disappeared from Major League Baseball and failed to appear consistently in the NBA and NHL. Outside of the NHL, dominance on any basis has diminished as most teams no longer tend to remain winners or losers for more than a few seasons (see Figure 5.4). These moves toward the performance consequences of the modern prototype have outpaced the development of national publics, and hence are likely to fuel internal tensions. Outside the NFL it still matters, from the standpoint of overall profits and publicity, who wins and loses in championship races. Hence there will be continued pressure to stack formal and informal league dynamics in favor of large-city teams, as well as counterpressure to cultivate a national, or international, public where the location of winners and losers no longer matters.

In trying to anticipate how the peculiar situation of the major leagues will resolve itself, an examination of at least two analytic issues is necessary. First, we need to look more closely at the process of organizational change. This has emerged as highly problematic, particularly where past success has occurred. Major League Baseball had the most difficult time adjusting to the vast new opportunities brought by network television. For change to have occurred, loyal constituencies had be denied and the power of those who served them had be undermined. This meant ending large-city dominance. In the next chapter, we look at how one particular relation among owners, that of player deal making, changed as Major League Baseball moved into the modern era of televised sport. Once serving to reinforce the dominance of large-city teams, these deal-making relations later began undermining this dominance. But did the changing informal relations make the formal "modernization" of 1965 possible, or were they a consequence of the formal changes? An answer here will help us anticipate where and how the impending reorganization of competition for international publics can best be made.

A second issue is the specific role of publics in affecting competitive performance. Much attention has been given to how major leagues have cultivated local, then national, publics. Yet these publics have been given no role outside of yielding profits and publicity for the owners. We need to look closely at what publics are accomplishing by showing up so regularly. The more successfully major leagues have pursued competitive balance among teams, the more energy publics have exerted in finding differences among them. Could publics themselves be the source of performance inequalities that persist even in the modern prototype of NFL football? By isolating the effects of local and national publics, we can more clearly see the real accomplishment of major leagues. This task is undertaken in Chapter 8. It should also aid our speculation on both the form and the role of international publics in the future of major league sports.

7

• • •

Changing Ways

Major league sports currently stand on the threshold of vast new opportunities, in the form of international publics. For anticipating the future, past threshold crossings provide valuable lessons. In earlier chapters, we have seen how local urban publics were once an enticing opportunity for sports organizers, and how early major leagues became vehicles for cultivating them in attaching professional teams to cities. Then the possibility of national publics arose, and modern major leagues became vehicles for attaching network television audiences to leaguewide competition. We have seen that the cultivation of each new kind of public required a reorganization of competition. To cultivate international publics, major changes must once again be made in the way major league competition is organized. Before prescribing specific changes, however, we need to examine how change can occur at all.

A striking fact about past changes is that they have invariably been forced on established major leagues by challenges from rival start-ups. When a major league has had such a tight grip on its sport that nobody would dare challenge it, change has had to come from another sport altogether. Early Major League Baseball was so dominant that the changes required by the modern era of televised sport had to develop within the marginalized NFL, and here mostly under the prompting of a rival challenge. Thus the transition from the early to modern prototype meant, for fans, a shift in interest from baseball to football. There is already much evidence from the current dynamism within the NBA and the NHL that a new prototype, for cultivating international publics, will be nurtured within (and will push forward) a new major league sport. Change has always been problematic within established leagues, and especially so in the ones that have best adapted to past and present opportunities.

In the past, sports owners and organizers came from a relatively small stock of American entrepreneurs who moved freely across leagues and sports. Rival leagues were mostly formed by men with legitimate but frustrated claims for membership in established leagues. Conversely, established leagues are filled with one-time rivals, through past mergers. Of the 103 major league franchises operating in 1991, 40 began as rivals (Quirk and Fort 1992). And a large number of owners and organizers can be found in multiple sports. Thus the failure of a major league to adapt to new opportunities often has little consequence for the cast of owners and organizers, who simply reappear elsewhere in major league sports, reuniting with fans who have also moved. In the future, however, failure to change may have more dire consequences. If the small stock of American entrepreneurs fails to cultivate international publics, control over the distinctly American industry of major league sports could move abroad.[1] We need to look more closely at how established leagues have changed, in order to grapple with how they can change in pursuing a new prototype.

There is no better example of the difficulty of change than Major League Baseball. Its success in cultivating local publics became an obstacle in the pursuit of national publics. The attachment of teams to cities reinforced the dominance of large-city teams, both on and off the field. In order to pursue a national public, however, this dominance had to be undermined. Major leagues that were dominated by large-city teams had to somehow eliminate large-city dominance. Herein lies the difficulty of change. We have seen how slow Major League Baseball was in moving into the modern era, and how partial its achievements ultimately were. Once change is viewed as problematic, we need to explain how it occurred at all.

Much attention has been given to the development of formal mechanisms that promote competitive balance and hence undermine large-city dominance. In 1965 Major League Baseball increased the sharing of gate receipts, adopted a reverse order amateur draft, and began to pursue equally shared network broadcast revenues in earnest. That same year the New York Yankee dynasty collapsed and the overall ordering of team performance by host population size disappeared for good. Both the policy and the performance developments marked a dramatic change in Major League Baseball, heralding the end of large-city dominance and the entry into the modern era. But how could this have come about? However effective, the policy changes themselves had to come from somewhere. In a prior decade, large-city teams could have easily blocked such changes. But they did not do so in 1965. Nor did they take advantage of their larger local publics in fielding superior teams.

Ultimately competitive balance is delicately tied to the informal dynamics within leagues. Formal mechanisms must themselves grow out of these dynamics, marking changes in underlying realities that have already occurred. The NFL was quicker than Major League Baseball in adopting centralized television contracting and revenue sharing because it lacked large-city dominance, and not vice versa. While policies that fit the underlying informal order may serve to reinforce this order, those that do not are often easily undermined. The informal status of owners in leagues not only shapes policy alliances but determines the efforts owners put into building winning teams. In this respect, competitive balance hinges on the absence of an informal hierarchy among owners that could discourage the winning ambitions of some. Unlike most social groups, where poor performance leads to lowered expectations and energies, owners must remain vigilant in the pursuit of winning, regardless of past results.

In this chapter, we look at how the relative ambitions of owners changed over time by examining the complete record of player deals that Major League Baseball owners cut with each other. Unlike in basketball and football, with top-notch college programs, baseball players rarely achieve national prominence before entering the major leagues. Hence the most immediate and visible way for a team to signal winning ambitions is through the trading and purchasing of already prominent players from other major league teams. From 1901 to 1987, there were 5,082 instances in which Major League Baseball teams purchased, sold, or traded at least one major league player among themselves. These deals, compiled by Joseph Reichler (1988), provide an ideal glimpse into the relations among, and ambitions across, baseball owners. City size should be crucial in early deal making, with larger-city owners engaging in a pattern of deal making that serves to reinforce the dominance of their teams. At some point, however, city size should cease to be crucial as owners move in and out of deal making purely on the basis of their team's performance, in their quest for winning teams.

By identifying when this change occurred, in relation to the formal policy changes, we can better understand the process of change in major leagues.

Deal Making in the Past

Player deals among owners were an unintended consequence of the reserve clause. First appearing in 1879, the reserve clause gave clubs exclusive rights to renegotiate with players after their contracts expired. By eliminating competitive bidding for such players, the reserve clause helped owners lower player salaries by 30 percent over the next few years. To conceal this obvious intent, owners claimed that the reserve clause was necessary to prevent talented players from drifting toward rich, large-city teams that could afford to pay higher salaries. Yet owners soon realized that their exclusive rights to negotiate with players had a definite economic value and hence could be bought, sold, or traded. While players could not move to large-city teams in pursuit of higher salaries on their own, they could be sold to these teams by owners. The reserve clause gave the owner the enviable option of re-serving the player or reserving the surplus from the player's transfer.[2]

In the decade after the reserve clause appeared, a "ten-day" rule, which predated the reserve clause, complicated player trades and sales by requiring clubs to wait ten days after a player was released to ne-gotiate with him. This was designed to give all teams a chance at re-leased players. But the ten-day rule was commonly circumvented by owners who wished to keep other owners away from a player. Players were sometimes sent out of the country for ten days, distracted with wine and women, or made to sign personal contracts with a club officer. As a result of conflicts among owners arising from the ten-day rule, the National League adopted a waiver rule. This gave clubs a formal op-portunity to declare their interest in a released player or to "waive" their right to negotiate with the player (allowing a direct transfer). When multiple teams made claims, a lottery was used to decide which team could negotiate with the player. Still, there was no direct provision for the sale of players. It was not until 1889, ten years after the first reserve clause was introduced, that open sales of players were allowed.

Until this time, most players regarded being placed on a reserve list as something of an honor, as lists were limited to at first five, and later up to fourteen, players. Yet open player sales made clear the full implications of the reserve clause, and inspired the ill-fated players' revolt of 1890 (see Chapter 2). But the right to buy, sell, and trade players is something that Major League Baseball owners clung to with remarkable tenacity. While owners have since lost some peripheral skirmishes, only recently have they lost any real control over the disposition of major league players.

Owners sometimes managed to reach "gentlemen's agreements" to thwart the limited remaining rights of players. The waiver rule, for example, still required other owners to waive their rights to a player before he could be sent to the minors (beyond a fixed number that could be held in the minors on "options"). Thus when two Brooklyn players were banished to the minors for refusing to accept a salary cut, their owner Charles Ebbetts wrote to National League owners, "I particularly request that you promptly waive on these players in order that I may properly discipline them. Please keep this strictly confidential" (quoted in Seymour 1971, p. 185). In another instance, National League owners helped St. Louis's owner Sam Breadon buy out player-manager Roger Hornsby's $100,000 stake in the club because Breadon could not stand Hornsby's tactless and aloof personality.

With owners firmly in control of player movement, the arena of conflict shifted from players to minor league owners. Selling players created numerous opportunities for minor league owners, who could rarely thrive on the basis of gate receipts alone. The National League had started its first minor league draft in 1889, claiming unlimited rights to purchase minor league players at a fixed price. As the minor leagues grew stronger, they limited the rights of the majors and raised the draft price. They also found ways to sell their best players, worth far more than the draft price, outside the draft. Organizing into the National Association of Professional Baseball Leagues during the National and American League trade war, the minor leagues proved so effective by 1921 that some major league owners began looking for alternatives to dealing with them.

Major league owners started sponsoring and buying teams at all levels of the minor leagues, creating farm systems. The larger farm systems, like those owned by the Cardinals and Yankees, flourished by selling players to other teams as well as developing their own talent. By increasing the number of players at the owners' disposal, farm systems greatly enhanced the major league owners' ability to barter in players among themselves.

Farm systems made mockery of old rules carefully designed to re-strict roster sizes and to limit the control, through options contracts, of major league teams over minor league players. Major league owners scuttled players around their farm systems to evade these rules, and even colluded with each other in transferring players between farm systems. In an under-the-table deal, Branch Rickey sent Pete Reiser to Larry MacPhail to be buried in the minors until he could be legally traded back to Rickey, but MacPhail's unwitting manager Leo Duro-cher "discovered" the star and brought him up to the majors, where he played spectacularly for a month before MacPhail forced Durocher to send him back down to the minors "for more experience." Curiously, not one of the other owners or staffs noticed, despite having read great things about Reiser for the past month (Parrott 1976). Commissioner Landis, angered by such abuses, could only harass the owners with overzealous enforcement of technicalities. The only challenge to Landis in court, from the owner Phil Ball of St. Louis, arose over a minor league player's contract decision.

Landis was not the first baseball leader to intervene in player deals. In 1904 the American League's Boston team traded a competent hitter to the New York Yankees for an untried infielder. The National League protested this one-sided exchange as a ruse to draw fans away from their own New York team. The National League president, Harry Pulliam, publicly criticized Ban Johnson for sanctioning the deal. Johnson was known to engineer player deals, arranging, for example, the sale of Ed Collins to Chicago. Chicago needed a star to rival Walter Johnson, who had recently defected to the Federal League's Chicago team. In this case, the Yankees were angered because they were denied an opportunity to bid on Collins. According to Eugene Murdock (1982, p. 78), "Johnson never hesitated to manipulate player transfers wher-ever he thought the situation justified it."

But commissioner involvement in player trades and sales was always a risky affair. The collapse of the National Commission was precipi-tated by a number of disputes arising from player transactions. Barney Dreyfuss, Pittsburgh's owner, became an enemy of Commissioner August Hermann over the latter's release of the star player George Sisler from a contract Sisler signed as a minor; Sisler had been sold twice before he got out of college. A dispute over a pitcher decided in favor of the Yankees fueled the enmity between the White Sox owner Charles Comiskey and Ban Johnson. Later, the Yankee owners Jacob

Ruppert and Tillinghost Huston also turned against Johnson when he suspended a newly acquired player for quitting his prior team during the second inning of a game. John Tener, president of the National League, resigned as a result of a rift between the leagues over the player Scott Perry.

With Landis's death in 1944 and the institution of rule changes that would undermine the power of future commissioners, the owners appeared unopposed in their control over the cultivation and exchange of talented players. The source of talented players, the minor leagues, had been largely subsumed by the major league owners. Among themselves, large-city owners commanded the best talent. The two New York teams played in the World Series twenty-one times during the Landis era, leaving only twenty-seven slots for the remaining fourteen teams. Just as the dominance of large-city teams was beginning to appear unshakable, however, television entered the sports scene. With the power to keep people at home, television quickly decimated the minor leagues, reducing their number from fifty-nine to twenty-one over the course of the 1950s. Major league owners often undermined their own farm systems by building local networks that brought major league games into minor league towns. With access to major league games, as well as rapidly improving nonbaseball programming, annual attendance at minor league games dropped from 42 million to 12 million during the 1950s. Once a money maker, the minor leagues soon had to be subsidized by the major league owners. A critical talent shortage had developed by the mid-1950s, resulting in escalating signing bonuses for players entering Organized Baseball.

The shortage provided inducement for owners to straddle league boundaries in their search for talent. During the 1950s, interleague deals escalated to the point where they were almost as likely as intraleague deals (see the top panel of Figure 7.1). An extension of the waiver rule in 1959 to encompass both leagues served to facilitate this trend. The increase in the number of teams who could claim a player placed on waivers made it extremely difficult for teams to collude in sending a player to the minors. Instead of giving a player up for the fixed waiver price, teams opted to deal them off in a sellers' market. Waivers rapidly disappeared (see the bottom panel of Figure 7.1).

Also spurring interleague deals, and the shift toward trades over cash deals, was the growing importance of the general manager. Charged with the procurement, recruitment, and development of players, the

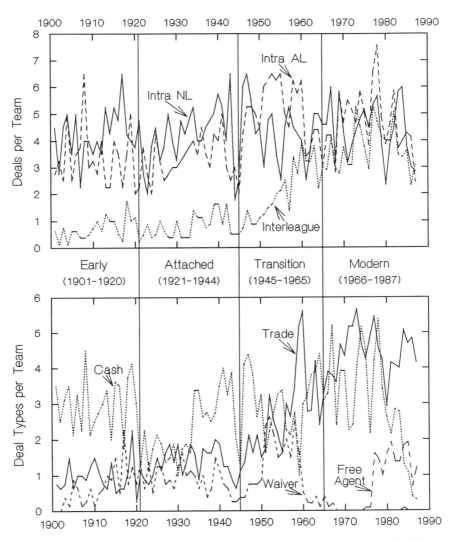

Figure 7.1   The number and type of player deals in Major League Baseball, 1901–1987. Deal-making barriers between leagues disappeared in the modern period, and trades came to predominate among transaction types. Waiver and free agent transactions are not treated as player deals in the top panel, or in subsequent analyses.

general manager first appeared with the hiring of Cleveland's Billy Evans in 1928 and had spread to most clubs by the late 1940s. The position became more common as corporate owners entered the game. Deal making moved out of the owners' league backroom as general managers began using deals to vie for status with field managers. General managers searched across both leagues for talent. They tended to rely on trades rather than on cash deals, because owner involvement was required for deals involving large amounts of money. Even today, however, when owners gather twice a year at league meetings (in June and December), there is a surge in deal making that bespeaks their continued involvement in this activity.[3]

Major League Baseball's reverse order amateur draft, initiated in 1965, was an outgrowth of the escalating competition for playing talent. Large-city teams, which in prosperous times often came out ahead in this competition, were suffering from the drain on resources imposed by their large farm systems. The draft eliminated the spiraling signing bonuses for new high school and college players. Yet because players were selected in reverse order of teams' prior season performance, the amateur draft helped spread talent throughout Major League Baseball. As this talent developed, many owners found themselves with premium players to trade or sell. Only one team had engaged in over 100 deals in a decade before 1960; nine teams did so during the 1970s, with St. Louis reaching an all-time high of 183 deals. Both playing talent and the search for it by owners and general managers spread rapidly throughout the leagues during the 1960s and 1970s. This produced the surge in deal making reflected in Figure 7.1.

In his efforts to modernize baseball, Commissioner Kuhn intervened in player deals on a number of occasions. He ordered one trade to stand, despite one player's announced retirement, because he wanted to strengthen the weak receiving franchise. In Kuhn's own account, he intervened "even though commissioners had infrequently involved themselves in owners' trades, certainly not in recent decades" (Kuhn 1987, p. 68). A few years later Kuhn announced a trade involving Denny McLain, marking "probably the only time a commissioner ever announced a trade" (ibid., p. 72). But his boldest intrusion into player transactions was in trying to prevent Oakland's Charles Finley from selling off his star players after his third consecutive World Series championship. Kuhn put a $400,000 limit on cash involved in a sale or trade among owners (Kuhn had no control over free agent purchases), stopping a trade of Oakland's Vida Blue for Dave Revering and $1.75 million. Blue ended up being traded for seven players and $390,000. This constituted the first legislative (versus judicial) control over owners by a commissioner. Kuhn's rule also virtually eliminated cash transactions among owners, as is shown in the bottom panel of Figure 7.1.

With characteristic self-justification, Kuhn insisted: "The laissez-faire days of baseball were gone. No more were the titans going to sell stars like peaches. Connie Mack had done it twice with two A's championship teams [1913 and 1929]. Yawkey had been a principal buyer the second time as Judge Landis benignly watched . . . Our 1965 rule that prevented clubs from selling amateur draft rights had exactly the same purpose and philosophy" (Kuhn 1987, p. 185). This boldness, however, brought about Kuhn's downfall. His insistence on compensation for teams that lost free agents—a device that had worked in the NFL to virtually eliminate the free agent market—divided the owners and incensed the players. Kuhn's ouster was just another instance of the owners protecting their ability to deal among themselves.

The advent of free agency in 1975 did more to destroy the laissez-faire days of Major League Baseball than any interventions of Kuhn. Power shifted toward the players, and not the commissioner. Although free agency is limited to players with six years of service in the majors, a sizable number of players have changed teams as free agents, as can be gleaned from the bottom panel in Figure 7.1. This again contrasts with the NFL, where free agents find it nearly impossible to get offers.[4] As a hedge against the escalating salaries won through free agency, many baseball owners started offering long-term contracts. Under the leadership of Peter Ueberroth, the owners were able to orchestrate a collective withdrawal from the free agency market, prompting a charge of collusion from the players. The dip in free agent transactions after 1985 provides support for this charge (see Figure 7.1). With help from the courts, the players were able to revive free agency by the late 1980s (and obtain a $280 million settlement from the owners). In the 1990s, free agency once again has produced a rapid succession of record-breaking salaries.

In view of past players' union victories, it is easy to see the owners as having lost control over the players and the game (Sands and Gammons 1993). But over the long haul, the success of the owners in protecting their ability to deal in players has been remarkable. Although particular types of transactions have been undermined by changing rules and conditions, others have replaced them. Sales surged as waivers disappeared. At least some of the slack from Kuhn's restriction on sales was picked up by a rise in trades. In the next section, we explore the meaning of these varying types of deals in order to understand what they tell us about the relations among owners.

The Meaning of Deals

Deal making takes the form of cash deals, where one team sends cash (and occasionally players also) for players in return, and deals involving only the trade of players and no cash.[5] The amount of cash and the stature of the players was not included in Reichler's (1988) compilation, and no effort is made here to evaluate the terms of any deal. Deals are the basic unit, which may involve widely varying amounts of cash or number and quality of players. Our interest is in who deals with whom, in terms of the relative city sizes and past season performances of the deal makers, and what types of deals (cash or trade) are used. In this stripped-down form, what do deals mean?

Cash deals have been treated by economists as the basis for large-city dominance, with cash flowing from large-city teams in exchange for emerging talent on smaller-city teams. Yet since deals are made over contracts (or the exclusive right to contract), and not over players themselves, there need be no talent symmetry in a trade. A team giving up rights to a star at the same time relieves itself of a considerable salary obligation and so may seek a lesser player, who comes with a lesser salary obligation, in return (though this risks alienating local fans). These payroll changes obscure the distinction between a trade and a sale, since a trade can significantly increase or decrease *future* payroll expenses. Trades, like cash deals, can alter relative performance prospects.

Because cash deals are often linked in complex webs, they need not alter relative performance prospects. With the strict limit on roster size, any purchase of a player necessitates the disposal of another player if the team has a full roster. A limited number of players can be sent to the minor leagues "on option"—the team reserves exclusive rights to call them back. Otherwise, extra players must be sold or released. Hence a player purchased from one team can be tied to a player sale from another, making the set of transactions seem like a trade.[6] The movement of players between major and minor league teams serves to bound interconnected webs of deals. A player sent down to the minors can trigger the purchase of a major league replacement, which in turn creates another major league vacancy. Such a "vacancy chain" (White 1970) is terminated by bringing a player up from the minors. Insofar as we look only at transactions between major league owners that involve at least one major league player, we omit the very events that begin and end webs of such deals. Some teams avoid deals with other major league owners entirely (for long periods) by relying exclusively on their farm systems (that is, the minors) for players. Others are enmeshed in endless webs through their incessant deal making with other major league owners. Moving into and out of the player market can be as important as whether one sells, buys, or trades once in. The volume of deal making, regardless of component deal types, may be the most useful way to distinguish teams.

Deals can be prompted by diverse motivations. Team owners obsessed with winning, like Connie Mack or Charles Finley, have also gutted their teams of stars for financial gain. Clark Griffith, owner of the Washington Senators, even sold his son-in-law and star shortstop along with his manager for $225,000 in 1934. Another owner traded a player for a coveted bird dog. Some deals simply appear unfathomable. "It can be safely said that the [California] Angels would be better off if they had never made a trade and kept [owner] Autry's checkbook closed" (Reichler 1984, p. 272). The catalogue of reasons is so diverse, and so conflicting, that any outcome can be justified. Moving into the market can undermine team performance to help team finances, or vice versa, or perhaps affect only the owner's peace of mind.

Yet once in the market, an owner who is gutting his team must rely on the same deal-making acumen as the owner who is out to strengthen his team. Each can be made into a sucker or emerge as a shrewd dealer. Every generation of baseball owners and general managers has had its share of suckers and shrewd dealers. Joseph Reichler (1984) comments that Bob Howsem (general manager of Cincinnati) "traded shrewdly to create the Big Red Machine." Chicago Cub deals, however, have "kept the club down," while the Houston Astros have an "abysmal record in the trading market." Although the Dodgers rely primarily on their farm system, "faith in the Dodgers' judgement runs so strong" that baseball people concluded a player the Dodgers traded "wasn't all he'd been cracked up to be." John McGraw, owner of the Giants, had "unerring judgement." Pittsburgh's early owner, Dreyfuss, was a "shrewd trader," but also "extremely fair in offering value in return." Horace Stoneham "gave them [good players] all away, and got next to nothing in return for his generosity." In twelve years as general manager of four clubs, "Frantic" Frank Lane had "no time for a farm system," making three hundred trades involving over four hundred players. And "if you trade with [Branch] Rickey, don't drink, and keep your hands in your pockets. He'll hornswaggle you."

Much besides money and talent is on the line in every deal between major league owners. Reputations and (general manager) careers are made or broken. Every deal based on mutual benefit carries the prospect of making one side look, especially in retrospect, shrewd and the other foolish. Close allies can ill afford to drop their suspicions in a deal, while foes may mutually benefit from deals. As a way to allay suspicions, deal making is often couched in terms of a relationship. In the five years after the Athletics moved to Kansas City, they engaged in sixteen deals involving fifty-nine players with the Yankees. By contrast, Clark Griffith's Washington Senators would not deal with the Yankees at all, "because of a deep and abiding hatred for them" (Reichler 1984). Deal making can both initiate and terminate trust.

Some insight into the complexity of deal making can be gained from observing how it is affected by factional divides. In Figure 7.2, four instances where factions surfaced are monitored in terms of intra- and interfactional deal making. Freedman's 1901 effort to syndicate the National League led to a bitter 4–4 division among owners. Deal making ceased altogether before the December meeting showdown, yet resumed soon after Freedman's defeat and quick exit from the league. The 1920 "insurrection" against Ban Johnson by three owners similarly put a damper on deal making, with only a single interfaction deal occurring in the following twenty months. These factional divides occurred amid the larger difficulties of a trade war and the dissolution of the National Commission, respectively. In the less critical deadlock over Heydler's 1909 renewal as National League president, the 4–4 divide, ending in agreement on a compromise candidate, does not appear to have had any impact on deal making. From these early cases, we see that serious divides erect barriers to deal making. Yet members of an oppositional faction do not appear eager to deal among themselves, as deal making can itself produce conflicts that can jeopardize the faction's ability to stick together.

In January 1976, amid a major labor crisis, nine teams from both

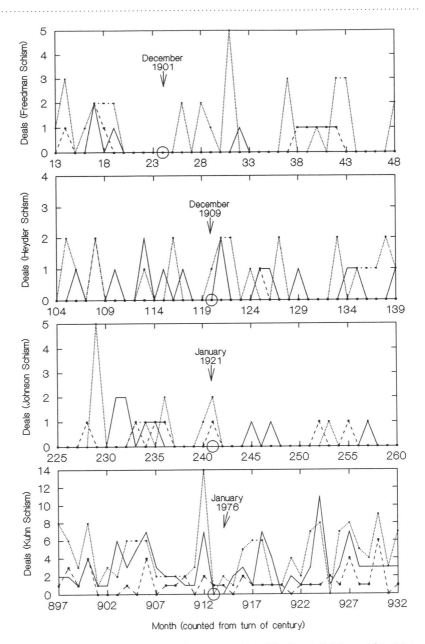

Figure 7.2 Monthly deal making during periods of factional division within Major League Baseball. Deals are broken down into interfaction deals (dotted line) and intrafaction deals among supporters (solid line) and opponents (dashed line) of the person around whom factions formed. A circle demarcates the month in which factional conflict surfaced.

leagues signed a letter calling for the resignation of Commissioner Kuhn. At the biannual meeting a month earlier, there had been a frenzy of deal making. Yet most of the deals were interfactional, and cosigners of the letter were the least likely to deal with each other (even taking into account their smaller numbers). Outside of a not atypical post-meeting lull in deals, the event had little subsequent impact on deal making. Deal making was random with respect to the factional division, with overall levels determined by the size of the groups. Something had changed in the relationship between owners and teams since the earlier period.

Owners or general managers have never been indifferent regarding whom they deal with. A pair of teams can be said to have an exchange relation if they engage in at least one player deal per season. This century's most enduring exchange relations are listed in Table 7.1, ranked by the number of deals made across an uninterrupted period of exchange.[7] Interleague relations appear distinctly modern. No enduring interleague exchange relations began before 1969, while four of the ten enduring relations beginning after 1965 were interleague. Oakland accounted for two of the four, including the most active relation of them all, involving nineteen deals over nine consecutive years with the Chicago Cubs. These relations, along with one enduring intraleague relation, helped Oakland win its three consecutive World Series in the early 1970s. Interestingly, the New York Yankee dynasty extending from the 1920s to the 1960s was built and maintained without a trail of enduring relations. Only one lasting relation was forged, and not until 1953, with the Philadelphia team that became the Kansas City club in 1955. The divergent market strategies of Oakland and New York, as small- and large-city teams amid changing opportunities, will be explored later in this chapter.

While some teams formed enduring exchange relations, others avoided exchange with each other. A list of the most enduring avoidance relations is entirely dominated by interleague relations, with some extending over seventy years. Only intraleague avoidance relations are used in Table 7.1, to underscore the fact that even league members may strongly differentiate among themselves when it comes to seeking or avoiding exchange partners. Surprisingly, nearly half begin on or after 1965, even though per team intraleague exchange remained constant (see Figure 7.1). The growth of interleague exchange evidently allowed certain league members to avoid each other more easily. Again Oakland

Table 7.1   The twenty most active transaction and avoidance relations in Major
              League Baseball

Top twenty	Began	Consecutive years	Number of transactions
Transaction Relations			
Chicago(NL)–Oakland(AL)	1971	9	19
Cincinnati(NL)–St. Louis(NL)	1931	7	18
Chicago(AL)–St. Louis(AL)[a]	1950	7	18
New York(AL)–Philadelphia(AL)[a]	1953	8	18
Cleveland(AL)–Washington(AL)[a]	1969	8	16
Oakland(AL)–Washington(AL)[a]	1969	6	15
St. Louis(NL)–San Diego(NL)	1969	10	15
Washington(AL)–Chicago(AL)	1948	8	14
Pittsburgh(NL)–Boston(NL)	1906	8	13
Milwaukee(NL)–New York(NL)	1962	4	13
Chicago(NL)–St. Louis(NL)	1962	7	13
Cincinnati(NL)–New York(NL)	1913	8	12
Chicago(NL)–Boston(NL)	1909	6	11
Brooklyn(NL)–Philadelphia(NL)	1941	3	10
Boston(NL)–St. Louis(NL)	1945	3	10
Cincinnati(NL)–St. Louis(NL)	1949	8	10
St. Louis(NL)–Houston(NL)	1972	5	10
St. Louis(NL)–Chicago(AL)	1973	5	10
San Diego(NL)–Cleveland(AL)	1977	7	10
San Diego(NL)–Montreal(NL)	1980	5	10

appears at the top of the list, having never dealt with the new Kansas
City team that occupied the city which it had abandoned. Next to Oakland, and far surpassing it when one-year interruptions to avoidance
are allowed, is the New York Yankees. Avoidance with Detroit extends
over most of the century. In the years leading to its dynasty, the Yankees
also did not deal with Chicago and Cleveland. Outside of the Yankees,
long-term avoidance relations appear rare in the first half of this century.

Ultimately the meaning of types of ties must be read from the patterns that crystallize around them. If strong large-city teams tend to
purchase players from weak small-city teams, then cash deals mean
something quite different from what they would if such deals occurred
irrespective of city size and performance. Patterns of deal making, with
respect to the relative city size and performance of transacting teams,

Table 7.1 (continued)

Top twenty	Began	Consecutive years	Number of transactions
Avoidance Relations (Intraleague Only)			
Oakland(AL)–Kansas City(AL)	1969	20+	0
New York(AL)–Detroit(AL)	1931	19	0
New York(AL)–Detroit(AL)	1951	17	0
New York(AL)–Detroit(AL)	1975	14+	0
Chicago(AL)–New York(AL)	1928	13	0
Chicago(AL)–New York(AL)	1951	19	0
Brooklyn(NL)–Milwaukee(NL)[a]	1954	19	0
Washington(AL)–Baltimore(AL)	1961	19	0
Cincinnati(AL)–Philadelphia(NL)	1965	19	0
Boston(AL)–Baltimore(AL)	1967	19	0
Chicago(NL)–New York(NL)	1921	18	0
Chicago(NL)–New York(NL)	1943	14	0
Minnesota(AL)–Boston(AL)	1968	18	0
New York(AL)–Cleveland(AL)	1914	16	0
Pittsburgh(NL)–Brooklyn(NL)[a]	1951	16	0
Baltimore(AL)–Kansas City(AL)	1971	16	0
Cincinnati(NL)–Boston(NL)	1923	14	0
Minnesota(AL)–New York(AL)[a]	1959	14	0
Philadelphia(NL)–San Diego(NL)	1969	14	0
Minnesota(AL)–Kansas City(AL)	1975	14+	0

Note: For inclusion, transactions (or avoidance) had to extend across consecutive years, and rankings were based on the number of transactions (or years) in the spells. Allowing one-year disruptions did not change the rankings substantially, suggesting that any stop (or start) marked the end of a transaction (or avoidance) relation.

a. When a team moved during relation period, original site is given.

can implicate deals and their types in perpetuating dominance or promoting competitive balance. The changing role of relative host population size and team performance in different types of deal making is explored below.

Structures of Deal Making

Twentieth-century Major League Baseball can be divided into four distinct periods. The first, 1901–1920, spans the birth and death of the National Commission. During this period a stable attachment of teams to cities was forged, yet ownership was unstable and the lack of strong central leadership made the sport vulnerable to crises. Next came the entrenchment of the Landis era, 1921–1944, when both ownership and leadership were most stable and local attachment to cities proved so strong that they endured the Great Depression and World War II. With the death of Landis and the end of the war, Major League Baseball entered its slow and difficult transition into the modern era of national publics. Although in many ways Major League Baseball has yet to fully enter this era, at least to the extent that the NFL has, much overt resistance to the needed changes crumbled in 1965. Hence what will be called the "transition" period spans the years 1945 through 1965. The fourth period, optimistically called the "modern era," runs from 1966 to 1987.[8]

Important quantitative changes have already been observed across the four periods. In the transition to the modern era, there was a rapid increase in the annual number of deals per team, made up almost entirely through an increase in interleague deals. The transition period also saw the ascendance of trades as the primary mode of deal making, although sales made a short-lived resurgence in the 1970s. These trends coincide with the growing importance of general managers in institutionalizing deal making. Providing evidence for this institutionalization, team differences in number of annual deals declined 25 percent between the years before World War II and the coming of the modern era.[9] Increasing stability in team deal making can also be seen in the correlation between a team's volume of deals across consecutive years. Using regression analysis (see Appendix B), the coefficients associated with the one-year lagged volume of deals rise dramatically for both leagues in the modern period (see Figure 7.3). There was a decrease in stability, however, in the transition period. This is the first of many ways it is distinguished.

To begin to account for what is driving deal making at the team level, we need to look at how deal making is related to a team's relative city size and to its performance in the season preceding the deals. In the shift from local to national publics, the role of city size and performance in driving deal making should also have changed. Using coefficients from a regression of these variables on overall deals, Figure 7.4 shows a sharp increase across periods in the importance of performance in driving deal making.[10] With the transition into the modern period, poor performance became the central instigator for engaging in player deals. By the modern period, an increase of seven in season win percentage

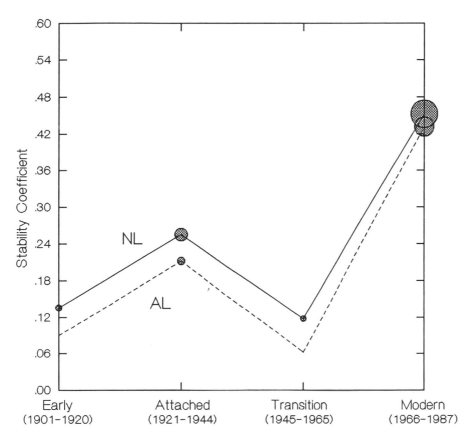

Figure 7.3 The stability of team deal making in four periods. Stability coefficients are obtained from regressing the number of team deals in each year with the number in the prior year, with past performance and the direction of performance included as controls. Zero denotes no relation, while one would denote no changes across time (perfect stability). Circle size indicates degree to which the relation is statistically significant.

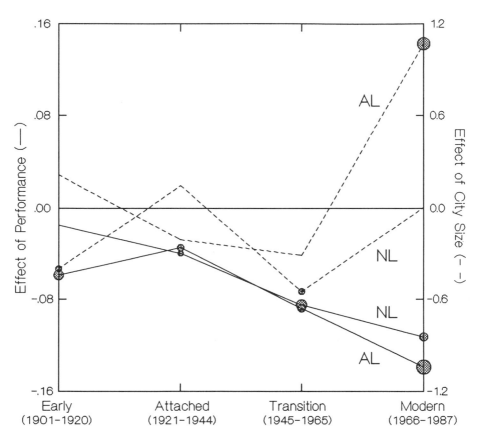

Figure 7.4 Effect of preceding season performance (—) and standardized city size (---) on the number of team deals each season, from a regression of team deals on the two variables. Size of circle denotes degree of statistical significance. Over time, the worse a team performed, the more deals it engaged in, the following season. City size had a less consistent effect.

led to one less player deal the next season. The impact of city size was less consistent, both across time and across leagues. Only in the transition period is the effect in both leagues clearly in the same direction. Here, teams in smaller cities were the most active participants in player deals. A revolt of the small and weak appears to have taken place in the transition period, with claims pressed in the arena of player deals. By the modern period, when winning was unrelated to city size, the small were no longer the ones revolting—as is particularly evident in the American League.

A dynamic aspect can be added by looking at the effect of the change in season performance between the two seasons preceding the focal year of deal making. Using a fourfold distinction between teams whose winning or losing records of the preceding season represented a rise or a fall, and looking separately at the teams above and below the median-city-size teams, interesting refinements emerge (see Figure 7.5). For almost everyone, rising performance and a winning record led to a relative withdrawal from deal making. This fact underscores its riskiness; teams do not engage in deal making if things are going well. Yet only once, among larger-city teams in the second period, did falling teams with a losing record engage in the most deal making. The most active deal makers, particular among smaller-city teams after World War II, were losing teams on the rise. For larger-city teams, preceding performance did not make much difference. In the transition period, large-city winners who were falling made the most deals. Although large-city winners who were falling were still active in the modern period, rising losers moved past them in dealing volume, which suggests a possible convergence between patterns for large and small cities.

From these results, it appears that after World War II small-city teams turned increasingly to deal making as a way to fuel upward mobility and to a somewhat lesser extent to halt downward mobility. Larger-city teams, in a less dramatic way, turned to the market to halt the deterioration of their winner roles and then, as this did not always work, to move back upward in the modern era. We have seen that small-city teams were ultimately successful in achieving competitive balance (Chapter 6), which suggests that they were more successful in their use of deal making than were large-city teams. This interpretation is bolstered by the fact that rising large-city teams tended to avoid the market in the transition period, leaving their falling counterparts to feed the rise or turnaround of small-city teams. Having lost their privileged

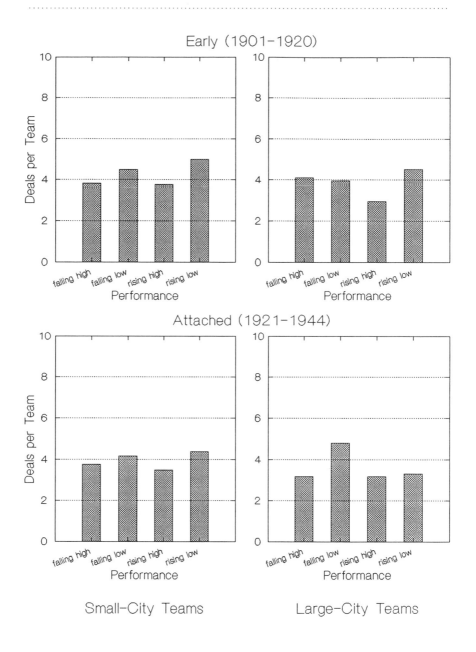

Early (1901–1920)

Attached (1921–1944)

Small–City Teams   Large–City Teams

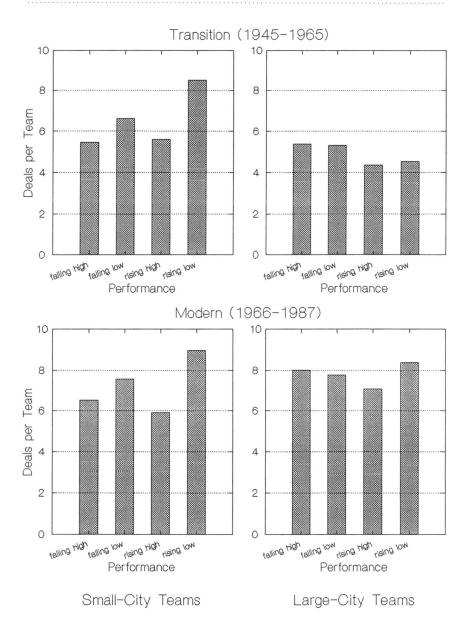

Figure 7.5 Average number of season deals for teams who rose or fell to their high (>.5) or low (≤.5) performance level in the season preceding deal making. Rising or falling was based on the performance difference between the preceding season and the one prior to it.

position on the field by the modern period, even rising winners among large-city teams had to engage in deals while, for the first time in the century, small-city teams remained more aloof.

Yet this neat picture of small-city teams somehow using deal making in the transition period to gain at least equal footing with large-city teams needs to be more closely and directly examined. First we need to look at which teams were actually dealing with each other. If large-city teams maintained their dominance in the first half of the century by purchasing talented players that surfaced on small-city teams, did the small-city teams seal themselves off from large-city teams in the transition period? The issue of who deals with whom can be approached in terms of relative team city size and relative performance levels in the season preceding the deals. Differences are used on both dimensions, and these are divided into three categories. For deals involving cash, the sender of cash can be from a larger, similar-sized, or smaller city than the receiver, and can be a better-, equal-, or worse-performing team.[11] With trades, senders and receivers cannot be distinguished, so not all combinations of these categories are distinct. For each distinct combination of these possibilities, we can observe how many of the possible partners in each joint category actually consummated a deal. Dividing the actual number of deals by the possible partnerships provides a useful measure of the kinds of teams that tend to deal with each other, although it is not a strict probability since a partnership could be activated more than once in a season.

Results for pure trades are shown in Figure 7.6. Trade partners can be either similar or different on the two dimensions of city size and preceding season performance. Where trading partners are different on both dimensions, the differences can be either positively (larger-better trading with smaller-worse) or negatively (larger-worse trading with smaller-better) correlated. Within these possibilities, striking changes occur over time. In the first period, some difference between partners is crucial for trades to occur. Trades are most likely when teams are different in both city size and performance, but here only when the differences reinforce each other. This is consistent with the argument that as teams were attaching to cities, patterns of deal making emerged that helped large-city teams maintain their dominance on the field. The pattern for deals involving cash, shown in Figure 7.7, provides further support. Larger-city teams are overall more likely to send cash for talent to smaller-city teams than vice versa, and here they are most likely to when the smaller team is also a worse performer. In cash deals as well as trades, similars on both dimensions are the least likely to deal.

Although the tendency for larger-city and better-performing teams to both trade with and purchase players from smaller-city and lesser-performing teams may have aided the ascendance of large-city teams, by the time this ascendance was achieved—in period two—the pattern of deals had changed somewhat. As was true in earlier analyses, transition periods reveal fundamental shifts that are often hidden when a situation stabilizes. By the second period, similarities between partners appear to facilitate trades, although deals are most likely when a difference remains on one of the two dimensions (with city size appearing slightly more important here). For cash deals, however, larger-city teams remain the more likely purchasers of players, although their purchases are most commonly from smaller teams that are performing better than they are. This is, of course, an anomalous possibility that presented itself almost half as often as the possibility for larger-better teams to deal with smaller-worse teams. Reciprocal purchases, from smaller-better teams to larger-worse teams, were the deals least likely to occur. It remains to be seen whether this very asymmetric flow of cash for players functioned to move the smaller-city teams back to a subordinate position in the competitive hierarchy.

Much evidence has already been offered for a revolt of the small and weak that largely characterizes the transition to the modern era. Figures 7.6 and 7.7 offer a more detailed glimpse into this revolt. Overall, trades became much more important. Differences reassert themselves somewhat as a basis for making trades, with performance differences appearing once again more important than city-size differences. But unlike in the first period, teams with negatively correlated differences are more likely to trade than teams with positively correlated differences. This puts them on a more equal footing in a trade. Smaller-city teams trading with larger-city teams are more likely to be better performers than their partners.

Cash deals reveal striking breaks with the past. For the first time, purchases of larger-city teams from smaller-city teams are no longer the most prevalent. Teams from similar-sized cities are most likely to transact cash deals, and hence these asymmetric exchanges can no longer function to sustain performance differences between large- and small-city teams. On the performance dimension, cash for players for the first time clearly and consistently flows from worse- to better-

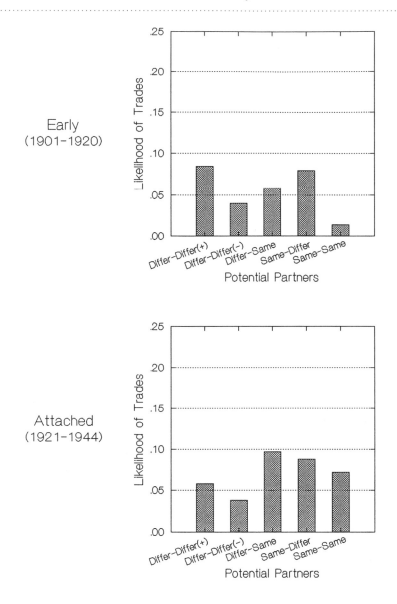

Early
(1901–1920)

Attached
(1921–1944)

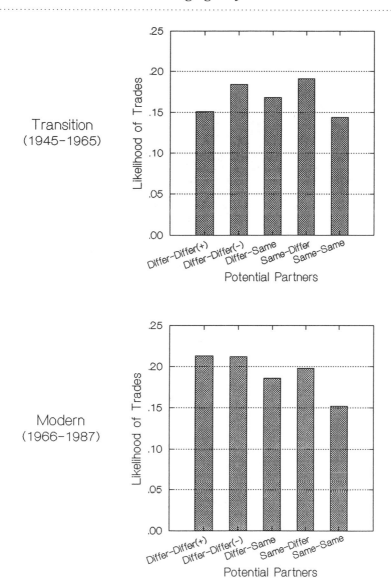

Figure 7.6 Tendencies for trades among Major League Baseball teams across four periods. Potential partners could be the same (within .4 standard deviations) or different in the size of their host cities (left of dash), and could be the same (within .05 in win proportions) or different in preceding season performance (right of dash). For teams different in both city size and performance, a distinction is made between larger-better teams trading with smaller-worse ones [Differ-Differ (+)] or larger-worse teams trading with smaller-better ones [Differ-Differ (−)]. Trading tendencies are the number of actual partnerings (counting multiple trades between teams) divided by the number of potential partners.

Early
(1901-1920)

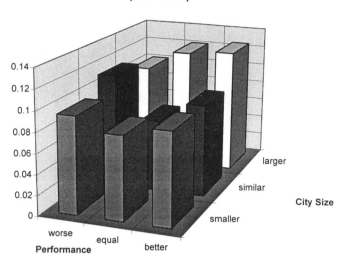

Attached
(1921-1944)

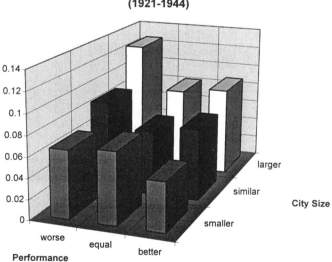

**Transition
(1945-1965)**

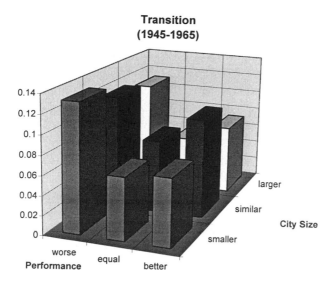

**Modern
(1966-1987)**

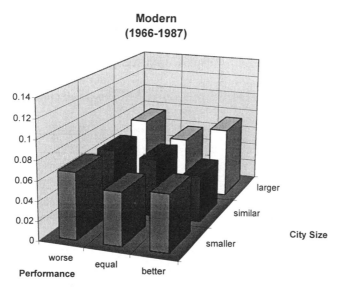

Figure 7.7   Tendencies for cash deals among Major League Baseball teams across four periods. Potential cash senders could be smaller, similar (within .4 standard deviations), or larger than cash receivers in host city size, and could be worse, equal (within .05 in win proportions), or better in preceding season performance. Tendencies are the number of actual partnerings (counting multiple cash deals between teams) divided by the number of potential partners.

performing teams. Interestingly, the single most likely possibility is for smaller, not similar-sized, city teams to purchase players from teams that are doing better than themselves. This marks a complete turn-around from the first period. It also appears to link directly the small-city rising low performers with the large-city falling high performers that both appeared in Figure 7.5. In addition, the overall heightened activity of lower performing teams was evident in Figure 7.4.

These qualitative changes seem essential for competitive balance to come about. Cash for talent had to stop flowing from large-city to small-city teams and start flowing from worse- to better-performing teams. Trades had to start occurring between teams on some kind of equal footing. By the time the modern era arrived, the clear strategies of the transition period had disappeared and a striking lack of pattern had settled in. Considering the high levels of trading in this period, there are very small differences among the possibilities. While similars on both dimensions clearly trade least, there is no difference between those with two positively or negatively correlated differences. Cash deals yield even less differentiation of deal makers. Overall, the level of cash deals is lower than in any other period. But even within their low levels, there are no substantial differences between any of the nine possibilities. The difference between the highest and lowest disposition to cash deal is only .027, compared with the .077, .078, and .054 of the prior periods. Hence, outside of a small tendency for teams to avoid trading with others just like themselves, in the modern era there is no pattern to deal making with respect to our two central dimensions. Teams buy, sell, and trade with each other largely irrespective of their city sizes or performance levels.

Further evidence for the decay of any ascribed hierarchy within Major League Baseball can be gleaned from free agency acquisitions. The rationale owners gave for resisting free agency was that rich large-city teams would use it to lure talent from poorer small-city teams through the offer of higher salaries. This rationale, however, is rooted in a by-gone era, when owners sent talent to larger cities through deals they cut among themselves. Analysis of the 211 free agent acquisitions between 1975 and 1987 reveals a higher incidence of smaller- to larger-city free agent acquisitions (.032 of possible partners) than vice versa (.028). Acquisitions among similar-sized cities had the lowest incidence (.021). With respect to performance, teams were least likely to acquire free agents from teams they were better than. If anything, it is the small and weak—now in appearance only—who make the free agent acquisitions.

As we look at who has engaged in deal making, a consistent theme emerges. Deal-making patterns that reinforced the domination of large-city teams before World War II began breaking down with the transition into the modern period. During this transition, however, large-city teams remained dominant in competition and successful in blocking regulatory changes that would undermine their position. Hence the revolt of the small and weak was a quiet revolution, evidenced only in shifting patterns of deal making. After the revolution, with entry into the modern period, who dealt with whom became largely independent of relative city sizes or performance levels among partners. Any team could deal with any other, at least with respect to city size and performance.

The Impact of Deal Making on Performance

If changes in the deal-making strategies of small and weak teams cannot be linked to prior changes in formal policies and immediate opportunities, can they at least be directly linked to performance improvement? In looking at the impact of deal making on performance, some caveats are necessary. First, we look only at the change in performance between the deal-making season and the season immediately following it.[12] To look further into the future would require controlling for too many intervening factors, including changes in deal-making strategies. Second, the average change in performance must be zero, because no matter how shrewd the deal makers or avoiders get, the number of wins must equal the number of losses.[13] Hence a "shrewd" strategy that improves performance must somewhere be counterbalanced by a strategy that in retrospect appears foolish, no matter how truly shrewd or foolish the deal makers may be. If all teams scrambled to adopt a "shrewd" strategy, then it would no longer appear shrewd. This may account for the disappearance of clear transition period strategies in moving into the early and modern forms the transitions help set up. A new strategy that triggers real change is quickly absorbed or evaded by those it unsettles. Finally, effects must be cast in terms of a regression to the mean since, if change occurs, high-performing teams can only fall and low-performing teams can only rise. Reducing or eliminating the regression to the mean serves high-performing teams well and low-performing teams quite poorly, as it keeps both in their place. The converse is true for enhancing the regression to the mean.

By graphing performance changes on past performance and overall deal making, we can observe the impact overall deal making has on the regression to the mean—the relation between past performance and performance change. Separate graphs were generated for smaller- and larger-city teams in each period. In addition, the different types of deal making were analyzed both separately and together. For each type, and the composite, the number of deals was rescaled so that the most active team each year was coded as 100.[14] In Figure 7.8, four graphs based on overall deal making are displayed to provide (using a quadratic smoothing function) a baseline for analysis of the effects of deal types.

Moving into and out of the player deal arena has had varied and sometimes perplexing effects on performance. In the first period, active deal making among smaller-city teams nearly eliminated the strong regression to the mean facing their deal-avoiding counterparts. When the deal types were viewed separately, purchases by smaller-city teams magnified the overall deal-making effect, while sales and trades weakened and eliminated it, respectively. Since there was some tendency toward low performance levels among active small-city purchasers, eliminating the regression to the mean was not a desirable outcome. Those most active in purchasing players were most likely to be held in their lowly place by their deal making. Active sellers of players were somewhat better performers, and hence disappointed by the persistence of the regression to the mean for themselves. Yet they tumbled no faster than those who refrained from player sales.

For larger-city teams, deal making had no effect on a mild regression to the mean experienced by all. This held for purchases, sales, and trades when examined separately, though for trades there was a slight rise in everyone's chances as trading activity increased. For the likely trading partners of better large-city teams with lesser small-city teams (see Figure 7.6), trades slightly thwarted decline for the large cities and helped keep the smaller cities in their lowly place. For likely partners in cash deals, however, no special impact was observed beyond the regressions to the mean experienced by nondealers alike. Thus there is no evidence, in period one, that cash deals held smaller-city teams in subordinate competitive positions (these positions did not materialize until the second period).

In the second period, overall deal making continued to eliminate a sizable regression to the mean for smaller-city teams. For larger-city teams, deal making began to moderate their mild regression to the mean. With larger-city teams increasingly coming to dominate in competition, these converging results for large and small indicate that deal making is helping to keep the large better and the small worse on the field. Curiously, for smaller-city teams, purchasing and selling players switched places in supporting the overall pattern, with player sales now eliminating the regression to the mean and purchases showing no effect at all (trades nearly eliminated the regression to the mean). For larger-city teams, both sales and purchases eliminated the regression to the mean while trades had no effect. In the most likely cash deal, a larger-city team purchasing players from a higher-performing smaller-city team, these patterns yield a puzzling outcome—the purchases do not help the larger-city team and do not hurt the smaller-city team, and hence do not function to rectify the anomalous situation of smaller-city teams performing better. With unequally performing larger- and smaller-city size teams no longer tending to trade, we cannot attribute the inequality between large- and small-city teams to this type of deal either.

Overall, deal making appears to reinforce inequalities between large- and small-city teams. Yet this effect cannot be traced to particular types of deals. We must remember that in isolating types of deals, we are leaving the other types free to vary.[15] Diverse kinds of overall deal-making strategies are possible even within the crude classification of types of deals. In the end, more detailed information on the deals themselves may prove essential to more fully account for the impact of deal making. Yet in moving toward the modern period, there are striking findings to be gleaned even at a crude level.

In terms of deal-making behaviors, the third period witnessed dramatic breaks with the past. Smaller-city and lesser-performing teams asserted themselves in deal making, moving into roles previously occupied only by their larger-city counterparts. Yet these newcomers did not achieve competitive equality until the fourth period. With respect to the third period transition, the short-term impact of their move into deal making was negative. Deal making had no effect on performance, for both overall deals and each isolated type. More perplexing, however, were the dismal improvement prospects for low-performing teams at all deal-making levels. Middling-performing teams had the best chances for improvement, with high-performing teams quickly re-

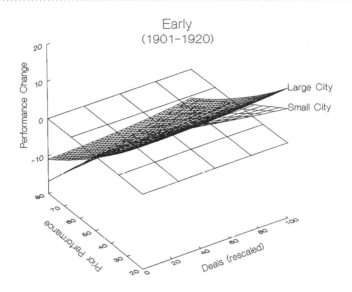

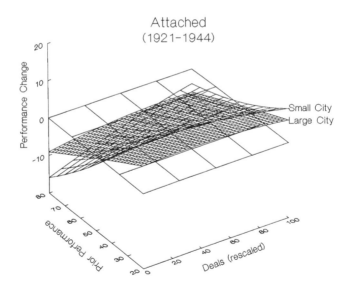

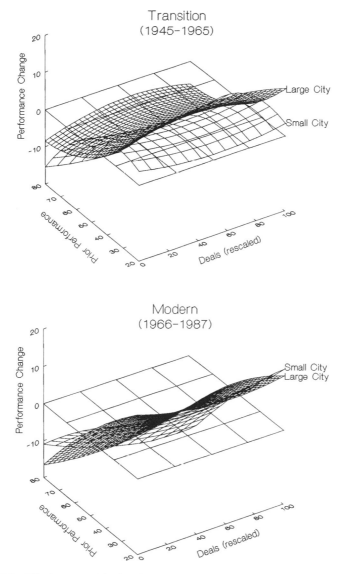

Figure 7.8 The impact of deal making on the next year's performance. Since high performers have less room to rise than fall, and conversely for low performers, performance change must be assessed relative to performance at the time of deal making. Deal making is scaled so that each season's most active deal maker had 100 deals. Quadratic functions are used to represent the impact of deal making, with the dense grid for teams from cities of above-median size and the sparser grid for teams from cities of below-median size. The sparsest grid represents the baseline of no impact.

gressing to the mean. Larger-city teams exhibited a more typical regression to the mean, though at moderate levels of deal making nearly all teams improved in performance—including the highest performers. Figure 7.9 reveals that these strange findings were at least partly due to a curvilinearity in the effect of city size.[16] The largest- and smallest-city teams are poorly served by deal making, and quite well served by refraining from it. Only middle-sized city teams at middling performance levels benefit from deal making.

These findings raise some perplexing problems. We saw earlier that falling large-city teams were more active deal makers than rising ones, whose restraint now appears quite prudent. Yet the actively dealing small-city teams with rising low performances seem only to be hurting themselves for their efforts. The only way to accommodate this finding is to invoke the long run. Although the observed shifts in deal-making strategy did nothing to improve performance immediately, they may have provided the foundation for gaining parity with large-city teams in the modern period. This would be the case if smaller cities went after young players with promising futures rather than star players facing future decline.

Modern period results are strikingly bland next to those of the transition period. Deal making slightly enhances a very mild regression to the mean for smaller-city teams. Hence it is most prudent for lower-performing teams to be active deal makers, because they stand to rise in performance quicker than their deal-avoiding counterparts. We have already seen the importance of performance in driving deal making in the modern period, especially among rising low performers, and the aloofness from deal making of rising high-performing small-city teams. Trading, now the predominant form of deal making, most sharply defines this composite result and shows high-performing teams to be especially hurt by engaging in trades. Selling players, by contrast, actually eliminates a mild regression to the mean and hence should appear attractive to high performers. Purchasing players has little effect, except for a very slight lift for moderation across the performance spectrum.

For larger-city teams, deal making mildly suppresses a moderate regression to the mean. This fact should make it most attractive to higher-performing teams, yet this is not a source of advantage that large-city teams have clearly pursued (though they are much less likely to let low performance be a catalyst for deal making). Player sales and purchases most sharply define this overall prescription, with trades actually sharp-

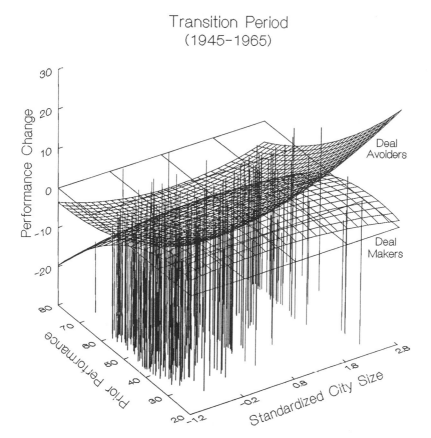

Figure 7.9 Another view of the transition period. Standardized city size is allowed to vary continuously, and deal making is dichotomized. Quadratic functions were used to fit less active (small grid) and more active (large grid) deal makers.

ening a mild regression to the mean. Here the results for large and small teams are quite similar, and hence should eventually produce a convergence in their deal-making strategies with the increasing predominance of trades. Engaging in trades enhances the circulation of winners and losers.

It is easy to be disappointed in the performance impact results. Yet clearer results would themselves raise problems. They would imply yearly changes in deal-making strategies as teams moved around in performance space. They would also rest on the willingness of some teams to engage in deals that harm their performance. Like the stock market, the arena of player deals is more likely sustained by the uncertainties that make false hopes possible. For many teams and in many periods, staying away from player deals altogether is the best way to improve performance. Less dramatic efforts put into player development are often much more prudent for long-term success. The arena of player deals serves a theatric purpose, not only in maintaining fan involvement outside the regular season but also in signaling the ambitions of owners among themselves. What comes from their dramatic performances, in terms of one season's performance change, may be at least partly incidental to the show.

To probe further, two exemplary teams were selected for more detailed examination. Both the New York Yankees and the Oakland A's have been immensely successful, the first as a large-city team in a period of large-city domination and the second as a small-city team in the modern period, where any team could pursue a winner role. The role of deal making in building and maintaining winning teams is quite different, however, across teams and periods (see Figure 7.10). During the 1915 season the Yankees purchased six players, including Dazzy Vance, Ensign Cottrell, and Bob Shawkey in addition to the three they acquired on waivers (not counted in Figure 7.10), and continued to rely mainly on purchases in the years preceding their dynasty. The main recipients of Yankee cash were teams in smaller cities like Pittsburgh, St. Louis, Cincinnati, and Boston, whose Red Sox sold Babe Ruth in 1920 for $125,000 and a $300,000 loan. Once their dynasty was in place, however, the Yankees largely withdrew from deal making, relying instead upon their extensive farm system for players. Until the 1940s, they jumped back in only during dips in performance, mainly to sell players.

As the Yankees moved into the transition period, both their perfor-

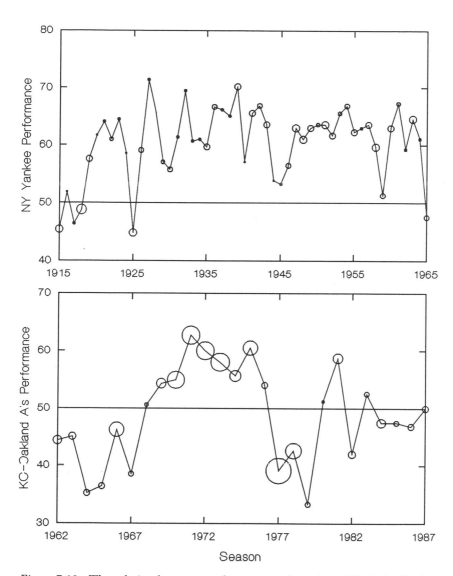

Figure 7.10 The relation between performance and number of deals for the dynasty period of the large-city New York Yankees and the modern triumphs of the small-city Oakland Athletics (who moved from Kansas City in 1968). Performances across time are graphed for each team, with the number of deals represented by the size of the circles.

mance and their deal making stabilized. They shifted from sales to trades, at modest levels relative to period averages, and maintained consistently high performance. There is little in Figure 7.10 that can account for the collapse of the Yankee dynasty in 1965. For this we would have to look at the deterioration of their farm system, which occurred with the general decline of the minor leagues, and at the other league developments that made it possible for smaller cities like Oakland to field winning teams.

Unlike the early Yankees, Oakland relied heavily on deal making in both its rises and its declines. After moving out of Kansas City after their 1967 season, the A's turned to trades to build a team that won three consecutive World Series (1972–1974). A strong correlation between the team's sales and purchases meant that these deals functioned as trades, with players sold helping to pay for players purchased. Oakland becomes an outlier to our overall results, however, insofar as it continues actively trading after achieving performance success. Performance success appears to ride directly on trading activity, waning when the team owner, Finley, slowed down in 1976 and collapsing when Finley opened his "meat market" for players in 1977.[17] This pattern certainly supports his reputation for trading acumen. With Finley's mounting health problems and the advent of free agency, Finley's magic sputtered out as the team entered the 1980s. No longer could Finley keep his players fired up with the threat, or for some the promise, of being traded.

Pursuing Opportunities

The results in this chapter apply at the level of tendencies. Buried in the deviations from these tendencies are colorful personalities who defied, sometimes for long periods, the logic of opportunities spelled out above. Pittsburgh's wealthy owner Barney Dreyfuss shelled out a great deal of cash to field a winning team for his relatively small local public in the 1920s and 1930s. He defied the odds, winning two pennants and finishing second twice. Most sports books focus exclusively on notable exceptions, ignoring the subtler pressures that eventually may rein in the most forceful personalities. Although virtually all rich owners enter sports with the intention of fielding a winner and hence garnering much favorable publicity for themselves and their home city, few remain willing, especially after several losing seasons, to squander their entire fortune on pursuing this aim.

Owners, for the most part, have operated within the constraints defined by the opportunities they have faced. When opportunities for support were defined in terms of local publics, smaller-city teams facing limited opportunities seldom tried to outspend larger-city teams in the pursuit of established talent. Low performance was not a strong catalyst for deal making of any kind. Mostly resigned to their disadvantaged position, smaller-city teams were content to cultivate their own talent and, when markedly successful, to sell it off to larger-city teams for needed cash. These deal-making relations between small- and large-city teams functioned to reinforce the dominance of the latter both on and off the field. Resisting this dominance was costly and, for the most part, foolish, as small-city publics could not long support the salary demands of winning teams—if they could be fielded at all. When opportunities were defined in terms of national publics, however, smaller-city teams found themselves facing opportunities more similar to those of large-city teams. Deal-making strategies of small- and large-city teams converged. Performance became the central instigator of deal making, as every team struggled to reach a national public through winning.

This simple accounting, however, ignores the central problem of change. Intervening between owners and opportunities is league organization. National publics did not appear from nowhere, but had to be first envisioned and then actively pursued. The NFL largely created national publics through its innovative television policy. Major League Baseball, however—by allowing individual teams to build up local and regional television networks that simply tapped local publics more fully—for a long time used television merely to reinforce the dominance of large-city teams. To create a national public, change had to occur in the organization of the owners. Somehow, small-city owners had to be first empowered to usher in the informal ambitions and formal policies that only later secured their equal standing.

Much of the NFL's modern success has been attributed to its early failure to develop large-city dominance and to the forceful leadership of Pete Rozelle in uncovering new opportunities. As Major League Baseball entered the television age, however, it was hampered by large-city dominance and weak leadership. The findings here indicate that change came from the bottom, through the growing ambitions (that is, heightened deal making) of small city–low performing teams. There is nothing in the immediate context of these teams that would give encouragement to these ambitions. Large cities dominated Major League

Baseball throughout the transition period (1945–1965), a situation that formal policies only reinforced. Nor were small-city ambitions rewarded on the field, as the heightened deal making if anything had deleterious effects on season performance. The growing ambitions of small- and second-city teams could only have been based on folly, or on a bold gamble on the future.

Major League Baseball's leadership and dominant teams were remarkably successful in resisting change. In the midst of flagging fan interest, an impending soccer invasion of the summer, and escalating subsidization of the minor leagues, Major League Baseball was finally jolted by the startling success of the NFL under the strong leadership of Rozelle. Only after the NFL defined the new opportunities for national publics and the organization needed to pursue them did Major League Baseball in 1965 tentatively set out on the course chartered by the NFL. Small-city teams stood ready to assume a new role, having been in preparation for almost twenty years. Over the next decade, teams from three smaller major league cities, Baltimore, Minneapolis, and Oakland, made regular appearances in the World Series.

In this more complex accounting, opportunities determine what kind of organization works best, but some inexplicable (at the time) organizational change is needed to realize new opportunities. Similarly, organizational power relations determine patterns of deal making, but prescient deal makers can deviate in starting early to maneuver for an improved position in a changed organization that will pursue new opportunities. Vision is essential, but this can easily appear as folly if organization and opportunities do not change. League organization is locked in place, and hence makes contexts strongly felt, when opportunities, organization, and deal making serve to reinforce each other. For context to be determinative, however, it must at times be capable of being changed. The more it can be adjusted to energize still other contexts, the more constraining it will appear.

Currently, Major League Baseball is in the midst of a new transformation. Network television has been increasingly upstaged since the mid-1980s by an array of cable, satellite television, and pay-per-view options. These rivals threaten to dismantle the national public formed around network television into a patchwork of local publics, based more on subscription patterns than on city residence. As the networks recede, the power of the commissioner is undermined. The 1992 firing of Commissioner Fay Vincent, and talk of dropping the position altogether, is reminiscent of 1919. But large-city team owners will not necessarily move into the power vacuum this time. Owners like Ted Turner use their own broadcasting systems (TBS and TNT) to pipe Atlanta Brave games to remote locations, and have built fan constituencies larger than some of those for large-city teams. Without the leverage provided by the networks, any new commissioner faces a daunting challenge in reining in so many ambitious owners.

8

• • •

Publics and Performance

From commissioner to commoner, everyone involved in major league sports has an interest in team performance. Sports enthusiasts track the standing of teams in pennant races much as investors track prices in markets. In the league office, more abstract features, like the competitive balance, or the tightness of pennant races, are monitored. Throughout this book, I have credited the degree of competitive balance to the way owners are organized into leagues. Before leagues appeared, competitive balance was a matter for extemporizing only, in isolated games or matches. Leagues introduced the careful selection and regulation of teams in extending competitive balance to whole sets of teams engaged in prolonged pennant races. But competitive balance was constrained by the need for large cities to field the strongest teams. It was not until the modern era of televised sports that complete competitive balance could be pursued in earnest. Past chapters have charted the long and difficult journey of major leagues toward this end.

Missing from the account, however, has been a role for publics in shaping the performance of teams. The profits and publicity gained from sports publics have, of course, been central to the way owners have organized into leagues. It was the uneven size of local publics that led to the dominance of large-city teams in early leagues. And it was the ability of a national television public to follow competition anywhere that ultimately decreased the importance of where winners were located, paving the way for real competitive balance. But it is not merely for the benefit of owners that publics exist. In focusing so intently on major league competition, they too play a part in shaping its course.

This chapter examines the impact of publics on performance. As with the owners, the impact is linked to how publics are organized.

As city dwellers began providing ongoing support for local teams in early leagues, teams were able to settle down and play half their games in the same home location. The resulting regularity with which broad spectrums of city populations were mobilized turned emerging cities into local publics, or markets for the owners. But local publics did more than provide revenue. They helped their teams win, in what has been called the "home advantage." If the impact of a partisan local public were uniform across teams, it would serve as a leveler of performance, helping each team win the half of its games played at home and hurting its chances in the half played away. In the extreme case of an absolute home advantage, each team would win (and lose) exactly half its games. Thus the attachment of teams to cities could have put cross-pressures on competition. Unevenly sized local markets gave large-city team owners an edge in fielding the strongest teams, but the uniformly partisan loyalty of local publics in every city may have worked to level season performances across cities. Both pressures flow from the successful attachment of teams to cities, and together may help account for the peculiar combination of large-city dominance and low performance inequality in the prototype for early leagues.

In the modern era of televised sport, both the major leagues and publics were reorganized along much different lines. Instead of following a local team only, the sports enthusiast was encouraged to follow leaguewide competition. That way, a single broadcast could attract a national audience as opposed to merely the local followings of the two engaged teams. As this audience developed and came to be regularly activated, the disparate sports enthusiasts combined into a national public that constituted a vast new market for owners. Unlike local publics, national publics are not partisan in nature. They are driven by expectations, as they scour league competition in search of winners to celebrate. Not particularly loyal to any team, they are constantly shifting in their momentary attentions. National publics stand ready to converge en masse on any team that happens to be doing better at the moment. The potential for converging gives them tremendous power.

In casting their attention toward winners and away from losers, national publics may actually function to stabilize these performance roles. Expectations that a team will win (or lose) may actually increase its chances of winning (or losing). As winning and losing become self-perpetuating, performance inequality increases over what it would otherwise be. If this is the case, a reverse cross-pressure would exist. While early leagues reinforced large-city dominance in cultivating local publics that then leveled performances, modern leagues pursue competitive balance in cultivating national publics that then induce performance inequality. The more successful modern major leagues have been, the more national publics have had to search throughout the league for winners to mobilize behind. Because the national television public can follow competition anywhere, it has become less important where winners (and losers) are located. In modern times, the ordering between team performance and host population size has largely disappeared. But even in the modern prototype of the NFL, performance inequality has persisted. Can the modern cross-pressure account for this persistence, as an instance of performance inequality among competitive equals?

In this chapter we explore the distinct cross-pressures that flow from local and national publics. This task is complicated by the fact that existing major leagues cater to a mix of local and national publics. And the distinct effects of local and national publics can flow largely from the same set of fans. Games are still played out before partisan crowds who support the home team. Yet the people in the stadium and at home increasingly follow leaguewide competition and hold strong nonpartisan expectations regarding who is likely to win, and these sentiments undoubtedly influence their behavior toward the contending teams. In short, much needs to be disentangled to isolate the performance effects of local and national publics.

At any given time, the four major league sports have differed substantially in the type of publics they attracted for regular season games. In the 1980 regular season, used in this chapter for in-depth analysis, opportunities for national publics peaked as network sports broadcasting was never stronger. The National Football League was the most successful in cultivating a national public, with almost 70 percent of team revenues coming from equally shared national broadcast revenues. At the other extreme, the National Hockey League, operating without a network contract, depended almost entirely on gate receipts and local broadcast rights. Major League Baseball uneasily straddled local and national publics, with a season that produced too many games and owners who produced too many local broadcasts for the networks to eagerly pursue national broadcasts. The National Basketball Association attracted only limited network attention for the 1980 regular season. The performance effects of publics should vary corresponding to the pronounced differences in the way publics are organized across the major league sports.

No Place Like Home

The home advantage is a starting point for exploring the impact of publics on competition. It is certainly the clearest evidence that publics have an impact. In this chapter, the home advantage is treated as the effect of partisan local publics (the partisan effect). In the modern era, local publics are diminishing in importance as major leagues pursue the modern (and now the future) prototype. One way to see that national publics have introduced a new dynamic is to connect them, as I will do, to the dampening of the partisan effect. In some situations, the partisan effect disappears entirely. We will also see that relative past performance levels, as the basis for expectations among the national public, become a better predictor of game outcomes where this publics has an impact on performance (the expectations effect). In short, the home advantage serves as a starting point, or baseline, in searching for the impact of national publics.

There is abundant evidence for the home advantage. In accounting for game outcomes in the major leagues, the *Chicago Tribune* made more references to home or away location than to such factors as talent, injuries, and momentum (Edwards 1979). The actual magnitude of the home advantage (home-win proportion minus away-win proportion) has been calculated for a variety of sports settings. Using a composite of prior studies, Kerry Courneya and Albert Carron (1992) calculated the home-win percentage and home advantage for four sports (using college and professional versions). Their results correspond closely to the major league results I calculated (see Table 8.1).

The sports vary dramatically in overall home advantage levels. Within each sport, the home advantage varies across teams inversely with season lengths, as might be expected from the greater sensitivity of performance to chance fluctuations in short seasons. Figure 8.1 provides a graphic display of the home- and away-win proportions for each season of every major league team. As the difference between home- and away-win proportions, the home advantage is the distance below the diagonal line. In hockey and, especially, in basketball, it is rare that

Table 8.1   Home advantage levels found in a composite of past studies and in the present study

Composite home advantage results[a]			
Sport	Studies	Games	Home-win percentage	Home advantage
Baseball	6	23,034	53.5	.070
Football	5	2,592	57.3	.146
Hockey	4	4,322	61.1	.222
Basketball	8	13,596	64.4	.288

Results for extant U.S. major leagues[b]			
Sport (seasons)	Team-seasons	Standard deviation	Home advantage
Baseball (1901–90)	1,672	.084	.085
Football (1960–90)	808	.232	.124
Hockey (1917–89)	671	.117	.196
Basketball (1949–89)	636	.129	.290

a. Courneya and Carron (1992).
b. Author's calculations.

a team will win a higher proportion of games on the road than it does at home. It is also clear that the home advantage can, and does, assume the greatest range the closer a team moves to a middling level of overall performance.

As Barry Schwartz and S. F. Barsky (1977) originally observed, the home advantage is strongest in the indoor sports of hockey and basketball, where partisan crowd support can be most intense. Of the two predominantly outdoor sports, the stronger home advantage of football seems consistent with its larger and more enveloping crowds. When major league football teams (1960–1990) have domed stadiums, the home advantage is .147 compared with .121 for teams with open stadiums. For Major League Baseball, R. A. Zeller and T. Jurkovac (1988) found a home advantage of .105 for teams with domed stadiums compared with .072 for teams with open stadiums, although I found only .089 versus .077 using a longer time frame (from the first domed stadium in 1965 to 1990). To pursue the apparent importance of partisan crowd intensity further, actual crowd size and behavior must be examined. But first, several less cumbersome possibilities should be ruled out.

Many efforts have been made to explain away the home advantage in terms that do not directly involve characteristics of partisan local publics. Travel fatigue among away teams is an obvious possibility, yet it fails on close examination. With 162 games played in less than six months, travel fatigue should be greatest in baseball. Yet the home advantage is weakest in that sport. Even within (minor league) baseball, Courneya and Carron (1991), in a detailed statistical examination of direct indicators of travel fatigue (length of visitor's road trip, length of home stand, series game number, and season game number), found no consistent evidence that travel is a major contributing factor to the home advantage. The same authors (1990) also eliminate a second possibility based on the notion that rules such as the home team's right to bat last confer an advantage. A learning factor, which traces the home advantage to the home team's superior knowledge of the local facilities and conditions, has fared little better (Pollard 1986). Baseball stadiums are among the least standardized of all playing arenas, with different turfs, playing field sizes, wall heights, and local weather conditions. Yet the home advantage is lowest in baseball.

Perhaps the most cynical way to explain away the home advantage would be to invoke the ancient practice of hippodroming. One could posit that teams who play each other more than once in a season have simply agreed to take turns winning before their home crowds. This would produce an extreme home advantage effect if practiced pervasively. Unfortunately, owing to the scheduling complexities in baseball, basketball, and hockey, which make it difficult to isolate pairs of home and away encounters, only football is amenable to a clear test of the hippodroming hypothesis. In the NFL, division teams play each other twice a season, once at home and once away. These paired encounters can be compared with the baseline of single encounters with nondivision teams (see Figure 8.2). No significant difference appears in the home-win proportions of single and paired encounters. As is evident from the quadratic fitting functions used to discern tendencies in the observations, paired encounters exhibit slightly less home advantage than single encounters.

It might be argued that a hippodroming agreement is no simple matter, given that enforcement would be highly problematic. Such agreements, if publicly exposed, would thoroughly undermine the integrity of a league. One might argue that if hippodroming could occur at all, it would have to be carried out across games that took place close

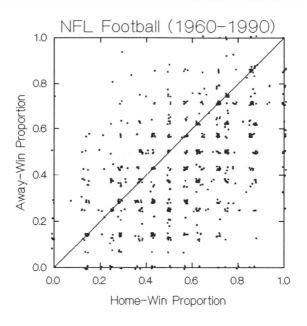

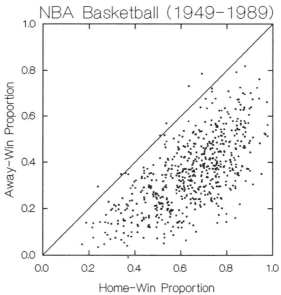

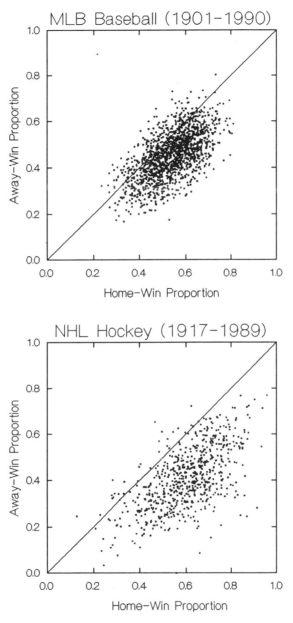

Figure 8.1 Variation in home advantage across teams and sports. A team's home advantage is the distance below the diagonal, or the difference between season home- and away-win proportions. Random noise was used in football to reduce exact overlap in observations.

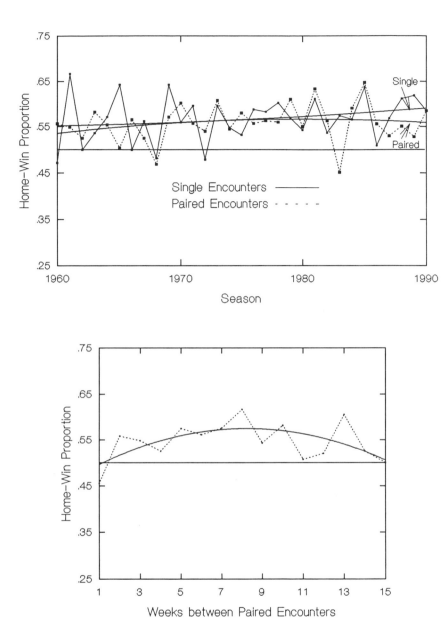

Figure 8.2 A test for hippodroming in football (National Football League and American Football League). Home-win proportions for single encounters (solid line) and paired encounters (dotted line) are compared. Paired encounters occur when two teams play twice during a season, once at each's home stadium, and offer the opportunity to exchange victories. Exchanges would be easiest to implement if games were close together in the season. In the bottom panel, the consequences of the number of weeks between paired encounters for home-win proportions are shown.

together in the season. Among the many corrosive effects of time, changes in league standing from the time of the agreement might be the most serious. A team that has since moved into contention for a pennant title is most likely to renege on its agreement to lose a game. The bottom panel in Figure 8.2 explores the effect of time between paired encounters, and we find that teams playing each other on adjacent weeks are actually more likely to win on the road than at home. There is, in sum, no evidence whatsoever of any hippodroming in the NFL.[1]

Using partisan crowd intensity to account for the home advantage is, however, no simple matter. Local publics are highly reactive, and fully capable of exerting multiple and not always consistent effects. Efforts to focus on a single dimension, such as crowd density, have failed to produce clear results across studies. Schwartz and Barsky (1977) found that home-win proportions increased from 48 percent when less than 20 percent of the stadium was filled to 57 percent when more than 40 percent was filled in Major League Baseball, although these overall effects varied depending on the prior performance levels of the teams. Smaller crowds turn out when there is a low expectation of winning, and hence may not have anything to do with the lesser performances associated with them. J. Dowie (1982) and R. Pollard (1986) failed to find any effect for crowd density in the English Football League.

J. Thirer and M. S. Rampey (1979) and Donald Greer (1983) studied the effects of spectator behavior on performance in college basketball games. Thirer and Rampey found that antisocial behavior, such as shouting obscenities and throwing objects on the court, negatively affected the home team more than the away team by inciting "dysfunctional aggression" by home players. Greer focused on sustained, but not antisocial, protest among spectators, analyzing the effect of such instances on a number of performance measures. Using observations from two enthusiastically supported college teams, he found that episodes of spectator protest were related to an increase in the performance advantage enjoyed by home teams. These findings support a "social reinforcement" theory, in which audience behavior interacts with task performance, rather than audiences having an effect merely by being present. Because much of the spectator protest was directed at referees, at least some of the home advantage may have been due to referee intimidation by the home crowd.

E. J. McGuire and colleagues (1992) introduce the reverse causal direction in their study of aggression in 840 hockey games. Finding that high levels of player aggression (measured in terms of penalties) boost the winning chances of the home team, they suggest that aggression is used to entice the crowd into more active involvement, from which the home team benefits. Away teams struggle to leave the home crowd out of the game by checking the escalation of aggression. Since aggressive penalties are remarkably balanced between home and away teams, game outcomes are significantly affected by the strategic struggle over mutual aggression levels.[2] This intriguing finding might help account for the across-sport usefulness of crowd intensity in explaining overall home advantage differences and the within-sport difficulties in linking crowd density to home advantage. Crowds of varying size may or may not produce an effect, depending on the dynamics of the competition on the field.

Crowd size, intensity, and support matter, and matter differently for pairs of teams at different performance levels. To make additional inroads, we must recognize that the partisan effect represented by the home advantage emerges from the interaction of three sides (two competitors and a public), and cannot be understood in terms of the attributes of each side viewed separately. Much effort has been wasted, for example, in trying to resolve whether the home team performs better or the away team performs worse before a partisan home crowd. Schwartz and Barsky (1977) look at both defensive and offensive performance measures in Major League Baseball (such as errors, double plays, runs per at bat) and, after finding that the home team had higher levels on offensive performance measures, claim that the partisan effect inheres exclusively in offensive superiority. John Andrew (1984) looked at five performance measures in Atlantic Conference basketball and found that significant differences existed between home and away performance measures in each measure except free throw percentage. Coaches' "expected" performance levels were then used to determine whether the observed measures were high at home or just low away, with support for the latter claimed.

These efforts ignore crucial interdependencies in the sports setting. One team's win is another's loss. A great defensive performance is facilitated by a poor offensive one, and vice versa. It is impossible to get two pieces of information out of a single performance measure in trying to determine how "good" each side was in producing it. Instead, publics should be thought of as affecting the nature of the competition between teams rather than their individual playing qualities. Publics don't make teams better or worse; rather, they alter the framework in which competition is interpreted and in so doing affect the course of competition itself. This allows the game to be the most basic unit, rather than teams, and allows a clear separation of the partisan effect from the playing qualities of teams. With this change of imagery, it becomes meaningless to ask which team is affected by a public. Competition is affected.

The interpretive framework imposed on competition depends on how publics are organized. Local publics are intrinsically partisan. Instead of seeking to identify winners and losers, local publics show up at games to provide support for the home team. One often hears a sense of guilt expressed by partisan fans if they fail to watch or attend a game involving "their" team, as if their absence could somehow be responsible for the team's loss. Like foot soldiers behind a mounted commander, the support they provide is part of their team's strength. And a loss is part of their own failings. Hence local publics actively seek to help the home team and hinder the away team in pursuing the opportunity and rewards of winning. Local publics encourage, distract, cheer, and ignore in a highly deliberate manner, and should this fail, they communicate only disappointment at the victory of an away team.

National publics are intrinsically not partisan. They approach games with expectations regarding outcomes based on the past performances of the teams engaged. Actual outcomes reshape these expectations, and therefore a strong team that happens to lose no longer appears as strong. Although national publics have memories, so that a single loss does not outweigh a whole string of past victories, the memories are not particularly long. With the resetting of performance records each season, a few early season wins can raise expectations despite many past seasons of poor performance. The national public is not averse to abandoning a team that does not live up to its expectations. To maintain a national public, a team must win consistently.

The importance of winning is reflected in the way contending teams are selected for network television broadcasts. In the forty-six network-televised NFL games in 1991 (plus eleven on ESPN cable television), one team (the Los Angeles Raiders) appeared eleven times while four teams (including the large-city New York Jets) appeared only once. Winning proved central in accounting for these inequities. In Figure 8.3 the number of nationally televised 1991 games for each NFL team is plotted over the team's 1990 season performance. Prior season per-

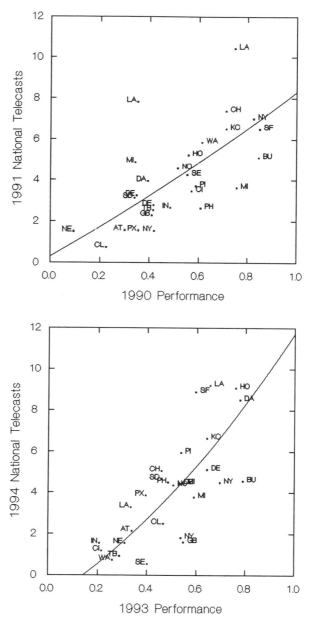

Figure 8.3 Relation between the number of nationally televised games scheduled for National Football League teams and their prior season performance. Random noise was introduced to scatter overlapping observations.

formance accounts for 43 percent of the variation in nationally televised games, with much of the unexplained variation attributable to the two Los Angeles teams. Interestingly, pre-1990 performance accounts for little additional variation. Performance in 1989 accounts for only 1 percent more variation, and average performance across the 1980s accounts for only 6 percent more variation. National publics have short memories and are unforgiving, at least in the assessment of league schedulers. Poor performance in the prior season is sufficient to bury a team from national public view. Denver, for example, outperformed the Raiders in the 1980s (.596 versus .592), yet its poor (5–11) 1990 showing earned it only four nationally televised games for 1991. Kansas City averaged only .425 for the 1980s, but a strong (11–5) 1990 showing earned it seven nationally televised games for 1991. While some teams, like the Los Angeles Rams (averaging .561 for the 1980s), can linger in the national limelight beyond what can be justified on past season performance grounds alone, winning is generally the basis for national exposure. Three seasons later, this conclusion received even stronger support, as is shown in the bottom panel of Figure 8.3. Los Angeles no longer received preferential treatment, and Houston and Dallas had earned a place in the national spotlight (though Buffalo remained underexposed).

Winning teams with national exposure are familiar wherever they play. The people who come see them play away games may be nominally part of a local public, but they may also be as familiar with the away team as with the home team. Although they may express a desire for the home team to win, they also hold more detached expectations regarding which team is actually likely to win.[3] A familiarity with leaguewide competition erodes the sharp distinction between home and away teams and confuses the simple partisanship of purely local publics. Once a home crowd can expect an away team to win, and admire its prowess in doing so, the home crowd ceases to be part of the strength of the home team. As part of a national public, people who show up at (or write about) games do so as part of a broader activity of following (and not intentionally shaping) leaguewide competition; they stand willing to recognize and acknowledge a winner wherever it may come from (within the closed circuit of a major league).

National publics closely monitor competition for signs of superiority among competitors. They may pick up perceived signs before the competitors themselves are aware of them, and hence put pressure on competitors to assume winner and loser roles within a game or pennant race that might not emerge otherwise. Timing is crucial here, given that stepping into a winner role before it is conferred is strategically unsound. Long ago, Clausewitz (1976 [1826]) analyzed the weakness of assuming the aggressor role in the absence of superior strength. Before the aggressor-defender roles that lead to winning and losing are assumed, teams must engage in probes and subtle ploys that can themselves conceal opportunities for clear action. Here national publics can play a decisive part in disrupting the stable equilibrium of balance, by latching onto apparent inequalities and convincing both sides of their reality. Under pressures from national publics, the subtle actions of competitive equals can give way to actions appropriate to a winner and loser.[4]

National publics have made the interpretive context of sporting competition relentlessly zero-sum, where winning and losing, and winner and loser, are sharply counterposed. Every play, every game, every series is used to sort and re-sort teams into winner and loser roles. Although teams have built into them all the painstaking league efforts to ensure competitive balance, they leave every game a winner or a loser (where no ties are possible), and hence much different. A bit of chance, like a favorable gust of wind or a lucky bounce, is enough to make two similar teams very different. In the winning locker room after a game it is completely forgotten that only minutes earlier either team could have won. The superiority that gets imposed on the winning team is the public's (including sportscasters' and writers') doing, and need not be based on any underlying reality at the moment it is generated.

A zero-sum interpretive context is something that must be imposed on competition and is by no means intrinsic, as it might sometimes seem in current sports. One alternative is reflected in the belief that it is not whether you win or lose that matters, but how you play the game. Here a well-played game is a gain for everyone. In times and places where local publics predominated, it was the show of support that was as important as the winning and losing, and a home team loss was hardly seen as a gain for the away team. Or imagine a much different world where fans appreciated, rather than undermined, the competitive balance of teams, getting enjoyment out of the delicate balance maintained by evenly matched teams. The events that would lead to the breakdown of this balance, that would produce a winner and loser, would be viewed as flaws that disrupted the delicate coordination and would evoke disappointment rather than cheers. In this world, public pressure would be directed toward suppressing the emergence of winners and losers, as both would be equated with failure. If we look at what sports enthusiasts actually do, this alternative world is not so strange. Enthusiasts are quick to leave sporting contests early, or to cease following pennant races, when the delicate balance is broken, whether the team they have supported is winning or losing. Their insistence on finding winners and losers only remains viable if leagues work hard to maintain a competitive balance. Far from being natural, the zero-sum context sports publics impose on competition is antithetical, and hence at cross-purposes, to the basis on which competition is organized.

In this scenario, the interpretive context affects competition and not the intrinsic abilities of either home or away teams. Just how it will affect competition in existing major leagues will depend on the interpretive context that prevails. We have seen that a mixture of national and local publics exists in every sport, with NFL football leading and NHL hockey trailing furthest behind in cultivating national publics. Anywhere local publics remain, however, their impact in the form of a partisan effect should be clearest when contending teams have failed to differentiate themselves in past performance so no clear expectations can cast a shadow over competition. Accordingly, the impact of national publics is most likely to be found where there are large differences in past performance between contenders, because here strong expectations may undermine any partisan effect. In the next section, performance boxes are used to examine nonuniformities in the home advantage across pairings of teams with all possible combinations of past performance. These allow us to disentangle the distinct impacts of local and national publics on competition, so that we can then explore the longer-term consequences of these publics for performance inequalities.

Game Outcomes

Game level attendance and outcome data were gathered for the 1980 regular season in Major League Baseball (2,092 games), the NBA (942 games), and the NHL (836 games), and, because of the short season, the 1974–80 seasons for the NFL (1,428 games). The 1980 season was selected because it was not disrupted by labor disputes in any of the sports. It also fell during the pinnacle of network domination of sport broadcasting, before the explosion of cable, satellite, and pay-per-view options that has since muddied the distinction between local and national publics. Overall, the home advantage was .078 for baseball, .136 for football, .192 for hockey, and .236 for basketball, making the 1980 season reflective of the long-term differences among the sports observed earlier.

Game outcomes were used to compute a running measure of performance that corresponds to season standings given in newspapers, from which fans follow the progress of teams throughout the sport season. Game attendances (reported in the *Los Angeles Times*) were used to compute crowd densities, or the proportion of stadiums or arenas that were filled for each game.[5] To assess the role of performance for mobilizing crowds, the particularities of each sport loom large. Baseball teams play eighty-one home games a season, during days and evenings of every day of the week. Even the most enthusiastic followers must be selective in the games they attend. At the opposite extreme, football teams play only eight home games a season, almost all conveniently scheduled on Sundays. Football can often fill stadiums with season ticket holders who commit themselves before the season even begins. To complicate matters, baseball and football teams sometimes share the same stadium, as do basketball and hockey teams, so that stadium capacities often bear little relation to actual ticket demand.

In Table 8.2, average crowd densities and attendance figures are given for each sport. From these figures alone, it can be expected that football and hockey will show less sensitivity to variations in performance than will basketball and particularly baseball, because stadium size sharply limits the number of people that might otherwise attend games. Despite these caveats, home crowds remain sensitive to performance in every sport, as is evident in Figure 8.4. Categories in Figure

Table 8.2 Average attendances and crowd densities for the four major league sports

Sport (season)	Crowd density	Attendance	Games (missing)[a]
Football (1974–80)	.822	54,152	1,423 (5)
Baseball (1980)	.414	21,596	2,086 (6)
Basketball (1980)	.619	10,005	941 (1)
Hockey (1980)	.840	13,445	834 (2)

a. Season games for which no attendance figure could be found.

8.4 are defined by the relation between the performance levels of home and away teams at the time of the game. From the lower left to the upper right of each performance box lie contests in which home and away teams had similar performance levels, and hence no clear expectations regarding the outcome were possible. Crowd densities were the highest where both home and away teams were high performers (upper-right corner), in every sport. As overall performance levels decline (lower-left corner), similarity ceases to attract large crowds relative to overall sport averages. In general, the size of crowds is more sensitive to home-team performance levels than away-team levels, as evidenced from the higher densities in lower-right cells than in upper-left cells. Proportions of sellouts (density greater than .98) are given in brackets. These are mostly consistent with crowd density figures.[6]

Some of the averages in Figure 8.4 are based on a relatively small number of games. To confirm the overall conclusions regarding performance effects without relying on an arbitrary categorization, regressions were run on home- and away-team performances and their multiplicative interaction, controlling for stadium size. The multiplicative interaction introduces an accelerated increase approaching the upper right of the performance box, consistent with the hypothesized impact of two high-performing contenders in mobilizing publics. Results, in terms of unstandardized beta coefficients (see Appendix B), are shown in Figure 8.5. Interaction coefficients, which tap the effect on crowd density of both contenders being high performers, are negative in the sports with the highest overall crowd densities. This is owing to the cap placed on attendance by stadium size. As home and away performance levels rise, increasing crowd density, the capacity cap increasingly comes into play. Where this cap rarely comes into play, as in baseball, the interaction coefficient is strongly positive.

Confirming this interpretation, the bottom panel in Figure 8.5 shows that sellouts are most likely where both teams are high performers (that is, where the interaction term is high). In no sport except football is the isolated impact of either home or away performance level statistically significant. Nor are intercepts significantly different from zero, except in hockey, where sellouts can occur between even the lowest-performing teams. These findings strongly suggest that the attendance potential for games between winning teams is much higher than stadiums are able to accommodate, outside of baseball.

(*Text continues on page 255*)

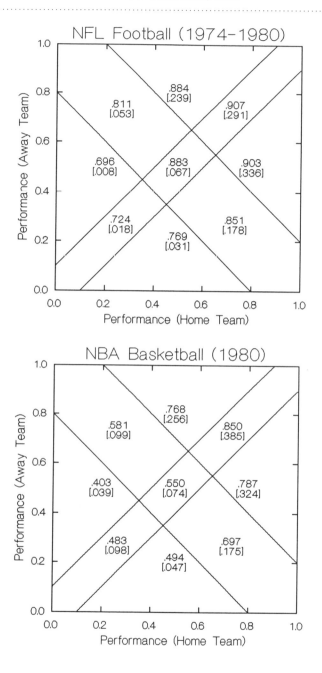

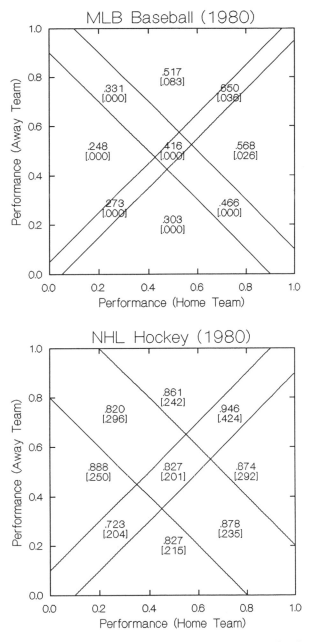

Figure 8.4 The effect of home- and away-team performance levels on average crowd density (unbracketed figures) and on the proportion of sellouts (bracketed figures). Because the dispersion of performance levels is lowest in baseball, a stricter criterion for similarity was used.

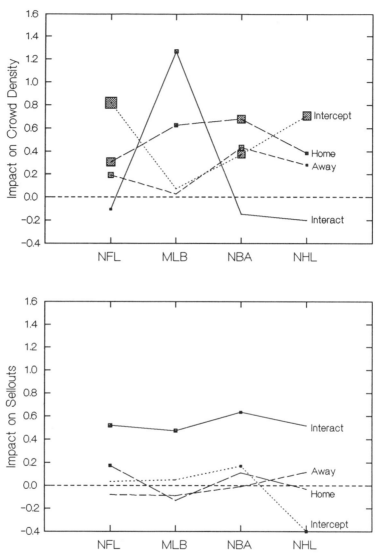

Figure 8.5 Regression estimates of the impact of home- and away-team performance, along with their multiplicative interaction, on crowd density and sellouts.
Stadium size was controlled for, and had a significant negative impact in all equa-
tions except for sellouts in hockey. Baseline densities, for teams with no wins or
ties, can be found in the intercept estimates. Size of square denotes degree of
statistical significance. MLB = Major League Baseball; NBA = National Basketball Association; NFL = National Football League; NHL = National Hockey
League.

In all major league sports, home-team performance has a greater impact than away-team performance in mobilizing publics. Local publics are clearly more sensitive to the performance of "their" team than to that of the away team. Winning home teams draw larger crowds no matter whom they play. For baseball, away-team performance level has no impact outside its interaction with home-team performance. Winning away teams draw larger crowds only when they come to play winning home teams. As local publics mobilize around winning home teams, particularly when they come up against winning away teams, what effect do they have on the home team's chances to win the game?

The simplest way to frame this issue is with the performance boxes used above. In the context of particular regions of the performance box, the home advantage becomes the difference between home and away winning chances for the same performance combinations at home and away. Home advantage is necessarily symmetrical around the equal performance level diagonal, as outcomes on both sides must be used in its calculation. Using a minimum of regions to stabilize estimates of winning chances, Figure 8.6 shows how dramatically home advantage can vary across different performance combinations. Contrasts between sports are even more striking. Compare, for example, the prototypical modern sport of NFL football with NHL hockey, the sport most lagging in the cultivation of national publics. In football, home advantage is relatively low in games between performance unequals (off the diagonal). In contests between performance equals (on the diagonal), home crowds have a sizable impact on helping the home team win, and this impact sharply increases as the performance level of both teams rises. Thus there appears to be a parallel between crowd density and home advantage, although the dense crowds that follow winning home teams have little added impact when the home team plays a weaker opponent. As shown below, stronger teams have similarly high prospects for winning wherever the game is played. Performance expectations prevail.

Yet hockey displays virtually the opposite home advantage pattern. Home advantage disappears entirely in games between high performers and increases as both teams' performance levels decrease. In matches between performance unequals, home advantage is relatively high. Although crowds were least sensitive to performance levels in hockey, the fact that a high overall home advantage should disappear where crowds are densest, and appear where they are most sparse (72.3 percent of

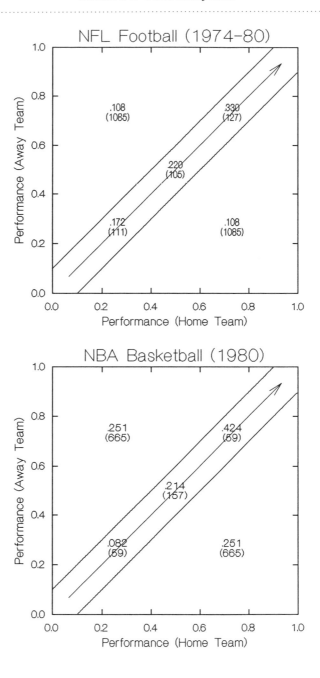

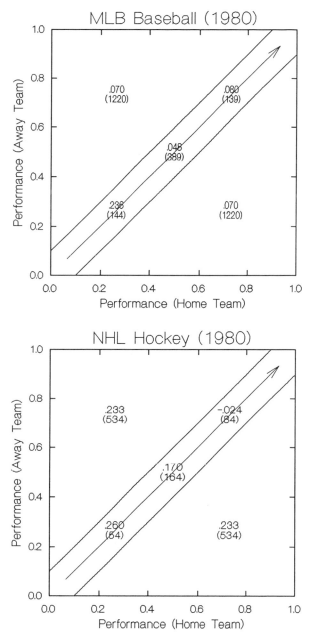

Figure 8.6 The effect of home and away performance levels on the home advantage. Because the same performance combinations were used to compare home and away winning chances, results are symmetrical around the similar performance axis. The number of games used to calculate home advantages is given in parentheses.

capacity), is indeed curious. As developed shortly, the result is not without function. Local publics, which predominate in hockey, are highly sensitive to where games are won. Losing teams can maintain local support by winning, albeit rarely, at home. Losses on the road are less debilitating than ones at home.

Baseball and basketball exhibit curious amalgamations of these extreme patterns. Basketball closely resembles football for games between performance equals, and hockey for games between performance unequals. With this combination, basketball displays the closest parallel with crowd density results. Dense crowds consistently appear to magnify home advantage in basketball. For baseball, however, the converse pattern of resemblances holds. Low performers exhibit the highest home advantage, as in hockey, but unequal performers exhibit relatively low home advantage, as in football. Aside from the slight rise in home advantage in games between high performers, the baseball results are more damning than hockey's for a straightforward crowd density hypothesis, since crowd density was more highly sensitive to performance levels in baseball.[7] Home advantage appears in performance regions where crowds are sparsest in baseball, in sharp contrast with basketball.

Basketball followed a developmental path similar to that of football, remaining primarily a college sport until the modern era, though basketball fell far short of football in cultivating a national public for its regular season play. Baseball shares with hockey a similar developmental path and a continuing dependence on local publics for support, yet it has made more substantial inroads in the creation of national publics. Before we try to link the distinctive role of publics in each sport to these distinctive home advantage patterns, the results need to be further elaborated.

Patterns in Figure 8.6 are tied to an artificial performance categorization, with some category results based on a relatively small number of observations. As in the crowd density case, regression analysis can be used to test for an underlying logic. In addition, it is necessary to link crowd density, or the lack of it, directly to home advantage patterns. Though in basketball home advantage was the highest in performance regions with the highest crowd densities, for example, the link has not been established at the level of individual games. In any given performance region, actual crowd densities need not be related to the home team's chances of winning.

To address these limitations, it is convenient to use home-team winning chances (HWC) as the dependent variable.[8] The winning chances of the home team are a function of the difference between home- and away-team performance levels, factors tied to the partisan effect, and the residual factors of chance and accident. The importance of performance differences can be interpreted in two ways. They may simply be an indicator for skill differences, and hence teams with higher past performance should beat teams with lower past performance. Yet teams play different schedules, so that the same performance levels could correspond to much different skill levels if one team had more skilled opponents than another. In addition, performance levels change with each game outcome, whereas there is no reason to believe skill would change with each win or loss. Performance differences would exist even if there were competitive balance. They could then operate on home-team winning chances only through the expectations they aroused in both teams and publics. National publics should magnify the role of expectations, as they allow away teams to be both known and admired by home crowds. The fact that higher performers tend to beat lower performers may have as much to do with expectations as it does skill.

Crowd density and stadium capacity were used as determining factors of the partisan effect. Because stadium capacity does not vary across games (within the 1980 season), it is only useful for addressing variation among teams. If we hold crowd density constant, additions to stadium capacity increase both the absolute size of the crowd and the average distance of the crowd from the competition. These can have opposite impacts on the home team's chances of winning. Yet differences in home advantage among sports suggest that the distance factor may be more important, because sports with the highest home advantage have the smallest and most intimate stadiums. According to the literature, crowd density is supposed to increase the home team's chances of winning when stadium capacity is held constant. To facilitate interpretation, stadium capacities were divided by the largest stadium in each sport, so the range of both variables falls between zero and one.[9] A multiplicative interaction was also constructed, allowing for large, full stadiums to have extra impact, but this was not significant except where noted below.

A two-step analysis was carried out. First, the difference between home- and away-team season performance at the time of each game were regressed on game outcomes (0 = lose, .5 = tie, 1 = win). As shown in Figure 8.7, the resulting intercepts mirror the overall home-

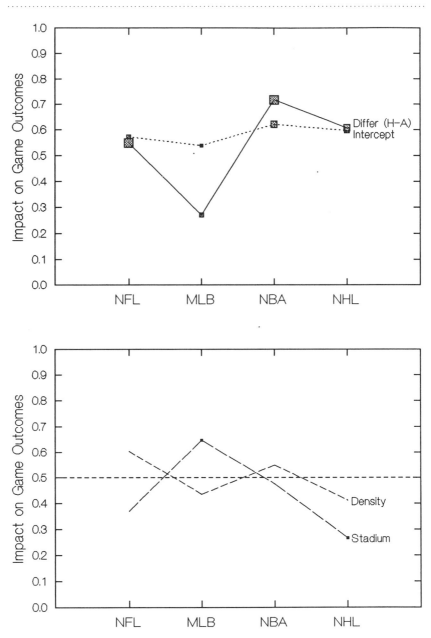

Figure 8.7   The impact of performance differences (top panel) and crowd intensity indicators (bottom panel) on game outcomes (0 = lose, .5 = tie, 1 = win). Performance differences were controlled for in the bottom panel results. Size of square denotes degree of statistical significance.

win team proportions of each sport, which, when differenced from .5, are one-half the overall home advantage. Performance differences show considerable variation in their impact on the home team's chances of winning. In baseball, for example, a home team that has won 70 percent of its past games playing an away team that has won only 30 percent of its games has only a .108 (.4 × .271) better chance of winning than it would playing a team at its own performance level. In basketball, the home team would have a .287 (.4 × .718) better chance in these same circumstances. The overall usefulness of performance differences in predicting game outcomes is measured by the proportion of variation in outcomes accounted for by performance differences, or R-squared (see Appendix B). This measure varies from .005 in baseball and .078 in hockey to .123 in football and .141 in basketball. If performance is no more than a measure of skill, sports with longer seasons should exhibit higher R-squared, because the performance measure would on average be based on more games and hence be more reliable. Yet the results go in the opposite direction, with football teams playing less than one-tenth the number of games as baseball teams.[10]

To allow for a nonuniform partisan effect, crowd density and stadium capacity were added to the regression equation. Results are shown in the bottom panel of Figure 8.7. Although the added impact of these variables on HWC was weak, the direction of the impact reinforces the emerging paradox. In football and basketball, home teams had greater chances of winning when denser crowds turned out to support them. Yet the opposite was the case for baseball and hockey, where home teams performed best before the sparsest crowds. In every sport except baseball, larger stadiums decreased home winning chances. A multiplicative interaction term between crowd density and stadium capacity proved insignificant in every sport except baseball, where its inclusion both changed the direction of the impact of stadium capacity (to −.157) and made the impact of crowd density (−.549) significantly negative. The interaction term, however, had a significant positive impact on home-team winning chances (.693), although it was not strong enough to overcome the negative effects of each of its separate components. This boost in home-team winning chances for sellouts in large stadiums was heavily influenced by a single team (see note 6).

The consistently negative impact of stadium capacity within each sport accords with differences among sports in overall home advantage. Where stadiums are large and fans quite distant from the competition, as in baseball and football, overall home advantage is lower than in the smaller, more intimate stadiums of hockey and basketball. Stadium variation within each sport is small relative to stadium differences between the sports, so the fact that within-sport variation still was able to reveal a consistent impact is quite noteworthy. Yet the finding that in baseball and hockey denser crowds of supportive fans can actually lower home winning chances poses a challenge to any straightforward interpretation of the home advantage.

Further analysis revealed that crowd density has a different impact depending on the performance levels of the competitors.[11] For both baseball and hockey, crowd density and stadium capacity had their strongest negative, and now significant, impact on the home team's chances of winning in contests involving performance equals. Among performance equals in football and basketball, large stadiums and dense crowds boosted (significantly in basketball) home winning chances (though in football crowds provided the strongest boost for home teams playing higher-performing away teams). In basketball, the impact of crowd density was actually weakly negative in games between performance unequals, confining the positive overall effect entirely to performance equals. Hence crowds tend to have their greatest impact in games between performance equals, although this impact can be channeled in opposite directions across sports. In the modern era, a partisan effect was expected to linger most clearly where no clear performance expectations are possible. Yet the fact that in this situation the partisan effect is sometimes negatively tied to the size and intensity of home crowds is new to home advantage research. The partisan effect appears precisely where it is most needed, among weak teams in sports still heavily dependent on local publics, whose small loyal followings have few rewards besides the knowledge that they make a difference.

Figure 8.8 summarizes the findings in this section. Home advantage patterns reduce neatly to two binary dimensions, with the four sports filling up the four possibilities. Among performance unequals, home advantage was found to be either low or high. Among performance equals, home advantage either increased or decreased with performance levels. Placement on these dimensions appears related to the predominance of national publics in a sport. Football stands in sharpest contrast to hockey with regard to publics, with baseball and basketball treading a middle ground in relying on both local and national publics. Hence the rise of national publics must be associated with low home advantage

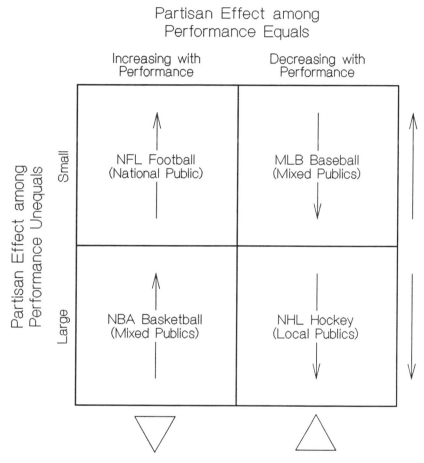

Figure 8.8 Summary of main findings. Major leagues differ in the size of the partisan effect for performance equals (columns) and unequals (rows), and in the size of the expectations effect for performance unequals as indicated by arrows through each sport (upward arrows denote a large effect). Since the expectation effect helps magnify performance inequality, and partisan effect lowers it, arrows (in cells and margins) also denote impact on performance inequality. Column triangles indicate whether the column effect promotes performance leveling at the top (▽) or bottom (△) of the performance distribution.

among performance unequals and increasing home advantage over performance levels among performance equals, as found in football. A third dimension, the impact of performance differences, drives outcomes where home advantage is low. In Figure 8.8, upward arrows through a sport denote relatively strong impacts and downward arrows denote weak impacts (assessed in terms of R-squared).

All three dimensions have implications for (re)generating patterns of performance inequality. Partisan effects, wherever they appear, function as a performance leveler. Hence small partisan effects among performance unequals open the way for the regeneration of performance inequality. Among performance equals, increasing partisan effects over performance levels will truncate the upper end of the performance distribution, yielding a small group of similarly performing teams at the top (with the opposite pattern yielding a similar group at the bottom of the performance hierarchy). This is because a strong partisan effect will produce a more exact win-lose split of the games played among top performers than would randomly occur, as half are played at home and half away. Insofar as performance differences have an impact, they will function to generate performance inequality—as winners tend to continue winning and losers continue losing. The use of up-down arrows in Figure 8.8 is in reference to these impacts on performance inequality (and triangles denote truncation at the top [∇] or bottom [$\triangle$] of the performance distribution).

In football, for example, winners will tend to split the games they play with each other, yet for the bulk of their games, when they play lesser-performing teams, they will tend to win wherever the game is played. Hence performance inequality is regenerated among performance unequals yet is clearly capped, because no team will happen to win all its games against other high performers. No such clear cap is induced at the bottom of the performance hierarchy, so some low performers may happen to lose all their games against other low performers. In hockey, these processes are entirely turned around. Low and unequal performers tend to split their games with each other and hence are subject to leveling. Among low performers in hockey, tendencies to win at home (and reserve losing for away games) may account for the unusually high fan support accorded losing teams.[12] Performance inequality must be generated among higher performers who win from and lose to each other on a random basis. The resulting lack of close races at the top can serve as an obstacle to cultivating national publics.

Basketball and baseball display peculiar mixtures of effects that represent built-in tensions. Basketball follows football closely, yet both home advantage and performance differences have an impact on outcomes among performance unequals. Figure 8.1 illustrated what this implies in terms of overall home- and away-win proportions. High performers may win nearly all their home games, but not much more than half their away games. Performance inequality is generated from the impact of performance differences and suppressed by the partisan effect. For a long time, the bulk of national attention was focused on two teams, the Boston Celtics and Los Angeles Lakers, and here mainly in the playoffs. As these teams falter, the large partisan effect among performance unequals will hinder basketball's ability to produce a new set of nationally hailed winners, because it levels the upper end of the performance distribution. In this respect, basketball's situation is more precarious than football's.

Baseball resembles hockey, except it shares with football the weakening of home advantage among performance unequals. Yet performance differences have only a weak impact, so that mostly random inequality is generated from games between performance unequals, as it is in games between equally high performers due to the weakness of the home advantage. The appearance of a partisan effect among equally low performers functions to truncate the bottom of the performance distribution, yet is not as effective in bringing out local fans as it is in hockey. Nascent national publics in baseball make overall winning too important for local fans to be satisfied with merely home-game wins, yet the predominant localism undermines the impact of performance differences in generating stable winners and losers. Baseball seems to be in the most precarious position of all sports, anchored more by its traditional popularity than its ability to produce a small group of rival superteams for national publics or a pattern of winning home games that draws local publics.

Publics and Performance Inequality

Actual performance inequalities may be affected by a variety of day-to-day factors, such as the entry of a new franchise or a few exceptional players in existing franchises. Individual games that make up season records are swayed by player injuries, coaching innovations, and a host of other factors we have ignored. If in the long run publics have the impact observed in the last section, however, this impact should at least apply pressure for particular patterns of performance inequality to emerge. To isolate these patterns in the clearest possible terms, a computer simulation was programmed to "play out" seasons of major league competition solely on the basis of the effects observed in the last section. This allows for an unequivocal interpretation of the patterns that emerge. These patterns will then be compared with actual patterns, to see how much of observed performance inequality can be attributed to the complex workings of the partisan and expectation effects.

Driving the simulation is an equation that determines the home team's chances of winning each scheduled game. To simplify, stadium capacity is assumed to be constant within each sport, and crowd density is assumed to be entirely a function of contending-team performance levels. Hence the equation can be specified entirely in terms of home- and away-team performance levels. In addition, a logistic specification is used to constrain home-team winning chances between 0 and 1. The resulting equation is:

$$\ln\left(\frac{\text{HWC}}{1 - \text{HWC}}\right) = b_0 + b_1 (\text{PFH} - \text{PFA}) + b_2 (\text{EQUAL})$$
$$+ b_3 (\text{PFH} + \text{PFA}) \times \text{EQUAL}$$

with
$$\text{HWC} = \text{home-team winning chances}$$
$$\text{PFH (PFA)} = \text{performance level of home (away) team}$$
$$\text{EQUAL} = \text{a variable that is '1' if teams have similar } (\leq.1)$$
performance levels and '0' if not.[13]

In this formulation, b_0 (>0) measures the partisan effect for unequal performing contenders, b_1 measures the expectations effect, b_2 measures the partisan effect difference between performance equals (at the diagonal base of the performance box) and performance unequals (b_0), and b_3 measures the effect of increasing performance levels among equals (along the diagonal of the performance box). The last two coefficients allow for the rising and falling partisan effect patterns we observed along the diagonal of the performance box, and hence will be called the diagonal base and diagonal effect, respectively. Although the logistic format requires interpreting the coefficients in terms of the nonintuitive logged odds ratio, actual estimates from the game-level data in Table 8.3 reveal relative levels that are clearly consistent with

Table 8.3 Estimates for the game outcome equation used in the computer simulation, based on a logistic regression of actual 1980 game outcomes (1974–1980 for football) in the four major league sports. (Standard errors are given in parentheses.)

Sport	b_0	b_1	b_2	b_3	Loss function
Football	.303	2.437	−.328	.522	661.70
	(.087)	(.266)	(.431)	(.397)	
Baseball	.205	.234	.596	−.583	712.80
(1st half)	(.165)	(.480)	(1.150)	(1.137)	
(2nd half)	0.65	3.216	2.02	−1.902	715.24
	(.220)	(.759)	(1.233)	(1.213)	
Basketball	.641	3.566	−.996	.848	553.06
	(.101)	(.363)	(.537)	(.533)	
Hockey	.525	2.741	.427	−.667	534.68
	(.108)	(.440)	(.643)	(.607)	

the home advantage patterns in Figure 8.6. A split baseball season reveals, however, a sizable change in game outcome dynamics after midseason. The weak expectations effect in the first half of the season cannot be attributed to any weakness in the performance measures, since these measures are based on at least as many games as those for the entire seasons of the other sports. Perhaps it is the case that national publics are mobilizing only near the end of the overly long season, in anticipation of the World Series.

To eliminate the problem of varying season lengths for cross-sport comparisons, and perhaps anticipate the future, a forty-eight-game season was used for all sports in the initial simulation. Toward the same end, twenty-eight-team leagues with no divisions were used for all sports. To assess the effect of these departures from actuality, the league structure and scheduling constraints (including the sixteen-game season) of the NFL were used in another set of simulations (for all sports). Every simulation was based on fifty seasons of competition. A season schedule was generated by the computer, and its rows and columns were randomly permuted (within divisional constraints, for NFL simulations) for subsequent seasons to guard against scheduling biases.

All teams started the simulation as perfect equals (that is, past performances of .5), and became differentiated only through the workings of the game outcome equation as the season progressed. Hence perfect competitive balance is assumed, and all systematic performance inequality can be attributed to the effects of publics. For subsequent seasons, however, past season performance was "remembered" with a weight of four games (two for the sixteen-game simulations) among current season results. Hence after four games into a new season, current season standing is equally weighted with past season results in determining performance levels. By the last game of the season, the prior season is forgotten entirely. The same algorithm was used to compute PFH and PFA in the empirical analysis, and is consistent with the earlier finding that the selection of teams for national broadcasts is primarily based on only one prior season of performance. Obviously, without any memory, there could be no relation between performances across seasons, as teams would enter each season as perfect equals and initial differences would occur on a purely random basis.

Four measures of performance are monitored in the simulation, each based on fifty seasons of competition. Season inequality is the average standard deviation of season performances across teams, and hence is a measure of the tightness of pennant races. Performance correlations across both one and four seasons gauge the extent to which winner and loser roles are stable across seasons. A high correlation across four seasons, for example, means that a winner (loser) in any given season has a high likelihood of still being a winner (loser) four seasons later. Finally, the skewness of the performance distribution is measured by the number of season performances below .5 minus the number equal to or above .5, divided by the maximum possible difference (one team winning all its games and the rest finishing just below .5). A positive value denotes runaway pennant races with a cap on the cellar, while negative values denote the opposite.

To establish baselines, preliminary simulations varied the levels of the expectation ($b_1 \geq 0$) and uniform partisan ($b_0 \geq 0$) effects (with $b_2 = b_3 = 0$). Figure 8.9 shows the impact of these varying levels on the four performance measures. As the expectations effect increases, season inequality sharply increases over the pure chance level (large grid). The partisan effect operates as a leveler, though to produce dramatic effects one must go beyond the levels observed in actual leagues. Similar conclusions can be drawn from looking at the performance correlations across seasons. Correlations spanning four seasons, however, are small

even for large expectation effects and small partisan effects (this atten-
uation is largely shaped by memory strength). With no inherent differences between teams (and a short memory for emergent differences),
national publics can succeed in creating only short-term differences
among them. Performance skewness was not systematically related to
either the expectation or the partisan effects. Because there is a perfect
symmetry between high- and low-performing teams in the baseline
simulations, there is no reason to expect skewness to be different from
zero.

Comparing actual leagues with the simulated leagues in Figure 8.9
is complicated by the use of a forty-eight-game season. Estimates for
the expectation effect (b_1) are sensitive to season length, with longer
seasons increasing the effect by enhancing the stability of the performance measure. Based on the difference between actual and simulated
season length and standard errors, projected (to a forty-eight-game season) estimates for b_1 were 2.750, .788, 3.235, and 1.977 for the sports
of football, baseball, basketball, and hockey, respectively. A combination of high expectation and low partisan effects generates the most
inequality, with the former dominating. Thus if public effects are the
only factor driving performance inequality, football and perhaps
basketball should exhibit the most inequality, and hockey and baseball
the least.

Nonuniformity in partisan effects were introduced through the diagonal base (b_2) and diagonal effect (b_3) coefficients, using actual estimates for b_0 and b_1 from the four league sports. The results for football
(using $b_1 = 2.750$) are shown in Figure 8.10. Since a low diagonal base
and negative diagonal effect, and vice versa, will affect the overall partisan effect level, attention should be directed to the upper-left, lower-
right diagonal along which the overall partisan effect remains constant.
Disappointingly, there is not much going on along this diagonal with
respect to the inequality measures. At least within the range of actual
partisan effect patterns, the nonuniformities are not sufficient to substantially affect long-term performance inequality. Results for the other
sports, which are not shown, lead to the same conclusion.

Skewness results were puzzling. Partisan effect nonuniformities in
football and basketball should have produced negative skewness by cap-
ping the upper end of performance and allowing spread in the lower
end. Positive skewness should be found for baseball and hockey simulations, where the high partisan effect among lower performers should

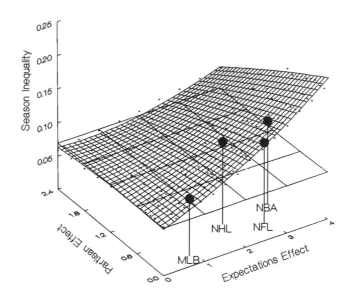

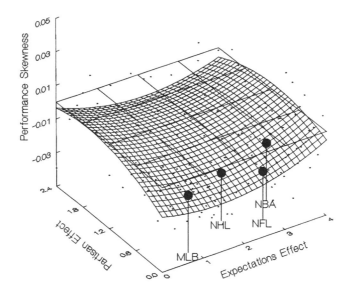

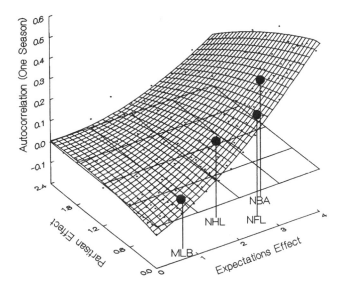

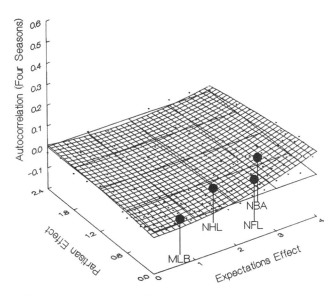

Figure 8.9 Simulated impact of uniform partisan and expectation effects on four performance measures. Each point used to estimate the small grid surface is based on a simulation of fifty seasons for twenty-eight hypothetical competitive equals playing forty-eight games each. The large grid surfaces are the expected results were publics to have no effect on competition.

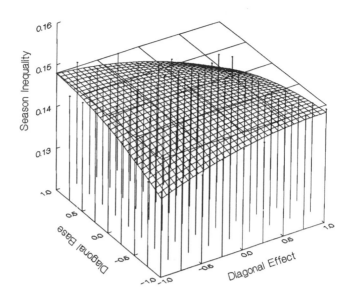

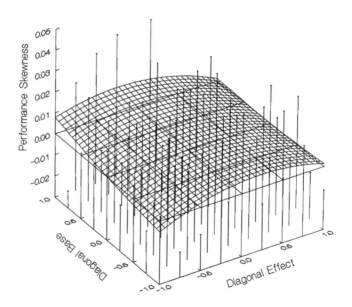

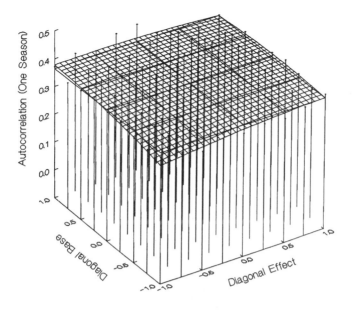

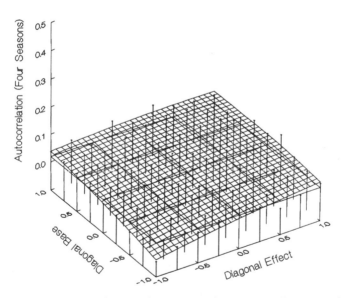

Figure 8.10 The impact of nonuniformities in the partisan effect on performance measures. Actual overall partisan and expectation effects from 1974–1980 NFL competition are held constant in the simulations (with twenty-eight teams playing forty-eight-game seasons), and partisan effects for similarly performing teams are allowed to vary with performance levels. Diagonal base is the partisan effect for two losing (zero performance) teams. Diagonal effect is the unit impact of increasing performance levels among similarly performing teams.

produce the opposite pattern of caps and spreads. It appears, however, that the magnitude of the actual nonuniformities was not sufficient to produce these predicted effects.

Although the nonuniformities in partisan effects do not appear dramatic enough to affect aggregate performance measures, overall partisan effects and particularly the expectations effect did have substantial impacts. Can these factors account for performance measures obtained from the four league sports? Actual performance correlations across up to twelve seasons, with solid lines used for recent decades, were given in Figure 5.4. In the two right-hand graphs in Figure 8.9, we see that football results most clearly fit the simulated results for season lags of one and four. Results from simulated sixteen-game seasons are even more accurate, with cross-season correlations of one and four seasons being .394 and .032 (and a season performance standard deviation of .188, which is within 5 percent of the actual amount). Hence virtually all of the persisting performance inequality in the modern prototype of NFL football can be accounted for by the impact of publics on competition. The other sports, however, should exhibit less inequality than football because they either have a weaker expectations effect (baseball) or greater home advantage (basketball), or both (hockey). Both baseball and basketball appear, in Figure 5.4, to be dramatically moving in this direction, considering their much higher inequality in the preceding period, but hockey, with the highest inequality, is moving in the wrong direction.

Missing from the simulation are any real skill differences among teams. Deviations between the simulated and actual results can be attributed to the persistence of such real differences. In this respect, the magnitude of the deviations corresponds closely to the extent to which the sport has entered the modern era of national public cultivation. It is only in this era that true competitive balance has become important, as it induces fans to search more broadly and deeply for winners than even past local loyalties would allow. The success of the NFL in cultivating national publics has been facilitated by the elimination of real differences among teams. Real differences keep hockey from moving beyond the local loyalties it still depends on.

Performance measures for individual seasons (1970–1990), with each horizontal line corresponding to a season, are shown in Figure 8.11. Season inequality is closely tied to season length in the top panel. Dotted lines provide the theoretically expected inequality were every game

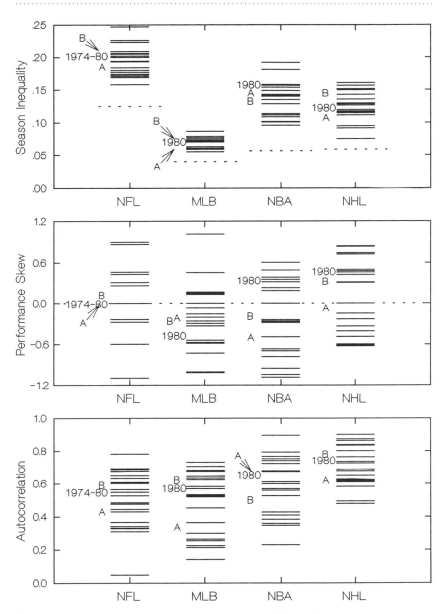

Figure 8.11 Actual performance measures for 1970–1990 seasons in the four league sports. The 1980 season (1974–80 in football) provided estimates for the partisan and expectations effects used in the simulation, and is marked along with averages for 1970–1979 (B) and 1981–1990 (A). Measures in the three panels are those used for the simulation results, except they are based on individual seasons rather than aggregated data for fifty seasons.

to be decided by a coin flip. Relative to this baseline, results conform to those for cross-season inequality except for hockey, which exhibits less inequality than basketball. Although this may be due to the difficulty of scoring in hockey and the admission of ties (which are prevalent), the fact that season inequality is decreasing (A < B) over the period should be noted. On this note, the season-to-season correlations (aggregated in Figure 5.4) in the bottom panel show the same pattern of decreasing inequality in the 1980s for hockey.

Again, skewness results (middle panel) prove hard to interpret, particularly in the absence of clear simulation results. The 1980 season, used to estimate the game outcome equation, is clearly an outlier for basketball and somewhat for hockey. Basketball shows a clear trend toward negative skew, implying a performance cap that makes for close pennant races combined with a large spread at the bottom of the performance distribution. But this pattern is only weakly found in football, where it was most expected, and the converse pattern is not to be found in baseball and hockey. Hence the actual and simulated results are consistent, but both fail to confirm the impact of publics that was predicted before the simulations were run.

In sum, the expectations effect dominated the simulation results, but could be muted somewhat by a strong overall partisan effect. No clear further impact could be found for nonuniformities in the home advantage that derive from complex mixes of local and national publics. Performance predictions based solely on public effects were most accurate for football, the sport that has most successfully cultivated national publics. Deviations for the other sports, in the form of real performance differences among teams, varied directly with the progress the sport had made in cultivating national publics. Hence the successful pursuit of competitive balance can be tied to entry into the modern era of national television publics. But the competitive balance remains beneath the surface, as national publics induce performance inequality through the expectations they impose on competition.

Publics in Perspective

Sports publics are the creation of major leagues. Throughout recorded history sporting events have been staged that have attracted large audiences. Gladiatorial contests in ancient Rome attracted more people than attend NFL games today. Yet major leagues devised the means for going beyond the gathering together of audiences for isolated events to the cultivation of enduring publics. The reliability with which publics are regularly activated has become the foundation on which concrete and steel stadiums are built and multiple-year television contracts are signed. Although sports publics have become sufficiently solid to elicit these sizable investments, they remain a rather mysterious phenomenon.

Nobody can deny the enjoyment the sports enthusiast gets from participating in a sports public by turning to the sports section in newspapers, reading sports magazines, wearing sports paraphernalia, tuning into sports broadcasts, or going to games. What is mysterious, however, is the powerful regularity with which major league sports are followed. Many activities that people need or enjoy can go unmissed when tending to other needs and enjoyments. But if a Monday night NFL game is missed there can be an uneasiness no matter what else was done instead. The impulse to take one's place in a sports public is so strong that even a brief lapse can arouse deep anxieties. There must be more to participation in sports publics than personal enjoyment.

We have searched for the roots of participation in what publics accomplish. Without some accomplishment, it would remain incomprehensible why so much energy is so regularly put into the very definite activities of being part of a public. In any collective where something gets accomplished, opting out becomes difficult and participating requires clear strictures on what is permissible. The myriad personal convictions and social pressures that narrowly define participation within sports publics are subordinate to a larger accomplishment. We have examined the impact of publics on performance because it is in this area that major leagues have left something important to accomplish.

Extensions of competitive balance, across teams and time, have been the vehicle for allowing publics to have an impact on performance. Audiences that gathered to watch the first traveling teams had little to accomplish. The traveling teams were vastly superior in skill to the pieced-together local teams they played. Audiences' lack of a role to play ensured that their attention would be short-lived, and hence hindered their transformation into publics. As early leagues attached teams to cities, however, emerging local publics found themselves with something important to accomplish. Because leaders in early leagues conspired to reinforce large-city dominance, the fate of small-city teams came to depend on the boost they received from the loyal support of local publics. In sports still largely dependent on local publics, we found the partisan effect to be highest among low-performing teams. This boost to the teams that need it the most helps the local public to maintain loyalty where it would otherwise be most in jeopardy, and hence to strengthen leagues where they are most vulnerable.

In the modern era of televised sports, local partisanship became an obstacle to the pursuit of national publics. A new breed of sports enthusiast had to be cultivated, one who was willing to follow leaguewide competition in search of winners to celebrate. Where winning teams were located mattered less than ensuring that they might emerge anywhere. For the first time, competitive balance was pursued in earnest by major leagues. To the degree major leagues succeeded, national publics acquired unprecedented control over performance outcomes. Local publics had to exert vigorous partisanship to give a weak home team some chance of upsetting a strong visiting team. National publics could tip the delicate balance between similarly skilled teams through the subtle workings of their expectations. As major league teams grew more similar in ability, it was left to national publics to accentuate performance differences among teams.[14] National publics create the winners they celebrate, from the inequality they help sustain among equals.

It was found that the influence of national publics diminished the partisan effect among performance unequals and increased the chance that the outcome would be decided on the basis of performance expectations. This pattern helps keep winners winning and losers losing despite underlying competitive balance. Only when no clear performance expectations existed, owing to similarity in past performances, did persisting local partisanship help the home team win. But here it was strongest among similarly high performers. This leveling among the best performers should work against runaway pennant races and hence help keep the national public involved. In the major league most successful in cultivating a national public, the NFL, the entire amount of actual performance inequality can be accounted for by the impact of its public on competition.

Involving publics has always been the aim of major league sports, and there is apparently no better way to involve them than to give them an actual role in affecting performance outcomes. We have found that this role, for both local and national publics, counters the effects of league policies on competition. Local publics level performance where leagues reinforce large-city dominance, while national publics induce performance inequality where leagues pursue competitive balance. These cross-pressures have been central in the success of major league sports. They give both leagues and publics much to do, without the prospect of a resolution. Early leagues worked to place strong teams in large cities, but smaller-city fans worked to help smaller-city teams sometimes win anyway. Modern leagues worked to make teams similar in abilities, but national publics worked to create winners to celebrate. And strangely enough, the more successful leagues were in pursuing their aims, the more energetic publics were in seeking success themselves.

In current major league sports the enthusiast is often caught in the middle of the distinct agendas of local and national publics. Those who reside in major league cities retain much of the partisan loyalty of an earlier era. They have a strong inner urge to support their local team, and would find that to do otherwise would elicit strong disapproval from their peers. Yet enthusiasts are also exposed to a good number of other major league teams through television and national magazines, and they may watch more games that do not involve the local team than do. The exposure to leaguewide competition can introduce an invidious objectivity that distances the enthusiast from the local team. Instead of being committed to helping the local team win, the enthusiast would rather separate from the team and announce that it does not have a chance. The complex and varied mix of these distinct orientations accounts for the equally complex and varied impact of publics on performance across the four major league sports.

In practice, there has never been a major league sport where only local, or only national, publics prevailed. Major League Baseball's New York Yankees were largely a national team well before television started bringing them into people's homes, and NFL teams remain attached to cities and play before tens of thousands of partisan fans each week. In recent times, the mix of local and national publics has provided a fallback for Major League Baseball, which has proved unable to muster the discipline required to more consistently pursue a national public. Nevertheless, the exercise of analytically isolating the distinct impact of local and national publics will prove useful for the incursion into the future in the next chapter. There I will argue that the attachment of teams to cities has become an anachronism that is hindering the cultivation of international publics. In the design proposed for future major leagues, teams are detached from geographical entities altogether. This will render cities, still the sites for competition, nonpartisan and hence will eliminate the partisan effect altogether. It will also greatly magnify the expectations effect as a huge international public searches for winners to celebrate. This chapter has offered a premonition of what these changes might mean for competition.

The stage is set for crossing the final frontier of international publics. Awaiting is a cross-pressure that will dwarf any that have been observed so far. With no local publics to cater to or fall back on, competitive balance will prove absolutely essential in keeping an international public involved in leaguewide competition. But the enormous weight of this public in converging on teams that happen to be winning will serve to stabilize winner and loser roles as never before. Heroic discipline will be required within major leagues to preserve the underlying competitive balance of teams, so that international publics will persist in creating stable winners and losers on the surface of competition.

9

• • •

The Accomplishment

Not long ago my father and I were walking through a locker room when we came upon four young men intently watching an NFL game on television. As we passed behind them, my father paused to look at the game. After a short while, he asked what the score was. One young man turned and answered, "21 to 7," quickly turning back to the game. After another short pause, my father asked who was winning. Again a perfunctory answer, this time without turning away from the screen. Then, after another short pause, my father asked who the winning team was playing. This time, in answering, the young man gave my father an odd glance. I too was struck by the sequence of my father's questions. How could he have been interested in the score without knowing the name of either team that was playing?

Few lines from major league sports are more quoted than the words attributed to Vince Lombardi: "Winning isn't everything, it's the only thing." Lombardi was coach of the Green Bay Packers during the NFL's dramatic entry into the modern era of televised sports. Winning had not always been as important as it became during Lombardi's time. When NFL teams were struggling to attach to cities, a certain amount of local loyalty could persist among fans even across many years of losing. This was particularly true in a small city like Green Bay, where the mere possession of a major league franchise was a big achievement. Winning was of course cherished, but mostly as a local affair. The national television exposure that Lombardi found himself receiving was something new. Green Bay was a cold place at season's end, where visitors got noticed just for showing up. When the national media came to Green Bay to help the nation celebrate Packer victories in the early 1960s, it must have seemed strange at first. But soon the absence of national media exposure after the Packers stopped winning was to seem more like abandonment than a return to normalcy. The lesson for achieving national exposure was clear. Winning was the only thing.

At the same time that Lombardi was learning about the importance of winning, a much less publicized development was taking place. Teams had stopped dying. If winning had become so important, why didn't losing have devastating consequences? Every win for one team is a loss for another in the closed circuit of a major league. The major leagues had, however, quietly figured out a way to accommodate so much losing at the same time that winning was becoming so important. Many years earlier, only four losses had destroyed the 1869–70 Cincinnati Red Stockings in the few months after they had tallied seventy-six consecutive wins. In early major leagues, losing teams continued to perish, or survived only by not finishing their scheduled games. Yet as winning became the only thing in modern leagues, teams stopped perishing because they had a losing record. With unrelenting regularity losing teams began playing out every game of the season, half at home and half away, season after season, imbuing season results with a remarkable orderliness. Even the New York Stock Exchange value of one of the few publicly traded franchises, the NBA's Boston Celtics, does not drop when performance declines (Gorman and Calhoun 1994).

The greatest accomplishment of major leagues is not the dollars they take in, or the memorable players, teams, and games they have produced, but the way they have quietly accommodated losing. There are much bigger businesses than major league sports in dollar terms, and independent teams have at times excelled over any the major leagues could produce. From the start, major leagues formed around the problem of improving the prospects of survival for a set of member teams across seasons. With every win producing a loss in closed circuits of competition, survival for the set of league teams rested on overcoming the destructiveness of so much losing. Many losing teams simply failed and were replaced, but sometimes losing teams in large cities dragged down whole leagues. Even support for winning teams could grow thin in games against losing teams, and only a small number of games could occur between teams with winning records. Although all major leagues have employed some form of subsidies to prop up economically weak teams, the subsidizers would be drained by the subsidized if sports publics were not somehow accommodated to losing. For this accommodation to occur, major leagues had to innovate in three areas.

First, major leagues extended the time frame of the "product" from isolated games and matches to carefully constructed pennant races restarted each season.[1] In an isolated game, a winner has to win to remain a winner. The coveted winner role could thereby be lost in a single afternoon, as happened to the Cincinnati Red Stockings. This possibility made the business of operating an independent team extremely precarious. In the pennant races that emerged in Major League Baseball, however, teams could lose over 40 percent of their games and still be winners. A team could even consistently lose to another team, yet still be declared the champion (by winning more against other teams), something that was inconceivable before major leagues appeared. By orienting fans to pennant races based on win percentages rather than on direct matches, winners became able to lose a substantial number of games and still remain winners. The relatively recent trend of including greater numbers of teams in the postseason playoffs has even turned some teams with losing records into "winners," in the sense of earning a playoff spot.

Extending competitive balance across teams was a second way major leagues accommodated losing. Traveling teams, who were far superior to the local teams they played, had demonstrated the liability of competitive imbalance. Winning was essential for attracting new crowds in new towns, but the definitive losses they inflicted undermined interest in their return. Early major leagues set out to trade the precarious and vagabond existence of traveling teams for the ongoing support of the largest cities. In the closed circuits they devised, teams played the same teams over and over. Competitive superiority or inferiority jeopardized the teams' ability to cultivate ongoing support. From the start, major leagues struggled to avoid serious competitive imbalances by selecting, and gradually regulating, teams to preserve a consistently high caliber of play across league teams.

As major leagues progressed toward competitive balance, however, publics intensified their search for winners to celebrate. I have argued that, by interpreting what might be initially random performance differences as ability differences, and imposing expectations on subsequent competition, publics can actually induce stable winner and loser roles among competitive equals. Without a score to work with, the names of competing teams would have meant little to my father in the story opening this chapter. The public can create (and destroy) the winners it celebrates, as long as major leagues impose competitive balance.[2] But at some level, where the makings for involvement reside, the members of the public must sense the underlying competitive balance (as they sensed the earlier imbalance between traveling and local teams). For while winning is taken as a sure sign of higher ability, losing does not destroy interest in a return match. The fact that losing teams play out their entire schedule and reappear each new season both reflects an accommodation of losing and provides an odd kind of reassurance to publics that losing does not matter. As long as losing does not destroy teams, and hence the league framework in which winning is relevant, winning can be unabashedly celebrated.

This book has chronicled the efforts of major leagues to impose a repetition across time and sameness across teams that is not broken by the built-in losing that must occur. After 125 years of experimentation, however, the intricate systems that have emerged in current major leagues are still far from perfect in their functioning. To get by in the always urgent need to accommodate losing, major leagues have had to pursue a third tack that has largely defined their character. Never having stood alone, the product of major league sports has always been attached to some outside entity. Major leagues initially set out to attach professional teams to cities. This attachment allowed many teams, particularly in smaller major league cities, to survive long stretches of losing. With local support essential for winning, fans were also willing to share in the blame for losing. To let down one's team, in not providing support, was to let down one's city once the attachment had taken hold. Jerry Gorman and Kirk Calhoun (1994) call this attachment "fan equity," because it is what remains for the owners to work with after all liabilities, like losing, are subtracted.

When major leagues began attaching league competition to network television, the new media was, like cities before it, in need of an identity. The attachment helped television largely supplant radio as a fixture in American households and, in the process, created a national television public that represented a vast new opportunity for major leagues. To nurture the new attachment, viewers had to be enticed into following the progress of remote teams so that viewers everywhere would focus on a limited stream of nationally broadcast games. A purely local partisanship had to be transformed into an eagerness to be wherever winners emerged. While the old attachment produced fans of local teams, the new one produced enthusiasts for a sport who followed leaguewide competition.

The attachment of league competition to network television, however, focused attention on winning and losing as never before. Although many viewers will watch television no matter who is playing (or what is on), tuning out carries none of the guilt found among local fans who fail to support their city teams. Nationally broadcast games must hold the interest of viewers by being close games between teams with real chances to be winners. The enormous challenges involved in both cultivating national publics and maintaining competitive balance across teams and time have often led major leagues to fall back on the original attachment of teams to cities. In practice, most television broadcasts have been used, like radio, to reinforce the bond between a city and its team through the local broadcasting of away games. The security offered by loyal local followings is, however, gained only by jeopardizing the much greater opportunities offered by a more fluid national public. Nothing better demonstrates this than Major League Baseball's failure to obtain a network contract (with guaranteed rights fees) for its 1994 season, because it had undermined the value of national broadcasts with a profusion of local and cable broadcasts.

Even where the attachment between league competition and network television has been most consistently pursued, in the NFL, teams still carry city names and continue to play half their games in the same home location. Despite the teams' relatively low dependence on gate receipts, considerable promotional energy is still directed at cultivating partisan local publics. The practice of maintaining local publics while pursuing a national public is associated with the geographic dispersion of major league teams. To involve the nation in televised sports, major leagues placed teams in all of its regions and largest cities so that most people had a nearby team to help draw them into the sport. But the use of locally rooted teams as bait to interest nearby residents in leaguewide competition has its limits. The goal of national coverage is already producing major leagues that are too large for even the most avid enthusiasts to follow. Undistinguished teams, with no widely recognized star players, are something that only a local public can love. As organizers continue to give legitimate new claimants franchises in increasingly unwieldy leagues, it grows harder to focus national attention on a limited stream of nationally broadcast games.[3]

There are simply too many potential major league cities for any major league to incorporate. As major leagues grapple with this problem by sporadically granting new franchises to cities with the most aggressive claims, they are backing toward what will prove an insurmountable impasse. As will be discussed below, every major league has recognized that the real frontier for expansion is international. Over the last three decades, the idea of placing teams in foreign cities has been entertained by both challenger and established major leagues. But if there are too many U.S. cities for a single major league to encompass for national coverage, how can international coverage be achieved by attaching teams to the much greater number of world cities? If anything, cultivating a diverse and unsophisticated international public will require major leagues that are smaller and simpler in structure than what currently exist. What has been the most secure feature of major league sports, the attachment of teams to cities, will have to be abandoned. If there is a single lesson to be taken from this book, it is that every major extension of publics is accompanied by a reorganization of competition. And the impending extension to international publics holds out prospects for the most radical reorganization since major leagues first appeared.

At every point in the historical development of major leagues, the future would have appeared fantastical. No independent team owners or organizers of the earliest leagues could have easily fathomed how modern leagues managed to incorporate so much losing without a single team dying, departing from a preset schedule, or even dropping in economic value. Progress toward the fantastical future has never been a smooth, gradual process. The transitions from club sports to independent professional teams, and then to early leagues and to modern leagues, have entailed momentous upheavals that have radically changed the way things are done and the relative importance of those doing them. The first appearance of professional players and teams in baseball triggered the countermobilization of amateur sports, which succeeded in marginalizing the subsequent professional versions of basketball and football for over half a century. For early leagues to establish their hold over cities, successful independent teams had to be destroyed. For major leagues to enter the modern era, the dominance of large-city teams had to be undermined. In the process, there were shifts in the relative popularity of whole sports as leagues that succeeded in adapting to one opportunity setting failed to re-adapt to the next.

Modern league sports is a strange phenomenon if one sees it through the lens of how it came to be. What seemed obvious had to be turned around, popularity had to be undermined, and powerful interests had to be resisted. The future of major league sports promises to be stranger still, and the challenges of getting there no less imposing. A vast new opportunity of international publics is being ushered in by progress in telecommunications and a new world order.

Facing the Future

Huge strides have been made in exporting major league sports to other countries. Every major league has an internal division devoted exclusively to international expansion. The NBA alone employs three hundred people in its pursuit of international sales and broadcasting, maintaining a fully staffed office in Geneva and satellite offices in Melbourne, Hong Kong, and Barcelona. But the emphasis has been on marketing rather than on reorganization. As has been true for many other American industries that have ultimately failed to penetrate international markets, the presumption has been that a product that sells well in the United States should be welcomed as is by the rest of the world. The success of preliminary marketing efforts has done little to discourage this presumption.

Most internationally generated revenues come from the sale of merchandise with major league logos. Major leagues license the right to use these logos for a commission of roughly 9 percent on retail sales. In the NFL, approximately 350 manufacturers are licensed to produce over 2,500 items that bring in over $2.3 billion in worldwide retail sales. Much of this licensing empire was built by John Bello, who came to the NFL in 1988 with marketing experience from General Foods and Pepsi. In Europe, NFL logos are so prevalent on clothing that one young German boy wearing a San Francisco 49ers jersey thought that the NFL was a clothing company. In Major League Baseball, commissioner and marketing wizard Peter Ueberroth centralized control over licensing in 1987, taking over from teams who had been making an average of $30,000 a year in this area. By 1992 retail sales of licensed products exceeded $2.3 billion, bringing in over $200 million in equally shared revenue to the owners.[4] The NBA, under Commissioner Stern's leadership, has developed a 248-page product catalog that generated $2.4 billion in worldwide sales for the 1992–93 season. With a later start, NHL-licensed products generated only $600 million in worldwide retail sales in 1992. But the marketing ideas that Commissioner Gary Bettman brought directly from the NBA are yielding rapid growth. Although domestic sales constitute almost 90 percent of hockey's worldwide figures, the potential for further growth lies primarily overseas.

In addition to the licensing of products, every major league sells broadcasts of its games abroad. Most of the sales, however, come from championship games. More than 400 million households in 93 countries watched the Chicago Bulls win the NBA title in 1992. In China alone, 100 million people watched the broadcast. By 1994 the NBA title game was being broadcast live in 117 countries. NFL Super Bowl games follow in worldwide popularity, being broadcast live in 35 countries. This success is remarkable, given that football is a distinctly American game. But Major League Baseball and the NFL have been working to build grass-roots support abroad by sponsoring clinics and little leagues for young people. In 1993, NFL clinics in Europe attracted 10,000 players and 1,000 coaches. And in Germany alone, over 200 amateur football teams have been created. Major League Baseball is targeting Japan and Latin America, as Europeans "are kickers, not throwers," and marketing the game as an American experience (*New York Times*, April 3, 1994).

As impressive as the marketing successes sound, they are minuscule next to what is possible. In many ways, the major leagues are no further along in exploiting the world market than the 1869 Cincinnati Red Stockings were in exploiting the potential of this country. The novelty of major league sports overseas, like that of the Red Stockings in the United States, is capable of arousing immense curiosity. Major leagues have been exploiting this curiosity with the most advanced modern marketing techniques. Yet they have not seriously begun to cultivate an international public, one that would follow the regular seasons of major league sports on a daily basis through newspapers, magazines, radio, and television. Instead, marketing efforts have focused on paraphernalia, players, playoffs, and championships. Once the novelty of these items wears off, the major leagues will find themselves without a way to keep the attention of international audiences returning over and over. The core product of the major leagues is the regular season, with all of its sameness and repetition, because only this is capable of bringing people into the major league fold on a regular basis. Everything else, however lucrative in the short term, is peripheral and possibly even damaging over the long haul.

Efforts to involve international publics in regular seasons have been tentative at best. To arouse interest in broadcasts, the major leagues have been sending teams overseas to play preseason exhibition games for some time. Catalyzed by the challenge of the World Football League, the NFL sent its St. Louis and San Diego teams to Tokyo in 1976, and two years later staged another exhibition game in Mexico City. Favorable responses to these ventures led the NFL, in 1986, to initiate an annual American Bowl in London, with a game between Dallas and Chicago in Wembley Stadium. Over the next few years, American Bowls were started in Tokyo, Berlin, and Barcelona. The four American Bowl games drew a total of 205,377 spectators in 1993. In the Barcelona game, San Francisco's quarterback observed, "The fans were tremendous . . . I'm not sure you need to provide them with any entertainment, they entertain themselves." In Tokyo, "the Japanese were so taken with [a 79-yard punt return] that [punt returner] Hughes was the subject of the postgame 'hero interview' broadcast from the field through the PA system." But the Philadelphia coach conceded that play "was sloppy . . . We played an awful lot of people. You want to win, but not at the expense of not evaluating people" (*USA Today*, August 3, 1993). Once the novelty of these exhibition games wears off, the use of second-string players in games that don't count (in pennant races) will prove no basis for a regular involvement.

Only the NBA and Major League Baseball have played any regular season games abroad, with the latter opening its 1992 season with a game in Tokyo. Major League Baseball, with its long 162-game regular season, is in the best position to export games that count without provoking a reaction from local publics at home. Yet even in baseball the large number of potential international sites and the games that would be required at each to cultivate a public limit the use of exported games without major changes at home. Equal treatment of domestic and international publics, necessary in the long haul, would require radical changes in the organization of sporting competition. Not only must international publics get their fair share of games, but they also must be provided a way of attaching themselves to teams and players. It is presumptuous to think that residents of world cities like London, Berlin, or Tokyo could be involved on a regular basis in rivalries between teams attached to American cities. As long as major league teams are attached to cities, international publics will require their own city teams. But this raises intractable problems concerning the size and composition of leagues, and even the visionary David Stern has ruled out establishing NBA teams overseas (Gorman and Calhoun 1994).

Some efforts have been made to form international leagues, beyond those extending to Canadian cities only. Until most recently, these plans have originated outside the major leagues. The organizers have all tried, and failed, to attach teams to cities. One such effort was initiated as early as the 1960s in baseball by Walter Dilbeck, Jr., a midwestern promoter and real estate investor who had tried to purchase the Kansas City Athletics from Charles Finley to keep the team from moving to Oakland. Dilbeck later toured Vietnam as an observer and writer and came back with much larger geopolitical baseball ambitions than keeping Major League Baseball in Kansas City. Dilbeck was concerned that Asians saw Americans as soft and decadent, and he believed that this perception was fueling the spread of communism. In organizing the Global League, Dilbeck would show Asia "just how good Americans can be" (Pietrusza 1991, p. 302).

Original plans for the Global League called for twelve American teams in two divisions with the later addition of teams in Tokyo, Puerto Rico, Manila, and Honolulu. By the time competition actually began in 1969, a year later than planned, the Global League consisted of teams "representing" Puerto Rico, two Japanese cities, the Dominican Republic, New York, and Los Angeles. All games, however, were played in Central and South America. The Global League collapsed three weeks into its first season, after a Caracas hotel stopped extending credit for meals and threatened to evict eighty-eight players. Dilbeck had secretly bailed out before the season began, selling the Global League to the Baptist Foundation of America (which was under investigation for fraud in its charitable mission). Needless to say, the Global League did little to show Asia just how good Americans can be.

Three subsequent international baseball leagues have been announced, but none has actually gotten under way. A World Baseball Association was formed in 1974 around five American cities and Mexico City. In January 1975 the number of cities had grown to thirty-two, including Taipei, but not a single game was ever played. A more modest North American Baseball League was announced a decade later, with Mexico City and Vancouver included among eight American cities, but this league never progressed beyond the planning stages. The same fate awaited Donald Trump's syndicated Baseball League, announced in 1989. Undoubtedly there were other efforts that did not even make it to the stage of being announced. What these failed dreams begin to make apparent, however, is that the design of an international league is by no means obvious. Any effort to attach teams to cities is likely to produce an odd collection of teams at the global level. As hard as some organizers might try, global leagues simply cannot look the same as current major leagues.

The most serious effort to form an international league is also the most discouraging, both because it failed and because it showed a reluctance to take international publics seriously. In the late 1980s, the NFL began organizing the World League of American Football with the support of twenty-six of its twenty-eight clubs (Chicago and Phoenix reneged on the required $200,000 investment). The World League was conceived by Tex Schramm, retired general manager of the Dallas Cowboys, and Schramm became the new league's first president. From the start, however, his conception was reined in by the NFL's fiscal conservatism and its insistence that the new league not compete in any way with the NFL. Like the failed United States Football League, the World League moved to the spring, with a schedule from March to May. And like the failed World Football League and the efforts in baseball, it situated most of its teams in U.S. cities lacking NFL franchises and an odd assortment of foreign cities. Franchise cities included Barcelona, Frankfurt, London, Mexico City, Birmingham (Ala.), Sacramento, Orlando, and San Antonio. Shramm sought a greater European presence and more sites, and his conflict with the seven-member board cost him his job in October 1990 (he was replaced by another former general manager, Mike Lynn, of the Minnesota Vikings).

World League competition began in March 1991, after much speculation that the economic recession and recent Gulf War would postpone the debut. Despite the innovations of placing chalk-sized cameras on player helmets and open mikes on coaches, the ratings of ABC and USA Cable telecasts were dismal. Ticket sales were also poor outside of the European sites, where the novelty of American football and a fondness for American culture among the young allowed some profits to be made. Boosting the success of the European teams was the fact that they won their first eleven home games against American teams. Overall, however, the World League lost $7 million its first season.

The main problem of the World League was the poor quality of play. At best, the World League was to serve as a feeder league for the NFL. Its season was scheduled to end in time for players to try out for the NFL's July training camps. Instead of using players fresh out of college, the World League used players who had been trying out for the NFL over the past five years. Only thirty-six players, however, ended up in the NFL training camps after the first season, raising fears that the World League would not even succeed as a feeder league. From the high number of minorities in management positions, the World League may have also have been conceived as a minority management trainee program for the NFL (whose players are 65 percent black). To improve its image, over one hundred NFL players agreed to play for the World League in its second season. But this proved too little and too late.

After a second season of dreadful television ratings and poor attendance, the World League folded, having cost the NFL a total of $45 million. Despite the loss, plans are being drawn up for a new World League to begin competition in March 1995. It consists of an all-European lineup of six teams, and has as equity partners Viacom's MTV Europe and Capital Cities/ABC Inc.'s ESPN International. These partners are helping to fashion the marketing image, but curiously, neither is expected to broadcast games (*Business Week*, February 7, 1994). Although the new World League has trimmed the deadwood of weak, smaller-city American teams, it will at best remain a feeder league for the NFL. Like Major League Baseball after World War II, the NFL appears committed to clinging to its three-decade-old formula for success. But just as national publics did not form around teams not good enough to play for prized local publics, international publics are not going to form around teams not good enough for the national public of the NFL.

Marginality was the springboard for the NFL's phenomenal success after World War II, and the NFL's current success is proving to be an obstacle in adapting to the new opportunities ahead (as was the case for Major League Baseball after World War II). If marginality is an asset, and success a liability, then the NHL and the NBA are in the best position to experiment with their basic structure in pursuing international publics. In addition, both hockey and basketball are longtime Olympic sports and hence have more solid international bases than either baseball or football.[5] NBA players became eligible to compete in the Olympics in 1992. The NBA's "Dream Team" in that year's Games was an important publicity coup for the league. Commissioner Bettman was able to persuade the somewhat reluctant NHL owners to follow the NBA's path. By early 1994 the commissioner had worked out an agreement with the International Olympic Committee to allow NHL players to compete in the Olympics in exchange for some restructuring of the competition to showcase and not overly impinge on the NHL, whose season is in progress during the games.

As a prelude to Olympic involvement, the NBA joined forces with the International Amateur Basketball Federation. Formed in 1932, the federation spearheaded the campaign to get amateur basketball into the Olympic Games starting in 1936. Working in conjunction with the NBA, the federation sanctioned the "McDonald's Open" in 1987, in which the host NBA Milwaukee Bucks played teams from the Soviet Union and Europe. The annual tournament moved on through Madrid, Rome, Barcelona, and Paris before becoming a biennial event to avoid conflict with the Olympics (it was played in Munich in 1993). In 1989 the federation removed restrictions that prohibited NBA players from competing in international events. This allowed foreign players to compete in the NBA and retain Olympic eligibility, which opened the way for all NBA players to gain Olympic eligibility in 1992. Following in the NBA's footsteps, Bettman struck his Olympic deal at the same meeting he forged an alliance with the International Ice Hockey Federation that made individual NHL players, and the Stanley Cup champion team, available for the World Championships in ice hockey.

These alliances with international governing bodies offer convenient vehicles for entering the international scene without modifying the domestic product. Both the NBA and the NHL are trying to avoid establishing teams overseas by sending their players out to draw international attention to the national leagues. Far from being the start of any reorganization of competition, the alliances are simply one more marketing ploy to promote the existing product. After baseball and football failed in their efforts to establish teams overseas, the NBA and NHL's alternative path appears quite prudent. Both Commissioner Stern and his protégé and now NHL Commissioner Bettman are intent on pushing marketing to its limits.[6] But no matter how far flung the marketing efforts of the NBA or the NHL are, marketing genius alone is not sufficient to cultivate an international public. It can sell products and lure people to broadcasts, but this is different from getting people to follow sporting competition enthusiastically on a regular basis. In the end, teams will have to be somehow "established" overseas without being attached to any particular location.

Marketing alone will not succeed in cultivating international publics. Nor will occasional excursions abroad of existing teams, or the creation of secondary teams and leagues for stationing abroad. Established major leagues must transform themselves in a way that offers the same grounds for involving both domestic and foreign publics. Considering the vast opportunities to be gained, international publics must be taken at least as seriously as the national public. Too many industries have slipped out of American control by doing otherwise. If the established major leagues do not take action, others will. It is time to start thinking about how future leagues and publics will be organized.

A Strange New World

Major league sports is on the verge of a fundamental reorganization. Like those of the past, the changes will be spurred by the opportunity to extend sports publics. The lure of international publics will bring pressures for change that dwarf those once brought by the prospect of local and then national publics. Major leagues have never enjoyed the isolation necessary to be complacent. Attachments to cities and network television have led civic leaders and television executives to concern themselves in major league affairs. Large corporations like Nike, Budweiser, and Gillette have become highly dependent on major league sports as an advertising vehicle for reaching desired markets. As word spreads of the potential for reaching 100 million Chinese with a single NBA broadcast, pressure will mount on the major leagues to achieve such success on a regular basis. The prospect of penetrating international markets is too alluring for any opportunity to be slighted.

A sense of urgency is apparent in the recent activities of major leagues. Although international expansion is coveted, the reorganization of competition is something every major league is still trying to avoid. Implicitly, sports enthusiasts are being reassured that future major league sports will look just like the present ones, except that they will be followed everywhere in the world. For a Royals fan in Kansas City, it might make sense that the whole world could share his own enthusiasms. But suppose it was the Japanese who were pursuing an international public for their own baseball league and were promoting a televised game between the large-city teams of Sapporo and Nagoya in Kansas City. Could the Kansas Citian share in the enthusiasm of Nagoyan residents, particularly on a regular basis? The Japanese league would be likely to worry about this issue. As pressures for international expansion mount, U.S. major leagues are going to have to worry about the Nagoyan market. Competition must be reorganized to get Kansas Citians and Nagoyans involved on the same basis.

Future major leagues must be built by sports organizers and followed by sports publics. Much is possible. The future, if it can be predicted at all, should represent the solution to a problem that currently exists. We are greatly aided by the clarity of the problem facing major leagues. How can international publics be cultivated? More specifically, how can involvement in major league sports be extended to regions of the world where there are potentially lucrative markets to penetrate? Ideally, the design for future leagues would allow some flexibility to accommodate shifts in the world economy.[7] In practice, the only publics that are actively pursued are the ones whom leagues and sponsors would like to reach on a regular basis.

A solution to the problem facing major leagues must be consistent with the three types of constraints that have shaped the development of major leagues from the start. The first are technological or demographic constraints on who can have access to games on a regular basis. These constraints define the potential opportunities facing major leagues. If anything, the problem posed by the future will be too much access rather than too little. The proliferation of television channels has weakened the league offices' control over broadcasting as well as diverted attention to new professional sports like beach volleyball. Satellite and cable technologies have, in addition, allowed live broadcasting around the globe. This creates pressure for a single framework of competition that can definitively resolve contentions among teams. With everyone watching, only one team can be champion in the end. Global television undermines subsidiary leagues, like the minors in baseball or the NFL's World League of American Football, by siphoning away attention.

The second type of constraints are social configurational, and affect what can realistically be accomplished at any given time. Much of what might be technically possible is blocked by the powers that be. Social configurational constraints have been central in accounting for why the major leagues, which shared the same opportunity context, have been so varied in exploiting the prevailing opportunities. We have seen, for example, that success under one set of opportunities turned into a liability when opportunities changed, as success gave rise to powerful interests that resisted change. The NBA and the NHL, by never enjoying the full success of the early or modern prototypes for organizing competition, may be in the best position to make the changes necessary to pursue international publics. No major league, however, will enjoy a smooth transition, as all enjoy more than enough success to resist change. But major leagues have changed in the past, and there should be some solution that they can implement in the present situation.

The third type of constraints comes from the need to involve publics. I have argued that involvement is much different from attention. It has come to rest on a repetition across time and a sameness across teams that is not disrupted by the winning and losing that occurs. The more uniform the product of major league competition has become, the more control over the creation of stable winners and losers has passed into the hands of publics. In the relatively small major leagues of the future, however they are organized, teams will unavoidably be more remote from the diverse and faraway peoples they seek to involve. Unless major leagues can involve international publics in the creation of winners and losers, they will stand the constant risk of losing them to more pressing concerns in their immediate locales. With too many locales in which to place teams, future major leagues will not be able to fall back on the deeply ingrained local loyalties that have allowed past and current major leagues to get away with a far from perfectly uniform product.

It will be an enormous organizational challenge to achieve repetition and sameness in a diverse and tumultuous international scene with all kinds of new unevennesses to overcome. A warm sunny afternoon in one city is at the same time a wintry night in another, so that any live international sports broadcast would have to occur at awkward times and in odd seasons in much of the world. In addition, local broadcasting customs, laws, and existing programming are so diverse that scheduling constraints on even nonlive broadcasts would be severe. The World League of American Football took pride in its local sensitivities, serving bratwurst at its concession stands in Frankfurt and fish and chips in London. Were teams to start traveling beyond western Europe on a regular basis, even smaller details would have to be tended to with great care.[8]

The major stumbling block to cultivating international publics, however, is the attachment of teams to cities. While the original attachment could continue into the modern era by serving as the basis for national coverage, it cannot serve as the basis for international coverage. There are too many major cities for this, and the size of future major leagues must be relatively small to involve an unsophisticated international public. The requirement that teams play half their games in a single locale (central in attaching teams to cities) would shut out unrepresented locales altogether from live competition. Prospects for building involvement based entirely on television exposure are not good, as demonstrated by the short-lived made-for-television United States Football League. Major league teams are going to have to start playing in many more locations than there are teams. They must be able to move throughout the world, stirring up local interest in the television broadcasts that will follow them. Major leagues have taken a tiny step in this direction with overseas exhibition games and even some isolated regular season games. But these are only leaks in a dam that will soon burst.

Were existing teams to start playing the bulk of their games abroad, should they still be attached in name to a city? The 1869 Cincinnati Red Stockings promoted their city this way, as did the short-lived Tokyo team in Dilbeck's South American–based Global League. City residents would still take pride in their teams, and follow them on television. This arrangement, however, is no longer sufficient, and has not been for almost fifty years. In the future the Nagoyans, and their counterparts throughout the world, have to be interested in following the competing teams on a regular basis. If Americans are unlikely to become involved in competition between Japanese-based teams, what makes us think that others will become involved in competition between U.S.-based teams? So far the major leagues have captured widespread attention abroad, but only as a novelty. Involvement is another matter, and will take years and reorganization to achieve.

In 1869 it made a lot of sense to promote the emerging city of Cincinnati with a national tour of the Red Stockings, just as it made sense for the emerging television networks to showcase major league competition in the 1950s and 1960s. What is the sense, however, of promoting cities like New Orleans, Charlotte, or Portland in China? What meaning could these cities, or rivalries between them, have to the Chinese? What meaning could Nagoya or Sapporo have to Americans? While some sense of connection can be created through vigorous marketing, there needs to be a rationale for the effort. In their day, the attachments to cities and networks created enormous synergies that benefited both sides. On the verge of the next great expansion of publics, a new attachment is needed that can enlist new kinds of support and spawn new identities in return.

Attaching teams to larger geographical entities might help alleviate the problem of international coverage, but the entities would have to be too large to easily capture the identification of both viewers and sponsors.[9] Events like the Olympics and the World Cup in soccer, which attach teams to countries, succeed mainly because of their infrequency. The Jamaican bobsled team can amuse the world as a novelty, but not as a regularity. On a regular basis, there are still too many countries to fit in a major league and they are too uneven in local market size. The problem of city-size differences in early major leagues is magnified many times over when countries are local publics. Most vexing, however, would be the transition problem should an existing major league try to redefine locales. If the Dodgers' move from Brooklyn to Los Angeles still seems outrageous to many Brooklynites, imagine the reaction to an announcement that the Yankees will now be representing Southeast Asia in an appropriately renamed American League. Even the Southeast Asians would be suspicious of the gift.

The time has come to recognize that major leagues have outgrown their original format of teams attached to locales of any form. Local loyalties have become a hindrance to the cultivation of broader publics. This fact could be ignored in past decades, because teams remained attached to cities. People could attend games as fans, and watch games on television as enthusiasts of a sport. Although people may see themselves as loyal fans, it is the quiet disloyalty in their willingness to watch games between remote teams that accounts for 70 percent of NFL revenues. As teams head out to cultivate followings throughout the world, there is no way they will also be able to cater to a local public—no matter how largely this is defined. Teams must detach from locales altogether and set out to captivate viewers on an international scale.

Major league teams are on the verge of reattaching themselves to a new kind of entity, one not rooted in locales. Multinational corporations are ideal for this purpose, and in many ways stand in need of clear identities much as cities and networks once did. These sprawling entities, with hundreds of products and operations spanning scores of countries, are exceedingly hard to think about and hence are vulnerable to the projections of others. The ships coming in and out of the harbor, the factory looming on the horizon, the office building towering over the cityscape evoke complex mixes of fear and hope for those passing by. Were major league teams to attach directly to multinationals, they would confer identities to the names of these corporations that would make them more a part of the landscapes they alter and provide some security for them in a tumultuous world.

As we saw for both football and basketball, attaching teams to corporations has been tried before. Local companies once used this sponsorship to strengthen their ties to the community on which they depended, and professional athletes gained access to managerial careers upon retirement from sports. Today, however, multinational corporations do not depend on local markets, and sports celebrities can hardly be motivated by the promise of managerial careers. The attachment of major league teams to multinationals would serve altogether different purposes. The international presence of multinationals gives them both the ability and the need to have an international identity. A Japanese league trying to enter the United States would have an easier time if its teams were attached by name to companies like Sony or Honda than to cities like Nagoya and Sapporo. Conversely, the names of McDonald's or Coca-Cola would arouse more passion in China than the names of San Diego or Kansas City. Rivalries in the global marketplace could spill over into the field of sporting competition. Even the American public might get more enthused over a showdown between Coke and Pepsi on the gridiron than another confrontation between Dallas and Buffalo.

As strange as this new attachment might sound, it is already in the making. One of the two new NHL franchises created in 1993 was purchased by Walt Disney & Company and was named the "Mighty Ducks." Soon after, Disney released a movie titled "Mighty Ducks," followed by a sequel, "Mighty Ducks II." The movies were about a group of ugly duckling kids who were formed into a hockey team called the Ducks and were gradually transformed into mighty ducks with the help of a lawyer turned coach. Both the team name and this open act of cross-promotion have the effect of attaching the Mighty Ducks to Disney. Many people who have heard of the Mighty Ducks may not even be aware that they are based in Anaheim, where they must play half their games. Should they ever be freed by the NHL to go out and build an international following, they would do well to call themselves the Disney Mighty Ducks rather than the Anaheim Mighty Ducks. Another NHL franchise created in 1993 was purchased by H. Wayne Huizenga, owner of Blockbuster Entertainment Corporation. Huizenga also owns a minority stake in the NFL's Miami Dolphins and a majority stake in Major League Baseball's newest franchise, the Florida Marlins.[10] His NHL team will be called the Florida Panthers, but again the Blockbuster name would have more meaning to an international public.

The lack of locale is the key virtue of multinationals. Major league teams attached to multinationals would no longer have a home location, and hence would be free to mobilize support internationally with live appearances. One could easily imagine many sets of teams passing through the same locations, much as teams pass through on the television screen. Live competition would thereby share with broadcast competition the ability to involve people in leaguewide competition. In the modern era, with teams still attached to cities, the only place local enthusiasts could welcome pairs of other city teams into their city was in the privacy of their homes on television. With teams attached to multinationals, there would be no automatic basis for a city to favor a single team, and therefore many teams could be welcomed in live appearances as well as on broadcasts. Teams would be freed of home locations, and home crowds would be freed of seeing the league entirely through the lens of a single team.

The lure of an international public is too great for teams to continue settling in a single place and spending half their exertions cultivating merely local support. Movement around the globe would aim to keep people in particular places involved in league competition as a whole, and hence stimulate widespread interest in television broadcasts. One way to conceive this movement is as slow shifts across major world regions. The teams of an entire league might compete in Asia, then in Europe, then in North and South America. As in the earliest basketball leagues, which split seasons in half, seasons could be segmented by these regional movements, with regional champions assured a place in the final season championships alongside overall division champions. This arrangement would allow regional favorites to emerge each season, and heighten international interest in the playoffs as each region tuned in to support "its" favorite team. Concurrent division races, however, are needed to keep television publics involved when competition has moved to distant locations.

Ideally, the season of each major league sport would be preserved, if only as a way to avoid direct competition between sports. A global itinerary would require a year-long season, because of seasonal variation across hemispheres. Movement across world regions could loosely follow the movement of seasons, so that live games could be played in the "same" season throughout the year. The different sports would continue to be staggered in their season starting dates, so that from the standpoint of the American public the season of live competition would not be significantly different. The different sports, at different stages of their own respective seasons and regional movement, would directly compete only in their televised form. Only one sport at a time would be engaged in postseason playoffs and championship series, given the staggering of season starting dates.

With a season extending across the entire (up to 48-week) year, the number of regular season games played should probably be decreased, except in football. Even with the regional confinement of league competition at any given time, the burden of travel and living adjustments on players would prohibit the 162-game season of Major League Baseball. But most important, the central purpose of live games is to arouse interest in telecast games. Promotional efforts involving players in a region could be as effective as games themselves for this purpose. A 48-game season, divided into three 16-game regional segments, would most likely be sufficient. The advantage of fewer games, as the NFL has amply demonstrated, is that it helps limit the number of broadcasts. When broadcasts are limited, each becomes an event that fans feel compelled to witness and hence television ratings soar. Limiting games also helps reduce television competition across sports, and perhaps different days might be given over wholly to particular sports.

Teams would play wherever stadiums were built and fans turned out. Stadium construction in the past has been entirely rooted in the attachment of teams to cities. Whether stadiums are financed by team owners or by municipalities, the investment is predicated on the fact that a team will play half its season games in the stadium. This security will be lost as teams detach from cities. Cities will no longer compete over securing a single franchise, but will compete over scheduling individual games among all the teams in a league. In this respect, both risk and opportunities increase for stadium owners. It is likely that multisport stadiums will be constructed in many new locations, as part of entertainment and shopping villages, and will compete year round for games in all the major league sports as they move through the region. As in any competition, there will be winners and losers. The magnitude of investment in stadiums and the intensity of local sentiments will make the issue of where games actually get played a highly contentious one. Major leagues will play cities off against each other on a regular basis, instead of only when new franchises are created, and city managers will have to become more creative in finding uses for stadiums.

The transition into this strange new world is likely to be triggered, at least as a pretext, by conflicts between publicly owned stadiums and team owners. In what has become routine, the owner of a popular team will demand renovations, luxury boxes, or perhaps a new stadium, and the city will not comply. The owner will then carry out the standard threat to abandon the stadium, only this time it will not be clear where the owner is planning to take the team. Perhaps some appearances in other major league stadiums (besides scheduled away games) will be ventured, but most likely the team will schedule games abroad. After more time has passed and more angry words are exchanged with the original stadium managers, the new road team will carry out its final threat and drop the city from its name in favor of a corporate attachment.

Meanwhile, the original stadium managers may have succeeded in scheduling the games of other major league teams who are up to the same antics as the team the city has just lost. This loss will, of course, create a new vacancy that may tempt still other teams to abandon their home location. In short order, city residents may find that they have fewer games to attend (because games played abroad will be lost to the system), but that a greater diversity of newly christened corporate teams seeks their support at the box office. The seeds for such fundamental changes have already been planted by the scheduling of isolated regular season games abroad and the open association of corporations with teams. Once the current system starts to unravel, it could take only a few seasons for a new prototype to emerge. Although at first the league office might distance itself from the process, and even express dismay, it will start to exploit the chaotic situation by pressing for major rule changes that could never be pushed through in normal times. In the end, of course, it will rename itself to acknowledge its new global scale.

The most difficult struggle in the transition to the future will be over television broadcasting. Television is most effectively exploited when sports enthusiasts everywhere can be focused on a limited number of broadcasted games. But achieving this requires tremendous discipline on the part of both the leagues and television. Commissioners must control broadcasting rights, and networks must control broadcast channels. Both broadcasting rights and broadcast channels, however, are becoming increasingly problematic. With teams attached to multinationals, it is unlikely that they will be any more docile in ceding broadcasting rights to the commissioner, especially where cross-promotion opportunities are concerned.[11] And the profusion of cable, satellite, and pay-per-view television options at the international level will provide even greater temptation for teams owners to cut their own deals. Hence the current struggles over broadcasting rights and policy are likely to be greatly magnified with international expansion.

As the market share of the major networks is declining in the United States, each is pursuing an aggressive strategy of acquisition of overseas broadcasting companies. It is unlikely, however, that anything resembling the one-time dominance of network television in this country will emerge at the global level. There are likely to be hundreds of channels in most countries, mostly differing in composition across countries and regions. These channels will extend localism to an international scale, with locales large enough to lure teams and leagues to broadcast virtually all of their games somewhere. Yet there will undoubtedly emerge stations that are truly international in scope. The challenge for future leagues will be to mobilize a truly international public around a limited number of games *and* to tap the sizable local publics around the globe with the large number of remaining games.

One way this might be done is to cultivate a sharp distinction between "event" broadcasts and "convenience" broadcasts. Games billed as events must be broadcast at the time they occur, which means they will appear at different times in different locations around the globe. Other broadcasts will be aired at the best, or most convenient, time slots that can be locally scheduled (which may be the same time in the day around the globe) or purchased directly by the viewer online. If event broadcasts are scarce enough, they could prompt viewers to adjust their own schedules around them. Given the movement toward round-the-clock economic activity, subcontracted work done at home, and flextime, this is not entirely far fetched. The electrifying idea that viewers throughout the world might all be focused on the same game would be enough to persuade some people to stay up past their normal bedtime for certain events. For the large number of other games, the selectivity and convenience of particular viewers must be paramount in marketing efforts. These games will be like Chinese food in New York City: available anytime you want, delivered to your door still warm, but never hot; something you like, but will not miss if you go out for an Italian meal.

The temptation will be great for future major leagues to create their own cable or satellite stations. Ever since this became technologically feasible, the NFL has been using this possibility as a threat in its negotiations with the networks. Acquiring the prime-time Monday Night Football slot on ABC, however, was more valuable to the NFL than the full possession of any cable channel could ever have been. By moving into the network's prime-time slot, NFL football gained legitimacy as well as viewers. Major League Baseball recently moved in the opposite direction. Having lost its network (CBS) contract for the 1994 season, it launched the Baseball Network in July 1994, only a month before a players' strike shut down the game for the season. None of these recent events is likely to help Major League Baseball. As major leagues begin to pursue international publics in earnest, gaining slots on popular preexisting channels will be crucial for success. Of course, this will by no means be easy. An overwhelming tangle of jurisdictions and regulations will have to be worked through. The politics waged over Sunday baseball in the United States will undoubtedly have to be waged over each day and hour of broadcast time somewhere in the world.

No aspect of the strange new world will be easy to bring about. More resistance is likely on the home front than abroad. In the United States change will be construed as a threat rather than an opportunity by many fans, cities, and team owners. Despite the decreasing dependence of teams on local support, the attachment of teams to cities has become too much a part of the natural order of things to be easily abandoned. Yet nearly everything that appears natural today would have seemed quite strange from the standpoint of earlier times, and the strange new world ahead, if it can be brought about, will quickly become the only one that makes sense. As an experiment, we need to situate ourselves in the strange new world and look back to current times.

A Voice from the Future

We fled the large cities long ago, and think back on them as failed social experiments. Most of us work out of our homes, in small, secure communities scattered throughout the countryside, doing work on a subcontracting basis mainly for large corporations. We live within an hour's travel by high-speed monorail of an entertainment village that includes a multisport arena and a vast array of amusement and shopping opportunities. Major league events at the arena draw people from great distances. The arena management is very aggressive in booking events, staging twelve live events last year that brought twenty-four of the best teams in four major league sports into the village. In addition, numerous major league games are telecast on a huge screen in the arena at all hours of the day and night. It's a great place to leave the kids while shopping, or to sit down yourself while the kids are pursuing other amusements. Of course, there are plenty of nonsports events like concerts and religious revivals.

Believe it or not, large cities used to build stadiums to house a single team, and people called fans would go see the same team play over and over. Now there are some teams we would like to see at the village more often, but there are many more that we would definitely not want to see play again and again. It is hard to imagine how fans could be persuaded to support such teams on such a regular basis, or why cities would make such large investments in the belief that they would. We are told that there was something called fan loyalty to city teams, and this must be true, because otherwise their actions don't make any sense. Frankly, we would be offended if the arena management expected us to come see the same losing team play over and over. We enjoy the variety and the chance to follow what is going on throughout the league. We even turn out for an occasional losing team because live games are scarce and would be scarcer if we did not show up.[12] And it's a good excuse to come into the village. Whatever the builders of the abandoned old city stadiums had in mind, they now serve as fitting monuments to the failed cities of the past.

Most of the year our favorite teams are playing in some remote part of the world. Though many of their games are telecast on the huge screen in the village, we mostly follow our favorite teams on home television. Most any game we might wish to see can be purchased on the information superhighway and piped directly to our televisions at a time that we request. These are low-budget productions. Each sport, however, broadcasts two special games a week live, around the world. Besides defining where the action is within a major league, the broadcasts take us all over the globe. During breaks, segments are inserted on the local cultures where the games are played as well as on the reception the teams and players have received as they travel around. In the past, only Olympic broadcasts expanded viewers' horizons in this way. But these were limited to one new location every four years, whereas the four major league sports now bring into our homes as many as eight games a week. Odd as it sounds, the major leagues of the past would not let teams venture outside a closed circuit of mostly U.S. cities. While claiming to produce "world champions," the major leagues never showed the viewer that their teams and players were known anywhere outside the circuit.

Today we celebrate winning teams and star players that are recognized throughout the world. Every time we see the reception given our favorite teams and stars in remote locations, they become larger in our own eyes. Players travel the whole world, and receive adulation wherever they go. So when they come to the entertainment village it is a major event, and we turn out to welcome them just as the rest of the world has. In the past, viewers could not so easily share in each other's celebration of winners and stars. Teams traveled only to the home locations of other teams, where they received no open support or adulation. Their arrival and stay was not much different from that of a mid-level manager on a routine business trip. Even outside the fixed and limited destinations, the element of travel was omitted from game broadcasts because it would have made the traveling team appear insignificant. The fact that home cities cheered for their teams did little to enhance their stature elsewhere. Past major leagues isolated viewers from each other. Although the best teams were presented as something the world celebrated, nobody actually got to see anyone in remote places doing any celebrating.

We have no immutable loyalties to particular teams. Players and teams constantly have to prove themselves to gain our attention and praise. We have our favorites, but there is no team or player who cannot fall from grace as far as we are concerned. The multinational corporations that teams represent encourage this insistence on excellence. We have grown up in a world where rivalries between multinational corporations permeate our daily life. In the daily battles waged over excellence in the marketplace, however, there are rarely any clear winners and losers. The rivalries go on indefinitely, in the marketplace and in protracted ad campaigns. But when the representative teams meet on the field, there is sure to be a winner and a loser. Although we know that a loss does not really mean that the sponsor corporation has been defeated, or even that its team will not get up and come back again, the playing of a game is still welcomed in rivalries that would otherwise have no resolution. Just the thought that people around the world are eagerly anticipating the outcome makes it seem all the more large and important.

Before teams were attached to multinationals, they were attached to cities. This evidently helped arouse local fan loyalty, and got public officials to build stadiums for teams. But especially after televised sports appeared, it is not clear why teams continued for so long to be attached to something that could only provide a limited base of support. Great teams can command attention regardless of the entity they are attached to, but the attachment to cities only seemed to discourage the attention of those outside the city. And the rivalries that developed between teams had no clear corollary in the relations between major league cities. Because the mere possession of a major league team helped promote a city, the real competition was between the cities who lacked teams and the ones who were trying to hold on to them. Whatever rivalries may have existed between major league cities, apart from their teams, were not apparent to the sports enthusiast and hence could not have helped stimulate interest in a game. Outside the cities, and especially outside the country, the attachment of teams to cities could only have been a liability for major leagues. With the attachment to multinationals, people everywhere are oriented to what teams represent and are wrapped up in the intense rivalries between them. Today we would rather be involved in the pursuit of excellence wherever it appears than be loyal to some team that happens to be based nearby and is not doing very well. There may have been a time when cities inspired enthusiasts to support anything in their midst, but it is long past.

This scenario for the future contains the seeds of a curious possibility. Could it be that one day the major leagues will be embarrassed over how competition was organized in the times in which we now reside? The *Official NFL Encyclopedia* presently omits all record of the NFL's first twenty-five years of existence. By current standards, these years are embarrassingly ragged. Yet for those who followed the NFL in the 1920s and 1930s, there must have been a good deal of pride in the accomplishments of the league both in terms of its great players and teams and in terms of the scale of its finances. But what was once a source of pride became an embarrassment in light of what followed. Could what we take so much pride in today suffer the same fate? Might the hard-fought pennant races that currently involve us so deeply someday be quietly dropped from the official record? Perhaps instead of the record some myth will be constructed about how the future teams came

into being. Disney may already be in the process of doing this for its
Mighty Ducks. The corporation's ugly ducklings were transformed into
mighty ducks by playing ice hockey for the honor and glory of a law
firm headed by a Mr. Duckworth, and not for a locale. Instead of pain-
fully evolving for more than a century, future teams, attached to corporations, appear destined to rise quickly from mythical humble origins
with a few gimmicks and a lot of help from smart lawyers.

Every element in the scenario for future major leagues can be found
somewhere in the present: the elements only need to be extended and
fit together into a new prototype. At this writing, plans are being laid
for a new football league to challenge the NFL, the "A League," tentatively scheduled to open with twelve franchises in the fall of 1995.
Teams will each have a corporate sponsor. Players will wear the colors
of the corporation, and display the corporate logos on their helmets (or
coach's cap). According to the organizers Mike Lynn (former president
of the World League) and Jim Spence (former ABC Sports vice president), "You aren't selling a franchise as much as you are a marketing
approach" (Pasquarelli 1994). By contrast, corporations are paying $40
million for 1996 Olympic sponsorship in Atlanta, plus another $40 mil-
lion in support. For a $10 million investment in the syndicated A
League, however, corporations not only get to display their logos on a
regular basis but also receive revenues and equity in return. To keep
teams from overspending on players, all players will sign with the league
and not with individual teams, and will be distributed via a draft.[13] As
of September 1994, Federal Express had signed on and Anheuser-Busch
was close to doing so. Disney, who had been trying to purchase the
NFL's Los Angeles Rams, had so far refused. Negotiations with CBS,
recently abandoned by the NFL for the new Fox network, were in
progress.

Despite the bold new attachment to corporations, the A League organizers have not been able to envision a detachment from cities. Corporate teams will be based in home cities and will parade their corporate
logos in front of a local public for half the games they play. Original
plans called for thirty-two franchises, with a whole division based in
Japan. This would, of course, have left other areas quite thinly represented. Unable to get very far in this international direction, the A
League seems to have fallen back on targeting cities that were left out
of the NFL's latest expansion, though permission was gained from CBS
to place one franchise in London. Hence the A League appears to be

falling into the mold of the World League, only it will be in head-on competition with the NFL in the fall. The power of the corporate attachment is lost in the search for leftover cities. Critics may be right in suspecting that A League games will simply be three-hour commercials for the corporation (Pasquarelli 1994). With teams still playing for cities in the minds of viewers, the corporate logos are likely to seem entirely out of place.

Challengers have never displaced an established major league. They have only propelled them into actions that are often much overdue. Although the established major leagues possess quite different propensities for change, they are in a much better position to usher in the strange new world than any challenger could ever be. Multinationals, or the individuals who control them, already own a large number of major league teams. And the major leagues have already developed teams and players whose names have gained international recognition. What major leagues must do, however, is detach teams from cities, and this is a huge step. The attachment of teams to cities was the idea around which major leagues first formed, and has served as a dependable fallback ever since. Abandoning the attachment will both open vast opportunities and create great risks. If the opportunities are not enough to propel the major leagues forward, a serious challenger inevitably will.

In the future, major league competition will be scrutinized as never before. Winning will be more important than ever in gaining teams and players international recognition. But as the world celebrates winners, major leagues will have to tend to the quiet business of ensuring the accommodation of losers. The quest for ways to extend the repetition across time and the sameness across teams will be more determined than ever. In this respect, the strange new world ahead will be a continuation of the past 125 years.

· · ·

Appendixes
Notes
References
Index

Appendix A

The Major Leagues

League	Years	Fate
Baseball		
National Association (NA)	1871–1875	Disbanded into NL
National League (NL)	1876–	Survives
American Association (AA)	1882–1891	Disbanded into NL
Union Association (UA)	1884	Dissolved
Players League (PL)	1890	Dissolved
American League (AL)	1901–	Survives
Federal League (FL)	1914–1915	Dissolved
Mexican League (ML)[a]	1946–1948	Dissolved
Basketball		
American B League (ABL)	1925–1931	Became regional
National B League (NBL)	1937–1948	Absorbed in NBA
Basketball Association of America (BBA)	1946–1948	Became NBA
Professional B League of America (PBLA)	1947	Dissolved
National B Association (NBA)	1949–	Survives
Continental League (CL)[b]	1961	Dissolved
American B Association (ABA)	1967–1975	Disbanded into NBA
Football		
National F League (NFL)	1920–	Survives
American F League (AFL1)	1926	Dissolved
American F League (AFL2)	1936–1937	Dissolved
American F League (AFL3)	1940–1941	Dissolved
All-American F Conference (AAFC)	1946–1949	Disbanded into NFL
American F League (AFL)	1960–1969	Merged with NFL
World F League (WFL)	1974–1975	Dissolved
U.S. F League (USFL)	1983–1985	Dissolved

League	Years	Fate
Hockey		
National H Association (NHA)[a]	1910–1916	Disbanded into NHL
Pacific Coast H Association (PCHA)[a]	1912–1925	Sold out to NHL
Western H Association (WHA)[a]	1921–1925	Sold out to NHL
National H League (NHL)	1917–	Survives
World H Association (WHA)	1972–1979	Dissolved

Note: Major league status was determined first by geographic and demographic criteria and thereafter by the action of raiding players from an existing major league.

a. Primarily foreign leagues not included in analyses.

b. Discovered too late to include in analyses.

Statistics Brief

Major league sports produce reams of data. To make sense of this data, statistics are often required. This book makes use of a variety of statistics. Below are brief explanations of the statistics and measures used. The term "variable" is used for anything that varies across "cases." For example, population size varies across cities and travel distance varies across pairs of cities, so population size and travel distance are variables while cities and pairs of cities are the cases they vary across.

Average (or Mean)

Averages are a commonly used measure of central tendency, or the middling level of a variable. For example, the average population size of NFL cities was 3,242,090 in 1993, with the total number of people in larger cities equal to the total number of people in smaller cities. An average is computed by adding together all the cases of a variable and then dividing by the total number of cases. For example, the average population size of league cities is the total number of people that reside in league cities divided by the number of cities. Deviations from the average of a variable sum to zero across all cases, a property that was used above to give intuitive meaning to average population size.

Moving Average

The value of a variable may fluctuate across time for a single case. In this situation, variation across time can be observed with time periods serving as cases. But sometimes short-term fluctuations obscure longer-term movements or trends. To reduce these fluctuations, averages over a number of adjacent values can be substituted for the actual values. For example, the number of 1977 player trades in baseball can be replaced by the average number of trades over 1975, 1976, and 1977 to form, when applied to every year, a "three-year moving average." Averages will fluctuate less than actual values as they move across time. The more past years used in computing a moving average, the smoother will be the trajectory across time (making trends easier to observe).

Standard Deviation and z-scores

Standard deviation is a measure of the amount of variation around the average of a variable. If all NFL cities had close to 3,242,090 people, for example, the standard deviation would be low. With very large cities like New York, Los Angeles, and Chicago, and smaller cities like Seattle, Pittsburgh, and Kansas City, the standard deviation is high. The standard deviation is the square root of the average squared deviation from the mean (the variance is the average squared deviation). Since deviations from the mean are squared (otherwise they would sum to zero), the standard deviation is strongly influenced by extreme cases. If a league establishes a team in New York, the standard deviation of league city population size will increase sharply. In a distribution that is roughly bell shaped, 64 percent of all cases will fall within one standard deviation from the mean, and 96 percent will fall within two standard deviations. In the case of season performance, a standard deviation of .1 means that 96 percent of the teams should finish with win proportions between .3 and .7 (average performance is always .5 if no teams drop out). A z-score is the value of a variable expressed in terms of standard deviations, so that in the above case a team with a .7 performance would have a z-score of 2 and a team with a .3 performance would have a z-score of −2.

Performance Inequality

The standard deviation provides the basis for assessing the "tightness" of pennant races or (conversely) the amount of season performance inequality. But by itself, the standard deviation of win proportions will be heavily influenced by season lengths, and thus will not permit comparisons across sports. For example, in a season of one game, each team will win either all or none of its games (without ties), and hence performance inequality will be at a maximum even if all teams were perfectly equal in ability. To allow comparisons across differing season lengths, performance inequality is measured by the standard deviation of actual win proportions divided by the standard deviation one would expect if all teams were perfectly equal in ability (that is, game outcomes were determined by a coin toss).

The Performance Ordering (Kendell's tau)

Besides describing individual variables, statistics are used to assess the relationship between variables. For example, a relationship between performance and city size, called the performance ordering, should be found if better-performing teams are located in larger cities. Kendall's tau, or tau, is a measure of the relation between the ordering of one variable and the ordering of another across cases. If, for example, all possible pairs of teams are examined, tau is the number of pairs where the larger city has a better team ("concordant" pairs) minus the number of pairs where the smaller city has a better team ("discordant" pairs) divided by the number of possible pairs (with N teams, there are $\frac{1}{2}N(N - 1)$ pairs). A correction must be made to the denominator if there are ties in the ordering. In the case of city size and performance, tau will be 1 if all larger cities have better teams than smaller cities and -1 if the reverse is true. If there is no tendency in either direction, a crucial indicator for competitive balance, tau will be around zero.

t-statistic

A *t*-statistic can be computed for virtually any statistic, including tau and the others discussed below. The *t*-statistic helps interpret the magnitude of a statistic's value. For example, even if there were no systematic tendency for large cities to have better teams than small cities, one would not expect tau to be exactly zero in any given year. Repeated calculations of tau across time would yield a distribution of tau values centered around zero. In general, any unbiased statistic based on a sample should be thought of as drawn from a distribution of possible values. The average of this distribution is the "true" population value, and the standard deviation (commonly called the standard error) is dependent on sample size (large samples reduce the fluctuation of the sample statistics). In research, only one sample is typically drawn, so this distribution is never directly observed. The *t*-statistic helps one decide whether any given statistic is "truly" different from zero, or whether it is the product of "sampling" fluctuation around zero. Let's say we observe a tau of .2. Is this part of normal fluctuation around a "true" average of zero, or is the true average actually different from zero? As the number of standard errors a sample statistic lies from zero, the *t*-statistic can be translated into the chances of the former possibility (formulas for computing standard errors vary for each statistic, and can be found in any statistics textbook). If a *t*-statistic is greater than 1.96 (or less than −1.96), there is less than a 5 percent chance the sample was drawn from a population where there was no relation between the variables. If a *t*-statistic is greater than 1.60 (or less than -1.60), there is less than a 10 percent chance. So if our tau of .2 had a *t*-statistic of 1.8, we would know that there was a 5 to 10 percent chance of observing a tau so large if there were actually no relation between performance and city size. A 5 percent level is commonly used in social science, though when the researcher is wary of wrongly dismissing an observed relation as due purely to sampling fluctuation a 10 percent level can be employed.

Covariance and Correlation

Tau measures the relation between variables using only information on the ordering of the variables. Hence, for example, New York City is treated as a larger city in all pairings, but whether it is larger by a few people or a few million people is not treated as important. While this may be appropriate for the prediction that larger cities will have better teams, on other issues absolute size differences may be important. Correlations make use of absolute size differences, measuring the extent to which variables co-vary around their average levels. To compute covariance, the distance from the average of each variable is multiplied and these products are summed across cases, and this sum is divided by the number of cases to get an average cross-product. If above-average cases on one variable are above average on the other variable, or below average on both (yielding two negative values), all products will be positive and this will produce a high covariance. But if, for example, both strong and weak teams can be found in large (and small) cities, the mix of positive and negative cross-products will cancel each other out, producing a near zero covariance. If large cities tended to have weak teams, and small cities possessed strong teams, the covariance would be negative. To constrain the range of the correlation between 1 and -1, the covariance is divided by the product of the standard deviations of the two variables. In most social science applications, a correlation above .7 (or below $-.7$) is considered very strong, particularly when it is based on a sizable number of cases.

In this book, cross-season correlations are used to measure performance stability across time. Performance in season t is correlated with performance in season $t + k$, where t is any given season and k is the number of seasons after season t, or the season lag. If, for example, performance is highly stable, then teams doing well in any given season should also be doing well a few seasons later, and conversely for teams doing poorly. This would yield a high positive correlation, computed on the basis of all teams and seasons. A near zero correlation implies that it is impossible to predict future performance on the basis of present performance, as teams doing well this season are just as likely to do poorly in the next as they are to do well again.

Beta Coefficients in Regression Analysis

In many cases, it is necessary to look at the impact of a number of "independent" variables on a single "dependent variable." At the grocery store, for example, the final bill is based on the quantity and price of each item we purchase. If we want to know how much the bill will change if we buy one more pound of apples, we look at the price of apples. Outside the grocery store, we often have to infer "price," or what we will call beta coefficients, by observing how much the dependent variable changes when an independent variable changes (but all others remain constant). For example, we can ask what impact both city size and performance have on the number of player deals a team makes in any given season. The beta coefficients are the expected change in player deals for unit increases in the two impact variables. Hence if city size is measured in units of one million, a beta of .6 would mean that for each additional million people in a city, the city teams should engage in .6 more trades.

Betas are dependent on the unit of measurement, so that had population in the above example been measured in hundred thousands the beta would have been .06 (so a city with a million more people would still be expected to have .6, or 10 × .06, more trades). In cases where comparisons between different betas are central, all variables in the analysis are standardized (that is, converted into z-scores) by subtracting the mean and dividing by the standard deviation (making the unit a standard deviation). This makes the beta coefficient the effect of increasing a variable by one standard deviation. Wherever possible, this book uses unstandardized betas, so that impacts can be assessed in intuitive terms. The t-statistic, or in some places the standard error of the sample beta distribution on which the t-statistic is based, is given to facilitate comparisons across betas. Regardless of the unit of measurement, variables with a direct impact on the dependent variable should have high (or low if negative) t-statistics.

Logistic Regression

Sometimes the dependent variable in regression analysis is binary, as in the analysis of game outcomes where teams either win or lose. Assigning a "1" for win and a "0" for lose, it is possible to use ordinary regression analysis to assess the impact of other variables, like home and away team performance levels, on game outcome. Expected outcomes, based on estimated beta coefficients, could be interpreted in terms of probabilities of winning. Hence an expected outcome of .6 would mean a 60 percent chance of winning. Yet this method could yield predicted probabilities that are below 0 or above 1, pointing to the unrealistic nature of the underlying linear regression model. In response to this inadequacy, a nonlinear logistic regression model is used. In logistic regression, what gets predicted is the natural log of winning chances (p) divided by losing chances ($1 - p$). A natural log (ln) of a number is the power to which e (2.718 . . .) must be raised to equal the number [that is, if $y = e^x$, then $\ln(y) = x$]. The natural log of $p/(1 - p)$ can range from positive to negative infinity, and is accounted for by the standard linear combination of independent variables found in ordinary regression (or a grocery bill). Since only the outcome, and not the chances of an outcome (p), is observed, estimating the beta coefficients requires an iterative search algorithm that uses considerably more computer time than ordinary regression. Because of the nonlinear transformation of the dependent variable, interpretation of the beta coefficients in terms of impacts on winning chances is also complicated. Because of these difficulties, logistic regression was used only to supply inputs for the computer simulation, which required winning chances to remain between 0 and 1. As shown in the text, estimates from ordinary and logistic regression were quite consistent.

R-squared

Regression analysis identifies the impact of any number of independent variables on a dependent variable. Sometimes, however, our interest is not in the individual impacts but in the overall usefulness of the particular set of independent variables. R-squared is a measure of the proportion of variation in the dependent variable that covaries with the linear combination of independent variables in ordinary regression. As a proportion, it ranges between 0 and 1. An R-squared of "1" means that the exact level of a dependent variable can be predicted on the basis of levels of the independent variables (and beta coefficients). For example, if the number of player deals a team engaged in was perfectly related to its city size and performance, the fact that a team was attached to a large city and had performed poorly would allow the exact prediction of its number of player deals. In the case of a zero R-squared, the levels of independent variables would be useless in predicting the dependent variable. Here one could not do better than predict the overall average number of player deals for every case. To the extent R-squared increases, predictions will vary across cases.

R-squared increases when more variables are added to the equation, since even an unrelated variable will account for some variation (that is, will not have an exactly zero beta coefficient) on the basis of sampling fluctuations alone. An adjusted R-squared is sometimes used to remove the amount of variance explained one would expect even if the independent variables had no explanatory power.

Additional Measures

In Appendix C, two additional measures are calculated for each major league each season of its operation. One is the site competition, or overlap, within cities between rival major leagues. For each case where two teams occupied the same city, one "overlap" was registered. Thus if three teams (A, B, C) occupied the same city, the three possible pairs (A-B, A-C, B-C) each added an overlap. A second measure, league stability, was computed by dividing the number of changes in league composition from the prior year by the number of possible changes. Thus a "0" means that team composition did not change. In the first year of operation, stability is always "1" since there is no overlap with the prior year. In the computation, major leagues that changed their name were treated as new leagues, and continuities with the past were ignored. The text contains sufficient information to correct this problem, if it is regarded as such.

Appendix C

League Statistics

(For an explanation of the statistics, see Appendix B.)

Baseball

Year	Average distance	Average pop. base	Site overlap	Perform. ordering (tau)	Tau t-stat.	League stability	Perform. equality
National Association (NA)							
1871	527.65	330.16	0	0.67	2.50	1.00	1.96
1872	321.53	547.26	0	0.09	0.39	0.36	2.81
1873	179.56	603.58	0	0.20	0.73	0.33	2.64
1874	352.64	693.23	0	0.30	0.99	0.40	2.53
1875	481.86	542.39	0	−0.04	−0.18	0.43	3.58
National League (NL)							
1876	613.71	481.98	0	0.00	0.00	1.00	3.49
1877	650.60	252.82	0	−0.20	−0.56	0.25	2.06
1878	615.20	221.77	0	0.33	0.94	0.67	2.21
1879	483.65	200.64	0	0.29	0.99	0.60	2.81
1880	499.53	207.88	0	0.00	0.00	0.22	2.92
1881	468.51	203.44	0	0.21	0.74	0.22	1.49
1882	468.51	216.38	0	0.58	1.98	0.00	2.32
1883	465.27	567.09	2	−0.07	−0.25	0.40	2.80
1884	465.27	588.58	5	−0.14	−0.50	0.00	3.51
1885	582.18	633.94	4	0.36	1.24	0.22	3.50
1886	692.82	652.33	4	0.43	1.49	0.40	4.14
1887	492.89	658.30	3	0.43	1.49	0.40	2.52
1888	492.89	679.33	2	0.71	2.47	0.00	2.06
1889	479.90	707.09	2	0.79	2.72	0.22	2.29
1890	463.78	1008.50	10	0.47	1.61	0.30	3.65
1891	463.78	1042.15	2	0.18	0.62	0.00	1.86
1892	498.18	828.47	0	0.11	0.48	0.33	2.66
1893	498.18	853.33	0	0.20	0.89	0.00	2.16
1894	498.18	878.18	0	0.50	2.26	0.00	2.79
1895	498.18	903.04	0	0.26	1.17	0.00	2.87
1896	498.18	927.90	0	0.01	0.07	0.00	2.64
1897	498.18	952.76	0	0.14	0.62	0.00	2.99
1898	498.18	977.62	0	0.05	0.21	0.00	2.96
1899	498.18	1002.48	0	0.32	1.44	0.00	3.52
1900	567.91	1369.25	0	0.04	0.12	0.33	1.37
1901	566.84	1406.51	3	−0.04	−0.12	0.00	2.41

Baseball *(continued)*

Year	Average distance	Average pop. base	Site overlap	Perform. ordering (tau)	Tau *t*-stat.	League stability	Perform. equality
1902	566.84	1443.78	4	−0.33	−1.11	0.00	2.62
1903	566.84	1481.04	6	0.04	0.12	0.00	2.69
1904	566.84	1518.30	6	0.04	0.12	0.00	3.07
1905	566.84	1555.56	6	0.11	0.37	0.00	3.30
1906	566.84	1592.86	6	0.33	1.11	0.00	3.55
1907	566.84	1630.09	6	0.11	0.37	0.00	2.79
1908	566.84	1667.35	6	0.04	0.12	0.00	3.11
1909	566.84	1704.61	6	0.04	0.12	0.00	3.68
1910	566.84	1741.88	6	0.26	0.87	0.00	2.51
1911	566.84	1783.58	6	0.33	1.11	0.00	2.56
1912	566.84	1825.28	6	0.11	0.37	0.00	2.86
1913	566.84	1868.98	6	0.33	1.11	0.00	2.46
1914	566.84	1908.68	11	0.33	1.11	0.00	1.56
1915	566.84	1950.38	11	0.11	0.37	0.00	1.14
1916	566.84	1992.08	6	0.56	1.86	0.00	2.25
1917	566.84	2033.78	6	0.26	0.87	0.00	2.09
1918	566.84	2075.48	6	0.11	0.37	0.00	1.98
1919	566.84	2117.18	6	−0.11	−0.37	0.00	2.70
1920	566.84	2158.88	6	0.11	0.37	0.00	1.61
1921	566.84	2196.13	6	0.04	0.12	0.00	2.20
1922	566.84	2233.38	6	−0.11	−0.37	0.00	2.15
1923	566.84	2270.63	6	−0.11	−0.37	0.00	2.51
1924	566.84	2307.88	6	0.33	1.11	0.00	2.48
1925	566.84	2345.13	6	−0.41	−1.36	0.00	1.54
1926	566.84	2382.38	6	−0.33	−1.11	0.00	1.59
1927	566.84	2419.63	6	−0.11	−0.37	0.00	2.50
1928	566.84	2456.88	6	0.11	0.37	0.00	2.96
1929	566.84	2494.13	6	0.18	0.62	0.00	2.09
1930	566.84	2531.38	6	0.26	0.87	0.00	2.27
1931	566.84	2553.78	6	0.47	1.61	0.00	2.14
1932	566.84	2576.18	6	0.18	0.62	0.00	1.40
1933	566.84	2598.58	6	0.18	0.62	0.00	1.98
1934	566.84	2620.98	6	0.33	1.11	0.00	2.36
1935	566.84	2643.38	6	0.26	0.87	0.00	3.11
1936	566.84	2665.78	6	0.11	0.37	0.00	1.93
1937	566.84	2688.18	6	0.33	1.11	0.00	2.30
1938	566.84	2710.58	6	−0.18	−0.62	0.00	2.15
1939	566.84	2732.98	6	−0.11	−0.37	0.00	2.52
1940	566.84	3984.00	6	−0.33	−1.11	0.00	2.29
1941	566.84	4025.59	6	−0.11	−0.37	0.00	2.87
1942	566.84	4067.18	6	−0.04	−0.12	0.00	3.23

1943	566.84	4108.76	6	−0.47	−1.61	0.00	2.30
1944	566.84	4150.35	6	−0.47	−1.61	0.00	2.42
1945	566.84	4191.94	6	0.11	0.37	0.00	2.67
1946	566.84	4233.53	6	0.04	0.12	0.00	2.11
1947	566.84	4275.11	6	0.11	0.37	0.00	1.86
1948	566.84	4316.70	6	−0.04	−0.12	0.00	1.62
1949	566.84	4358.29	6	0.18	0.62	0.00	2.07
1950	566.84	4399.88	6	0.40	1.36	0.00	1.90
1951	566.84	4436.75	6	0.26	0.87	0.00	1.98
1952	566.84	4473.63	6	0.47	1.61	0.00	2.72
1953	551.77	4330.44	5	0.11	0.37	0.22	2.60
1954	551.77	4367.88	4	0.26	0.87	0.00	2.25
1955	551.77	4405.31	3	0.26	0.87	0.00	1.74
1956	551.77	4442.75	3	−0.26	−0.87	0.00	1.99
1957	551.77	4480.19	3	−0.33	−1.11	0.00	1.80
1958	1305.09	3165.85	1	−0.44	−1.49	0.00	1.19
1959	1305.09	3229.68	1	0.07	0.25	0.00	1.17
1960	1305.09	3293.50	1	−0.29	−0.99	0.00	2.03
1961	1305.09	3333.59	2	−0.36	−1.24	0.00	2.32
1962	1315.60	3816.00	3	−0.29	−1.16	0.20	3.00
1963	1315.60	3858.10	3	−0.07	−0.27	0.00	2.09
1964	1315.60	3900.20	3	−0.39	−1.52	0.00	1.96
1965	1315.60	3942.30	3	−0.11	−0.45	0.00	2.19
1966	1315.60	3991.52	3	0.07	0.27	0.18	1.81
1967	1315.60	4036.64	3	−0.16	−0.63	0.00	1.74
1968	1315.60	4081.76	4	−0.29	−1.16	0.00	1.13
1969	1453.47	3773.72	4	0.24	1.10	0.17	2.43
1970	1453.47	3818.42	4	0.12	0.55	0.00	1.49
1971	1453.47	3830.98	4	0.12	0.55	0.00	1.55
1972	1453.47	3843.53	4	−0.09	−0.41	0.00	1.99
1973	1453.47	3856.09	4	0.12	0.55	0.00	1.55
1974	1453.47	3868.65	4	−0.28	−1.23	0.00	1.88
1975	1453.47	3881.21	4	0.06	0.27	0.00	1.80
1976	1453.47	3893.77	4	0.09	0.41	0.00	2.10
1977	1453.47	3906.33	4	0.06	0.27	0.00	1.96
1978	1453.47	3918.88	4	0.06	0.27	0.00	1.53
1979	1453.47	3931.44	4	−0.27	−1.23	0.00	1.76
1980	1453.47	3944.00	4	0.03	0.14	0.00	1.52
1981	1453.47	3950.28	4	−0.06	−0.27	0.00	1.50
1982	1453.47	3956.56	4	0.18	0.82	0.00	1.48
1983	1453.47	3962.84	4	0.24	1.10	0.00	1.29
1984	1453.47	3969.12	4	0.03	0.14	0.00	1.12
1985	1453.47	3975.40	4	0.12	0.55	0.00	2.12
1986	1453.47	3981.68	4	0.18	0.82	0.00	1.82
1987	1453.47	3987.95	4	0.09	0.41	0.00	1.44
1988	1453.47	3994.23	3	0.12	0.55	0.00	1.83

Baseball *(continued)*

Year	Average distance	Average pop. base	Site overlap	Perform. ordering (tau)	Tau *t*-stat.	League stability	Perform. equality
1989	1453.47	4000.51	3	0.21	0.96	0.00	1.43
1990	1453.47	4006.79	3	0.16	0.69	0.00	1.39
1991	1453.47	4006.79	3	−0.12	−0.55	0.00	1.49
1992	1453.47	4006.79	3	−0.58	−2.61	0.00	1.60
1993	1453.47	4006.79	3	0.12	0.60	0.16	2.29
1994	1453.47	4006.79	3	0.14	0.71	0.00	1.48
American Association (AA)							
1882	471.24	377.03	0	−0.07	−0.19	1.00	2.21
1883	461.88	537.95	2	0.29	0.99	0.25	2.98
1884	427.56	523.68	9	0.09	0.43	0.31	3.22
1885	489.09	810.56	4	−0.18	−0.62	0.39	1.99
1886	489.09	830.83	4	−0.11	−0.37	0.00	2.18
1887	499.87	841.01	3	−0.18	−0.62	0.22	2.97
1888	592.49	603.75	2	0.79	2.72	0.13	3.11
1889	581.40	597.63	2	0.64	2.23	0.22	3.44
1890	481.98	310.63	2	−0.18	−0.62	0.55	2.46
1891	574.65	394.03	2	0.50	1.73	0.55	2.61
Union Association (UA)							
1884	627.75	270.98	8	0.42	1.92	1.00	3.18
Players League (PL)							
1890	422.42	1003.25	10	0.69	2.35	1.00	2.40
Federal League (FL)							
1914	595.28	1215.50	8	−0.14	−0.50	1.00	1.49
1915	623.51	1256.69	8	0.07	0.25	0.22	2.03
American League (AL)							
1901	495.17	680.91	3	0.58	1.98	1.00	1.49
1902	538.37	735.28	4	0.50	1.73	0.22	2.03
1903	558.50	1100.31	6	0.14	0.50	0.22	2.25
1904	558.50	1129.38	6	0.57	1.98	0.00	2.95
1905	558.50	1158.44	6	0.14	0.50	0.00	2.05
1906	558.50	1187.50	6	0.57	1.98	0.00	2.52
1907	558.50	1216.56	6	0.14	0.50	0.00	2.45
1908	558.50	1245.63	6	−0.29	−0.99	0.00	2.12
1909	558.50	1274.69	6	0.07	0.25	0.00	2.81
1910	558.50	1303.75	6	0.21	0.74	0.00	2.63
1911	558.50	1340.79	6	−0.07	−0.25	0.00	2.54

1912	558.50	1377.83	6	− 0.29	− 0.99	0.00	2.92
1913	558.50	1414.86	6	− 0.29	− 0.99	0.00	2.23
1914	558.50	1451.90	9	− 0.14	− 0.50	0.00	2.26
1915	558.50	1488.94	9	− 0.07	− 0.25	0.00	3.26
1916	558.50	1525.98	6	0.21	0.74	0.00	2.62
1917	558.50	1563.01	6	− 0.07	− 0.25	0.00	2.39
1918	558.50	1600.05	6	− 0.43	− 1.49	0.00	1.61
1919	558.50	1637.09	6	0.43	1.49	0.00	2.88
1920	558.50	1674.13	6	0.14	0.50	0.00	2.74
1921	558.50	1706.54	6	− 0.07	− 0.25	0.00	2.28
1922	558.50	1738.95	6	0.29	0.99	0.00	1.81
1923	558.50	1771.36	6	0.21	0.74	0.00	1.72
1924	558.50	1803.78	6	− 0.07	− 0.25	0.00	1.62
1925	558.50	1836.19	6	− 0.21	− 0.74	0.00	2.29
1926	558.50	1868.60	6	0.43	1.49	0.00	2.28
1927	558.50	1901.01	6	0.50	1.73	0.00	2.86
1928	558.50	1933.43	6	0.43	1.49	0.00	2.41
1929	558.50	1965.84	6	0.29	0.99	0.00	2.40
1930	558.50	1998.25	6	0.14	0.50	0.00	2.57
1931	558.50	2011.91	6	0.00	0.00	0.00	2.91
1932	558.50	2025.58	6	0.29	0.99	0.00	3.44
1933	558.50	2039.24	6	0.14	0.50	0.00	2.19
1934	558.50	2052.90	6	0.21	0.74	0.00	2.36
1935	558.50	2066.56	6	0.21	0.74	0.00	1.88
1936	558.50	2080.23	6	0.29	0.99	0.00	2.35
1937	558.50	2093.89	6	0.50	1.73	0.00	2.77
1938	558.50	2107.55	6	0.00	0.00	0.00	2.53
1939	558.50	2121.21	6	0.21	0.74	0.00	3.16
1940	558.50	3116.38	6	0.22	0.74	0.00	2.04
1941	558.50	3160.75	6	0.45	1.49	0.00	1.71
1942	558.50	3205.13	6	0.14	0.50	0.00	2.40
1943	558.50	3249.50	6	− 0.07	− 0.25	0.00	2.15
1944	558.50	3293.88	6	0.07	0.25	0.00	1.34
1945	558.50	3338.25	6	− 0.21	− 0.74	0.00	1.71
1946	558.50	3382.63	6	0.00	0.00	0.00	2.58
1947	558.50	3427.00	6	0.36	1.24	0.00	1.85
1948	558.50	3471.38	6	0.00	0.00	0.00	2.81
1949	558.50	3515.75	6	0.29	0.99	0.00	2.86
1950	558.50	3560.13	6	0.21	0.74	0.00	2.94
1951	558.50	3615.26	6	0.21	0.74	0.00	2.37
1952	558.50	3670.40	6	0.21	0.74	0.00	2.21
1953	558.50	3725.54	5	0.14	0.50	0.00	2.64
1954	444.95	3740.13	4	0.21	0.74	0.22	3.42
1955	613.84	3414.25	3	0.43	1.49	0.22	2.57
1956	613.84	3464.35	3	0.57	1.98	0.00	2.33
1957	613.84	3514.45	3	0.64	2.23	0.00	2.16

Baseball *(continued)*

Year	Average distance	Average pop. base	Site overlap	Perform. ordering (tau)	Tau *t*-stat.	League stability	Perform. equality
1958	613.84	3564.55	1	0.64	2.23	0.00	1.32
1959	613.84	3614.65	1	0.50	1.73	0.00	1.58
1960	613.84	3664.75	1	0.29	0.99	0.00	1.98
1961	1029.43	3742.06	2	0.38	1.52	0.20	2.45
1962	1029.43	3788.62	3	0.38	1.52	0.00	1.51
1963	1029.43	3835.18	3	0.20	0.81	0.00	2.05
1964	1029.43	3881.74	3	0.56	2.24	0.00	2.17
1965	1029.43	3928.30	3	0.02	0.09	0.00	2.18
1966	1029.43	3974.86	3	−0.29	−1.16	0.00	1.32
1967	1029.43	4021.42	3	0.11	0.45	0.00	1.49
1968	1309.53	4245.58	4	−0.16	−0.63	0.18	1.78
1969	1423.75	3800.13	4	0.03	0.14	0.17	2.17
1970	1205.54	3483.67	4	0.12	0.55	0.15	2.30
1971	1205.54	3842.97	4	0.06	0.27	0.00	2.03
1972	1205.54	3805.38	4	0.33	1.51	0.15	1.66
1973	1254.19	3808.41	4	−0.03	−0.14	0.00	1.64
1974	1254.19	3811.43	4	0.09	0.41	0.00	1.09
1975	1254.19	3814.46	4	−0.03	−0.14	0.00	1.79
1976	1254.19	3817.48	4	−0.09	−0.41	0.00	1.50
1977	1339.18	3587.87	4	0.08	0.38	0.14	2.42
1978	1339.18	3593.84	4	0.05	0.27	0.00	2.13
1979	1339.18	3599.81	4	0.03	0.16	0.00	2.22
1980	1339.18	3605.79	4	−0.12	−0.60	0.00	1.97
1981	1339.18	3608.77	4	0.03	0.16	0.00	1.69
1982	1339.18	3611.76	4	−0.12	−0.60	0.00	1.71
1983	1339.18	3614.74	4	0.10	0.49	0.00	1.65
1984	1339.18	3617.73	4	0.39	1.92	0.00	1.53
1985	1339.18	3620.71	4	0.41	2.03	0.00	1.78
1986	1339.18	3623.70	4	0.39	1.92	0.00	1.34
1987	1339.18	3626.69	4	0.03	0.16	0.00	1.57
1988	1337.78	3235.67	3	0.08	0.38	0.13	1.86
1989	1337.78	3238.93	3	−0.14	−0.71	0.00	1.60
1990	1337.78	3235.71	3	0.21	1.04	0.13	1.40
1991	1337.78	3325.71	3	0.19	0.93	0.00	1.49
1992	1337.78	3325.71	3	0.17	0.82	0.00	1.55
1993	1337.78	3325.71	3	0.32	1.59	0.00	1.34
1994	1337.78	3325.71	3	0.19	0.93	0.00	1.40

Basketball

American Basketball League (ABL)

1925	440.35	1439.78	0	−0.11	−0.42	1.00	1.96
1926	412.57	1654.45	0	0.14	0.50	0.46	2.62
1927	425.76	2423.51	0	0.04	0.12	0.30	2.15
1928	420.47	2077.43	0	0.11	0.37	0.40	1.85
1929	430.69	1568.71	0	0.33	1.05	0.25	1.90
1930	424.10	1607.00	0	0.05	0.15	0.25	1.10

National Basketball League (NBL)

1937	274.59	243.60	0	−0.14	−0.62	1.00	2.05
1938	308.93	320.33	0	0.00	0.00	0.67	2.04
1939	277.70	752.91	0	−0.08	−0.25	0.40	1.24
1940	273.63	1153.00	0	−0.37	−1.05	0.13	1.35
1941	262.07	904.59	0	−0.50	−1.50	0.56	2.07
1942	220.87	1112.44	0	−0.32	−0.74	0.29	1.50
1943	292.92	411.18	0	−0.18	−0.34	0.50	2.32
1944	317.53	1461.47	0	−0.14	−0.38	0.33	2.08
1945	348.83	1021.00	0	−0.47	−1.61	0.44	2.31
1946	365.01	865.60	2	−0.03	−0.14	0.46	2.17
1947	421.25	312.18	1	0.02	0.08	0.36	2.77
1948	555.92	460.72	0	−0.66	−2.59	0.69	2.41

Basketball Association of America (BAA)

1946	511.20	2823.22	2	0.05	0.23	1.00	2.44
1947	553.08	3151.13	1	0.08	0.25	0.42	2.11
1948	615.44	2320.30	0	0.09	0.41	0.33	2.49

Professional Basketball League of America (PBLA)

1947	645.15	790.71	2	0.42	2.13	1.00	1.44

National Basketball Association (NBA)

1949	691.28	1683.99	0	0.02	0.12	1.00	2.76
1950	582.56	1935.55	0	0.16	0.70	0.35	1.66
1951	580.47	2105.18	0	−0.07	−0.27	0.25	1.99
1952	580.47	2136.46	0	−0.11	−0.45	0.00	3.06
1953	575.57	2334.20	0	0.06	0.21	0.10	2.47
1954	599.90	2464.60	0	−0.22	−0.74	0.11	1.30
1955	649.94	2595.50	0	0.30	0.99	0.22	0.97
1956	649.94	2626.00	0	0.30	0.99	0.00	0.86
1957	665.64	3135.54	0	0.00	0.00	0.40	1.92
1958	665.64	3177.65	0	0.14	0.50	0.00	2.39
1959	665.64	3219.76	0	0.21	0.74	0.00	2.98
1960	1078.90	3817.00	0	−0.21	−0.74	0.22	2.34
1961	1017.28	4126.66	0	−0.11	−0.42	0.11	2.79

Basketball *(continued)*

Year	Average distance	Average pop. base	Site overlap	Perform. ordering (tau)	Tau *t*-stat.	League stability	Perform. equality
1962	1366.30	3980.51	0	−0.45	−1.67	0.20	2.72
1963	1388.93	3949.23	0	−0.39	−1.46	0.36	2.81
1964	1388.93	3990.64	0	−0.11	−0.42	0.00	2.74
1965	1388.93	4032.06	0	−0.17	−0.63	0.00	2.29
1966	1303.83	4333.58	0	0.02	0.09	0.10	2.95
1967	1566.78	3864.52	1	0.34	1.51	0.17	2.93
1968	1554.38	3452.03	3	0.41	2.03	0.27	2.65
1969	1554.38	3492.87	2	0.21	1.04	0.00	2.10
1970	1522.45	3170.12	1	0.44	2.47	0.18	2.56
1971	1473.50	3218.58	1	0.30	1.65	0.11	3.29
1972	1484.08	3221.15	1	0.31	1.73	0.11	3.48
1973	1483.51	3281.32	1	0.30	1.65	0.11	2.34
1974	1474.82	3169.97	1	0.11	0.64	0.06	2.07
1975	1474.82	3180.44	1	0.09	0.49	0.00	1.85
1976	1412.44	3204.96	0	0.23	1.47	0.14	1.74
1977	1411.73	2876.89	0	−0.02	−0.14	0.05	1.98
1978	1472.59	2910.46	0	−0.12	−0.76	0.09	1.83
1979	1481.58	2912.39	0	0.07	0.42	0.09	2.69
1980	1460.76	2928.65	0	0.00	0.03	0.04	2.84
1981	1460.76	2936.72	0	0.00	0.03	0.00	2.84
1982	1460.76	2944.79	0	0.07	0.45	0.00	2.71
1983	1460.76	2952.86	0	−0.03	−0.18	0.00	2.86
1984	1460.76	2960.93	0	0.12	0.82	0.00	2.03
1985	1460.76	2969.00	0	0.14	0.92	0.00	2.57
1986	1460.76	2977.07	0	0.12	0.77	0.00	2.54
1987	1460.76	2985.14	0	0.12	0.82	0.00	2.75
1988	1598.98	3225.32	0	0.10	0.63	0.12	2.79
1989	1535.62	3073.28	0	0.27	1.85	0.08	2.88
1990	1518.45	2965.09	0	0.17	1.25	0.07	3.09
1991	1518.45	2965.09	0	0.17	1.23	0.00	2.81
1992	1518.45	2965.09	0	0.11	0.77	0.00	2.83
1993	1518.45	2965.09	0	−0.01	−0.10	0.00	2.81
1994	1518.45	2965.09	0	−0.08	−0.60	0.00	3.15

American Basketball Association (ABA)

Year	Average distance	Average pop. base	Site overlap	Perform. ordering (tau)	Tau *t*-stat.	League stability	Perform. equality
1967	1325.57	1680.45	1	0.02	0.08	1.00	2.28
1968	1404.69	2826.64	3	−0.42	−1.79	0.43	2.51
1969	1202.79	2762.66	2	−0.24	−1.01	0.43	2.01
1970	1045.45	1994.00	1	−0.20	−0.86	0.43	2.15
1971	1045.45	2001.84	1	−0.09	−0.39	0.00	2.74
1972	1176.87	1985.20	1	−0.43	−1.70	0.25	2.68

1973	1216.38	1835.26	1	0.07	0.27	0.18	2.30
1974	1154.03	2022.48	1	0.29	1.16	0.18	3.33
1975	895.38	2425.79	1	0.33	1.05	0.30	3.02

Football

National Football League (NFL)

1920	318.76	631.43	0	0.02	0.11	1.00	1.18
1921	332.46	722.32	0	−0.04	−0.18	0.31	1.66
1922	366.89	493.90	0	0.12	0.68	0.52	1.35
1923	375.98	519.85	0	0.23	1.40	0.19	1.43
1924	426.98	703.52	0	0.07	0.38	0.48	1.51
1925	448.85	739.35	0	0.02	0.12	0.33	1.62
1926	699.35	1136.86	8	0.21	1.33	0.44	1.53
1927	551.70	1824.18	0	0.25	1.10	0.52	1.52
1928	516.38	2217.30	0	−0.02	−0.09	0.31	1.57
1929	593.98	1443.74	0	0.20	0.89	0.50	1.77
1930	594.60	2017.27	0	0.13	0.55	0.29	1.50
1931	526.26	2236.60	0	−0.34	−1.34	0.25	1.62
1932	578.91	2528.90	0	−0.37	−1.24	0.36	1.21
1933	533.79	2343.79	0	0.25	0.98	0.36	1.29
1934	559.49	2362.13	0	0.32	1.32	0.25	1.73
1935	532.33	2766.50	0	0.06	0.21	0.18	1.28
1936	532.33	2787.36	6	−0.35	−1.25	0.00	1.60
1937	464.37	2599.47	3	−0.12	−0.45	0.27	1.50
1938	464.37	2619.88	0	0.02	0.09	0.00	1.29
1939	464.37	2640.29	0	−0.16	−0.63	0.00	1.83
1940	464.37	3699.60	2	−0.02	−0.09	0.00	1.45
1941	464.37	3743.51	2	0.12	0.45	0.00	1.80
1942	464.37	3787.42	0	−0.16	−0.63	0.00	2.06
1943	497.73	4205.66	0	−0.38	−1.24	0.20	1.69
1944	518.27	3889.22	0	−0.17	−0.63	0.36	1.93
1945	498.89	3236.65	0	−0.28	−1.07	0.10	1.64
1946	933.09	3514.24	5	0.38	1.43	0.18	1.26
1947	933.09	3564.28	5	0.14	0.54	0.00	1.23
1948	933.09	3614.32	5	0.32	1.25	0.00	1.79
1949	898.00	4372.46	5	0.07	0.27	0.09	1.69
1950	1064.62	3800.08	0	0.49	2.20	0.23	1.63
1951	1109.70	4058.32	0	−0.06	−0.27	0.08	1.56
1952	1174.07	3399.47	0	0.21	0.89	0.08	1.29
1953	1095.00	3506.74	0	−0.11	−0.48	0.15	1.79
1954	1095.00	3568.85	0	0.14	0.62	0.00	1.39
1955	1095.00	3630.96	0	−0.05	−0.21	0.00	1.16
1956	1095.00	3693.07	0	0.33	1.44	0.00	1.13
1957	1095.00	3755.18	0	−0.08	−0.34	0.00	1.12
1958	1095.00	3817.28	0	0.02	0.07	0.00	1.55

| | | | | Perform. | | | |
Year	Average distance	Average pop. base	Site overlap	ordering (tau)	Tau *t*-stat.	League stability	Perform. equality
1959	1095.00	3879.39	0	−0.11	−0.48	0.00	1.50
1960	1151.35	3458.39	4	0.13	0.61	0.15	1.16
1961	1130.27	3369.46	3	0.15	0.71	0.07	1.44
1962	1130.27	3413.41	3	0.01	0.05	0.00	1.83
1963	1130.27	3457.37	2	−0.03	−0.16	0.00	1.76
1964	1130.27	3501.33	2	−0.49	−2.35	0.00	1.36
1965	1130.27	3545.29	2	−0.19	−0.93	0.00	1.30
1966	1114.80	3444.97	2	−0.23	−1.14	0.07	1.49
1967	1126.19	3333.56	2	0.14	0.72	0.06	1.49
1968	1126.19	3375.56	2	0.02	0.09	0.00	1.76
1069	1082.75	3297.42	2	−0.04	−0.25	0.06	1.76
1970	1284.07	3123.46	0	0.11	0.77	0.27	1.51
1971	1284.07	3131.81	0	0.05	0.38	0.00	1.35
1972	1284.07	3140.16	0	0.02	0.11	0.00	1.67
1973	1284.07	3148.51	0	−0.11	−0.73	0.00	1.69
1974	1284.07	3156.86	3	0.03	0.20	0.00	1.45
1975	1284.07	3165.21	2	0.02	0.11	0.00	1.85
1987	1357.32	3050.85	0	0.16	1.19	0.07	1.85
1977	1357.32	3060.97	0	0.20	1.42	0.00	1.56
1978	1357.32	3071.09	0	0.12	0.87	0.00	1.36
1979	1357.32	3081.20	0	0.08	0.55	0.00	1.37
1980	1357.32	3091.32	0	0.13	0.91	0.00	1.47
1981	1357.32	3096.43	0	−0.01	−0.08	0.00	1.36
1982	1345.13	3253.48	0	0.00	0.00	0.00	1.26
1983	1345.13	3259.12	0	0.10	0.71	0.00	1.37
1984	1331.24	3228.45	12	0.17	1.23	0.07	1.65
1985	1331.24	3234.00	6	0.39	2.77	0.00	1.54
1986	1331.24	3229.55	0	0.27	1.98	0.00	1.64
1987	1331.24	3245.10	0	−0.03	−0.20	0.00	1.33
1988	1383.80	3228.87	0	0.07	0.47	0.07	1.32
1989	1383.80	3235.48	0	0.00	0.00	0.00	1.43
1990	1383.80	3242.09	0	0.07	0.47	0.00	1.59
1991	1383.80	3242.09	0	0.17	1.22	0.00	1.71
1992	1383.80	3242.09	0	−0.12	−0.85	0.00	1.63
1993	1383.80	3242.09	0	0.12	0.83	0.00	1.26

American Football League 1 (AFL1)

| 1926 | 1003.24 | 2166.07 | 8 | 0.31 | 1.15 | 1.00 | 0.97 |

American Football League 2 (AFL2)

| 1936 | 343.82 | 2656.53 | 6 | 0.00 | 0.00 | 1.00 | 1.38 |

| 1937 | 1205.46 | 1730.00 | 3 | −0.07 | −0.19 | 0.43 | 1.44 |

American Football League 2 (AFL2)

| 1940 | 536.59 | 2293.67 | 2 | −0.33 | −0.94 | 1.00 | 1.61 |
| 1941 | 470.58 | 2345.28 | 2 | −0.21 | −0.49 | 0.17 | 1.10 |

All-American Football Conference (AAFC)

1946	1596.94	4000.93	5	0.19	0.62	1.00	1.66
1947	1411.93	4170.59	5	−0.11	−0.37	0.22	2.07
1948	1411.93	4232.85	5	−0.47	−1.61	0.00	2.21
1949	1500.03	3556.03	5	−0.05	−0.15	0.00	1.68

World Football League (WFL)

| 1974 | 1914.59 | 2014.72 | 3 | −0.09 | −0.41 | 1.00 | 1.76 |
| 1975 | 1891.64 | 1782.05 | 2 | −0.36 | −1.48 | 0.23 | 0.90 |

United States Football League (USFL)

1983	1512.94	3376.95	10	0.31	1.37	1.00	1.53
1984	1287.33	2671.18	12	0.16	0.87	0.42	1.80
1985	1519.62	2067.52	6	0.19	0.93	0.48	1.43

American Football League (AFL)

1960	1656.12	3290.75	4	0.21	0.74	1.00	1.31
1961	1656.12	2702.33	3	−0.07	−0.25	0.22	1.81
1962	1656.12	2739.65	3	−0.21	−0.74	0.00	1.61
1963	1636.92	2680.54	2	0.07	0.25	0.22	1.34
1964	1636.92	2711.93	2	0.00	0.00	0.00	1.60
1965	1636.92	2743.31	2	0.07	0.25	0.00	1.36
1966	1688.95	2592.49	2	0.17	0.63	0.11	1.58
1967	1688.74	2624.09	2	0.34	1.25	0.00	1.76
1968	1596.74	2526.44	2	0.16	0.63	0.10	1.94
1969	1688.95	2687.29	2	0.28	1.04	0.10	1.67

Hockey

National Hockey League (NHL)

1917	210.77	453.73	0	0.20	0.34	1.00	1.21
1918	254.53	397.07	0	−0.33	−0.52	0.00	1.22
1919	294.91	328.35	0	0.33	0.68	0.25	1.89
1920	310.00	342.25	0	0.00	0.00	0.40	1.44
1921	310.00	350.95	0	−0.33	−0.68	0.00	1.23
1922	310.00	359.65	0	0.00	0.00	0.00	1.42
1923	310.00	368.35	0	0.00	0.00	0.00	1.12
1924	290.00	494.73	0	−0.55	−1.50	0.17	1.67
1925	342.17	1304.93	0	−0.29	−0.90	0.38	1.48
1926	440.51	1944.96	0	−0.11	−0.45	0.20	1.54

| | | | | Perform. | | | |
Year	Average distance	Average pop. base	Site overlap	ordering (tau)	Tau *t*-stat.	League stability	Perform. equality
1927	440.51	1983.52	0	− 0.25	− 0.98	0.00	1.79
1928	440.51	2022.08	0	0.16	0.63	0.00	1.75
1929	440.51	2060.64	0	− 0.21	− 0.81	0.00	2.35
1930	435.52	2227.30	0	− 0.16	− 0.63	0.18	2.22
1931	463.00	2554.05	0	0.00	0.00	0.20	0.78
1932	438.67	2311.18	0	0.00	0.00	0.11	1.22
1933	438.67	2337.77	0	0.06	0.21	0.00	1.23
1934	565.53	2440.47	0	− 0.29	− 1.04	0.20	1.61
1935	463.00	2672.75	0	− 0.31	− 0.99	0.11	1.06
1936	463.00	2702.43	0	− 0.30	− 0.99	0.00	1.22
1937	463.00	2732.10	0	− 0.08	− 0.25	0.00	1.77
1938	482.23	3016.46	0	− 0.10	− 0.30	0.00	1.86
1939	482.23	3047.51	0	− 0.10	− 0.30	0.00	2.13
1940	482.23	4139.57	0	− 0.39	− 1.20	0.00	1.90
1941	482.23	4190.16	0	− 0.10	− 0.30	0.00	1.31
1942	522.55	3471.27	0	− 0.33	− 0.94	0.00	1.36
1943	522.55	3515.73	0	− 0.47	− 1.32	0.00	2.76
1944	522.55	3560.20	0	− 0.60	− 1.69	0.00	2.58
1945	522.55	3604.67	0	− 0.33	− 0.94	0.00	1.18
1946	522.55	3649.13	0	− 0.73	− 2.07	0.00	1.46
1947	522.55	3693.60	0	− 0.33	− 0.94	0.00	1.43
1948	522.55	3738.07	0	− 0.20	− 0.56	0.00	1.25
1949	522.25	3782.53	0	− 0.20	− 0.56	0.00	1.24
1950	522.25	3827.00	0	− 0.47	− 1.32	0.00	2.63
1951	522.25	3886.53	0	− 0.33	− 0.94	0.00	2.10
1952	522.55	3946.07	0	− 0.21	− 0.56	0.00	1.41
1953	522.25	4005.60	0	− 0.33	− 0.94	0.00	2.21
1954	522.25	4065.13	0	− 0.33	− 0.94	0.00	2.30
1955	522.25	4124.67	0	− 0.20	− 0.56	0.00	1.92
1956	522.55	4184.20	0	− 0.07	− 0.19	0.00	1.75
1957	522.55	4243.73	0	0.20	0.56	0.00	1.72
1958	522.25	4303.27	0	− 0.33	− 0.94	0.00	1.25
1959	522.55	4362.80	0	− 0.47	− 1.32	0.00	1.58
1960	522.55	4422.33	0	− 0.33	− 0.94	0.00	2.13
1961	522.55	4474.37	0	− 0.20	− 0.56	0.00	2.29
1962	522.55	4526.40	0	− 0.33	− 0.94	0.00	1.70
1963	522.55	4578.43	0	− 0.20	− 0.56	0.00	1.71
1964	522.55	4630.47	0	− 0.07	− 0.19	0.00	1.77
1965	522.55	4682.50	0	− 0.33	− 0.94	0.00	1.98
1966	522.55	4734.53	0	0.07	0.19	0.00	1.87
1967	1225.95	4141.60	0	0.24	1.10	0.50	1.34

1968	1225.95	4189.07	0	0.00	0.00	0.00	1.96
1969	1225.95	4236.53	0	0.03	0.14	0.00	2.23
1970	1324.88	3845.64	0	0.28	1.37	0.14	2.50
1971	1324.88	3844.96	0	0.28	1.37	0.00	2.65
1972	1275.00	4081.63	7	0.08	0.41	0.06	2.52
1973	1275.00	4078.41	5	0.21	1.13	0.00	2.40
1974	1224.54	3859.34	4	0.08	0.46	0.11	2.78
1975	1224.54	3857.61	2	0.12	0.68	0.00	2.88
1976	1084.62	3796.53	1	0.17	0.99	0.20	2.56
1977	1084.62	3794.90	0	0.16	0.91	0.00	2.71
1978	1129.15	3902.75	0	0.23	1.28	0.06	2.27
1979	1198.77	3205.69	0	0.31	1.96	0.19	2.00
1980	1272.06	3205.19	0	0.15	0.94	0.09	2.12
1981	1272.06	3204.76	0	−0.01	−0.09	0.00	2.10
1982	1214.17	3218.56	0	0.10	0.63	0.09	2.26
1983	1214.17	3217.00	0	0.10	0.63	0.00	2.31
1984	1214.17	3215.45	0	−0.06	−0.39	0.00	2.33
1985	1214.17	3213.89	0	−0.13	−0.82	0.00	2.07
1986	1214.17	3212.34	0	−0.07	−0.45	0.00	2.15
1987	1214.17	3210.78	0	−0.01	−0.09	0.00	1.34
1988	1093.10	3209.23	0	−0.01	−0.09	0.00	1.44
1989	1093.10	3207.67	0	0.03	0.21	0.00	1.60
1990	1093.10	3206.12	0	−0.17	−1.06	0.00	1.55
1991	1093.10	3206.12	0	0.17	0.06	0.00	1.82
1992	1219.96	3211.52	0	0.30	0.92	0.05	1.67
1993	1226.60	3053.77	0	0.10	0.67	0.09	2.61
1994	1375.46	3014.15	0	0.22	1.54	0.09	1.84

World Hockey Association (WHA)

1972	1377.94	3326.98	7	−0.12	−0.55	1.00	1.15
1973	1497.37	2389.07	5	−0.06	−0.27	0.59	1.57
1974	1484.24	1830.60	4	−0.05	−0.27	0.38	1.98
1975	1466.35	1295.32	2	−0.01	−0.05	0.35	1.76
1976	1569.49	1147.60	1	0.21	0.96	0.27	1.41
1977	1334.40	1053.30	0	−0.29	−0.99	0.33	1.51
1978	1268.70	827.64	0	−0.71	−2.25	0.13	1.35

Notes

Introduction

1. Major league status was assessed on the basis of geographic and demographic criteria for the first claimant in a sport. Before air travel, the "national" ambitions that distinguished major leagues in practice meant including a few populous midwestern sites like Chicago and St. Louis among a predominantly northeastern menu of large city sites. Once a major league was established, challenges to major league status were made by raiding players from existing major leagues.

2. To "thrill in victory" was given as the primary motive for viewing sports in a study by Gantz (1981). Secondary motives included "letting loose," "getting psyched," and having a beer or drink. "Learning about sports" was less important, and "passing time" was a highly unusual response. These priorities are strongly reflected in sports reporting, which emphasizes how players and coaches feel about winning (or losing) rather than the mechanics of the actual competition.

3. Over 57,000 Cleveland fans per game turned out to watch the Cleveland Browns dominate the newly formed All American Football Conference in 1946, its premier year. By 1949, under 30,000 Cleveland fans per game were turning out to see their team continue to dominate the league. The absence of serious rivals undermined the attachment of Cleveland fans to the Browns and contributed to the collapse of the entire league before the 1950 season (Quirk and Fort 1992).

4. Player salaries command the most attention in the business of major league sports. For most people (and even most corporate chief executive officers), star player salaries exceeding $10 million a year may seem shockingly high. Yet relative to the other media icons that players compete with, such as movie stars, rock musicians, and comics, these salaries are not particularly high. Michael Jackson and Bill Cosby, at the extreme, make nearly $100 million per year.

5. In major league pennant races, winning is defined on the basis of overall

won-lost percentages so that winning teams can get away with a substantial amount of losing. Before leagues, however, this was inconceivable, as champions were determined only through direct matches. The modern idea of winning rests on an immense amount of regularity and comparability in season schedules across teams.

6. Economists have largely ignored the last three decades of major league sports in basing their theory of performance inequalities entirely on the size of potential local markets, or city size. They have also ignored early major leagues outside of baseball, where teams failed to attach successfully to cities. In the recent work of the economists James Quirk and Rodney Fort (1992), city size is quietly replaced by the actual drawing power of teams as a way to avoid acknowledging the failure of their model. Since winning teams draw more fans, it is a fairly safe prediction that teams drawing more fans are likely to be winners.

7. Baseball, whose games are canceled for something as benign as rain, is the major league sport most vulnerable to nature's perversity. Yet doubleheaders allow lost games to be quickly made up, so that the sanctity of season schedules is nearly always preserved. It took the San Francisco earthquake during the pregame warmups of the 1989 World Series to bring major disruption. Although football is also mostly played outdoors, games are played despite the weather.

8. Coverage of the four major league sports is even more lopsided than these numbers suggest, as the quality of scholarship varied directly with the number of entries. The lack of serious historiography in hockey seriously handicapped this study. Unfortunately, biases in existing coverage are perpetuated in works that depend on secondary sources.

9. When Ted Turner, owner of the Turner television network and Atlanta's major league baseball and basketball teams, was asked at a congressional hearing whether there were any significant differences between baseball and football, he replied, "Well, football is played in the fall, and it uses a different shaped ball" (quoted in Quirk and Fort 1992, p. 192).

10. Consider the organization of most modern markets, where bitter rivalries between competitors sometimes conceal the civility of their co-relations. It might appear, for example, that Coke and Pepsi are out to destroy each other, yet the attachments that consumers have to either brand depend deep down on the ongoing rivalry between them. Were either to destroy the other, consumer involvement in the cola market could drop precipitously. Although attachments are invariably described in terms of brands, as they are to specific teams in sports, they depend on the menu of brands that constitutes a market. It may be no accident that the number of branded firms in most modern markets shares the same range as the number of teams in major league divisions (see Leifer and White 1987).

1. Laying the Groundwork

1. The Civil War was largely responsible for baseball's remarkable growth during the 1860s. A single Christmas game during the war, played at Hilton Head, South Carolina, attracted a soldier audience of 40,000. Soldiers brought home tales of baseball throughout the war-weary nation. Later, the years after World Wars I and II were to see similar booms in sports interest.

2. As late as 1820, three-quarters of American families were rural. While most sports of the day were better suited for open rural areas, the commercialization of sport required the concentrations and new types of persons that only urban areas could produce.

3. Publicans played a central role in the earliest efforts to commercialize sports. Large crowds of heavy drinkers could be drawn to inns and saloons by staging blood sports involving animals (bear baiting, cockfights, ratting) or humans (boxing or gouging matches). Gate receipts eventually relieved contestants of their reliance on the patronage of rural elites. But the end of elite sponsorship removed any semblance of restraint from the events, producing excesses that triggered opposition from the "respectable" classes.

4. Interest in baseball's origins developed with the sport's commercialization at the end of the nineteenth century. Interest in baseball's history among team owners, however, was aimed at making baseball a purely American invention. Based solely on an octogenarian's recollection of an event occurring sixty years back, the story of Abner Doubleday's invention of the game in Cooperstown in 1839 was eventually legitimated by a 1907 commission that included two U.S. senators and the president of the National League. Careful research by Robert Henderson in the 1930s revealed that Doubleday, who went on from his alleged Cooperstown experience to become a major general in the U.S. Army, a writer, and a friend of the National League president, never mentioned Cooperstown (he was at West Point during the late 1830s) or his invention of the national game in his writings. Furthermore, Robin Carver published a rulebook in 1834 for a game called baseball, noting the game was "generally adopted in our country." The rules were the same as those published in London by William Clerke in 1829 for English rounders (Brasch 1970). None of these findings daunted the baseball owners. A 1939 centennial celebration in Cooperstown unveiled baseball's Hall of Fame, which joined the Baseball Museum, the first baseball field, and numerous plaques as centerpieces of Cooperstown's commercial life.

5. After professional teams emerged, locally rooted professionals would sometimes supervise preseason practice before their own season began, establishing links that later became the basis for recruiting. But once the season began, students would be largely on their own in the conduct of play (Cagnon 1989). Although help from administrators and alumni grew steadily as the publicity value of sports teams became apparent, students were the driving force

behind college athletics. The Intercollegiate Amateur Athletic Association of America was formed in the 1870s entirely through student initiative. Perhaps the most impressive student initiative was a tour by Harvard's baseball team that went as far west as Milwaukee and Chicago, scoring victories over numerous college and professional teams (and almost defeating the great Cincinnati Red Stockings).

6. To understand how this identity creation works, the reader only needs to stop and consider how he or she "knows" of distant cities in the United States. Outside of natural disasters or heinous crimes, most people remain aware of cities they may have never visited by constantly hearing about the activities of major league teams associated with them. Cities that lose major league teams, like Pottsville or Keokuk, quickly drop from the national landscape, even though they may otherwise be quite similar to cities like Green Bay, which few people would have ever heard of were it not for its National Football League team. Yet when the Cincinnati Red Stockings were formed, there were no major leagues and professionals were stigmatized. Bold vision was required to see what now appears obvious.

7. Gambling interests appeared at work in producing the tied game with the Troy Haymakers. The Cincinnati pitcher, alleged to have received $500 to throw the game, allowed thirteen runs in the first two innings. But the Cincinnati team fought back to a 17–17 tie by the seventh inning. Worried over an alleged $60,000 bet on the game, the Troy president withdrew his team from the field, ostensibly over an argument concerning a foul ball (Ryczek 1992, p. 50).

8. Remaining strictly amateur has always been difficult for amateur sport as its scale of organization has increased. Some kinds of player compensation, such as scholarships and professional coaching, are openly accepted, while money payments and eligibility rule evasions occur more secretly. In the New York Athletic Club (NYAC), the flagship of amateur ideals, "special athletic memberships" (not requiring dues) were given to college men who played for the club. When, in 1893, these players would not be available until July 1, the NYAC's June *Journal* issue revealed that "a professional battery has been engaged to play in games prior to that date," adding blandly, "the nine will otherwise remain strictly amateur" (quoted in Seymour 1990, p. 157). Forty years later, an ostensibly amateur tournament (with large cash prizes) sponsored by the American Baseball Congress was won by a traveling professional team, the bearded House of Davids, with the help of the legendary black professional pitcher Satchel Paige.

9. Such victories helped Crowell push through curriculum changes. But ringers, brutality, and postgame parties ultimately proved too much for the conservative Methodist faculty to accept. A frustrated Crowell left Trinity in 1894.

10. For its first seven years the NCAA was called the International Athletic Association of the United States. The exclusion of the word "football" from its title was deliberate, as the association had aspirations to regulate all college sports (Falla 1981).

11. But the NCAA failed to eliminate fatalities—33 players died in 1909—though the number of games had increased substantially. In 1930, 40 of the 750,000 persons who played the game died of football injuries (Weyland 1955).

12. Efforts to define amateur sports have been from their beginning part of a countermobilization against professional sports. While much attention is given to the restrictions placed on professional athletes' ability to realize their full financial worth, as in the struggle over free agency, few have worried about the amateur athlete's failure to receive any official compensation at all. The definition of amateur athletics, as play without pay, has enriched many a college—especially with the added plum of television broadcast revenues.

13. Baseball players at the time, forging the reputation of the sports profession, were for the most part a poorly educated group (though they had on average slightly more education than the general population, who were very poorly educated by modern standards).

14. Numerous studies have documented wage discrimination against blacks in basketball (see Kahn and Scherer 1991). Although on average blacks in the sport receive higher pay than whites, the differential tips significantly in favor of whites when skill is controlled for. Owners justify paying white players more than comparable black players on the basis of their ability to draw more (white) fans to games. It is obviously crucial that white fans be able to see sometimes all-black teams as "their" teams, a feat that is possible only when race or ethnicity is not a central issue. For basketball leagues to attach teams to cities, race and ethnicity had to be circumvented as bases for attachment.

15. Hockey clubs formed in New York (1895), Pittsburgh (1897), and Boston (1898), and soon initiated inter-city rivalries. During these same years Columbia, Dartmouth, Harvard, Princeton, and Yale formed teams and had organized the Intercollegiate Hockey League by 1900. The hockey clubs drew heavily on college teams for players and competed frequently with them on the ice. It was not until 1920, however, that the amateur clubs formed a league "of any importance," the U.S. Amateur Hockey League (Farrington 1972).

2. Getting Established

1. Steamboat and rail transportation made it possible for some sporting events to be staged outside of urban settings. In the early days of professional boxing, for example, local legal restrictions often forced organizers to move fights to remote locations accessible only by river or rail. Such events, however, had to be of championship caliber to draw large numbers of people from distant locations.

2. Competition for players is treated as a constant here, because the definition of major league status includes competing for major league players. It should be remembered, however, that there were numerous minor leagues which, by definition, did not compete for major league players but which, at any time, could start to compete for them and hence lay claim to major league status.

3. On nine of the teams, players were paid entirely through a share of the gate receipts. On two others, including a Washington, D.C., team, they were "appointed to office" (Pietrusza 1991).

4. The effort for both purity and survival failed, mainly from pressures to charge admission and pay players. The amateur NABBP died in 1874, with $4.05 in its treasury. Goldstein (1989, p. 126) writes, "The essence of amateurism may very well be the effort itself . . . the chance to breathe in the emotional atmosphere of that world serves, at least for a time, as its own reward." As primarily a reaction against professionalism, amateurism lost its character when it tried to mimic the high degree of organization that professional teams attained in leagues.

5. Left on their own to negotiate financial arrangements, large-city teams often demanded guarantees before traveling to the homesite of smaller-city teams. The latter often found themselves in a poor position to absorb this risk.

6. In finding this treatment of the National Association puzzling, Ryczek (1992, p. xi) points out that "the first time Wilbur Wright attempted to defy gravity, he crashed unceremoniously at the end of the takeoff ramp . . . Yet no one scoffs at [the Wright brothers] and compares their primitive aircraft to Boeing's 767s."

7. Performance inequality is a ratio of the standard deviation of actual season win percentages divided by the standard deviation of win percentages were all games determined by a fair coin flip [(.5 × .5/average number of games played).5]. See Appendix B for an explanation of standard deviation.

8. With an eye to his future, Al Spaulding, newly appointed secretary (and still player) of the Chicago club, insisted that players should no longer have any responsibility to "secure grounds, erect grandstands, lease and own property, make schedules, fix dates, pay salaries, assess fines, discipline players, make contracts, or control the sport in all its relations to the public" (Pietrusza 1991, p. 27). The secret coup among owners did not sit well with the eastern press. No notice of the new league appeared for three days, and then it was given less space than an article on pigeon shooting. The sportswriter Harry Chadwick called it a "sad blunder" because "reform should not fear the light of day" (Pietrusza 1991, p. 28).

9. In 1886 Louis Hauck, owner of the Cincinnati team which had resurfaced in the rival American Association, banned Sunday games because they "attracted a crowd that were unable to attend during work days" (Sullivan 1990).

Hauck had in mind working-class rowdies, who had instigated riots on more than one occasion. Sunday games drew an average of over four thousand people, more than twice that of any other day (Sullivan 1990).

10. The effect of the ban was to give rise to all-black teams, mostly owned by white entrepreneurs. By 1920, however, a Negro National League had been organized by black businessmen. Although this league was shaky from the beginning to its end in 1931, a second Negro National League organized by black bankers was financially sound. In 1937, a Negro American League was founded. Both leagues benefited from the large numbers of blacks who moved to the cities to pursue war industry opportunities during World War II. Major League Baseball took note of the large attendances, often including many whites. When Jackie Robinson became the first black to return to Major League Baseball in 1947, so many fans of both races came to see him play that the columnist Mike Royko has commented: "It was probably the first time blacks and whites had been so close to each other in such large numbers" (quoted in Riess 1989, p. 120). Owners responded cautiously. Boston did not sign its first black until twelve years later, and by then the move of stadiums out of the inner city to the white suburbs was assuaging owner concerns over the racial integration of stadium audiences.

By the 1960s, the television audience was becoming as important as the stadium audience. Here there could be no concern over physical intermingling, because the audience never left home. The racial integration of Major and Minor League Baseball, which led to the demise of the black leagues, greatly expanded the potential size of this audience. When the gender barrier is broken in major league sports, the first entrants will surely bring a sizable audience with them.

11. It took some time before the full implications of the reserve clause were recognized. Initially, players felt honored to be placed on the reserve list and a stigma was attached to those left off. On the owners' part, the trading and selling of players began some years after the reserve clause was introduced and was most likely an unanticipated consequence for the drafters of the clause.

12. Hulbert died of heart failure in 1882. After the short tenure of A. G. Mills, known mainly for his later role in creating the myth of baseball's American origins, the jovial and compliant Nicholas Young (known as Uncle Nick) reigned from 1884 to 1900.

3. The Early Prototype

1. In 1900, a year before the Western League changed its name to the American League and broke with the National Agreement, the Western League sought permission from the National League to move into Chicago (already occupied by the National League's Chicago Cubs). The request was granted

under the conditions that the White Sox had to play on the far south side and could not use "Chicago" in their name (Sullivan 1990a, p. 37).

2. During the three-year trade war with the National League, the American League did not raid the 1901–1903 pennant-winning Pittsburgh team. Some speculate that Johnson's idea "was to create such an imbalance of talent in the National League that the pennant race would be uninteresting and attendance would decline" (Murdock 1982, p. 60). Yet Johnson later claimed that the hands-off policy was part of his efforts to lure Pittsburgh into the American League, and was abandoned as soon as Pittsburgh explicitly refused (Murdock 1982).

3. Hermann had been in the National League only five months, and was selected mainly because his business pragmatism had been instrumental in ending the trade war. Hermann presided over the National Commission until it disintegrated in 1919. Although he earned the reputation of "Ban's Boy," many American League owners suspected him of a National League bias.

4. The budding movie industry used the World Series to popularize the new media, and in turn introduced new audiences to the game. Although the Series was shown in movie houses as early as 1908, actual rights to show it were not sold until 1910 (for $500, and for $3,500 the next year).

5. As things turned out, by mid-season 1918 attendance had dropped so low that owners shut down six weeks early because of dwindling gate receipts. Players were released, with owners agreeing not to tamper with the freed players of other teams.

6. Landis had higher regard for owners who had themselves played major league baseball, like Connie Mack and Clark Griffith.

7. A rival "Continental League" was nearly organized by the Boston promoter George Lawson in 1921, but failed even to start the season. It was to be based on the novel idea of attaching teams to states, rather than cities, though each team would play its home games in a single city. In addition, the Continental League sought out talented black and Cuban players and teams in an effort to draw the growing urban populations of blacks and Cubans to the games.

8. In 1910, only 40 percent of the minor league teams could survive on gate receipts alone (Seymour 1971, p. 406).

9. Seymour (1971, p. 407) notes that draft-exempt leagues made "fantastic profits" from selling players. Jack Dunn's minor league Baltimore Orioles sold Jack Bentley to the New York Giants for $72,500 in 1922, and two years later sold Lefty Grove to Connie Mack's Philadelphia Athletics for a record $100,600. Yet to command such prices, players had to be held in the minors long after they were ready to move up—Lefty Grove spent five years with the Orioles while Dunn held out for the right price. Given ballplayers' limited

playing lives and the ever-present possibility of injury, such holding strategies were not without risks.

10. But after the Giants and Yankees met for the third straight time in the 1923 World Series, Landis complained about never being able to leave New York for the series! (Lieb 1951).

11. Economic theory provides a clear rationale for lower-right outcomes in the performance figures. Talent is worth more in larger cities, and hence tends to flow there regardless of whether players or owners control the movement of players. Diminishing returns, however, limit the extent of the resulting inequality. The only function of leagues in this market-based rationale is to ensure territorial monopolies, guaranteeing that larger-city teams will have larger markets. But this rationale does not account for upper-left outcomes, where territorial monopolies are also maintained. Nor will it account for lower-left outcomes in the modern era. For the presumed "market-based" dynamic to work, it takes a league that can exert strong internal controls (see Leifer 1990a).

4. Attachment Failures

1. It was not until 1967 that another team sport, soccer, challenged baseball's hold on the summer. As the world's most popular sport, the soccer challenge had baseball owners so alarmed that five bought into the soccer league as a hedge on their investment. But major league soccer did not take hold in the United States, although the success of the 1994 World Cup games in the United States followed shortly by the baseball player strike may reopen this issue. The only other challenge to baseball came from the U.S. Football League, a made-for-television league that was more concerned with challenging the NFL's hold on the fall than baseball's hold on the summer.

2. In 1925, the Maroons edged ahead of the Chicago Cardinals in the season's final game. Soon after they played an exhibition game outside Philadelphia, billed as a world championship, with Notre Dame and won 9–7. (Averse to professional football, Knute Rockne told his former players he would not attend but broke his vow when he slipped into the stadium and stood behind a press box pole.) But the local Frankford team claimed that the game had violated their territorial rights, which Commissioner Carr used as a pretext for stripping the Maroons of their 1925 NFL title. This was accomplished by having the Cardinals play two more games against weak league teams whose players had mostly gone home, so their win percentage again bettered that of the Maroons. Pottsville residents protested for years, prompting NFL action as late as 1963, when the league's executive board voted against Pottsville's claims 12–2 (see Gudelunas and Couch 1982).

3. It has been argued that the elimination of black players from professional football from 1934 to 1946 resulted from efforts to strengthen ties with college

football (Smith 1988). With only a few exceptions, college players were white through the 1930s. The stigma of the professional game was partially linked to the use of black players before 1934, and efforts to broaden its appeal beyond the working class were essential in attracting college players into the game.

4. Effects of reverse drafts on competitive balance are complicated by the fact that draft choices can be sold or traded. In football, draft choices are especially valuable because average playing careers are so short (under four years)—a draft choice can be worth more than an established star. Hence owners can use draft choices to enhance their talent pools or their own financial standing.

5. Currently, drafted college players are comparable to AA players, one level below the top level of the minors. College players need an average of three more years experience before entering the majors. The "stigma" of college is just about gone. Of active major leaguers in 1982, 72.8 percent had attended some college, compared with 11.6 percent in 1938 (Voigt 1987).

6. With ten teams in 1933, the NFL subdivided into an Eastern and Western division. It is interesting that the new idea of divisions came as NFL membership was decreasing and not increasing. As peripheral towns were eliminated and more control over the schedule asserted, the NFL could begin to think about providing orderly pennant races. Only then did ten teams became a bit unwieldy.

7. The Celtics' organizer was in no position to protest, as he was at the time imprisoned on an embezzlement charge. An earlier backer, whom the team had only met once in his three years (1914–1917) of support, had been gunned down by some of his rivals in the brewery business.

8. World War II may have played a role in the ascendancy of major leagues over independent teams. Lacking corporate sponsorship, the latter were more vulnerable to the effects of the military draft on both players and fans. The war may have also facilitated the rise of the "big man" in basketball that took place during this period, because men over 6'6" tall were exempt from the draft.

9. Owned by one man, the Professional Basketball League of America had suspiciously low performance inequality and a strong ordering between performance and population. Central ownership invariably raises suspicions over the integrity of competition, and these performance results certainly do little to allay these fears.

10. Lest there are any doubts over the relative playing strengths of the merging leagues, ex-National Basketball League teams won the 1948–49 Basketball Association of America championship and then six consecutive NBA championships.

11. Children, according to Edmund Vaz (1979), are "given no formal instruction in obeying rules. They do receive informal instruction in violating

rules in the use of illegitimate tactics, and they are taught conditions under which these acts are expected."

5. The Modern Prototype

1. The issue of pooled television contracts proved more controversial in college football, where top teams have more to lose by sharing revenues. Within the NCAA, Division I revenues are shared with Division II and III, as well as with some non-revenue-producing sports. In the 1970s the universities of Georgia and Oklahoma successfully challenged the NCAA's right to control their television contracts. But as a result the market was flooded with college football games, and the rights for them fell in value to the point where it was not clear whether top universities gained anything from their hard-earned autonomy (Klatell and Marcus 1988).

2. ABC pioneered the slow-motion replay, first used in an NCAA game at halftime, but CBS must be credited with the first truly instant replay in December 1963.

3. With Roone Arledge's introduction of the Wide World of Sports, Ron Powers (1984, p. 160) notes that television made a seminal discovery: "Instead of telecasting events because people were interested in them, they could make people interested in events because they were on television." Through television people were drawn into not only football but arcane sports like wrist wrestling and tobogganing.

4. Opportunities for further expansion were limited, as the NFL had agreed to leave Saturdays for college football and Friday evenings for high school football.

5. Having lost money on its prior four-year contract, CBS was seeking reductions in rights fees. Fox's huge bid could be justified only in terms of the legitimacy the NFL contract gives it as a network, which will greatly boost its viewership for the rest of its sports and nonsports programming.

6. Revenue variation is mainly attributable to differing stadium capacities (sellouts are common) and the number of luxury boxes available (yielding revenues not subject to league sharing rules). Fierce political battles are waged over stadium and luxury box construction with city officials. From the league's standpoint, locating teams in smaller cities rather than larger ones has the advantage of freeing the latter for more television broadcasts. Home games not sold out cannot be broadcast locally, and therefore a large city with multiple teams stands a high risk of blackouts and hence lost revenues. It was for this reason that Rozelle rejected the Stanford Research Institute's recommendation that the league place its expansion teams in the suburbs of New York, Chicago, or Los Angeles in 1977 (Harris 1987). Pressure from CBS to free up Chicago for broadcasts had led to the movement of that city's second team, the

Cardinals, to St. Louis in 1960, at a time when all home games were blacked out.

7. This residue of localism is suggested in Klatell and Marcus's (1984, p. 226) claim that "it is no secret that [the networks] root for teams from major cities. The continued interest of audiences in the ten largest markets constitutes an absolutely vital ingredient in the success of any sports program. There is pressure . . . for leagues to maintain the competitive excellence and promote [the] high profile of teams in those markets . . . [if not,] the networks are not pleased, and say so." In the concluding chapter here, a design for future leagues is offered that detaches teams from all geographical entities and hence undermines localism entirely.

8. At the time Hunt conceived the AFL, Commissioner Bell was participating in hearings for the limited antitrust exemption. In "one of the more naive thoughts in the history of sports," Hunt asked Bell to be commissioner of his new league as well, since he had no wish to do battle with the NFL. Bell politely refused, but asked permission to mention the new league in the antitrust hearings where he promised to "foster and nourish" the new competition (Harris 1987, p. 90). This first public announcement of the AFL, by the NFL commissioner, started the new league in motion (as nobody had yet invested any money in the new league).

9. The United States Football League tried to get ABC to subsidized the Walker contract, on the grounds that the network would be the main beneficiaries of his participation in the league. But ABC refused because of commitments to NCAA football (Byrne 1986). The modern complementarity between college and major league sports rests on the latter's respecting the former's eligibility rules. Dealing with both sides, television networks have a substantial interest in cultivating this complementarity.

10. Given the advantage of playing at home and the momentum that comes from winning, a string of home games early in the season would seem to give a team an edge in the competition for the championship. Green Bay had the most early home games (most likely owing to its harsh weather late in the season) during the years of its dynasty, and the New York Jets had the longest string of consecutive home games (seven) in modern football history the year they won the Super Bowl (1969) as the AFL underdog. Overall, however, there is no significant relation between earliness of home games and season performance (Leifer 1990b).

11. This panoramic view of scheduling conceals a great deal of close-up political maneuvering. Scheduling is an area where many battles between owners and the league office are played out. Rosenbloom, owner of the Los Angeles Rams, saw his team's 1976 schedule as "a punishment and a warning to other teams that if they criticize Pete Rozelle, they will also be punished . . . Every team that is a contender, we play away from home . . . If Rozelle could have

arranged to have us play at midnight in Nome, Alaska, he would have done it" (quoted in Harris 1987, p. 232).

12. During the 1987 player strike, television ratings fell dramatically when the owners started fielding teams of semi-professionals. Some of the players seemed to lack a clear understanding of the game rules, and play, with the memory of NFL standards still fresh in the public mind, was painful to watch.

13. Actual ownership is highly scattered across individuals and corporations, and in the case of Green Bay, is even public. But each team must select one person to represent it at league meetings, and this person is invariably the one who comes to be viewed as "the" owner by other league members and the press and public.

14. The "national public" is far from homogeneous in the eyes of the networks. Large cities are disproportionately catered to, because they consume a disproportionate amount of advertised products.

6. Modernization

1. The economists James Quirk and Rodney Fort appear on the jacket of their recent book (1992) wearing caps with team logos. Though they assume throughout the book that teams depend entirely on local markets for revenue, the logos on their caps are for teams not even in the states where each resides. Quirk and Fort are, in appearance, part of a national public which may cast its support anywhere. Territorial monopolies lose their economic relevance when they no longer limit peoples' access (now through television) to games.

2. Returning players, however, found themselves blacklisted. Only after the player Danny Gardella brought a lawsuit against Organized Baseball was the ban on returning players lifted, in June 1949.

3. Frick's habit of avoiding controversial issues by leaving them for the two leagues to resolve led the maverick owner Bill Veeck to suggest that Frick's autobiography should be entitled *Armageddon Is a League Matter*. Instead, Frick titled his autobiography *Games, Asterisks, and People: Memoirs of a Lucky Fan*. Only the word "asterisks" reflects Frick's leadership role. When Roger Maris hit sixty-one home runs in 1961, Frick insisted that an asterisk be entered next to this accomplishment in the record books because it was facilitated by a 162-game season. Babe Ruth's famous sixty home runs were hit in a 154-game season. Frick, it turns out, had been Babe Ruth's ghostwriter before entering baseball management (Lowenfish 1991). Frick's asterisk brings embarrassing attention to changes in the game, which affect virtually every record but mostly go unmentioned to enhance the stature of the current record holder.

4. To enhance the institution's ability to equalize player talent on teams, the sale of draft rights was prohibited. Thus poor-performing teams could not sell their draft rights to stronger teams. Yet players, once drafted, might not

be signed (if the player's salary demands were not met), or might be signed and then sold or traded to another team. Thus the reverse draft, in itself, may help only to equalize the revenue of teams as they "give" weaker teams a valuable resource that stronger teams can only obtain through purchase.

5. The main issue that undermined Kuhn was his costly struggle with the players' union over the right of the commissioner to require teams losing free agents to receive compensation from teams purchasing them. This compensation, in the form of draft choices, was used effectively by Rozelle to undermine the competitive bidding for players between teams that accompanies free agency. But in Major League Baseball, rich teams—unfazed by escalating player salaries—were against paying compensation. These were, of course, the same teams that were going to have to share their national television revenues with poorer teams, so Kuhn's television coup did little to secure his position among them.

6. One lull occurred in 1980, but the next season the player strike eliminated the commissioner's main tool in thwarting free agency, compensation of teams losing free agents. A lull from 1985 to 1987 became the basis for a lawsuit charging the owners with collusion, which resulted in a $280 million settlement against them. When the courts effectively declared that self-control among owners was illegal, the owners had little choice but to place their hopes on salary caps. This precipitated the 1994 player strike and the cancellation of the World Series.

7. The short period where a positive ordering of team performance by host population size emerged in the American League, in the mid-1980s, occurred when collusion among owners thwarted free agency. The fact that the trend toward competitive balance did not reverse itself when the reserve system fell in the mid-1970s has been used as major support for the economic theory of performance inequality. Gerald Scully (1989, p. 191) confidently asserts: "Playing talent always migrates toward its highest-valued use. The dominance of the New York Yankees, the Brooklyn Dodgers, and New York Giants testified to the impotence of the reserve clause as a device for equalizing the distribution of playing talent. The lack of big city dominance in the period of post-free agency is further evidence of the fact that player reservation per se has nothing to do with the distribution of playing talent." Scully neglects to tell us, however, how the "lack of big city dominance" in the modern period ever came about if talent "always migrates to its highest value use" (that is, big cities). The economic model is based on an attachment of teams to cities that even Major League Baseball has managed to partially transcend.

8. After Fay Vincent told the owners they were fools if they went to war with the players' union again, the owners brought in an aggressive negotiator, Richard Ravitch, at a salary higher than Vincent's. Ravitch promised the owners they could win, but only if they got Vincent out of the way (Feinstein 1993).

9. The move west was prompted by the formation of a new version of the American Basketball League in 1960 (organized by Abe Saperstein), with teams in Washington, D.C., Cleveland, Chicago, Pittsburgh, Kansas City, San Francisco, Los Angeles, and Hawaii. Cleveland's team was owned by George Steinbrenner (future owner of the American League's New York Yankees), who hired and shortly thereafter fired the first black coach in league sports on the way to winning the league title. At the end of the season, Steinbrenner tried to defect to the NBA but was blocked by Saperstein's threat of an antitrust suit. Although the American Basketball League had signed a few players drafted by the NBA, it was never a serious threat and quietly perished, shortly into its second season (Quirk and Fort 1992).

10. The racial balance of the 1960s was lost in the 1970s, as NBA players became over 75 percent black.

11. In addition to shared network revenues, however, NBA teams actively pursue (unshared) local broadcasting revenues. These varied from less than $1 million to $5 million per team per year during the early 1980s.

12. Interestingly, the NBA became the first league to consider a women player when the Indiana Pacers signed Ann Meyers in 1979. Meyers was a four-time UCLA All American and an Olympic star, but she failed to make the Indiana team and was quietly dropped. A year before, the Women's Professional Basketball League had begun operation, and soon (1982) there would be an NCAA championship for women's teams. In 1985 a professional minor league was launched on the East Coast with a summer schedule. In its second season, Nancy Lieberman joined the Springfield (Massachusetts) team to become the first woman to play in a previously male professional league. Clearly, the first major league sport to incorporate women without compromising the quality of play will stand to expand its audience. For the NBA, pushing in this direction was only one of the many experiments to come.

13. Just ahead and behind Stern in the rankings were Phillip Knight (Nike's CEO), Ted Turner, and Jerry Reinsdorf (television magnates and basketball owners), all men whose power also serves the interests of the NBA. In fifth place, Donald Fehr (head of the players' union in Major League Baseball) was the highest-ranking person serving that sport's interests, much to the consternation of the owners. Nobody connected with the NFL appeared in the top ten.

14. Citing thuggishness in the 1994 NBA playoffs (even involving an owner) and a 30 percent drop in television ratings for the conference finals, the sports reporter E. M. Swift labeled NHL hockey as "the place to be." The once-thuggish NHL even got into the "Style of the Times" section of the *New York Times* as "hip," "sexy," and "cutting edge" (see *Sports Illustrated*, June 20, 1994).

15. On the one hand, with almost three-quarters of all teams qualifying for

the playoffs, local fans may wonder why they are maintaining an interest in the regular season. On the other hand, the members of a national public have little time to familiarize themselves with the teams and players, and hence may wonder why they are interested in playoffs involving so many unknown players and teams.

16. Another threat stems from a recent antitrust ruling against the NFL, which if sustained through the appeal process would outlaw the NFL's restrictions on franchise ownership. Current bylaws prohibit corporate and public (with the exception of Green Bay) ownership. With ownership in the hands of individuals, unrestrained bidding over players and other forms of noncooperation have been easier to control than in the other major league sports.

7. Changing Ways

1. International audiences for sports have long existed, and have been largely outside the control of U.S. interests—as in the case of the Olympics and the World Cup in soccer. Locating the 1994 World Cup in the United States was part of an attempt to bring this country into the international soccer fold. Yet there is no international public in soccer in the sense of a regularly activated international audience that is cued into an ongoing set of events. International tournaments draw a worldwide audience, but these are infrequent special events as opposed to the frequent regular events of a major league season. Should U.S. major leagues succeed in their international ambitions, they will have international publics following league competition on a daily, year-round basis, with outcomes reported as news and analyzed in a highly regular flow of newspapers and magazines. It is a mistake to assume, as have many other industries that have moved abroad, that only U.S. entrepreneurs can pull off such an achievement. Countries as far off as Korea are already producing players of major league caliber, and by now nobody should doubt that they can produce organizers as well.

2. For almost four decades, economists have been maligning the reserve clause on the grounds that it does nothing to stop "property" from flowing to large cities, where it is worth the most (Rottenberg 1956; El-Hodiri and Quirk 1971; Holohan 1978; Quirk 1980). Ironically, the end of large-city dominance has done little to dampen economists' enthusiasm for the argument.

3. For at least one owner, the maverick Charles Finley of Oakland, the rise of general managers seemed to enhance his own deal-making latitude. According to Kuhn, Finley "very effectively picked the brains of other clubs on player matters. Because this was like Ford's getting General Motors to help on a new car design, I was always puzzled by the amount of help he got. He called general managers and sought their evaluation of trades or player moves he was considering. And they helped him! This was all the more remarkable when

you realize that most of their bosses could not stand Finley" (1987, p. 129).

4. The issue of who controls trades and acquisitions has become more complex in the 1980s and 1990s. Players who have spent ten years in the majors, and the last five with the same team, can veto a trade. As a response to free agency, long-term contracts have become common, with some containing no trade clauses. Added to the legal obstacles is heightened uncertainty over drug use and drug policies in Major League Baseball. Though some sports writers prophesy an end to player deals among owners (with a greater reliance on farm systems for cultivating talent), it is too early to assess the impact of these developments (see Reichler 1984).

5. Instances where players were placed on waiver and purchased at a fixed waiver price, or were purchased as free agents, are not treated as deals. Deals involving both a trade and a cash payment are treated as cash deals, and the team sending cash is distinguished from the team receiving cash.

6. There were fourteen instances of "generalized exchanges" in this century, where, say, team A would transfer players to team B, B would transfer players to C, and C would send to A. Two instances involved four teams, and the rest three. In the main analyses, these exchanges were classified as trades and broken into their constituent dyads, with, say, team A "trading" n players for zero players from B, and so on.

7. In making this tabulation, I also tried less stringent definitions, allowing one or two one-year breaks in exchange or avoidance. Interestingly, durations increased much more for avoidance relations than for ties. Long periods of avoidance may be punctuated by a rare deal, but once a long spell of deal making is interrupted it is evidently never reinstigated with the same staying power.

8. Reichler's (1988) compilation of deals ends with December 1987. Since September (when acquired players cannot be used in winding up pennant races) to August is used to demarcate a year, the last months of 1987 were not used and 1901 included only January to September deals.

9. The coefficient of variation is the standard deviation divided by the mean (see Appendix B). It was used to take into account the rise in the volume of deals. For the first two periods, the average coefficient of variation across teams was .582 and .580 around overall averages of 3.969 and 3.672 deals per team-year. These dropped in the last two periods to .496 and then .441 around overall averages of 5.501 and 7.532 deals per team-year (third-period figures exclude the four late-entering expansion franchises, which all had consistently high volumes of deals).

10. Since mean performance and city size were constrained to 50 percent and 0 (z-scores were computed for each year—see discussion of standard deviation in Appendix B), respectively, it seemed prudent to constrain the yearly number of deals. Using yearly deal-making z-scores, the same results as in

Figure 7.4 were obtained with respect to signs and statistical significance. The rise in the impact of performance after World War II was, however, slightly less sharp. Because effects are more intuitive in terms of actual deal levels and the periodization removes the long-term fluctuation of means, the unstandardized results are presented.

11. Teams whose city sizes were within .4 standard deviations of each other were coded as "similar." Performance "equals" had to have season-win proportions within .05 of each other. These criteria produced a fairly balanced distribution of cases across categories.

12. Deal-making seasons run from September to August. Obviously, players acquired during the off-season may affect performance of the deal-making season itself, so change here would be better measured by comparing this season with the preceding one. To address this problem, it might be desirable to define the deal-making season as running from May through April. Yet this would raise objections when the focus is on past performance, as performance in the deal-making season itself would now be most relevant for off-season deals. In looking at years, rather than individual deals, there is no single definition of the season that is immune to objections.

13. When new teams enter the leagues, as they did in 1960, 1961, 1969, and 1977, the constraints may appear violated in the analysis because the lack of a preceding season performance yields missing values for the new franchises. Since these franchises invariably perform less well than older teams, their entry improves the performance of existing teams.

14. It is important to retain a meaningful zero point to be able to identify readily those teams who avoid deal making. Hence for each year's deals, each team's deals are divided by the most active team's deals and multiplied by 100.

15. An effort was made to isolate overall deal-making strategies. In the glimpse at types of deals above, there was no way to assess the impact of a team's behavior across types of deals. A trade avoider may be an active purchaser of players, and hence it would be desirable to assess the separate impact of each behavior. Some broad types of deal-making strategies were distinguished—deal avoidance, trade focused, cash focused, and deal seeking (active in both trades and cash deals). For the latter two types, involving cash deals, those who engage in more purchases than sales of players (that is, cash senders) are separated from those who do not. With the team-year as the unit, however, the cases available to assess average impacts rapidly thinned out when looking at the different relative city size and performance tendencies regarding whom teams deal with within strategy types. The results, perhaps like the deal making itself, were disappointing with respect to impacts on performance and based on too few cases to take seriously.

16. This analysis was done for the earlier periods. The only curvilinearity that appeared was for frequent deal makers in the second period, where middle-

sized city teams did slightly worse in terms of performance change across performance levels than either large- or small-city teams. This effect was weaker and opposite to that found for the third period.

17. Exacerbating Oakland's problems was the loss of stars through the onset of free agency (not counted in Figure 7.10). Oakland's star pitcher, Catfish Hunter, was the first player to be signed as a free agent in Major League Baseball on December 31, 1974 (1975 season). Between November 16 and December 14, 1976 (1977 season), Don Baylor, Joe Rudi, Bert Campaneris, Sal Bando, Rollie Fingers, and Gene Tenace left Oakland as acquired free agents.

8. Publics and Performance

1. Another way to avoid invoking publics is to make the home advantage a stable characteristic of teams, though in practice these may be hard to disentangle from the characteristics of their publics. There is considerable variation in home advantage within sports as well as between them. Much attention, for example, is given to the advantage enjoyed by the Boston Celtics at the Boston Garden owing to the irregularities of the court surface. The Celtics' lifetime home advantage (.263) is, however, less than the NBA average. Team-based explanations are naive because they ignore the simple fact that game outcomes always involve two teams, and a home team's tendencies may not be consistent with an away team's tendencies. For Boston to exhibit a high home advantage, for example, its opponents must do poorly at Boston and do well when the Celtics visit them (that is, they must also have strong tendencies for a home advantage). In trying to account nevertheless for home advantage tendencies with such factors as host population, alternative sports franchises, and stadium capacity, I was able to explain less than 2 percent of the variance in home advantage in football and baseball, but 18 percent in basketball and 7 percent in hockey (where team home advantages are more stable across time). Most of the significant effects, however, could be interpreted in terms of the intensity of partisan local publics.

2. Gary Ronberg (1975, p. 36) notes, "The referees are striving for what the league refers to as consistency. That's how they are rated and judged. Consistency, according to the NHL, is giving out roughly an equal number of penalties to each team . . . The NHL cites the relatively small discrepancy in penalties against the different teams as proof of the referees' fairness." Ronberg traces much of hockey violence to this brand of "fairness," as players who are unjustly singled out for punishment in the referees' balancing act mete out their own justice in moments when they are sheltered by this same act.

3. On rare occasions local publics in modern times have turned against the home team. In one 1975 game, Detroit fans started cheering for the visiting

Tampa Bay Buccaneers when their own team, with a disappointing 5–5 record at the time, trailed Tampa Bay by seven points in the first quarter. Tampa Bay had lost all twenty-three of its games since entering the NFL as an expansion franchise the year before. The Tampa Bay coach was "surprised" by this reception, which deep down was one more sign that his team was not viewed as a serious rival. When Tampa Bay finally won a game three weeks later, the losing coach, Hank Stram, called the event a "nightmare." But when the expansion team won again the next week, the losing coach Don Corjell gave Tampa Bay credit for a "job well done." They had, in short, entered into the league of serious rivals.

4. For a more thorough treatment of how balance comes to be sustained and disrupted among rivals, see Leifer (1991).

5. Ideally, the size of a stadium should be based on local tendencies to support a home team. If the size of local stadiums stood in direct relation to the size of crowds that would show up for the most appealing games, then actual crowd density would be an indicator for the relative appeal of different pairings. Crowd densities of, say, .6 would mean the same everywhere—that 60 percent of potential support was being tapped by the particular contestants (ignoring the consequences of the particular day and time they meet). Unfortunately, the politics of stadium construction do not always yield close fits between stadium size and potential support. Overall, large stadiums prove harder to fill, regardless of where they are located or the teams that play in them. Hence in trying to account for crowd density, stadium size had to be (re)introduced as a control variable.

6. In Major League Baseball there were only seventeen sellouts, of which the Kansas City Royals (the pennant winner) accounted for seven and the Texas Rangers for four. Though sporadic with regard to home-away performance balance, all sellouts were elicited by games where average performance levels were high.

7. When the National and American leagues are analyzed separately, the rise is entirely confined to the National League (.130 versus .000, respectively), making the phenomenon entirely league specific. Because there is no reason to expect league differences here, any explanation would be hazardous without more data.

8. The dependent variable is actually game outcomes (code 0, .5, and 1 for losses, ties, and wins). Home-team winning chances are predicted values. Technically, logistic regression should be used to ensure that these values do not stray outside the 0,1 range. This was done for the computer simulation discussed below, but ordinary regression coefficients are used here because they are easier to interpret (and yielded the same conclusions as the logistic coefficients).

9. During 1980, basketball's Seattle Supersonics played in the Kingdome (where its baseball team played), which was almost twice as large as the second-largest arena (40,248 versus 22,422 capacity). I used the second largest to scale

capacities for basketball, and ran analyses involving stadium capacity both with and without Seattle. The text notes where this exclusion made a difference.

10. Within each sport, performance as a measure of skill would imply greater predictive ability in the second half of the season than the first. Yet only in baseball was this the case, where the R-squared rose from .000 to .024. In the other three sports, R-squared declined by from 15 percent to 25 percent in the second half of the season.

11. When the impact of stadium capacity and crowd density was allowed to vary across performance regions, the impact of performance differences entirely disappeared in baseball. This was not the case in any of the other sports, where performance differences continued to be influential (becoming even more so in hockey and not changing in football). Although separate intercepts for each performance region could absorb regional variation in game outcomes, the fact that this undermined the impact of performance differences only in baseball is quite puzzling.

12. While national publics are indifferent to where winning and losing occur, constituents of local publics expect the home team to win in return for their showing up and hence logically should be inclined to view the loss of an away game as justified by their not showing up. If this is so, the worst thing a team could do is win away games and lose home games, because this would greatly confuse local publics as to their own role. When Tampa Bay broke its twenty-six-game losing streak in an away game at New Orleans (see note 3), it was not only a personal "nightmare" for the home team coach but an occasion for being "ashamed of our people, our fans, our organization." Hence fans were implicated in the loss (only 40,124 showed up, leaving 28,941 seats empty). Tampa Bay's victim the next week may have been more gracious because the loss occurred in Tampa Bay before 56,922 delighted fans (in a 74,315-seat stadium).

13. To eliminate any abrupt discontinuities between equals and unequals, an interpolation between the two levels was used for contenders whose performance levels differed by from .1 to .2.

14. Competitive balance is a dangerous thing if it rises to the surface of competition. In Major League Baseball, a progression toward competitive balance has outpaced the cultivation of national publics. The resulting precipitous decline in performance inequalities has many commentators alarmed, because there are no stable winners for enthusiasts to identify with and celebrate (Hoffman 1985).

9. The Accomplishment

1. Records have provided a way for major leagues to involve publics in stretches of competition even longer than pennant races. For example, the number of division titles teams win is tracked over the past decade (or even

century), or aspects of entire individual playing careers are monitored. In this way, the whole sports public can be mobilized around issues such as when Hank Aaron would hit his 715th home run, breaking Babe Ruth's record. Without the record keeping, the home run would have seemed just like all the others and been attended to by far fewer people.

2. As long as the expectations effect is not absolute, and games cannot end in ties, expected winners will sometimes lose and expected losers will sometimes win. This will cause publics to readjust their assessment of team ability. Thus a losing team that wins a few games will attract favorable attention, and this may help it continue to win. Conversely, a winning team can start a long slide after a few fortuitous losses. These possibilities are, of course, central in sustaining uncertainty over future prospects, even where stability in winner and loser roles has emerged.

3. This trend is only being exacerbated by the declining market share of network television in the face of proliferating cable, satellite, and pay-per-view television alternatives. At the core of the modern attachment of leagues to networks are powerful commissioners who control broadcasting rights and powerful networks who can promise huge audiences and big dollars for those rights. With both powerful commissioners and powerful networks in decline, national publics (for regular season games) are threatened with dissolution into a patchwork of localities based on cable subscriptions as much as geography.

4. There is no relation between the sales of individual team logos and team performance (and all revenues are equally shared among teams). In the words of Anne Occi, the designer of fourteen Major League Baseball team logos in the early 1990s, "a club can transcend its own geographic area by having a mark whose color or whose depiction is in at the time" (quoted in *Maclean's*, October 18, 1993). While losing has been accommodated, unappealing colors and designs have not been.

5. Baseball became an Olympic sport in 1992, and the International Baseball Federation is now organized in eighty-six countries. This makes American football the only non-Olympic major league sport. Given NFL efforts to spread interest in the game at a grass-roots level, it should not be long before football enters the Olympics.

6. According to a *Los Angeles Times* reporter (October 10, 1993), the NHL's new operating plan sounds much like the NBA's, marketing the NHL as an "aggressive entertainment machine." Bettman is also trying to decrease hockey violence so that the game might appeal to a broader audience.

7. With teams still attached to cities, the only way a major league can follow economic growth is by adding franchises or violating the attachment by relocating existing ones. Major leagues that cultivate unsophisticated international publics will have to maintain strict limits on the number of franchises, and

hence will have to find a way to allow existing franchises to remain fluid without the pain associated with current relocations.

8. The growth of the television news industry has paralleled the growth of television sports, and shares similar problems in international expansion. A central player in the news industry (and owner of two Atlanta major league franchises), CNN's Ted Turner, asserts, "Nationalism is not growing. Internationalism is growing . . . The Cold War is over, nations are no longer forced to choose sides, and CNN can be a single, common international carrier of news." But then he admits, "Localism is strong. I know that" (*New Yorker*, August 2, 1993). CNN broadcasts overseas in English, both because "the beauty of one language is that is spreads the costs," and because "we don't want to alienate the American traveller who wants to know how his ball team did last night" (ibid.). Although CNN clings to the idea of producing a uniform product, it fully recognizes the importance of having a local presence, as was exemplified in its Gulf War coverage. There is a lesson here for the organization of sporting competition.

9. As noted earlier, over the last few decades major league teams have sometimes tried to attach to states, like the California Angels or Texas Rangers, or even regions, like the New England Patriots. By claiming to represent such large areas, these teams try to tap partisan loyalties among people who can connect with the teams only through television. Television, however, is best used when these partisan loyalties are weakened. If someone in Maine was only interested in televised Patriots games (played in Massachusetts), he or she would not register as part of a national public when a game between, say, Kansas City and Oakland was nationally broadcast. Partisan loyalties were useful only to get people to attend games, as once people had potential access to only a single team, one that needed their support.

10. Huizenga is planning to bring his franchises together into an "entertainment village" called Blockbuster Park (southwest of Fort Lauderdale). Huizenga has made overtures to purchase the Miami Dolphins and Joe Robbie Stadium, which is six miles from the park site. If successful, the resulting entertainment sprawl would be one more form of cross-promotion that the attachment of corporations to teams would facilitate. As has happened with Disney World, there is no reason why Blockbuster Parks could not begin appearing abroad and, were the major leagues willing, be graced by the visits of Disney and other major league teams.

11. This is a complex issue, and hinges on how ownership is structured. It is quite possible that in the future teams may not be owned by the corporations to which they are attached. Even more likely, efforts to syndicate future major leagues will be made in which shares in the league, and not individual teams, are sold. Some assurance must be given to shareholders in the corporations that fiscal responsibility will be exercised in the pursuit of winning teams.

12. Future major leagues will be smaller in size than current ones, but will have at least as many star players. Losing teams will be more likely to have at least one star player who has international recognition and hence attracts attention wherever he or she goes. The NBA has fully recognized the value of star players, particularly for attracting unsophisticated viewers. Many of its games are promoted as showdowns between individual stars, which obviously oversimplifies the complexities of team competition. International publics will make star promotion essential.

13. Only a challenger league, the Federal League in baseball, got away with such a syndicated arrangement in the past, and it is questionable in the long term whether credibility in the authenticity of competition can be established.

References

Abolofia, Mitchel Y. 1985. "Structured Anarchy: Formal Organization in the Commodity Futures Markets," in *The Social Dynamics of Financial Markets*, ed. P. Adler and P. Adler. New York: JAI Press.

Adelman, Melvin. 1981. "The First Modern Sport in America: Harness Racing in New York City, 1825–70," *Journal of Sport History*, 8(1): 5–32.

—— 1986. *A Sporting Time: New York City and the Rise of Modern Athletics, 1820–1879.* Urbana, Ill.: University of Illinois Press.

Adomites, Paul D. 1989. "The Fans," in Thorn and Palmer (1989).

Allen, Michael P., Sharon K. Panian, and Roy E. Lotz. 1979. "Managerial Succession and Organizational Performance: A Recalcitrant Problem Revisited," *Administrative Science Quarterly*, 24: 167–180

Andrew, John A., Jr. 1984. "An Analysis of Home and Away Game Performance of Atlantic Coast Conference Basketball Teams." Ph.D. dissertation, Department of Physical Education, University of North Carolina, Chapel Hill.

Baade, Robert A., and Richard F. Dye. 1990. "The Impact of Stadiums and Professional Sports on Metropolitan Area Development," *Growth and Change: A Journal of Urban and Regional Policy*, Spring: 1–14.

Baker, Wayne. 1985. "Floor Trading and Crowd Dynamics," in *The Social Dynamics of Financial Markets*, ed. P. Adler and P. Adler. New York: JAI Press.

Barber, Red. 1982. *1947—When All Hell Broke Loose in Baseball.* Garden City, N.Y.: Doubleday & Co.

Barron, Bill, et al., eds. 1982. *The Official NFL Encyclopedia of Pro Football.* New York: New American Library Books.

Baumeister, Roy F., and Andrew Steinhilber. 1984. "Paradoxical Effects of Supportive Audiences on Performance under Pressure: The Home Field Disadvantage in Sports Championships," *Journal of Personality and Social Psychology*, 47(1): 85–93.

Becker, Michael A., and Jerry Suls. 1983. "Take Me Out to the Ballgame: The Effects of Objective, Social, and Temporal Performance Information on

Attendance at Major League Baseball Games," *Journal of Sport Psychology*, 5: 302–313.

Bellamy, Robert V. 1993. "Issues in the Internationalization of the U.S. Sports Media: The Emerging European Marketplace," *Journal of Sport & Social Issues*, 17(3): 168–180.

Bennett, Tom, et al. 1977. *The NFL's Official Encyclopedic History of Professional Football*. New York: Macmillan Publishing Co.

Berlew, David E., and Douglas T. Hall. 1966. "The Socialization of Managers: Effects of Expectations on Performance," *Administrative Science Quarterly*, 11: 207–223.

Berry, Robert C., and Wong, Glenn M. 1986. *Law and Business of the Sports Industries*. 2 vols. Dover, Mass.: Auburn House.

Besanko, D. A., and Simon, D. 1985–86. "Resource Allocation in the Baseball Players' Labor Market: An Empirical Investigation," *Review of Business & Economic Research*, 221: 71–84.

Betts, John R. 1974. *America's Sporting Heritage, 1850–1950*. Reading, Mass.: Addison-Wesley Publishing Co.

Brasch, Rudolph. 1970. *How Did Sports Begin: A Look at the Origins of Man at Play*. New York: David McKay Co.

Brown, M. Craig. 1982. "Administrative Succession and Organizational Performance: The Succession Effect." *Administrative Science Quarterly*, 27: 1–16.

Burkitt, B., and S. Cameron. 1992. "Impact of League Restructuring on Team Sport Attendances: The Case of Rugby Leagues," *Applied Economics*, 24: 265–271.

Byrne, Jim. 1986. *The $1 League: The Rise and Fall of the USFL*. New York: Prentice-Hall.

Cagnon, Cappy. 1989. "College Baseball," in Thorn and Palmer (1989).

Carlson, Kenneth N. 1986. *Pro Football Scorebook*. Lynnwood, Wash.: Rain Belt Publications.

Cashman, Richard. 1980. *Patrons, Players, and the Crowd: The Phenomenon of Indian Cricket*. New Delhi: Orient Longman.

Canes, M. E. 1974. "The Social Benefits of Restrictions on Team Quality," in Noll (1974).

Chambliss, Daniel F. 1987. "The Mundanity of Excellence: An Ethnographic Report on Stratification and Olympic Athletes." Unpublished paper, Hamilton College.

Chase, Ivan D. 1984. "Social Process and Hierarchy Formation in Small Groups: A Comparative Perspective," in *Social Hierarchies: Essays toward a Sociophysiological Perspective*, ed. P. R. Barchas. Westport, Conn.: Greenwood Press.

Clausewitz, Carl von. 1976[1826]. *On War*. Princeton, N.J.: Princeton University Press.

Coleman, Charles L. 1972. *The Trail of the Stanley Cup*. Sherbrooke, Quebec: National Hockey League.

Cope, Myron. 1970. *The Game That Was: The Early Days of Pro Football*. New York: World Publishing Co.

Courneya, Kerry S., and Albert V. Carron. 1990. "Batting First versus Last: Implications for the Home Advantage," *Journal of Sport & Exercise Psychology*, 12: 312–316.

——— 1991. "Effects of Travel and Length of Home Stand/Road Trip on the Home Advantage," *Journal of Sport & Exercise Psychology*, 13: 42–49.

——— 1992. "The Home Advantage in Sport Competitions: A Literature Review," *Journal of Sport & Exercise Psychology*, 14: 13–27.

Covick, Owen. 1986. "Sporting Equality in Professional Team Sports Leagues and Labour Market Controls," *Sporting Traditions*, 2(2): 54–73.

Cymrot, Donald J. 1983. "Migration Trends and Earnings of Free Agents in Major League Baseball, 1976–1979," *Economic Inquiry*, 21(4): 545–556.

Dabscheck, B. 1975. "Sporting Equality: Labour Market versus Product Market Control," *Journal of Industrial Relations*, 17(2): 174–190.

Daly, G., and Moore, W. J. 1981. "Externalities, Property Rights, and the Allocation of Resources in Major League Baseball," *Economic Inquiry*, 19(1): 77–95.

Danzig, Allison, and Peter Brandwein. 1948. *Sport's Golden Age: A Close-up of the Fabulous Twenties*. Freeport, N.Y.: Harper & Row.

Davenport, D. S. 1969. "Collusive Competition in Major League Baseball: Its Theory and Institutional Development," *American Economist*, 13 (Fall): 6-30.

Davis, Lance E. 1974. "Self-Regulation in Baseball, 1909–71," in Noll (1974).

Daymont, T. N. 1975. "The Effects of Monopsonistic Procedures on Equality of Competition in Professional Sports Leagues," *International Review of Sport Sociology*, 10(2): 83–99.

Dellinger, Harold. 1989. "Rival Leagues," in Thorn and Palmer (1989).

Demmert, Henry G. 1973. *The Economics of Professional Team Sports*. Lexington, Mass.: Lexington Books.

de Werra, D. 1985. "On the Multiplication of Divisions: The Use of Graphs for Sports Scheduling," *Networks*, 15: 125–136.

Dowie, J. 1982. "Why Spain Should Win the World Cup," *New Scientist*, 94: 693–695.

Drahozal, Christopher R. 1986. "The Impact of Free Agency on the Distribution of Playing Talent in Major League Baseball," *Journal of Economics and Business* 38: 113–121.

Dunning, Eric, and Kenneth Sheard. 1979. *Barbarians, Gentlemen, and Players: A Sociological Study of the Development of Rugby Football*. Oxford: Martin Robertson.

Eccles, Robert G., and Dwight B. Crane. 1988. *Doing Deals: Investment Banks at Work.* Boston, Mass.: Harvard Business School Press.

Eccles, Robert G., and Harrison C. White. 1986. "Firm and Market Interfaces of Profit Center Control," in *Approaches to Social Theory,* ed. Siegwart Lindenberg, James S. Coleman, and Stefan Nowak. New York: Russell Sage.

———. 1988. "Price and Authority in Inter-Profit Center Transactions," *American Journal of Sociology* 94(Supplement): S17–S51.

Edwards, John. 1979. "The Home Field Advantage," in *Sports, Games and Play: Social and Psychological Viewpoints,* ed. J. H. Goldstein. Hillsdale, N.J.: Lawrence Erlbaum Associates.

El-Hodiri, M., and Quirk, J. 1971. "An Economic Model of a Professional Sports League," *Journal of Political Economy,* 70: 1302–1319.

Elias, Norbert. 1987. *Involvement and Detachment.* Oxford: Basil Blackwell.

Elias, Norbert, and Eric Dunning. 1986. *Quest for Excitement: Sports and Leisure in the Civilizing Process.* New York: Basil Blackwell.

Enright, Jim, ed. 1976. *Trade Him: 100 Years of Baseball's Greatest Deals.* Chicago: Follett Publishing Co.

Eskenazi, Gerald. 1974. *The Fastest Sport.* Chicago, Ill.: Follett Publishing Co.

Falla, Jack. 1981. *NCAA: The Voice of College Sports.* Mission, Kans.: National Collegiate Athletic Association.

Farrington, Kip. 1972. *Skates, Sticks, and Man: The Story of Amateur Hockey in the United States.* New York: David McKay Co.

Feinstein, John. 1993. *Play Ball: The Life and Troubled Times of Major League Baseball.* New York: Villard Books.

Figone, Albert J. 1989. "Gambling and College Basketball: The Scandal of 1951," *Journal of Sport History,* 16(1): 44–61.

Filichia, Peter. 1993. *Professional Baseball Franchises: From the Abbeville Athletics to the Zenesvilk Indians.* New York: Facts on File.

Fischler, Stan. 1985. *Offside: Hockey from the Inside.* Toronto: Methuen Press.

Fischler, Stan, and Shirley W. Fischler. 1983. *The Hockey Encyclopedia.* New York: Macmillan Publishing Co.

Gallagher, Daniel J. 1976. "An Economic Analysis of the Player Reservation System in the Professional Team Sports Industry in the United States." Ph.D. dissertation, University of Maryland.

Gamson, William A., and Norman A. Scotch. 1964. "Scapegoating in Baseball," *American Journal of Sociology* 70: 69–72.

Gantz, W. 1981. "An Exploration of Viewing Motives and Behaviors Associated with Television Sports," *Journal of Broadcasting,* 25: 283–286.

Goldstein, Warren. 1989. *Playing for Keeps: A History of Early Baseball.* Ithaca, N.Y.: Cornell University Press.

Gorman, Jerry, and Kirk Calhoun. 1994. *The Name of the Game: The Business of Sports.* New York: John Wiley & Sons.

Gorn, Elliott J., and Warren Goldstein. 1993. *A Brief History of American Sports*. New York: Hill and Wang.

Granovetter, Mark. 1985. "Economic Action and Social Structure: The Problem of Embeddedness," *American Journal of Sociology*, 91: 481–510.

Greenstein, Theodore N. 1981. "Factors Affecting Attendance of Major League Baseball: Team Performance," *Review of Sport & Leisure*, 6(2): 21-34.

Greer, Donald L. 1983. "Spectator Booing and the Home Advantage: A Study of Social Influence in the Basketball Arena." *Social Psychology Quarterly* 46(3): 252–261.

Grusky, Oscar. 1963. "Managerial Succession and Organizational Effectiveness." *American Journal of Sociology* 69: 21–31.

Gudelunas, William, and Stephen R. Couch. 1982. "The Stolen Championship of the Pottsville Maroons: A Case Study in the Emergence of Modern Professional Football," *Journal of Sport History*, 9(1): 53–64.

Guttmann, Allen. 1986. *Sports Spectators*. New York: Columbia University Press.

———— 1988. *A Whole New Ball Game: An Interpretation of American Sports*. Chapel Hill, N.C.: University of North Carolina Press.

Halberstam, David. 1981. *The Breaks of the Game*. New York: Alfred A. Knopf.

Harris, David. 1987. *The League: The Rise and Decline of the NFL*. New York: Bantam Books.

Henderson, Robert W. 1947. *Ball, Bat, and Bishop: The Origin of Ball Games*. New York: Rockport Press.

Hill, J. R., and Spellman, W. 1983. "Professional Baseball: The Reserve Clause and Salary Structure," *Industrial Relations*, 22(1): 1–19.

Hoffman, Rich. 1985. "Major League Baseball Is Moving Toward Parity?" *Baseball Digest*, 44: 47–59.

Hollander, Zander, ed. 1989. *The Official NBA Basketball Encyclopedia*. New York: Villard Books.

Hollander, Zander, and Hal Bock. 1983. *The Complete Encyclopedia of Hockey*. New York: New American Library Books.

Holohan, W. H. 1978. "The Long Run Effects of Abolishing the Baseball Player Reserve System," *Journal of Legal Studies*, 19: 129–137.

Hunt, J. W., Jr., and Lewis, K. A. 1976. "Dominance, Recontracting, and the Reserve Clause: Major League Baseball." *American Economic Review*, 66(5): 936–943.

Isaacs, Neil. 1984. *All the Moves: A History of College Basketball*. New York: Harper & Row.

Jable, J. Thomas. 1991. "Social Class and the Sport of Cricket in Philadelphia, 1850–1880," *Journal of Sport History*, 18(2): 205–223.

James, Bill. 1988. *The Bill James Historical Baseball Abstract*. New York: Villard Books.

Johnson, William. 1969. "TV Made It All a New Game," *Sports Illustrated*, December, pp. 86–98.

Jones, J. C. H. 1969. "The Economics of the National Hockey League," *Canadian Journal of Economics*, 2(1): 1–20.

——— 1984. "Winners, Losers, and Hosers: Demand and Survival in the National Hockey League," *Atlantic Economic Journal*, 12(3): 54–63.

Kahn, Lawrence M., and Peter D. Scherer. 1991. "Racial Discrimination in the National Basketball Association," in *The Business of Professional Sports*, ed. Paul D. Staudoher and James A. Mengan. Urbana, Ill.: University of Illinois Press.

Kirsch, George B. 1989. *The Creation of American Team Sports: Baseball and Cricket, 1838–72.* Urbana, Ill.: University of Illinois Press.

Klatell, David A., and Norman Marcus. 1988. *Sports for Sale: Television, Money, and the Fans.* New York: Oxford University Press.

Kmenta, Jan. 1971. *Elements of Econometrics.* New York: Macmillan Publishing Co.

Koch, James V., and Wilbert M. Leonard II. 1978. "The NCAA: The Development of the College Sports Cartel from Social Movement to Formal Organization," *American Journal of Economics and Sociology*, 37(3): 225–239.

Kowet, Don. 1977. *The Rich Who Own Sports.* New York: Random House.

Kuhn, Bowie. 1987. *Hardball: The Education of a Baseball Commissioner.* New York: Random House.

Landau, Saul G. 1951. "On Dominance Relations and the Structure of Animal Societies: I. Effect of Inherent Characteristics." *Bulletin of Mathematical Biophysics*, 13: 1–19.

Larson, Andrea. 1990. "Social Control and Economic Exchange: Conceptualizing Network Organizational Forms," manuscript, Darden Graduate School of Business Administration, University of Virginia, Charlotteville, Va.

Lehn, Kenneth. 1982. "Property Rights, Risk Sharing, and Player Disability in Major League Baseball," *Journal of Law & Economics*, 25: 343–366.

Leifer, Eric M. 1990a. "Inequality among Equals: Embedding Market and Authority in League Sports," *American Journal of Sociology*, 96(3): 655–683.

——— 1990b. "Enacting Networks: The Feasibility of Fairness," *Social Networks*, 12(1): 1–25.

——— 1991. *Actors as Observers: A Theory of Skill in Social Relationships.* New York: Garland Publishing Co.

Leifer, Eric M., and Harrison C. White. 1987. "A Structural Approach to Markets," in *Intercorporate Relations: The Structural Analysis of Business*, ed. Mark S. Mizruchi and Michael Schwartz. Cambridge: Cambridge University Press.

Levine, Peter. 1985. *A. G. Spalding and the Rise of Baseball: The Promise of American Sport*. New York: Oxford University Press.

Lewis, Robert M. 1987. "Cricket and the Beginnings of Organized Baseball in New York City," *International Journal of the History of Sport*, 4(3): 315–332.

Lieb, Frederick G. 1951. *The Baseball Story*. New York: G. P. Putnam's Sons.

Lowenfish, Lee. 1991. *The Imperfect Diamond: A History of Baseball's Labor Wars*. New York: Da Capo Press.

Lucas, John A., and Ronald A. Smith. 1978. *Saga of American Sport*. Philadelphia: Lea & Febiger.

Mann, Steve. "The Business of Baseball," in Thorn and Palmer (1989).

Markham, Jessie W., and Paul V. Teplitz. 1981. *Baseball Economics and Public Policy*. Lexington, Mass.: Lexington Books.

McFarlane, Brian. 1973. *The Story of the National Hockey League*. New York: Charles Scribner & Sons.

———— 1989. *One Hundred Years of Hockey*. Toronto: Deneau Publishers.

McGuire, E. J., Kerry S. Courneya, W. Neil Widmeyer, and Albert V. Carron. 1992. "Aggression as a Potential Mediator of the Home Advantage in Professional Ice Hockey," *Journal of Sport & Exercise Psychology*, 14: 148–158.

Meserole, Mike, ed. 1994. *Sports Almanac*. Boston: Houghton Mifflin.

Metcalfe, Alan. 1992. "Power: A Case Study of the Ontario Hockey Association, 1890–1936," *Journal of Sport History*, 19(1): 5–25.

Miller, James Edward. 1990. *The Baseball Business: Pursuing Pennants and Profits in Baltimore*. Chapel Hill, N.C.: University of North Carolina Press.

Mizruchi, Mark S. 1985. "Local Sports Teams and Celebration of Community: A Comparative Analysis of the Home Advantage," *Sociological Quarterly* 26: 507–518

Morrow, Dan. 1986. "A Case Study in Amateur Conflict: The Athletic War in Canada, 1906–1908," *British Journal of Sport History*, 3(2): 173–190.

Murdock, Eugene C. 1982. *Ban Johnson: Czar of Baseball*. Westport, Conn.: Greenwood Press.

Neale, Walter C. 1964. "The Peculiar Economics of Professional Sports." *Quarterly Journal of Economics*, 78 (Feb.): 1–14.

Neal-Luneford, Jeff. 1992. "Sport in the Land of Television: The Use of Sport in Network Prime-time Schedules," *Journal of Sport History*, 19(1): 56–76.

Neft, David S., Richard M. Cohen, and Jordan Deutsch, eds. 1975. *The Sports Encyclopedia: Pro Basketball*. New York: Grosset & Dunlap.

———— 1982a. *The Sports Encyclopedia: Pro Football, the Modern Era—1960 to the Present*. New York: Simon and Schuster.

———— 1982b. *The Sports Encyclopedia: Baseball*. New York: Grosset & Dunlap.

Nells, Humbert S. 1989. "The Kentucky Basketball Survey," *Journal of Sport History*, 16(2): 186–189.

Noll, Roger G., ed. 1974. *Government and the Sports Business.* Washington, D.C.: Brookings Institution.

—— 1977. "Major League Team Sports," in *The Structure of American Industry,* ed. Walter Adams. New York: Macmillan Publishing Co.

Ouchi, William G. 1980. "Markets, Bureaucracies, and Clans," *Administrative Science Quarterly,* 25: 129–140.

Parrott, Harold. 1976. *The Lords of Baseball.* New York: Praeger Publishers.

Pasquarelli, Len. 1994. "Latest NFL Challenger: The A League," *Atlanta Constitution,* May 4, p. G3.

Patton, Phil. 1984. *Razzle-Dazzle: The Curious Marriage of Television and Professional Football.* New York: Doubleday & Co.

Pearson, Daniel M. 1993. *Baseball in 1889: Players vs. Owners.* Bowling Green, Ohio: Bowling Green State University Popular Press.

Perrin, Tom. 1987. *Football: A College History.* Jefferson, N.C.: McFarland & Co.

Perrow, Charles. 1986. *Complex Organizations: A Critical Essay.* 3d ed. New York: Random House.

Peterson, Harold. 1973. *The Man Who Invented Baseball.* New York: Charles Scribner's Sons.

Peterson, Robert W. 1990. *Cages to Jumpshots: Pro Basketball's Early Years.* New York: Oxford University Press.

Pietrusza, David. 1991. *Major Leagues: The Formation, Sometimes Absorption, and Mostly Inevitable Demise of 18 Professional Baseball Organizations, 1871 to Present.* Jefferson, N.C.: McFarland & Co.

Pollard, R. 1986. "Home Advantage in Soccer: A Retrospective Analysis," *Journal of Sport Sciences,* 4: 237–248.

Powers, Ron. 1984. *Supertube: The Rise of Television Sports.* New York: Coward-McCann.

Quirk, James P. 1973. "An Economic Analysis of Team Movements in Professional Sports," *Law and Contemporary Problems,* 38(1): 42–66.

—— 1980. "The Reserve Clause: Recent Developments," in *Current Issues in Professional Sports,* ed. M. E. Jones. Durham, N.H.: University of New Hampshire Press.

Quirk, James P., and Rodney D. Fort. 1992. *Pay Dirt: The Business of Professional Team Sports.* Princeton, N.J.: Princeton University Press.

Rader, Benjamin G. 1984. *In Its Own Image: How Television Has Transformed Sports.* New York: Free Press.

—— . 1992. *Baseball: A History of America's Game.* Urbana, Ill.: University of Illinois Press.

Reichler, Joseph L. 1984. *The Baseball Trade Register.* New York: Macmillan Publishing Co.

Reichler, Joseph L., ed. 1988. *The Baseball Encyclopedia.* 7th ed. New York: Macmillan Publishing Co.

Riess, Steven A. 1980. *Touching Base: Professional Baseball and American Culture in the Progressive Era.* Westport, Conn.: Greenwood Press.

—— 1981. "Power without Authority: Los Angeles Elites and the Construction of the Coliseum," *Journal of Sport History*, 8(1): 50–61.

—— 1989. *City Games: The Evolution of American Urban Society and the Rise of Sports.* Urbana, Ill.: University of Illinois Press.

Riffenburgh, Beau. 1986. *The Official NFL Encyclopedia.* New York: NAL Books.

Riordan, James. 1977. *Sport in Soviet Society.* Cambridge: Cambridge University Press.

Rivett, P. 1975. "The Structure of League Football," *Operational Research Quarterly*, 26(4): 801–812.

Ronberg, Gary. 1975. *The Violent Game.* Englewood Cliffs, N.J.: Prentice-Hall.

Rosen, Sherwin. 1986. "Prizes and Incentives in Elimination Tournaments," *American Economic Review*, 76(4): 701–715.

Rosenbaum, James E. 1976. *Making Inequality.* New York: Academic Press.

—— 1984. *Career Mobility in a Corporate Hierarchy.* New York: Academic Press.

Rottenberg, S. 1956. "The Baseball Player's Labor-Market," *Journal of Political Economy*, 64(3): 242–258.

Ruck, Rob. 1987. *Sandlot Seasons: Sport in Black Pittsburgh.* Urbana, Ill.: University of Illinois Press.

Ryczek, William J. 1992. *Blackguards and Red Stockings: A History of Baseball's National Association.* Jefferson, N.C.: McFarland & Co.

Sage, George H. 1990. *Power and Ideology in American Sport: A Critical Perspective.* Champaign, Ill.: Human Kinetics Books.

Sammons, Jeffrey T. 1990. *Beyond the Ring: The Role of Boxing in American Society.* Urbana, Ill.: University of Illinois Press.

Sands, Jack, and Peter Gammons. 1993. *Coming Apart at the Seams: How Baseball Owners, Players, and Television Executives Have Led Our National Pastime to the Brink of Disaster.* New York: Macmillan Publishing Co.

Schofield, John A. 1984. "Performance and Attendance at Professional Team Sports," *Journal of Sport Behavior*, 6(4): 197–206.

Schwalbe, Michael L. 1989. "A Humanist Conception of Competition in Sport," *Humanity & Society*, 13(1): 43–60.

Schwartz, Barry. 1983. "George Washington and the Whig Conception of Heroic Leadership," *American Sociological Review*, 48: 18–33.

Schwartz, Barry, and S. F. Barsky. 1977. "The Home Advantage," *Social Forces*, 55(3): 641–661.

Scully, Gerald W. 1989. *The Business of Major League Baseball.* Chicago: University of Chicago Press.

Seymour, Harold. 1960. *Baseball: The Early Years.* New York: Oxford University Press.

—— 1971. *Baseball: The Golden Age*. New York: Oxford University Press.

—— 1989. *Baseball: The People's Game*. New York: Oxford University Press.

Shell, Ellen R. 1985. "Making Up Sports Schedules Is One Game Nobody Wins," *Smithsonian*, 15(11): 125–133.

Sloane, P. J. 1976. "Restriction of Competition in Team Sports," *Bulletin of Economic Research*, 28(1): 3–22.

Smith, Ronald A. 1981. "Harvard and Columbia and a Reconsideration of the 1905–6 Football Crisis," *Journal of Sport History*, 8(3): 5–19.

—— 1985. "The Historic Amateur-Professional Dilemma in American College Sport," *British Journal of Sports History*, 2(3): 221–231.

Smith, Thomas G. 1988. "Outside the Pale: The Exclusion of Blacks from the NFL, 1934–1946," *Journal of Sport History*, 15(3): 255–281.

Sobel, Lionel S. 1977. *Professional Sports and the Law*. New York: Law-Arts Publishers.

Spink, J. G. Taylor. 1947. *Judge Landis and Twenty Five Years of Baseball*. New York: Thomas Y. Crowell Co.

Staudohar, Paul D. 1986. *The Sports Industry and Collective Bargaining*. Ithaca, N.Y.: ILR Press.

Stern, Robert N. 1979. "The Development of an Interorganizational Control Network: The Case of Intercollegiate Athletics," *Administrative Science Quarterly*, 24: 242–266.

—— 1981. "Competitive Influences on the Interorganizational Regulation of College Athletics," *Administrative Science Quarterly* 26: 15–32.

Sullivan, Neil J. 1990a. *The Minors: The Struggles and the Triumph of Baseball's Poor Relation from 1876 to the Present*. New York: St. Martin's Press.

—— 1990b. "Faces in the Crowd: A Statistical Portrait of Baseball Spectators in Cincinnati, 1886–1888," *Journal of Sport History*, 17(3): 354–365.

Summer, Jim L. 1990. "John Franklin Crowell, Methodism, and the Football Controversy at Trinity College, 1887–1894," *Journal of Sport History*, 17(1): 5–20.

Taylor, Ralph B., and Joseph C. Lanni. 1981. "Territorial Dominance: The Influence of the Resident Advantage in Triadic Decision Making," *Journal of Personality and Social Psychology*, 41(5): 909–915.

Thirer, J., and M. S. Rampey. 1979. "Effects of Abusive Spectators' Behavior on Performance: Visiting Intercollegiate Basketball Teams," *Perceptual and Motor Skills*, 48: 1047–1053.

Thorelli, Hans B. 1986. "Networks: Between Markets and Hierarchies," *Strategic Management Journal*, 7: 37–51.

Thorn, John, and Pete Palmer. 1984. *The Hidden Game of Baseball*. Doubleday & Co.

Thorn, John, and Pete Palmer, eds. 1989. *Total Baseball*. New York: Warner Books.

Varca, P. 1980. "An Analysis of Home and Away Game Performance of Male College Basketball Teams," *Journal of Sport Psychology*, 2: 245–257.

Vaz, Edmund. 1979. *The Professionalization of Young Hockey Players*. Lincoln, Nebr.: University of Nebraska Press.

Vincent, Ted. 1981. *Mudville's Revenge: The Rise and Fall of American Sport*. New York: Seaview Books.

Voigt, David. 1983. *American Baseball: From Postwar Expansion to the Electronic Age*. University Park, Pa.: Pennsylvania State University Press.

——. 1987. *Baseball: An Illustrated History*. University Park, Pa.: Pennsylvania State University Press.

Watterson, John S. 1981. "The Football Crisis of 1909–1910: The Response of the Eastern Big Three," *Journal of Sport History*, 8(1): 33–49.

Wenner, Lawrence A., ed. 1989. *Media, Sports, and Society*. Newbury Park, Calif.: Sage Publications.

Weyland, Alexander M. 1955. *The Saga of American Football*. New York: Macmillan Co.

White, Harrison C. 1970. *Chains of Opportunity: System Models of Mobility in Organizations*. Cambridge, Mass.: Harvard University Press.

——. 1992. *Identity and Control: A Structural Theory of Social Action*. Princeton, N.J.: Princeton University Press.

Whyte, William F. 1946. *Street Corner Society*. New York: Free Press.

Wilkins, Alan L., and William G. Ouchi. 1983. "Efficient Cultures: Exploring the Relationship between Culture and Organizational Performance," *Administrative Science Quarterly*, 28: 468–481.

Williamson, Oliver. 1981. "The Economics of Organizations: The Transaction Cost Approach," *American Journal of Sociology*, 87(3): 548–577.

——. 1985. *The Economic Institutions of Capitalism*. New York: Free Press.

Young, Scott. 1989. *100 Years of Dropping the Puck: A History of the OHA*. Toronto: McClelland & Stewart.

Zak, Thomas A. 1979. "Production Efficiency: The Case of Professional Baseball," *Journal of Business*, 52(3): 379–392.

Zeller, R. A., and T. Jurkovac. 1988. "Dome-inating the Game." *Psychology Today*, October, pp. 19–22.

Zimbalist, Andrew. 1992. *Baseball and Billions: A Probing Look inside the Big Business of Our National Pastime*. New York: Basic Books.

Zingg, Paul J. 1990. "The Phoenix at Fenway: The 1915 World Series and the Collegiate Connection to the Major Leagues," *Journal of Sport History*, 17(1): 21–31.

Index